APPLIED BEHAVIOURAL ECONOMICS

VOLUME I

APPLIED BEHAVIOURAL ECONOMICS

VOLUME I

EDITED BY
SHLOMO MAITAL

NEW YORK UNIVERSITY PRESS
Washington Square, New York

First published in the U.S.A. in 1988 by
NEW YORK UNIVERSITY PRESS
Washington Square
New York, NY 10003

Library of Congress Cataloging-in-Publication Data

Applied behavioural economics/edited by Shlomo Maital.
p. cm.
Bibliography: v. 1, p.
Includes index.
ISBN 0-8147-5437-6 (set) ISBN 0-8147-5439-2 (v. 1).
ISBN 0-8147-5440-6 (v. 2)
1. Economics—Psychological aspects. I. Maital, Shlomo.
HB74.P8A66 1988
330'.01'9—dc19 88-4971
CIP

Printed in Great Britain

CONTENTS

INTRODUCTION

Shlomo Maital

The American philosopher and essayist Ralph Waldo Emerson was known to detest small talk. In greeting visitors, he chose to come straight to the point:

"What has become clearer to you since we last met?"

Emerson's pointed question comprises the agenda of most scientific conferences, but is especially apt in defining that of the International Conference on Economics and Psychology, held at Kibbutz Shefayim, Israel, July 9-11, 1986. The conference was sponsored jointly by two organizations, I.A.R.E.P. (International Association for Research in Economic Psychology, based in Europe, and S.A.B.E., Society for the Advancement of Behavioral Economics, based in the United States). Some 100 scholars from 14 countries, representing a broad range of behavioral and social sciences, met to discuss aspects of the young and burgeoning discipline, behavioral economics. Of some 60 papers presented at the conference, 49 appear in this volume. They portray what has become clearer to behavioral economists, and in more than a few cases, what has become more obscure.

In summarizing and integrating this book, I will discuss briefly the nature of behavioral economics, the type of questions it addresses and the tools it uses to answer them. The papers referred to below are all drawn from these two volumes.

Proust once said that any mental activity is easy, if it need not take reality into account. In reality, economic behavior is rich and complex in nature. The simplifying behavioral assumptions made by conventional economics—justified in part by the principle that the more abstract a theory, the more general (hence more powerful) it is—have become increasingly unacceptable to many scholars and students.

One recalls Albert Einstein's advice to thinkers: "Simplify as much as possible . . . but not more so." Behavioral economics for the most part finds it necessary to complicate, rather than simplify, in order to capture the intricate, often internally contradictory structure of human choice; it subscribes to William James' adage that "man's chief difference from the brutes lies in the exuberant excess of his subjective propensities" and seeks to explain "irrational", perverse or paradoxical behavior, rather than deny their existence (see Treisman's analysis of the St. Petersburg paradox, an attempt to explain "how people actually reason", or Wahlund & Warneryd's analysis of perverse saving behavior following tax reform in Sweden).

It is particularly appropriate that the keynote paper of the conference and first paper of this book, by Harvard psychologist Richard Herrnstein, challenges the foundation of modern economics, the postulate that individuals act in order to maximize utility. Herrnstein offers instead the principle of "melioration":

> . . . Maximization as a descriptive . . . theory of behavior fails because it presupposes organisms to be sensitive to total utility or to changes in marginal utility. As a general principle, however, they are not. . . . They are sensitive to the average utilities associated with the competing alternatives for behavior. . . . Allocation shifts toward any behavioral alternative earning a higher average utility than other alternatives.

Herrnstein supports his thesis with a compelling array of experimental evidence on both animal and human choice behavior. His paper illustrates an important attribute of behavioral economics: the strong belief in the value of direct observation through experiments, surveys or even introspection, resulting in data that is often generated by the researcher himself or herself (Bolle; Hey; Guth).

Behavioral science often discovers its theories in the course of observations and data collection (as Herrnstein himself did), a laudable methodology that behavioral economics embraces. Goethe once observed that thinking is more interesting than knowing, but looking is far more interesting than thinking. Increasingly, "looking" leads one to what Leibĕnstein has termed "micro-micro" data, revealing the behavior of individuals or small groups.

Most of us who attended Shefayim would gladly go to battle under Goethe's banner, believing as he did that wisdom is nearer when you stoop than when you soar. Many of the issues addressed in this volume relate to everyday phenomena encountered in shopping malls, shop floors and offices, within families (Phelps; Grossbard-Shechtman; Kirchler; and Neumark) and among small and large groups—phenomena best seen by stooping.

Behavioral economics is eclectic, searching for useful ideas in psychology, sociology and anthropology (Saldanha and Lancry make effective use of opponent-process theory in modeling consumption; Lampert applies biology to the study of mate selection). Moreover, practitioners believe, together with James Thurber, that it is at least as important to ask good questions as it is to find the right answers: What do people hope to get out of life? What things are important to them? What are their values? How have values changed? (Levy, Scholz, Sevon, Montgomery & Johansson). How have motives changed? (Albanese). How is the nature of society and democracy itself changing? (Raven). Why do people seek change and variety? (Middleton). Why do people move? (Ayal).

The adjective "applied" in the book's title is not misused. Many papers contain theories and empirical results that are applicable to problems faced by managers (Sokolowska; Tyszka & Gasparski; Hellman; Bar-On & Niv) and address practical issues such as productivity (Tomer), labor relations (Meltz), or quality (Windieck). Nor are small businesses (Schwartz) or entrepreneurs (Gilad, Kaish & Ronen; O'Higgins) neglected. Papers on tax evasion (Webley & Robben; Elffers & Hessing; and Hessing, Elffers & Weigel), public services (Francken & Kuylen) and social security (Schoormans & von Grumbkow; Poiesz & Sol; van Praag) contain results useful for policy-makers. Yet despite the emphasis on applications (or perhaps because of it), the central role of human passion and emotion is not neglected; the implications of caring for others (Phelps; Grossbard-Shechtman) and of emotions (Frank) are extensively treated. Two papers focus on "relativity": how comparisons with others (Stark & Yitzchaki) and with the past (van Praag) influence choice and behavior.

Behavioral economics attaches great importance to perception and information—how people see the world and learn about it, as opposed to how the world really is. Papers by Levin and by Messick, Allison & Samuelson treat the phenomenon of "framing"; Kotowitz places information within a model of advertising and learning; and the perception of time is treated by Jungerman and by Winston. Several papers deal with the nature and uses of information, in the context of consumer behavior (Olander), policymaking (Graziano), and inflation expectations (Shapira & Friedman).

Novelist Peter de Vries once wrote that gluttony is a sure sign that something is eating you. Western society has attained unprecedented affluence, yet something *is* eating us: high levels of consumption have not created a serene, collectively content society. Why has the shower of post-War affluence left anomie and discontent in its wake? Three papers treat the economics of anxiety, over health (Westman & Gafni), environmental episodes (Shechter) and nuclear power (Pieters). Behavioral economists accept Samuel Johnson's dictum, that a man searching for his dinner and trembling over his creditors is unlikely to think great thoughts, yet find few links between the abundance of "dinners" and credit and the prolificacy of great thoughts and challenge the very foundation of economics, that "more is better than less".

Alfred North Whitehead once said that a clash of doctrines is not a disaster, it is an opportunity. The clash of doctrines within this volume, among various assumptions and disciplinary points of view, and between this volume and conventional economics, should indeed by seen as an opportunity—a chance to reexamine the very foundations of economics, the agenda of questions it addresses and the set of tools it uses to answer them.

LIST OF CONTRIBUTORS

Paul Albanese, Middlebury College

Scott Allison, University of California (Santa Barbara)

Eliezer Ayal, University of Illinois (Chicago)

Dan Bar-On, Ben Gurion University

Friedel Bolle, University of Hamburg

Charlotte Demonte Phelps, Temple University

Henk Elffers, Erasmus University

Dick Francken, S.W.O.K.A.

Robert H. Frank, Cornell University

Abraham Friedman, Hebrew University

Amiram Gafni, Tel Aviv University and McMaster University

Peter Gasparski, Polish Academy of Sciences

Benjamin Gilad, Rutger's-Newark

Loretta Graziano, California State University

Amyra Grossbard-Shechtman, San Diego State University

Amir Helman, Ruppin Institute

Richard Herrnstein, Harvard University

Dick J. Hessing, Erasmus University

John D. Hey, University of York

Ulla-Stina Johansson, University of Goteborg

Helmut Jungerman, Technische Universität (Berlin)

Stanley Kaish, Rutger's-Newark

Erich Kirchler, University of Linz

Yehuda Kotowitz, University of Toronto

Tom Kuylen, S.W.O.K.A.

Pierre-Jean Lancry, Université Paris

Ada Lampert, Ruppin Institute

Irwin P. Levin, University of Iowa

Shlomit Levy, Israel Institute of Applied Social Research

Noah M. Meltz, University of Toronto

David Messick, University of California (Santa Barbara)

Elliott Middleton, College of St. Thomas

Henry Montgomery, University of Goteborg

Ira Morris, University of Exeter

David Neumark, Harvard University

Amittai Niv, Ruppin Institute

Eleanor O'Higgins, Radio Telefis Eireann

Folke Olander, Aarhus School of Business Administration

Rik G. M. Pieters, Erasmus University

Theo Poiesz, Tilburg University

John Raven, Consultant (Scotland)

Henry Robben, Erasmus University

Joshua Ronen, New York University

Charles Samuelson, University of California (Santa Barbara)

Mordecai Shechter, University of Haifa

Joachim Scholz, Free University of Berlin

Jan Schoormans, Tilburg University

Hugh H. Schwartz, Inter-American Development Bank

Guje Sevon, Swedish School of Economics (Helsinki)

Zur Shapira, Hebrew University

Joanna Sokolowska, Polish Academy of Sciences

Jopy Sol, Tilburg University

Oded Stark, Harvard University

John F. Tomer, Manhattan College

Michel Treisman, Oxford University

Tadeusz Tyszka, Polish Academy of Sciences

Bas Verplanken, University of Leiden

Jasper von Grumbkow, Open University

Richard Wahlund, Stockholm School of Economics

Karl-Eric Warneryd, Stockholm School of Economics

Paul Webley, University of Exeter

Russell H. Weigel, Amherst College

Mina Westman, Tel Aviv University

Gerd Windieck, University of Cologne

Gordon C. Winston, Williams College

Shlomo Yitzchaki, Hebrew University

Keynote Paper
A Behavioural Alternative to Utility Maximisation

R. J. Herrnstein

Harvard University

Economic Man is held to be self-interested and rational in pursuit of his interests. When Real Man behaves otherwise, economic theory is inclined to blame defects of memory, understanding, reasoning, patience, and the like, rather than the theory itself. The utility-maximizer of economic theory is viewed as description, not prescription -- a model of how people actually behave (except for their errors and inadequacies) not how they ought to behave.

In economic theory, self-interest is couched in the concept of utility, the subjective valuation of the commodities or goods that flow from behavior. Rationality then amounts to the maximization of utility. Economic theory thus contains two psychological subtheories -- a motivational theory that yields at least an ordinal scale of subjective utility corresponding to the objective consequences of action, and a decision theory that states that, given the utilities, an optimal course of action is chosen. Both of those psychological subtheories are in considerable empirical trouble. Many economists recognize troubles with the motivational theory (e.g. Frank, 1985, 1986; Hirshleifer, 1985; Kornai, 1986; Leibenstein, 1976; Maital, 1982; Scitovsky, 1975); few appear aware of any general difficulty with the decision theory (with notable exceptions, such as the seminal work of Herbert Simon on bounded rationality, and the recent and related work of Ronald Heiner, about both of which more later). I will suggest below that the problems with the decision theory are fundamental to economics as a science of human behavior. In this paper, I will discuss both sets of problems from the standpoint of empirical psychology.

Utility and Its Complexities

The power of economic analysis comes in part from its subtle explanations of social life. It is not the butcher's benevolence, explained Adam Smith, that accounts for the meat in our dinner; it is the butcher's regard for his own self-interest. He sells meat for the opportunity to reap the pleasures of his own utility functions.

Economic theory traditionally conceived of individual utility functions that are, on the whole, stable, universal, and narrowly egoistic and hedonistic, then showed ingeniously how, prompted only by self-interest, individual actions may concatenate into collective, often socially beneficial, behavior. But the less narrow, egoistic, and hedonistic individual utility functions are, the less ingenuity it may take to weave them into social behavior. The power of economic analysis declines in inverse relation to the extent that individual utility functions already embody social parameters and also in inverse relation to their unpredictability and variability. Described below are six kinds of evidence arguing against the conventional economic theory of self-interest.

1. Sociality. Organisms are motivationally complex. The butcher may be self-interested in the normative economic sense, but perhaps not entirely so. Nothing we know about human motivation suggests that he must be emotionally indifferent to the well being of his customers. Biology provides many examples of innate social instincts (Wilson, 1975, 1981) -- "moral sentiments," in the vocabulary of Adam Smith's time. Considering the importance and antiquity of human social life, evolutionary considerations suggest innate social drives for mankind (Brown & Herrnstein, 1975). Butchers, like people in general, may be driven by innate social motives as well as by narrowly egoistic ones. The social drives are hard to identify, first, because learning obscures what is universal about them. In addition, they blend, perhaps interacting complexly (e.g., Maslow, 1955), with the egoistic drives in determining behavior. The parsimonious assumption is, nevertheless, that social drives motivate human behavior to some extent, the way they do the behavior of other social species. The hard-core economist may try to reduce every instance of human generosity, heroism, love, parenthood, martyrdom and philanthropy to egoistic self-interest, but he has neither evolutionary biology nor the evidence of everyday experience on his side. Some economists (e.g., Frank, 1986; Hirshleifer, 1985) have incorporated evolutionary considerations into their thinking about utility functions, in effect, shifting the locus of "interest" from the self to the gene pool. Sociality has obvious adaptive value to a social species. Having broadened the meaning of self-

interest by assuming an optimization process within natural selection, some economists then grant that love, generosity, a concern for fellow man, and so on, may be fundamental human motives. This approach may be plausible, but it also betrays the defects of the traditional economic view of self-interest as applied to individuals.

2. Diversity. Motivational complexity leads to variability and instability. It is unlikely that any pair of people could have, at a given moment, the same set of drives at the same levels of intensity, hence the same utilities. It is even unlikely, given the dynamic character of motivation, that a given person would have the same utilities at different moments. Psychopathology often shows up as odd or atypically intense or feeble drives, hence odd or atypical utilities -- e.g., kleptomania, pyromania, necrophilia, nymphomania, impotence, anorexia, and so on. The concept of "self-interest" loses explanatory value if it must be recalibrated for each individual at each moment. An individual may have mutually contradictory drives. He may have no integral self-interest at all, but many interests pushing in different directions. Behavior is the resultant of the motivational forces, varying from person to person and from moment to moment. Stable, universal utility functions may be an expedient assumption for large aggregations of people, but, as a theory of motivation, it omits far more than it includes.

3. Conventionality. Between the innate drives and behavior comes conditioning, the molding of values and habits by the

contingencies of an environment. Custom, convention, manners, and so on, are the terms we use for the arbitrary aspects of social behavior. In economic theory, this behavior may be considered self-interested, earning egoistic benefits for conformity. If all such arbitrary acts were in fact sustained by egoistic drives, it would be reasonable to label them self-interested in the economic sense. But, to the extent that they are sustained by social drives, they violate traditional economic theory. There is every reason to suppose that social drives are, at least in part, responsible for the conventional behavior of a culture. We have no better evidence that people behave "correctly" because it earns them food, water, shelter, safety, and so on, than because it earns them the company, admiration, and good will of others.

4. Self-Image. People learn not only to behave in socially correct ways, but also to approve of the social behavior of others. They become not only exemplars of a culture, but agents in its transmission. They reward politeness, heroism, generosity, and other virtues, and disapprove of avarice, sloth, and other sins. Their own behavior, as well as the behavior of others, is seen through the prism of cultural values. Each individual is constrained to some extent by internalized standards of conduct (see Wilson & Herrnstein, 1985, for a fuller discussion and an application to criminal behavior). We may refrain from cheating not just because of the risk of getting caught, but because we disapprove of cheaters. We go on a diet not just because obesity is unhealthy and unpopular, but because we admire slimness no less

in ourselves than in others. The human capacity for internalizing values modulates egoistic drives by adding or deducting motivational strength to them, no doubt to varying extents for different people. A butcher may occasionally reduce the price of meat for a poor customer because he feels generous, not just because it is good business to do so. What may seem to be generosity may be so in fact, rather than "enlightened self-interest."

5. Maladaptation. Some drives violate self-interest in any non-tautological sense; some are clearly self-destructive. The chemical addictions are obvious examples; subtler ones may foster overworking, overeating, and other maladaptive behavior. According to the opponent-process theory of motivation (Solomon and Corbit, 1974), new drives may be created simply by indulging in stimulation that produces transient positive or negative feelings. An emotional state is homeostatically counteracted by an internally generated emotion of the opposite sign, according to the theory. This may itself be an evolutionary adaptation arising to dampen the effects of extreme emotion, but it apparently can have maladaptive long-term consequences. With repetition, the theory says, the rebounding emotion becomes strong relative to the initially elicited emotion. We find strenuous exercise or mountain climbing disagreeable or frightening at first, but, eventually, we become addicted to it in order to experience the newly exhilarating rebound emotion, while the fear or the disagreeable emotions nearly disappear. Or, the initial pleasures

of cocaine or heroin produce a counteracting depression. With repetition, the depression becomes so profound that the addict indulges to escape temporarily from the rebound emotion, experiencing almost none of the initial pleasurable emotion any longer. In the limit, according to the opponent-process theory, a large fraction of a person's behavior may be drawn into the pursuit of dubious or obviously counterproductive "utility." Whether or not the theory is precisely correct, people are obviously vulnerable to motivational traps that belie any plausible interpretation of self-interest.

6. Interdependence. Interpersonal comparisons are a major source of motivation. Modern social science refers to the Aristotlean principle of distributive justice as equity, or exchange, theory (Adams, 1965; Blau, 1964; Hatfield, Walster, & Berscheid, 1978; Homans, 1974). A sense of fairness is violated -- and a motivational state thereby created -- when we sense an inbalance among people or groups of people in the ratio of gains to investments. We are unlikely to be angry at someone for failing to do us a favor until there is an unreciprocated favor outstanding. It is less annoying to be stuck in a traffic jam when the lanes on either side of us are stuck too, than when ours is the only one stuck. An individual views his gains from an activity as fair or unfair by the standard of what others are earning from comparable activities. We may think we are underpaid until we discover that we are earning more than others doing the same work, at which point we may feel overpaid. The "norm of

reciprocity," based on implicit calculations of ratios of gains to investment, colors virtually all interpersonal relations (Brown, 1986). People are not commensurately pleased by increases in personal standards of living, if they merely maintain their relative position in society (Easterlin, 1974). To feel happy about an improvement apparently requires an improvement in relative position. Romance is plausibly depicted as an exchange of gains and investments between the partners, taking into account not only mutual actions, but such individual traits as physical attractiveness, intelligence, social status, and, in some contexts, ethnic and religious background (Hatfield, Traupmann, & Walster, 1978; Hatfield, et al., 1978; Rubin, 1973). The criminal may see his crime as rectifying inequity -- a grievance against a particular individual or against society in general, which has, as he perceives it, done him wrong. When society disagrees with his view of what is equitable, the offender is punished by paying his "debt to society," in theory restoring the balance after his inequitable gain. Frank (1985) has noted that employees at the tops of firms are paid smaller salaries, and those at the bottom, larger salaries, than their contributions to productivity would justify. This, he argues, is because the top positions carry the extra compensation of high status, and those at the bottom, the cost of low status. Dollars combine with status to determine the utility of the returns from the job. But status as a source of utility is inexorably interpersonal, based on comparison with others. The universal, potent social motivation known as envy

(Schoeck, 1966) also depends on comparison. To the extent that interpersonal comparison affects utility, it is meaningless to speak of individual utility (hence self-interest) without taking account of social context.

These examples hardly exhaust the complexities of human motivation, but they prove that the conventional economic notion of self-interest, if not vacuously tautological, rests on shaky empirical foundations. Nor is it satisfactory to suggest, as economists sometimes do (Friedman, 1953), that there exists some significant area of human behavior where self-interest in the economic sense holds sway -- markets, perhaps, or the workaday world -- and Economic Man dwells and economic theory works, if not perfectly, then well enough. As the next section shows, an individual's behavior constitutes a field, like a physical field of force, where each point is influenced by motivational events at all points. Except as a crude approximation, a person's behavior cannot be viewed as if were composed of mutually independent domains. The empirical laws of behavior force us to consider individual behavior as a whole.

If not Maximization, What?

The heart of modern economic theory is the formal analysis of utility maximization. Any change in the allocation of behavior (usually represented as a portion of one's assets spent on a commodity) may or may not cause a marginal change in total utility. A little less bread and a bit more wine may increase, decrease, or leave unchanged, overall utility. Behavior seeks a point of zero slope, to use the formal language of economic theory, a maximum in the function relating behavioral allocation to total utility. Given the proper limitations on the objective functions, this is the point at which no re-allocation of behavior can increase total utility. Figure 1 (from Vaughan & Herrnstein, in press) illustrates the economic theory of behavior for the simple case in which there are only two commodities available, and where a smooth total utility function has only a single maximum. Complications multiply rapidly as the situation approximates reality -- many commodities whose utilites may interact, complex total utility functions, uncertainties about outcomes, varying levels of assets, and so on. Economics has tamed many of those unruly complications.

Nothing will be said here to challenge the preeminence of economics in formalizing the intuition that people, in some way, obey the "felicific calculus," which is to say, that they behave so as to foster pleasure and reduce pain. Nor can economics be challenged as providing the normative definition of rational choice -- of how we should behave if we wish to maximize utility. The challenge is to a literal maximization of overall utility as a scientific law of behavior. People (as well as other species) do obey a law of behavior that can be reconciled with utilitarianism, but the evidence now strongly argues against literal maximization and in favor of a process that has been called melioration (Herrnstein & Vaughan, 1980; Herrnstein, 1982; Heyman & Herrnstein, 1986; Vaughan, 1981, 1985; Vaughan & Herrnstein, in press).[1]

Maximization as a descriptive (as opposed to a prescriptive or normative) theory of behavior fails because it presupposes organisms to be sensitive to total utility or to changes in marginal utility. As a general principle, however, they are not. It is not that they are random in their choices or irrationally wedded to past choices (as Becker, 1962, suggests), but that they are attuned to the wrong variable to be maximizers. They are sensitive to the average utilities associated with the competing alternatives for behavior, as the principle of melioration implies. Allocation shifts toward any behavioral alternative earning a higher average utility than other alternatives. According to the principle of melioration, behavior comes into equilibrium at an allocation at which each alternative earns equal utility, as Figure 2 illustrates for the simple case in which there are only two alternative behaviors competing. The maximum point in Figure 1 may or may not correspond to the equilibrium point in Figure 2, depending upon characteristics, to be elucidated later, of functions like those in Figure 2.

---

1 Numerous behavioral scientists have formulated theories resembling what is here called melioration. Besides the works cited in the text, I should call attention to Myerson & Myezin, 1980, and Rachlin, 1973.

Matching

Let us first consider the evidence bearing on behavioral equilibrium. In these experiments, subjects work for reinforcement -- the behaviorist's term for utility -- under fixed conditions for as many experimental sessions as it takes to estimate the strength of each behavior. Thus, a hungry pigeon may spend 45 minutes per day in a chamber containing two response keys, pecking either of which will produce a bit of food intermittently. The rate of reinforcement is typically so low that the pigeon's level of hunger does not change during the course of the session.

A significant feature of such experiments is the schedule of reinforcement. On a variable-interval schedule, for example, a a peck earns reinforcement at varying and unpredictable times since the preceding reinforcement. In a typical experiment on pairwise choice, each key will be governed by mutually independent variable-interval schedules, differing only in the rate at which they yield reinforcement. A pair of reinforcement rates will be chosen for the two keys, and left in force long enough to provide a stable estimate of the subject's frequency of responding to each, then a new pair is chosen and allowed to stabilize, and so on through subsequent schedule values. The results of such experiments are well approximated by the "matching law:" for each alternative, the proportion of responses emitted matches the proportion of reinforcements received (Herrnstein, 1961, 1970, 1971). A pigeon may, for example, earn a total of 100 reinforcements in 45 minutes, having pecked 3000 times at one key or the other. It will have distributed the 3000 pecks in approximately the same proportion as the reinforcements were earned. However the reinforcements are distributed, the pigeon will have spent 30 pecks per reinforcement.

The matching law applies to two or more choices, and to any subset of choices within some larger set of choices. It has been demonstrated scores of times with numerous species, including human (Bradshaw & Szabadi, in press; de Villiers, 1977; Herrnstein, 1970, 1971; Williams, in press), and it describes the behavior of individual subjects, as in Figure 3, not just averages of subjects. It may be represented as follows:

(1)

Here, B is a measure of the frequency of a behavior (or of the time spent engaging in some behavior); R is the count of reinforcements actually obtained from each of the behavioral alternatives. The denominators may represent the total behavior occurring, and the total reinforcements received, during some observation period, or some subset of each, so long as the same subscripts appear on either side. This discussion ignores the problem of measuring, on single scales, behaviors of different topography and differing quantities or qualities of reinforcement, but these have been dealt with elsewhere (see Herrnstein, 1974, 1982; Williams, in press).

Equation 1 represents proportions of reinforcement and behavior. Many experiments have, further, shown that the time rate of a behavior is a hyperbolic function of the reinforcement it earns (Bradshaw & Szabadi, in press; de Villiers & Herrnstein, 1976; Williams, in press), as follows:

(2)

Figure 4 (from Bradshaw & Szabadi, in press, their Fig. 5) illustrates typical findings for individual rats, pigeons, and human subjects (the last working for small amounts of money), along with the variances accounted for by equation 2.

Equations 1 and 2 can be reconciled with each other by interpreting the parameter, k, as total behavior measured in the units of B_1, and the other parameter, R_e, as all reinforcement being received in the situation exclusive of R_1, measured in the units of R_1 (Herrnstein, 1974, 1979). Implicitly, Equation 2 says that the absolute rate of a behavior is determined by its topography -- represented by k -- by the context of total reinforcement surrounding it -- represented by R_e -- and by the matching relation expressed in Equation 1 applying to all the behaviors occurring during the observation period. Each of those behaviors occur at a rate that is directly proportional to its own reinforcement and inversely proportional to total reinforcement. Because every behavior is influenced by all reinforcement, we may speak of a behavioral field analogous to a physical field.

Equation 2 is a familiar formalism for biological systems (e.g., Heyman, in press; Lehninger, 1970; Mansfield, 1976; Naka & Rushton, 1966) for which a finite receptor structure can be stimulated by potentially unlimited stimulus intensities. In biochemistry, where it is called the Michaelis-Menten equation, it is often applied to enzymatic reactions. It has also been applied to drug reactions and to the response of a sense organ, such as the retina. In each case, a finite substrate reacts to potentially unbounded stimulus intensities -- e.g., chemical reagents acting on limited amounts of catalyst or light energies acting on limited numbers of photoreceptors. As the receptor structure saturates with higher stimulus intensities, response increments decline hyperbolically. In the case of Equation 2, it is a matter of reinforcement acting on a limited capacity for behavior in any finite period. All behaviors will be in the same ratio to their reinforcement (the basic matching relation), but, given the finiteness of behavior, the size of the ratio must decline as the total amount of reinforcement rises.

Equation 2 is a simplification for natural environments in that it presupposes that a single category of behavior, B_1, can be observed against the background of an unchanging context of reinforcement, R_e. In the laboratory, however, where such conditions can be approximated, many studies have substantiated the hyperbolic relationship between behavior and its reinforcement and some of the other implications of Equation 2 (see Bradshaw & Szabadi, in press; de Villiers &

Herrnstein, 1976; Williams, in press), for human subjects as well as animal. It has been shown, for example, that a shift in drive level for R_1 causes, not only a change in the absolute rate of B_1, but a change in the curvature of the function relating behavior to reinforcement. If the drive is increased, making each unit of R_1 more valuable, then R_e, which is measured in units of R_1, shrinks, and vice versa if R_1 is devalued by a reduction in motivation. The empirically confirmed result, illustrated in Figure 5, is a family of functions for which curvature is inversely related to drive level.

For economists, the question must be whether Equations 1 and 2 maximize reinforcement. Consider a pigeon pecking a single response key and earning food reinforcement on a variable-interval schedule. The value of the schedule's average interval is explored parametrically. For each value, some function relates the obtained rate of reinforcement to the subject's rate of responding. The specific shape of this "reinforcement feedback function" depends upon the distributions of time intervals in the schedule and of the subject's interresponse times. Figure 6 shows typical functions for range of schedule values. The crosses mark typical rates of responding, given that Equation 2 holds, which is to say that the responding is a hyperbolic function of reinforcement rate, indicated by the dashed line connecting the crosses.

For the performance to be maximizing, we would have to suppose that the crosses fall at the point where the marginal effects of a change in peck rate (presumably in the slight change in earned reinforcement) are exactly offset by the change in the effects of not pecking (presumably in the change in leisure). However, Vaughan and Miller (1984) have shown that the performance is insensitive to the slope of the feedback curves in Figure 6 (see also Vaughan, 1976). They used a reinforcement schedule for which the reinforcement feedback function is sloped negatively over the range of observed response rate, as shown by the interrupted lines. Although the pigeons could have responded at a much lower rate and gained both more food and more leisure, they still approximated the rates of responding indicated by the crosses.

Departures from reinforcement maximization are commonplace with certain procedures. On a variable-ratio schedule, each response has a predetermined probability of reinforcement, but the probability varies unpredictably from reinforcement to reinforcement. This is the standard schedule for gambling situations, where there is some average ratio between numbers of responses and reinforcements. Variable-ratio schedules may be distinguished from variable-interval schedules, where, for a given schedule value, the ratio between responses and reinforcements varies inversely with response rate. Let us consider a choice procedure that allows the subject to earn reinforcement on two response keys -- one governed by a variable-interval schedule and the other, by a variable-ratio schedule. Figure 7 illustrates the reinforcement feedback functions for the procedure and shows why it is especially relevant to the question of reinforcement maximization.

Figure 7 plots, along the x-axis, the percentage of time during a period of observation spent working on the variable-interval alternative, the complement of which is the time spent working on the variable-ratio alternative (time spent working at neither can be disregarded, see Heyman & Herrnstein, 1986). The rising curve repeats a feedback function for variable intervals, such as those in Figure 6. Increasing times spent on the schedule earn more reinforcement at a decreasing rate. For the variable ratio, the relationship is a direct proportionality -- each increment of time earns a fixed increment in reinforcement. Reinforcement maximization -- shown by the left vertical line -- is earned where the negative of one slope equals the positive of the other, for that is where marginal changes in time allocation to the two alternatives balance each other. The right vertical line shows the matching performance, where the ratios of reinforcement to behavioral allocation are equal for the alternatives.

Several versions of the interval-ratio choice procedure have been examined, with about the same outcome (DeCarlo, 1985; Herrnstein & Heyman, 1979; Heyman & Herrnstein, 1986; Williams, 1985). Subjects match rather than maximize. Matching often exacts a considerable cost in overall reinforcment, which subjects appear to be indifferent to since they match as well when it is costly as when it is not. They match even when doing so earns the smallest possible rate of overall reinforcement (see Heyman & Herrnstein, 1986, for the special version of the procedure that allows such a possibility). Maximization typically calls for spending most of the time on the ratio alternative, visiting the interval only occasionally to collect any reinforcement that has come due since the last visit to it. Optimal performance, with its asymmetry in the proportionality between invested behavior and reinforcement for the competing alternatives, violates the matching law and is, it seems, psychologically unfeasible for interval-ratio choice. It has been observed (Houston, 1986) that the natural foraging behavior of a bird (pied wagtail) is analogously suboptimal when one source of food is ratio-schedule-like and another is interval-schedule-like.

Melioration

Matching, William Vaughan and I have suggested, is an equilibrium state produced by a behavioral process we call melioration (Herrnstein, 1982; Herrnstein & Vaughan, 1980; Vaughan, 1981, 1985; Williams, in press). A meliorating organism invests more time in better alternatives, until all less lucrative alternatives are precluded or until all remaining alternatives are equal in their returns (see Figure 2), thereby conforming to the matching law. Melioration resembles, but only slightly, Herbert Simon's concept of "satisficing," which holds that subjects seek behavioral allocations that are good enough to attain some goal or level of aspiration, not necessarily the best possible (Simon, 1955, 1956, 1979). Related to satisficing is Ronald Heiner's "reliability criterion," which attempts to define conditions for less than optimal performance (1983): a behavior is added or subtracted from a repertoire as a joint function of its likelihood, given limitations of perception, of occurring appropriately, the costs and benefits of inappropriate and appropriate occurrence, and the frequency of opportunities for appropriate occurrence. Heiner has, in effect, spelled out how a behavior may or may not be "good enough," in the satisficing sense of the term.

Melioration stipulates a general equilibrium state, namely matching; satisficing does not. Nothing more characterizes the satisficing allocation than that it satisfices; the level of aspiration or the reliability criterion varies with circumstances that are external to the decision rule itself. Melioration takes place at the same level of analysis, involving the same variables, as matching. Satisficing is a form of rationality, which has been called bounded or approximate; melioration is "rational" at the level of the behavioral alternative, not at the level of the organism as a whole.

For any pair of behaviors, the process of melioration takes into account the results of the following comparison:

(3)

The ratio, R_i/T_i, is the rate of reinforcement earned while engaging in the behavior represented by the subscript; the difference in reinforcement rate earned by the two behaviors is R_D. Allocation of time to B_1 increases when $R_D>0$; that to B_2 increases when $R_D<0$, and it achieves equilibrium when $R_D=0$. At $R_D=0$, the two behaviors are obeying the matching law:

(4)

Equilibrium is also attained when R_D is above or below 0 at all allocations, for then B_1 totally predominates over B_2 or vice versa. This form of equilibrium also conforms to the matching law, albeit trivially:

(5)

Given any variability in time allocation, equilibrium at $R_D=0$ depends on the values of R_D in the neighborhood of zero. Figure 8 illustrates the three classes of relationship relevant to melioration. In case A, R_D is nonzero at all time allocations, so one behavior becomes totally prepotent and the other behavior disappears. In case B, R_D passes through zero, resulting in equilibrium. The equilibirium is stable because deviations on either side of it are self-correcting: the function has negative slope in the neighborhood of $R_D=0$. In case C, because of the positive slope in that neighborhood, deviations are self-amplifying, so even though the function passes through zero, it will not produce a stable equilibrium if there is any variation in time allocation.

Whether or not a stable equilibrium point is also maximizing is fortuitous. From the curves in Figure 8, it is impossible to deduce the location of the maximization point, hence an organism controlled by R_D could not, on that basis, maximize. Figure 9 shows (from Herrnstein & Vaughan, 1980) the relevant function for the interval-ratio choice procedure described above, and adds an additional function, R_T, for the total reinforcement earned by the two alternatives. To maximize reinforcement, the subjects should have spent substantial time on the ratio schedule, but to do so would have meant tolerating a higher rate of reinforcement on the interval schedule, in violation of melioration. The subjects matched, hence they approximated the equilibrium point dictated by melioration, at considerable costs in overall reinforcement.

The decision rule embodied in melioration presupposes nothing about the nature, or even the sign, of the marginal utility function. The R_D functions involved in melioration depend on external circumstances -- the reinforcement feedback functions associated with the competing alternatives -- and on motivational processes -- the interactions between consumption of a reinforcer (or other motivational changes) and its value (or utility). Some reinforcers weaken with consumption at some rate, others strengthen, and still others are unchanged. Likewise, some environments yield poorer, some better, and some fixed, rates of return as a subject works at them. As a practical matter, certain relationships may be so common that understanding their dynamics may be worthwhile, but, theoretically, any configuration is equally well accounted for by melioration.

Vaughan and Herrnstein (in press) discuss the four configurations in Figure 10, for they illustrate the contrasting ways in which melioration and maximization may interact. First, one behavior may be more lucrative at all allocations, but overall reinforcement is unaffected by which is chosen. Melioration implies preference for one of the behaviors; maximization implies indifference to the choice between them. Second, one behavior may be more lucrative at all allocations, but result in the lowest overall reinforcement when chosen exclusively. The two decision rules make opposite predictions about preference. Third, the two behaviors are equally lucrative at all allocations, but overall reinforcement is maximal when one of them is exclusively chosen. Melioration implies indifference; maximization implies exclusive choice of one of the alternatives. Fourth, the two behaviors are equally lucrative at all allocations and overall reinforcement is unaffected by which is chosen. Both decision rules imply indifference. At least a small amount of data (in some instances only for animal subjects) for each configuration confirms the control of melioration, and the irrelevance of maximization (Vaughan & Herrnstein, in press).

Species Differences

The question of species differences is most likely to arise among economists in regard to humans compared to rats or pigeons. The short answer we do not know as much about species differences as we would like. Humans match in the basic procedures as well as other animals do, and their response rate functions are appropriately hyperbolic (see Bradshaw & Szabadi, in press, for a general review, and Takahashi & Iwamoto, 1986, for a representative experiment). But this is weak evidence for non-maximization, based on the inference that an organism that matches when it is not costly in overall reinforcement to do so will also match when it is.

Human subjects have not often been tested in procedures that pit matching against maximization. A parametric experiment on interval-ratio choice, for example, requires many sessions under reasonably stable motivational conditions -- an impracticality for human subjects in the psychological laboratory. It is, however, possible to devise acute tests that probe whether human subjects, like animals, are guided by the reinforcement rates associated with competing responses rather than the impact on overall reinforcement of marginal changes in allocation.

Drazen Prelec, William Vaughan, and I have studied various procedures that we refer to as intrapersonal prisoner's dilemmas; in the melioration scheme of things, each behavioral alternative is a "player" in its own right. In one procedure, volunteer human subjects worked for a single session. They chose one alternative or the other (i.e, depressing one of two telegraph keys) on a series of trials. Either choice earned a few cents on every trial (paid at the end of the session). The only difference between the choices was in their effects on the duration of the time interval between successive trials. The duration of the intertrial interval after a choice of one alternative, B_q, was: $d = 2 + 4x$. The intertrial interval, d, is measured in seconds; x is the proportion of trials that B_q was chosen over the last 10 trials (including the current one). The duration of the intertrial interval after a choice of the other alternative, B_s, was always two seconds longer than what it would have been after B_q. The duration in seconds of the intertrial interval is therefore described in general by the equation: $d = 4 + 2x$. If the subject always chooses B_s, the intertrial interval is four seconds; if always B_q, it is six seconds. Between the two extremes, the duration rises linearly with proportion of choices of B_q. Figure 11 shows the contingencies in the usual coordinates for melioration.

The function for B_s is two seconds above that for B_q at all allocations. The average intertrial interval for any allocation is shown by the dashed line. Maximization of reinforcement would have required exclusive choice of B_s; melioration, exclusive choice of B_q. Sixteen subjects worked for one session each. They were told at the start that they could earn more money by getting through trials rapidly and they had a ten-minute practice period to familiarize themselves with the contingencies before they started accumulating money. After the practice period, the median subject responded to B_q on .785 of trials (interquartile range from .590 to .935). Instead of earning \$6.15 in a session, the typical subject earned \$4.66; the least he could have earned, assuming a choice on every trial, was \$4.25.

Subjects working for just a single session probably do not reveal asymptotic choice. We cannot say whether, with additional experience, they might have moved toward maximization (i.e., toward B_s) or further toward melioration (i.e., toward B_q). However, it is clear from these results (as from other intrapersonal prisoner's dilemma procedures) that human subjects, like animals, are spontaneously disposed to be guided by the reinforcements per behavior, rather than by overall reinforcement. They, like pigeons and rats, shift away from optimality if melioration pushes that way.

Up to this point, I have taken for granted what the competing behavioral alternatives are -- depressing one telegraph key, or pecking one pigeon key, or another. Now, we need to examine the structure of the behavioral field more critically. Figure 11 showed a procedure involving a pair of response keys; it implicitly assumed that the environment was to be described in terms of those two alternatives, with their respective contingencies of reinforcement. It is, however, always possible to construe an environment in many ways. In this experiment, each allocation of choices within a sequence of 10 trials could be considered a distinct alternative.

Strategies involving multiple trials have reinforcement contingencies, among which subjects may choose. There are, in fact, 11 such behaviors, or strategies, defined by the reinforcement contingencies -- from 0 to 100 percent of B_q choices in steps of 10 percent. The subject could be choosing among, say, B_q on all 10 trials versus B_q on 60 or 40 or 20 percent within 10-trial sequences, and so on. In other words, the alternatives are not necessarily confined to one telegraph key or the other on a trial-by-trial basis. Figure 12 shows the procedure from the standpoint of strategies involving 10-trial sequences.

Because 10 trials are used to set intertrial intervals, the functions in Figure 12 are flat. A given 10-trial strategy earns a certain intertrial interval no matter what the subject does at other times. As long as the subject responds exclusively to B_s over 10 trials, the intertrial interval will be at its minimum, namely four seconds. Strategies involving choices of B_q produce longer intertrial intervals, reaching the maximum of six seconds when it is chosen exclusively in a 10-trial run. By the process of melioration applied to the behaviors represented in Figure 12, B_s should be chosen exclusively. This is also the reinforcement-rate-maximizing strategy.

Subjects do not, however, maximize reinforcement rate with this procedure. They behave as if they do not make contact with the representation in Figure 12 even though it is as accurate a description as the one in Figure 11. The representation in Figure 12 is more complex in that it involves 11 behavioral categories rather than the two in Figure 11; it cuts across the natural division between the two telegraph keys, and it involves delayed consequences stretching over 10 trials. It may fail to take hold because subjects are unable to detect the reinforcement contingencies at the relevant level, or because of implicit costs in doing so that wipe out the obvious benefits in additional reinforcement (see Heiner, 1983, for a systematic cost-benefit analysis of adding or subtracting behavioral entities from a repertoire). If the representation in Figure 12 did take hold, melioration applied to it would result in maximization of the programmed reinforcement.

Three general points are being made here. First, melioration can be applied, not only to the allocation across existing alternatives, but to the formation of the alternatives themselves. Behavior flows in a continuous stream; it is not, in principle, divided into sharp, fixed entities. New behaviors can be shaped out of this continuous stream by the process of melioration if there are differences in the reinforcements earned by different ways of partitioning the stream. Second, although behavior is not in principle divided into entities, it seems, in fact, to be more or less easily cut up in particular ways. Given two telegraph keys to depress, we tend to see the situation as a choice between them, rather than as choices among the many hybrids of sequential choices of the two keys, let alone hybrids that might include all the other activities that could added in (e.g., pressing with the left index finger while standing on the right leg).

Different subjects may subdivide the behavioral stream in different ways, depending upon past experience or sensitivities of various sorts. The acquisition of skills -- playing a violin or flying an airplane, for example -- consists of shifting toward more complex and abstract behavioral entities guided by the process of melioration. But for any subject at a given time, there are limits in the plasticity of behavioral classes, hence in the possibility of discovering still more lucrative strategies than the ones we may initially adopt.[2] These limits may vary not only within, but also across, species. Species with less flexibility in their behavioral classes are species for which behavior is more constrained by instinct.[3] Third, maximization would be achieved by the process of melioration itself if there were no limits to plasticity. However, whatever behavioral field an organism settles on -- or whatever field it is given by instinct -- it will be driven toward equilibrium -- the matching relationship -- by melioration.

---

[2] The interaction beteen contingencies of reinforcement and the molding of behavioral categories is illuminated by the experiments on "framing," by Tversky and Kahneman (1981). Those authors do not place their work in the matching law framework, but Rachlin, Logue, Gibbon, and Frankel (1986) have recently done so.

[3] Unusual among economists is Ronald Heiner, who draws on the study of animal behavior and notes that the rigidity of instinct in animals has implications for the economic theory of choice (1983). If choice were optimal except for errors of memory, perception, etc., then, suggests Heiner, we might expect behavior to be less orderly the more it deviates from optimality. On the contrary, he points out, the most orderly and predictable behavior is not that which adapts to changing circumstances in order to maximize, but that which is fixed in instinct. There must, he infers, be some other principle besides maximization that accounts for orderly behavior.

Advantages of a Valid Theory

Even if maximization is not a valid scientific theory of choice, it will survive as a normative principle. People express a desire to maximize, whether or not they succeed in doing so in action. So, an economist may ask, what if utility maximization is not a valid theory of behavior, does it not remain a valid formalization of rationality. My first answer would be "Yes, but ..." -- if it is not a valid theory, what is. Behavioral scientists should seek a better description of behavior than maximization gives us, even after taking account of the complexities and vagaries of utility functions.

A second answer is that, if maximization is a poor theory, it may give the wrong results when it is used to infer utility functions, as it often is. Utility functions are mapped out by assuming that subjects are indifferent to bundles of choices that have equal total utility. But subjects have been shown to match, regardless of the impact on total utility. Subjects will not be indifferent to bundles of choices that earn the same total utility, if the behavioral alternatives constituting some bundles conform to matching and others do not. They shift from bundle to bundle, not because of the changes in total utility, but because of meliorizing comparisons across the behaviors (or commodities) that constitute those bundles. Only for that class of feedback functions for which maximization occurs at the matching point is the standard economic procedure correct. For feedback functions that fail to yield maximization at the matching point, the inferences about utilities based on standard economic analysis will be wrong.

Consider a choice between alternatives reinforced on variable-ratio schedules -- a pair of slot machines in a gambling casino, for example. The probability of reinforcement for each alternative is fixed, not dependent upon the rate of responding, as it is for variable-interval schedules. The time rate of reinforcement for each alternative is thus also fixed (assuming no changes in the local rates of responding). How much we win (or lose) per unit time at a machine is independent of how much time we spend playing it. Figure 13 presents, in the same coordinates used earlier, the contingencies arranged by concurrent variable-ratio schedules with different values. This, then, is an example of a situation in which melioration and maximization make the same prediction -- exclusive choice of the alternative with the higher probability of reinforcement.

Competing variable-ratio schedules are, at least to a fair approximation, commonplace in nature -- alternatives that offer approximately direct proportionalities between behavioral input and reinforcement output. They are also the schedules that economists, and others who take a rationalistic approach to behavior, often postulate for theoretical and empirical consideration. It is an important feature of melioration that it reduces to maximization in the very situations that we intuit will elicit rational choice. But, by the same token, rational choice in these situations is no more evidence for maximization as a general decision rule than for melioration, and vice versa. Nevertheless, such situations are special because they are appropriate for the formal methods of optimization theory.

For variable-ratio schedules, it is correct to assume maximization, thence to infer the underlying utilities. But now suppose the environment shifts to interval schedules. The economist still assuming maximzation will be forced to infer different utilites for the same commodities. But under the assumption of melioration and matching, the data would force no change in either the decision rule or the inferred utilities when the reinforcement schedule changes. A formal structure, comparable in all respects to that of neoclassical economics but based on matching rather than maximization at equilibrium, is a possibility yet to be realized (but see Prelec, 1982, 1983, for some beginnings).

A third answer is heuristic -- not decisive but perhaps worth considering anyway. Given the continuity of species, it would not be surprising to find continuity in behavioral processess. But can evolutionary continuity be reconciled with the universal intuition that humans and other higher species are more rational, which is to say, they maximize better, than lower species? Melioration seems to do the job, for it permits any point on the continuum between irrationality and rationality. Within the framework of melioration, species may vary in their sensitivity to deferred or abstract or novel relationships between behavior and its consequences. Longer time horizons, and greater flexibility and abstractness in behavioral entities provide a broader set of behavioral categories upon which melioration may operate, hence it provides choices closer to the rational end of the continuum. Assuming the appropriate genetic variance and selection pressures, evolution may push a meliorizing species incrementally toward theoretical Economic Man, without a decision rule other than melioration itself or a sudden leap to perfect rationality.

Overview

Neither matching nor maximization can account, without ad hoc adjustments, for all the facts we have about behavior. The ad hoc adjustments differ. For melioration, the main problems arise from ambiguities in the set of behavioral alternatives, examples of which were described above. The notion is that melioration itself shapes the behavioral stream, but only to a limited degree. Given a set of behavioral alternatives, the very same process of melioration governs allocation, yielding matching at equilibrium. Maximization theory is saddled with the same ambiguity in defining a choice set, but has, in addition, problems with the equilibrium state. Individuals often fail to maximize, given any plausible definition of utility or reinforcement. Economic theory provides no general characterization of the actual equilibrium states individuals attain, but instead must suppose that individuals would have maximized except for limitations in perception, memory, time horizons, reasoning ability, etc. Matching theory, in contrast, provides a general characterization of the equilibrium state -- namely, matching itself across whatever behavioral entities have been formed. This asymmetry seems to me to favor matching theory.

Economic theorists frequently invoke perceptual or cognitive limitations to explain failures to maximize. The experimental procedures or natural situations that yield non-maximizing choices are often dismissed as being too complex, usually with no further elaboration of what makes them complex besides the fact that the subject failed to maximize. The limitations in performance are not usually taken to have any deeper meaning. But an organism's perceptual and cognitive capacities are likely, on evolutionary grounds, to be adapted to the processes that guide its behavior, just as its digestive system is adapted to what it eats or its locomotor system to where it lives. That organisms seem to be perceptually and cognitively adapted for matching rather than maximizing also seems to me to favor matching theory.

References

Adams, J. S. (1965) Inequity in social exchange. In L. Berkowitz (ed.), Advances in Experimental Social Psychology, vol. 2. New York: Academic Press.

Becker, G. S. (1962) Irrational behavior and economic theory. The Journal of Political Economy, 70, 1-13.

Blau, P. M. (1964) Exchange and Power in Social Life. New York: Wiley.

Bradshaw, C. M., & Szabadi, E. (in press) Quantitative analysis of human operant behaviour. In G. C. L. Davey (ed.), Chichester, U. K.: Wiley.

Brown, R. (1986) Social Psychology: The Second Edition. New York: Free Press.

Brown, R., & Herrnstein, R. J. (1975) Psychology. Boston: Little Brown.

DeCarlo, L. T. (1985) Matching and maximizing with variable-time schedules. Journal of the Experimental Analysis of Behavior, 43, 75-81.

de Villiers, P. A. (1977) Choice in concurrent schedules and a quantitative formulation of the law of effect. In W. K. Honig & J. E. R. Staddon (eds.), Handbook of Operant Behavior. Englewood Cliffs, N. J.: Prentice-Hall.

de Villiers, P. A., & Herrnstein, R. J. (1976) Toward a law of response strength. Psychological Bulletin, 83, 1131-1153.

Easterlin, R. (1974) Does economic growth improve the human lot? Some empirical evidence. In P. David & M. Reder (eds.), Nations and Households in Economic Growth: Essays in Honor of Moses Abramovitz. New York: Academic Press.

Frank, R. H. (1985) Choosing the Right Pond. New York: Oxford University Press.

Frank, R. H. (1986) The nature of the utility function. In A. MacFadyne & H. MacFadyen (eds.), Economic Psychology. North Holland.

Friedman, M. (1953) Essays in Positive Economics. Chicago: University of Chicago Press.

Hatfield, E., Traupmann, J., & Walster, G. W. (1978) Equity and extramarital sexuality. Archives of Sexual Behavior, 7, 127-142.

Hatfield, E., Walster, G. W., & Berscheid, E. (1978) Equity: Theory and Research. Boston: Allyn & Bacon.

Heiner, R. A. (1983) The origin of predictable behavior. American Economic Review, 73, 560-595.

Herrnstein, R. J. (1961) Relative and absolute strength of response as a function of frequency of reinforcement. Journal of the Experimental Analysis of Behavior, 4, 267-272.

Herrnstein, R. J. (1970) On the law of effect. Journal of the Experimental Analysis of Behavior, 13, 243-266.

Herrnstein, R. J. (1971) Quantitative hedonism. Journal of Psychiatric Research, 8, 399-412.

Herrnstein, R. J. (1974) Formal properties of the matching law. Journal of the Experimental Analysis of Behavior, 21, 159-164.

Herrnstein, R. J. (1979) Derivatives of matching. Psychological Review, 86, 486-495.

Herrnstein, R. J. (1982) Melioration as behavioral dynamism. In M. L. Commons, R. J. Herrnstein, & H. Rachlin (eds.), Quantitative Analyses of Behavior, Vol. II: Matching and Maximizing Accounts. Cambridge, Mass.: Ballinger.

Herrnstein, R. J., & Heyman, G. M. (1979) Is matching compatible with reinforcement maximization on concurrent variable interval, variable ratio? Journal of the Experimental Analysis of Behavior, 31, 209-223.

Herrnstein, R. J., & Vaughan, W., Jr. (1980) Melioration and behavioral allocation. In J. E. R. Staddon (ed.), Limits to Action: The Allocation of Individual Behavior. New York: Academic Press.

Heyman, G. (in press) How drugs affect cells and reinforcement affects behavior: Formal analogies. In R. Church, M. L. Commons, J. Stellar, & A. Wagner (eds.), Quantitative Analyses of Behavior: Vol. 7. Biological Determinants of Reinforcement and Memory. Hillsdale, N. J.: Erlbaum.

Heyman, G., & Herrnstein, R. J. (1986) More on concurrent interval-ratio schedules: A replication and review. Journal of the Experimental Analysis of Behavior, 46, 331-351.

Hirshleifer, J. (1985) The expanding domain of economics. American Economic Review, 75, 53-68.

Homans, G. C. (1974) Social Behavior: Its Elementary Forms, Rev. Ed. New York: Harcourt Brace Jovanovich.

Houston, A. I. (1986) The matching law applies to wagtails' foraging in the wild. Journal of the Experimental Analysis of Behavior, 45, 15-18.

Kornai, J. (1986) Contradictions and Dilemmas: Studies on the Socialist Economy and Society. Cambridge, Mass.: MIT Press.

Lehninger, A. L. (1970) Biochemistry. New York: Worth.

Leibenstein, H. J. (1976) Beyond Economic Man: A New Foundation for Microeconomics. Cambridge, Mass.: Harvard University Press.

Maital, S. (1982) Minds, Markets, and Money. New York: Basic Books.

Mansfield, R. J. W. (1976) Visual adaptation: Retinal transduction, brightness and sensitivity. Vision Research, 16, 679-690.

Maslow, A. H. (1955) Deficiency motivation and growth motivation. In M. R. Jones (ed.), Nebraska Symposium on Motivation: 1955. Lincoln, Nebr.: University of Nebraska Press.

Myerson, J., & Miezin, F. M. (1980) The kinetics of choice: An operant systems analysis. Psychological Review, 87, 160-174.

Naka, K. I., & Rushton, W. A. H. (1966) S-potentials from luminosity units in the retina of fish (Cyprinidae). Journal of Physiology, London, 185, 587-599.

Prelec, D. (1982) Matching, maximizing, and the hyperbolic reinforcement feedback function. Psychological Review, 89, 189-230.

Prelec, D. (1983) The empirical claims of maximization theory: A reply to Rachlin and to Kagel, Battalio, and Green. Psychological Review, 90, 385-389.

Rachlin, H. (1973) Contrast and matching. Psychological Review, 80, 217-234.

Rachlin, H., Logue, A. W., Gibbon, J., & Frankel, M. (1986) Cognition and behavior in studies of choice. Psychological Review, 93, 33-45.

Rubin, Z. (1973) Liking and Loving. New York: Holt, Rinehart & Winston.

Schoeck, H. (1966) Envy: A Theory of Social Behaviour. Translated by M. Glenny and B. Ross. New York: Harcourt, Brace & World.

Scitovsky, T. (1975) The Joyless Economy: An Inquiry into Human Satisfaction and Consumer Dissatisfaction. New York: Oxford University Press.

Simon, H. A. (1955) A behavioral model of rational choice. Quarterly Journal of Economics, 59, 99-118.

Simon, H. A. (1956) Rational choice and the structure of the environment. Psychological Review, 63, 129-138.

Simon, H. A. (1979) Rational decision making in business organizations. American Economic Review, 69, 493-513.

Solomon, R. L., & Corbit, J. D. (1974) An opponent-process theory of motivation: I. Temporal dynamics of affect. Psychological Review, 81, 119-145.

Takahashi, M., & Iwamoto, T. (1986) Human concurrent performances: The effects of experience, instructions, and schedule-correlated stimuli. Journal of the Experimental Analysis of Behavior, 45, 257-267.

Tversky, A., & Kahneman, D. (1981) Framing of decisions and the psychology of choice. Science, 211, 453-458.

Vaughan, W., Jr. (1976) Optimization and reinforcement. Unpublished doctoral dissertation, Harvard University.

Vaughan, W., Jr. (1981) Melioration, matching, and maximization. Journal of the Experimental Analysis of Behavior, 36, 141-149.

Vaughan, W., Jr. (1985) Choice: A local analysis. Journal of the Experimental Analysis of Behavior, 43, 383-405.

Vaughan, W., Jr., & Herrnstein, R. J. (in press) Stability, melioration, and natural selection. In L. Green & J. Kagel (eds.), Advances in Behavioral Economics, vol. 1. Norwood, N. J Ablex.

Vaughan, W., Jr., & Miller, H. L., Jr. (1984) Optimization versus response-strength accounts of behavior. Journal of the Experimental Analysis of Behavior, 42, 337-348.

Williams, B. A. (1985) Choice behavior in a discrete-trial concurren VI-VR: A test of maximizing theories of matching. Learning and Motivation, 16, 423-443.

Williams, B. A. (in press) Reinforcement, choice, and response strength. In R. C. Atkinson, R. J. Herrnstein, G. Lindzey, & R. D. Luce (eds.), Handbook of Experimental Psychology. New York: Wiley.

Wilson, E. O. (1975) Sociobiology: The New Synthesis. Cambridge, Mass.: Harvard University Press.

Wilson, E. O. (1981) On Human Nature. Cambridge, Mass.: Harvard University Press.

Wilson, J. Q., & Herrnstein, R. J. (1985) Crime and Human Nature. New York: Simon & Schuster.

Figure Captions

Figure 1. Total utility (U_{a+b}) as a function of allocation to C_a, which is one of two mutually exclusive and exhaustive commodities, C_a and C_b. Assume that initial allocation is at $C_a{}^*$. A utility maximizer would shift allocation to $C_{a(max)}$ by noting how U_{a+b} changes with small shifts in allocation. (From Vaughan & Herrnstein, in press.)

Figure 2. Melioration across two behavioral alternatives, a and b, in terms of the proportion of time allocated to a (assuming no other alternatives). Reinforcements per unit time for each alternative is given by V_a and V_b. Assume that the initial allocation is at $T_a{}^*$. Melioration produces equilibrium at T_a where $V_a=V_b$. (From Vaughan & Herrnstein, in press.)

Figure 3. Percent of pecks at one of two response keys as a function of percent of reinforcements obtained by pecking at that key, for three pigeons. Diagonal line plots Equation 1. (From Herrnstein, 1961.)

Figure 4. Time rate of responding as a function of time rate of reinforcement for a pigeon, a rat, and a human being. Parameters are best-fitting values for Equation 2, with percent of variance accounted for. (From Bradshaw & Szabadi, in press.)

Figure 5. Time spent at a behavioral alternative as a function of its reinforcement rate, for three levels of motivation, according to Equation 2.

Figure 6. Obtained reinforcement rate as a function of response rate on variable-interval schedules. Crosses show typical observed rates of responding with this schedule (as predicted by Equation 2). Changing the reinforcement feedback function to the negatively sloped dashed lines has negligible effects on behavior, showing the irrelevance of marginal rates of reinforcement.

Figure 7. Reinforcement rate during an observation period that provides access to concurrent variable-interval and variable-ratio schedules. The abscissa is the proportion of time spent at the variable interval; its complement is the proportion of time spent at the variable ratio. Vertical line at the left is the reinforcement maximization point; that at the right is the matching point.

Figure 8. Given two behavioral alternatives, 1 and 2, the reinforcement-rate difference between them, R_D, may depend on time allocation, $T_1/(T_1+T_2)$. According to melioration, case A should produce exclusive choice of 1; case B should produce stable equilibrium at $R_D=0$; and case C should, given any variation in time allocation, produce exclusive choice of 1 or 2, depending on whether allocation slips to the right or left of $R_D=0$.

Figure 9. Reinforcement-rate difference (R_D) and total reinforcement (R_T) as functions of time allocated to the variable-interval alternative on a concurrent variable-interval variable-ratio schedule. Melioration predicts equilibrium at the cross on the R_D function; maximization, at that on the R_T function. Subjects consistently meliorate, at the cost of substantial losses in reinforcement. (From Herrnstein & Vaughan, 1980.)

Figure 10. Various configurations showing possible interactions between melioration and maximization for a pair of competing behavioral alternatives, a and b. See text for explanation. (From Vaughan & Herrnstein, in press.)

Figure 11. An intrapersonal prisoner's dilemma procedure for human subjects. There are two alternatives, B_q and B_s. Each alternative reinforces every time it is chosen, but the intertrial interval following B_s is always two seconds longer than that following B_q. However, the absolute duration of the intertrial interval grows linearly with the proportion of selections of B_q over the preceding ten trials.

Figure 12. An alternative way to represent the procedure illustrated in Figure 11. Consider 10-trial sequences defined by the proportion within them of selections of B_q. The panel on the right shows the intertrial intervals associated with these 10-trial sequences.

Figure 13. Reinforcement rate per unit time for a concurrent variable-ratio variable-ratio schedule. Alternative a has the smaller ratio, hence the higher reinforcement rate. The abscissa shows investment in alternative a; that in b is the complement. The dashed line is the overall rate of reinforcement. (From Vaughan & Herrnstein, in press.)

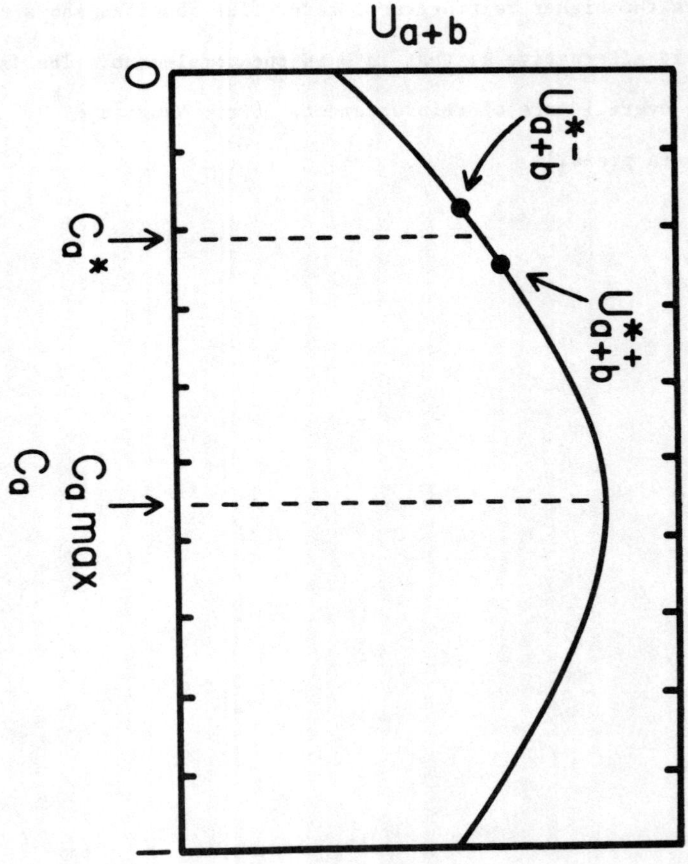

Figure 1

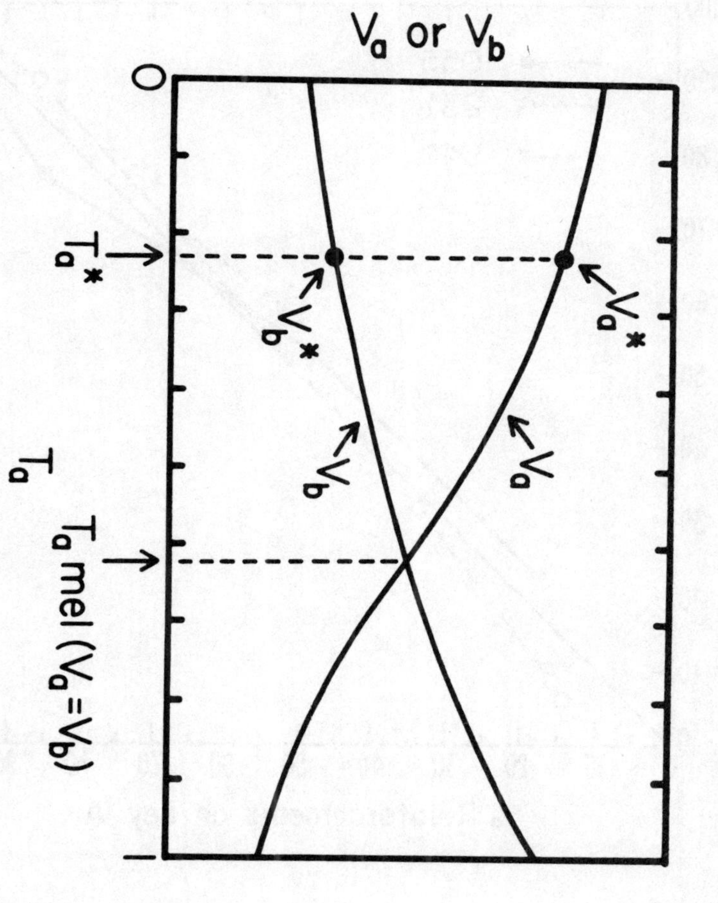

Figure 2

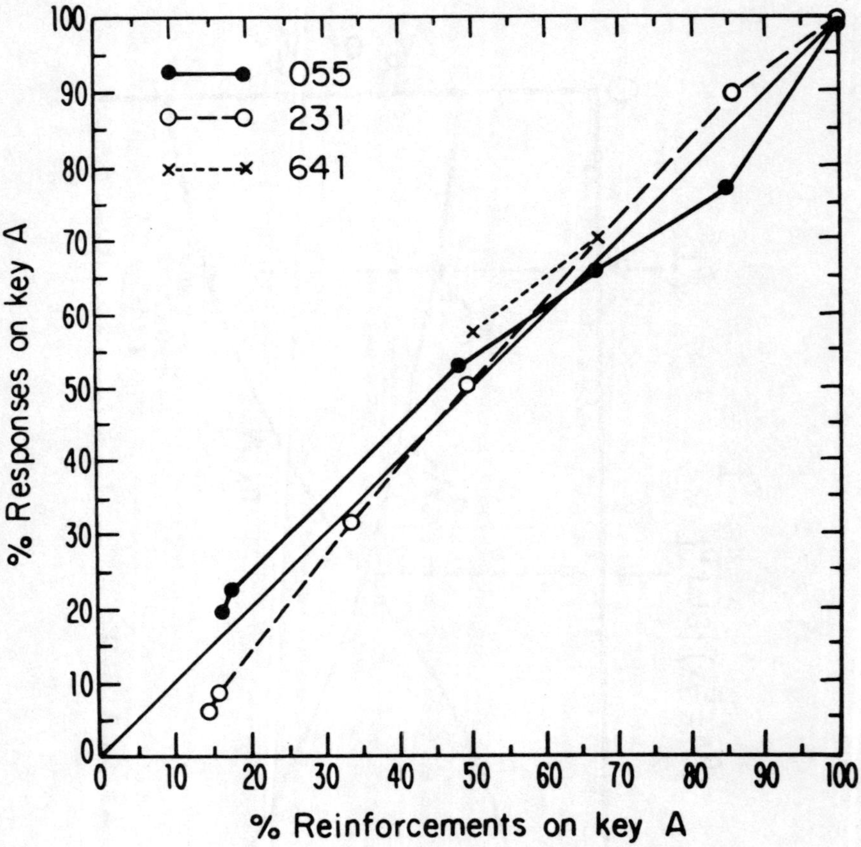
055
231
641
% Responses on key A
% Reinforcements on key A
0
10
20
30
40
50
60
70
80
90
100

Figure 3

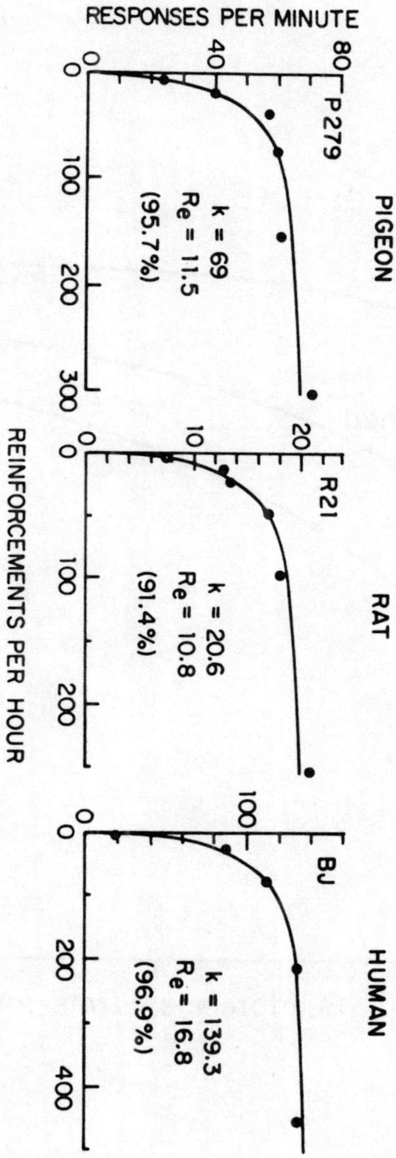

PIGEON
RAT
HUMAN
RESPONSES PER MINUTE
REINFORCEMENTS PER HOUR
P279
k = 69
R_e = 11.5
(95.7%)
R21
k = 20.6
R_e = 10.8
(91.4%)
BJ
k = 139.3
R_e = 16.8
(96.9%)

Figure 4

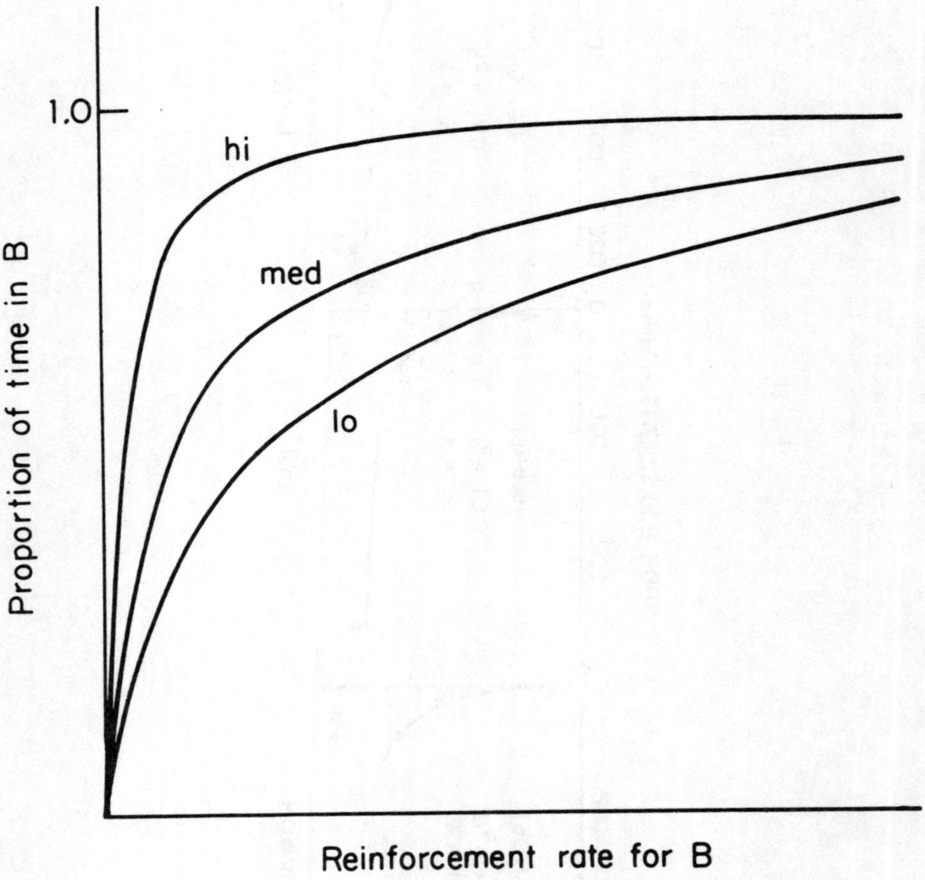

Figure 5

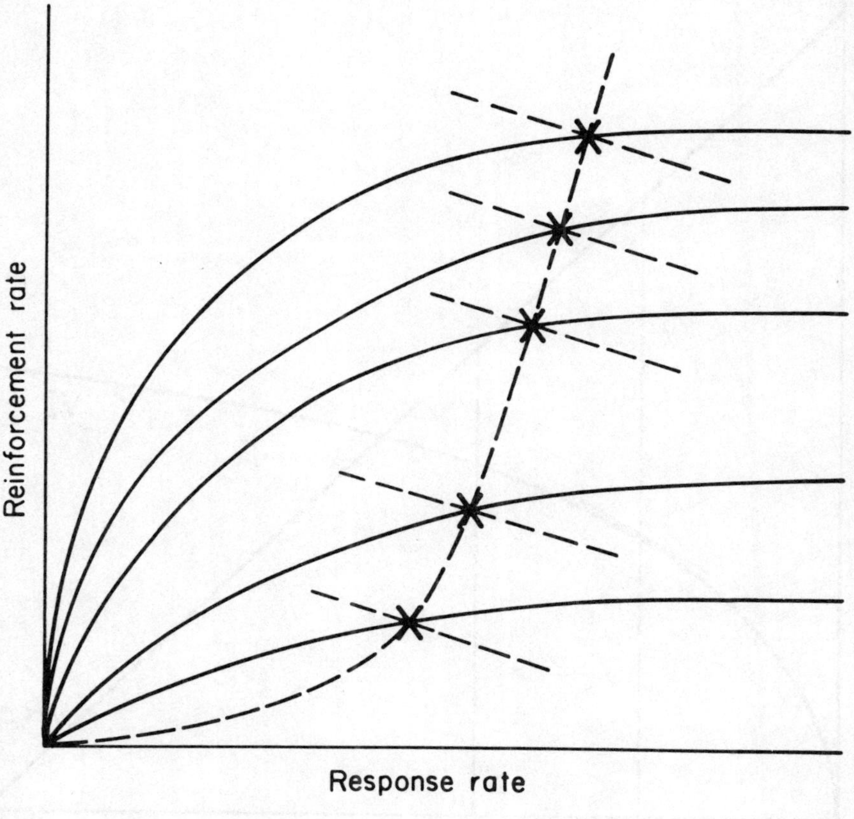

Figure 6

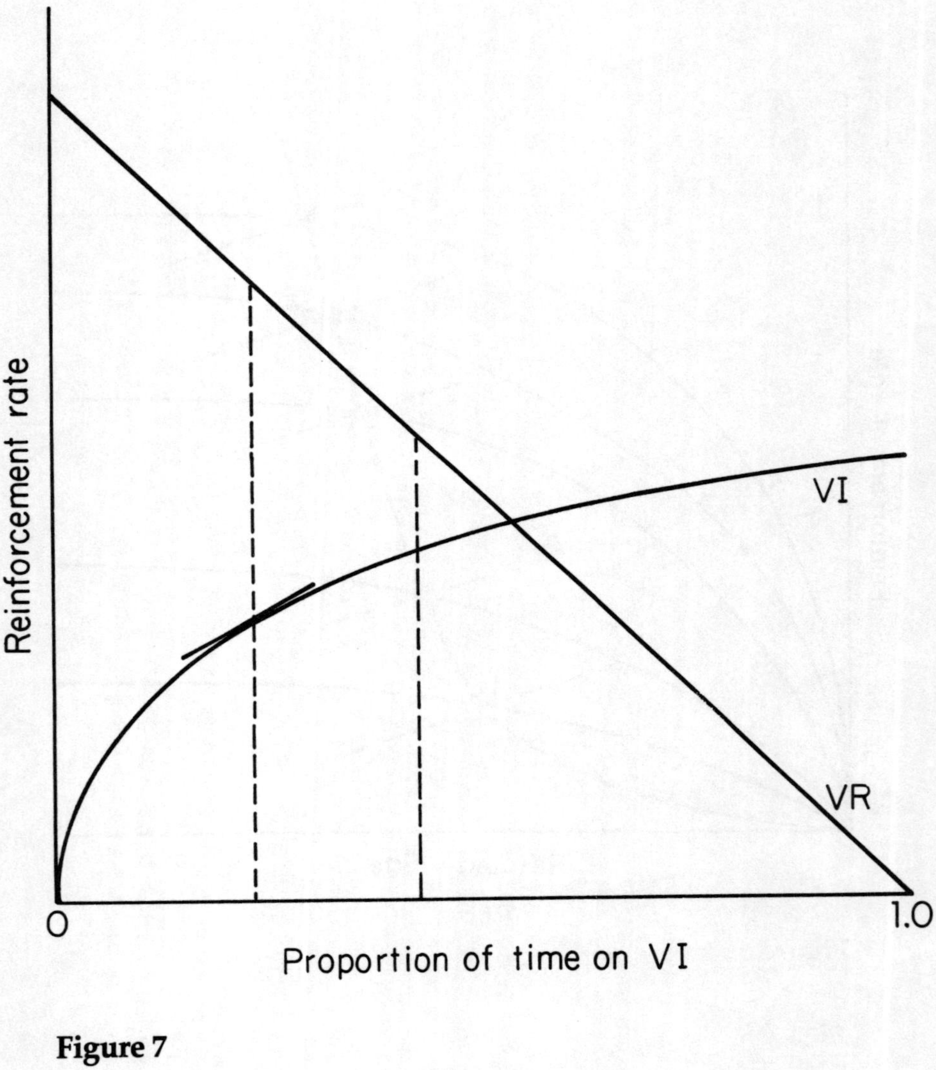

Figure 7

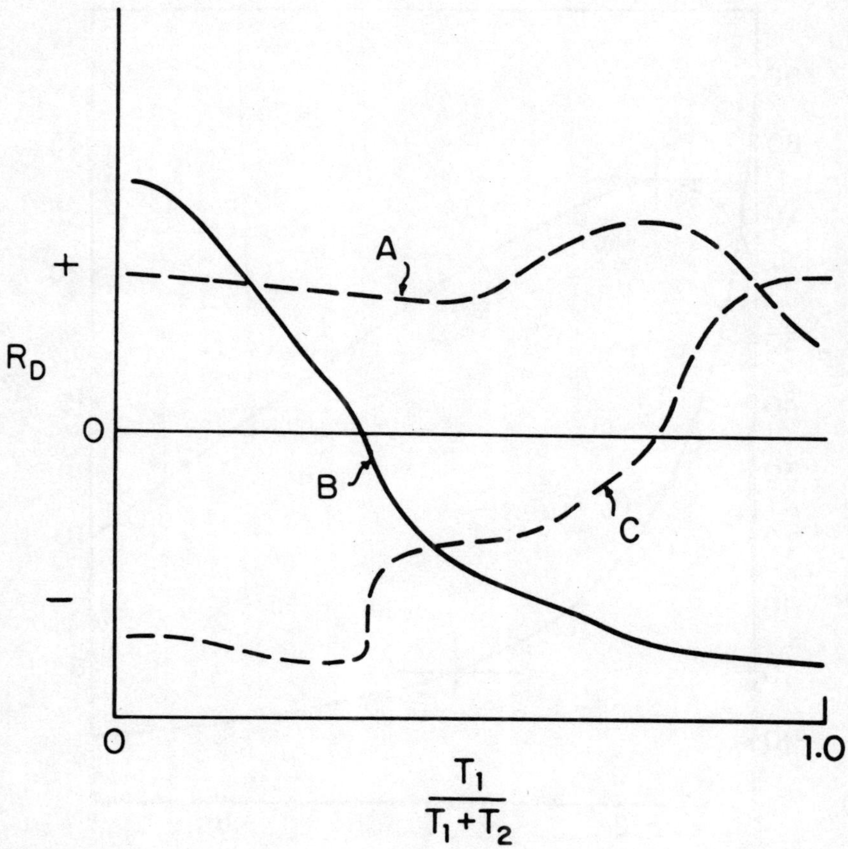

Figure 8

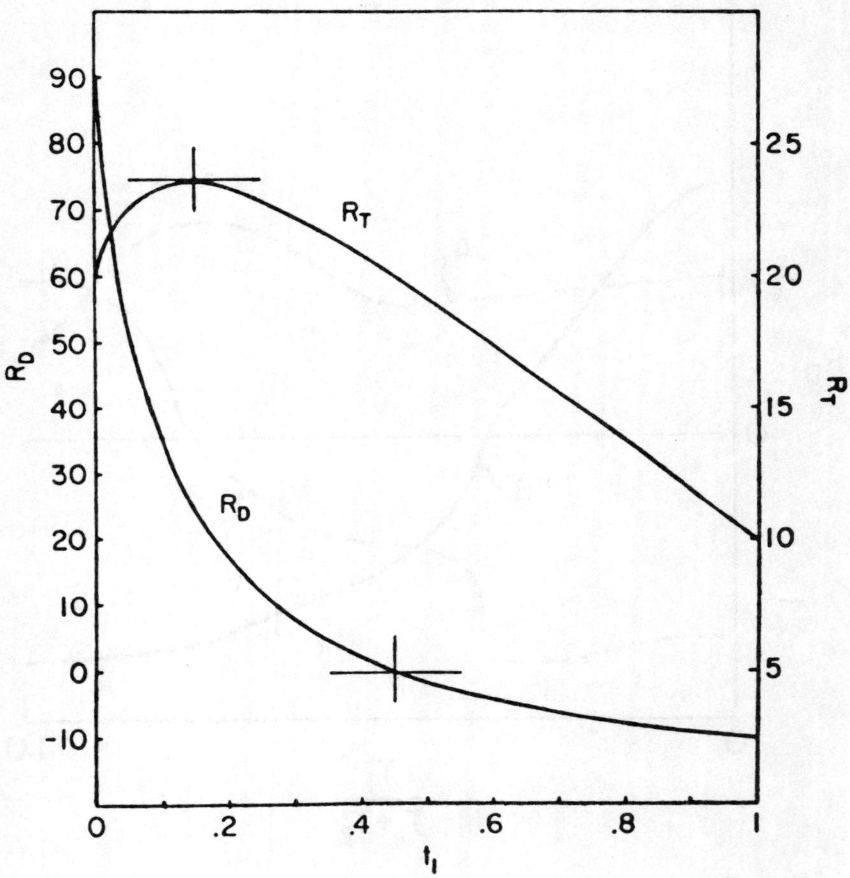

Figure 9

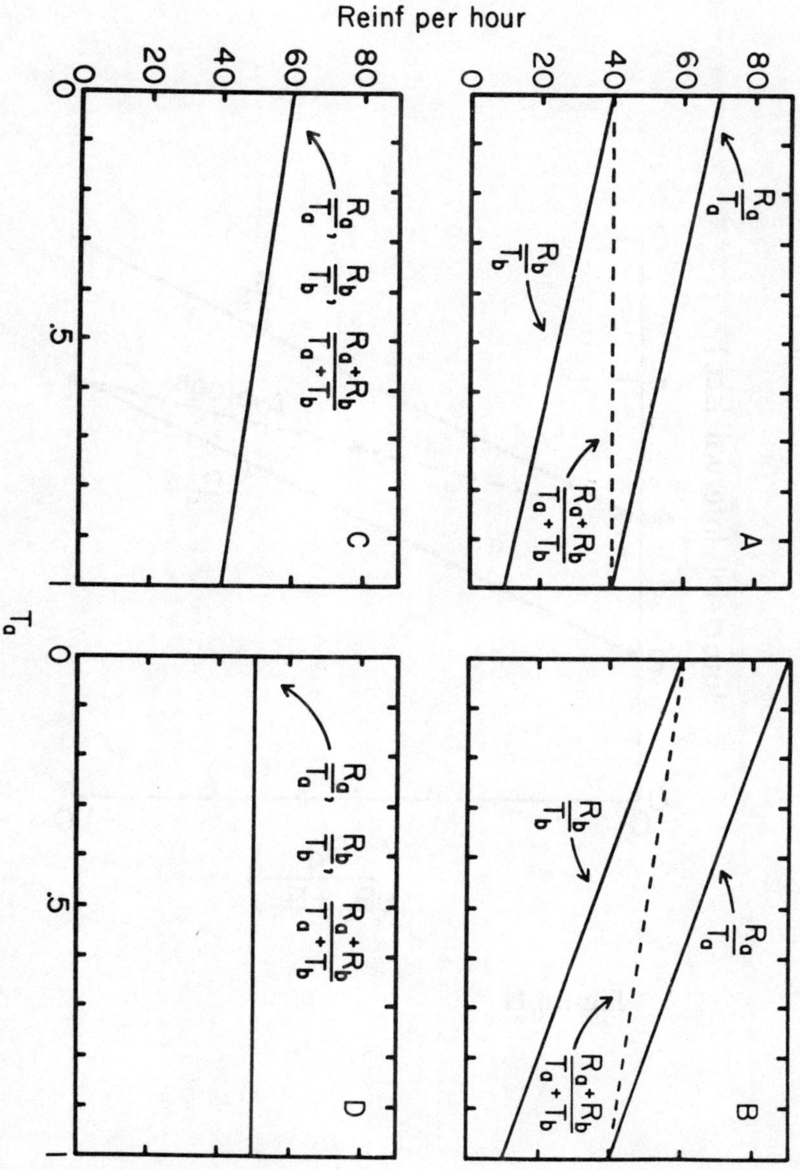

Figure 10

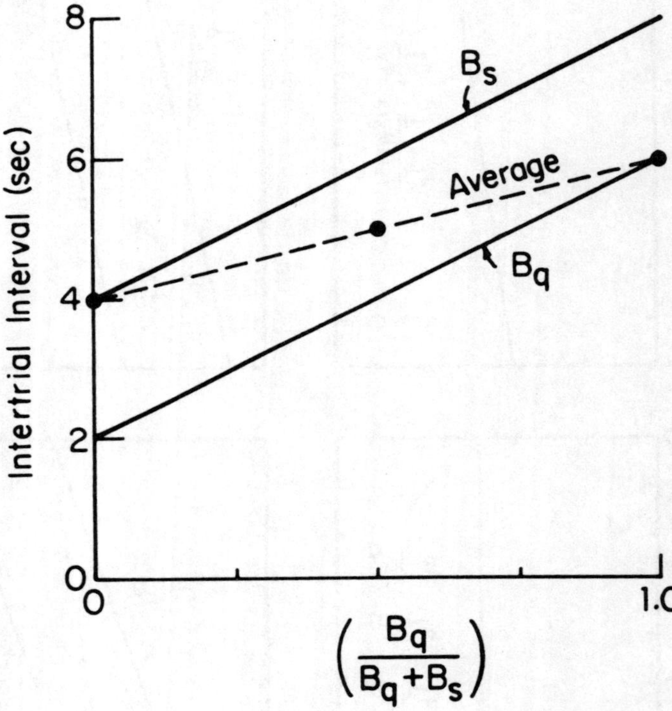

Intertrial Interval (sec)
8
6
4
2
0
B_s
Average
B_q
0
1.0
$\left(\frac{B_q}{B_q + B_s}\right)$

Figure 11

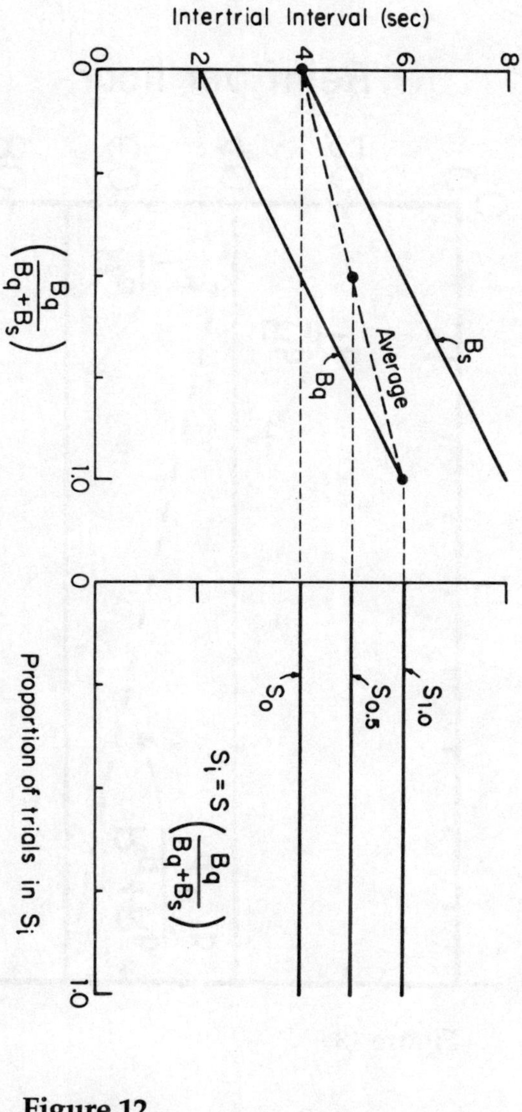

Intertrial Interval (sec)
0
2
4
6
8
0
1.0
B_s
Average
B_q
$\left(\frac{B_q}{B_q+B_s}\right)$
0
1.0
$S_{1.0}$
$S_{0.5}$
S_0
$S_i = S\left(\frac{B_q}{B_q+B_s}\right)$
Proportion of trials in S_i

Figure 12

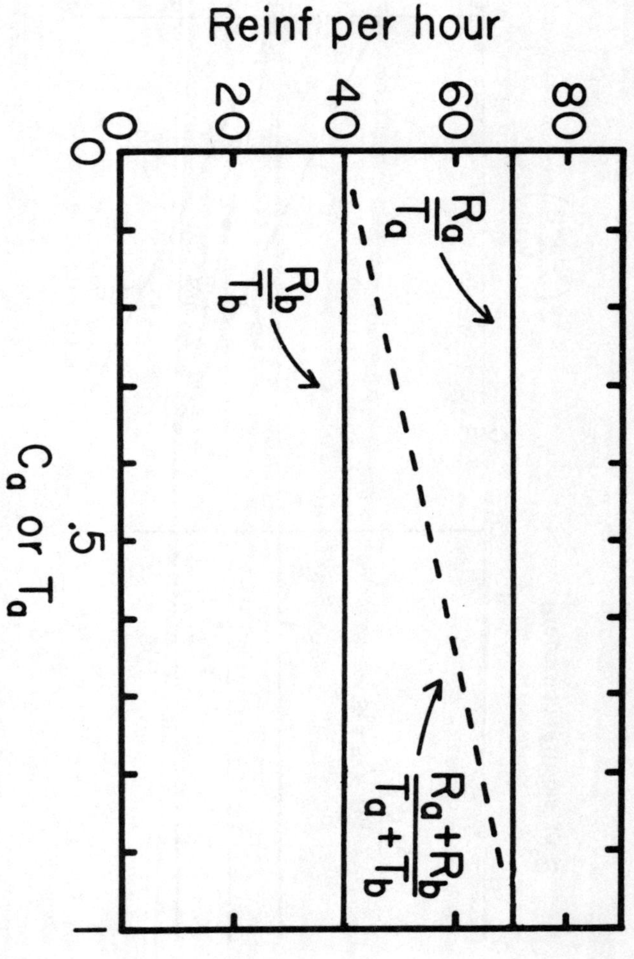
Reinf per hour
0
20
40
60
80
$\frac{R_a}{T_a}$
$\frac{R_b}{T_b}$
$\frac{R_a+R_b}{T_a+T_b}$
0
.5
1
C_a or T_a

Figure 13

Part One
The Role of Perception and Information in Consumption and Saving

Consumer Information in the Electronic Data Media

Folke ÖLANDER

Aarhus School of Business Administration and Economics
Ryhavevej 8
DK-8210 Aarhus V, Denmark

The new electronic data media (teletext, videotex, cabletext, other database access) are briefly described, as well as the present use of these media for neutral consumer information, i.e., information originating from public agencies and consumer organizations.

The main purpose of the paper is to discuss factors having an impact upon the future of neutral consumer information in these media. Most of these factors seem to work counter to an increased dissemination of such neutral consumer information through the data media, teletext being a possible exception. The rate of diffusion of the electronic media among households is likely to be much slower than previously predicted, and to the extent that households will become subscribers to, and users of, electronic data media, it is clear that the totally predominating part of consumer information will take the form of advertising and sales promotion.

1. INTRODUCTION

The new electronic media for the conveyance of text material - teletext, videotex, cabletext, computer databases - have sometimes been hailed as media excellently suited for neutral consumer information. Particularly great hopes have been set in videotex (unlimited capacity, easy to use for laymen without computer know-how, available day and night, use of home television screen as monitor, interactive features). The business community has also been interested in spreading information through these new electronic media for commercial purposes; in particular, the interactive features of some of the electronic media have provided hopes for a great increase in home selling.

This paper is based on a 400 page report (Sepstrup & Ölander, 1986 b; for a summary in English, see Sepstrup & Ölander, 1986 a), prepared for the Nordic Council of Ministers, in which we set out to identify those advantages and disadvantages for consumers which follow from the introduction of electronic transmission of information. The aim has been to provide Nordic public agencies and consumer organizations with a background which should make it possible to assess how consumer policy and consumer information could and should be adapted to the developments taking place in information technology. The sources we have built upon are an extensive survey of the literature (scientific and trade media) and personal interviews with about 50 experts in the U.K., West Germany, and the Nordic countries.

In the report, a basic distinction is made between those electronic media that carry text (and simple graphics) - electronic data media - and those that carry moving pictures - electronic visual media. In contrast to the report, this paper deals exclusively with the data media.

Consumer information in our terminology comprises all information that is transmitted to consumers, independently of the source from which it comes. For information originating from public agencies and consumer organizations we use the label neutral consumer information. For information which is distributed by commercial enterprises with a view to fostering demand for the product or service with which the information deals, we use the label advertising.

Whereas a substantial part of the full report is devoted to a description and discussion of the ways in which the new electronic data media are - or can be - used for purposes of advertising and selling, due to reasons of space the present paper is limited to reporting and discussing their use as carriers of neutral consumer information.

2. THE ELECTRONIC DATA MEDIA

2.1. Teletext

Teletext is a technique for transmitting text pages to the TV screen at the same time as the normal television picture so that the viewer can choose between watching a programme and a text on the TV screen. Some of the lines of the TV signal are not used for producing the living picture and can thus be made to carry the information which constitutes teletext. The viewer uses the remote control to select pages which are transmitted from the sender station in a pre-set order. To receive teletext the TV set has to have a decoder. This equipment is relatively cheap as is the production of teletext, and once a household possesses a decoder, the use of teletext is free of charge.

Teletext is spreading rapidly over Europe. In 1986, over 15% of all households, for example, had access to teletext in both the U.K. and Sweden, and the amount of use is also pretty high (the ITV teletext Oracle, only one of Britain's two teletext systems, is on average used for about 15 minutes per day, Ogilvy & Mather's Euromedia, September 1985).

Most experts point to simplicity and cheapness as very important advantages of the teletext medium, while the lack of interactive features, the limited amount of simultaneously available information, and access time (now often 20 seconds on the average) are seen as clear disadvantages. The capacity and access time problems will however be overcome in the not too distant future by the use of more TV signal lines for transmission and by the inclusion of a memory in the individual TV set which will make it possible to store a large number of teletext pages which can then be called up without any delay at all.

2.2. Videotex

Videotex is a system for information and communication. Via a telephone, a user gets connected with one or more databases, the contents of which can be made to appear on the TV screen. The screen can be a computer terminal, but in the original conception, it is thought of as the ordinary TV set already existing in the home. The TV set needs to be fitted with a decoder and a so-called modem, which today means that one has to pay a substantially higher price for the TV set. The user communicates with the database by means of the remote control belonging to the TV set or a special alpha-numeric keyboard. The information is retrieved with the aid of a tree-like search system or by typing keywords. A videotex system can give its user access to (a) information retrieval, (b) transactions (such as ordering goods and making payments), (c) programmes for carrying out certain calculations, and (d) an electronic mail service.

Many prognoses have been made for the diffusion of videotex among households, but they have all turned out to be much too optimistic (both in the U.S. and in Europe). In recent times, expectations have been substantially lowered. There seems to be a common feeling in most Western countries today that videotex is <u>not</u> going to turn into a medium for the ordinary citizen/consumer. The new strategy is to market videotex as a medium for communication within and between business firms in the hope that it will possibly later spread also among private households.

After the closing down in March 1986 of the only two fully operating videotex systems in the U.S. (Goldberg, 1986 a, b), systems which had been backed by some very large companies in the media industry, videotex no longer exists as a household medium in the U.S. In West Germany, the U.K., and the Nordic countries there are very few private users. France is an exception. Here, the fact that a simple terminal, in black-and-white, is provided free of charge with a telephone subscription (in order eventually to get rid of the need to print telephone books, the system holds all French telephone numbers) has caused a much quicker and broader diffusion also among households (Mayer, 1986; Nahon, 1985).

Nothing points to a major break-through for videotex as a household medium in the near future, or even by the end of this century, but one has to acknowledge that this opinion is based on present technology. Technical developments may, e.g., lead to the improvement of videotex pictures to photographic quality, and the use of personal computers for receiving videotex is already in full swing as far as business users are concerned. But with such developments one is rapidly abandoning the original idea of using the domestic TV set as a simple and almost universally spread data medium.

2.3. Cabletext

Cable television can be used for transmitting text in various ways. According to McIntyre (1984) we can distinguish between the following text services:

1. Cycling pages giving the user no possibility to select or freeze those pages he or she especially wants to see.
2. Teletext in local cable channels (which provides for quicker access/more text pages than in ordinary teletext, since more TV signal lines can be used than on airborne television).
3. A whole cable channel devoted to teletext (which means using all 625 lines and providing access to 5,000-10,000 pages without prolonging the access time).
4. Interactive services (transactions, etc.) of the same kind as are available in videotex systems.

The number of households reached by cable differs a lot among European countries (it is high in the Nordic countries and highest in the Benelux) with the U.S. at the top of the world list. It should be noted, however, that even in the U.S. very few households are linked to a cable system in such a way that the TV set can be used for truly interactive purposes (level 4 above). The experiments that were made in the U.S. with interactive uses have all ceased to exist (apart from some modest 'pay-per-view' activities). As far as Europe is concerned, it is mainly in the U.K. that one contemplates the use of cable for establishing interactive services, but only two or three systems of that sort are expected to exist before the end of the century. Full channel teletext (level 3 on the above list) is expected within the next five to ten years. The fastest growth is expected to take place at level 2. In the Nordic countries, there is some cabletext transmission at the simplest level 1; in Helsinki, there are some fairly advanced plans for a whole channel being devoted to an 'electronic newspaper' (level 3).

2.4. Other Database Access

Both teletext and videotex provide the user with access to databases. Teletext does not make it possible to interact with the database (except in the very limited sense of choosing the pages one wants to see). Videotex and other databases, on the contrary, allow for interaction. It is still useful to make a distinction between videotex and other database access because videotex was originally intended as the household variant of database access, has usually been regarded as a medium of its own, has some special features such as more characters and better colours and graphics, and can be received by a TV set, whereas other database access requires that a computer and a monitor are available.

As a consumer medium 'other database access' is uniquely American. In 1986, the two most consumer oriented systems are 'CompuServe' with 250,000 and 'Source' with 60,000 subscribers, corresponding to about .4% of U.S. households. These systems provide information and transaction services very similar to videotex services.

3. THE USE OF ELECTRONIC DATA MEDIA FOR NEUTRAL CONSUMER INFORMATION

3.1. Teletext

This medium has so far hardly been used for neutral consumer information. The exception is West Germany, where the main organization for comparative product testing, Stiftung Warentest, offers a short form of its test protocols through the medium. This belongs to one of the most popular categories in German teletext (Media Perspektiven 6/1985).

3.2. Videotex

To the consumer organizations which have tried to use this medium for the conveyance of information to individual households belong some of the major European consumer organizations and institutions: Consumers' Association in the U.K., Stiftung Warentest, Arbeitsgemeinschaft der Verbraucher, and the largest regional advice centre (North Rhine Westphalia) in Germany, l'Institut de la Consommation in France. In Scandinavia, the Danish Government Home Economics Council has been involved in videotex since the system was introduced in 1982.

These organizations have either believed that videotex would very quickly develop into a mass medium, or they have thought that the medium has to be explored because theoretically, it must be the perfect medium for consumer information. Naturally, those basing their involvement on the former belief have a different view today and show much less occupation with videotex. Although several of the organizations, to whom we have talked, feel that it was right to get involved at the time, no one could see a future for videotex as a consumer information medium within its current planning horizon.

3.3. Use of Other Electronic Data Media for Neutral Consumer Information

There are very few experiences with the other media (cabletext, direct access to databases) as instruments for the transmission of neutral consumer information directly to consumers. (A little more experience exists with the use of database information as an aid for consumer advisers, acting as middlemen between the source of information and the end user. Such use is described in the report on which this paper is based, but space restrictions prevent me from going into it here.)

4. FACTORS HAVING AN IMPACT UPON THE FUTURE OF NEUTRAL CONSUMER INFORMATION IN THE NEW ELECTRONIC DATA MEDIA

When it comes to predicting the future of the new electronic data media as carriers of consumer information, two lines of inquiry must be combined. One has to do with the assumed rate of diffusion of the new media in general. The other has to do with the particular possibilities and problems encountered when attempting to use the media for the transmission of (neutral) consumer information.

In the rest of the paper, I will mainly concentrate on factors belonging to the second set of issues.

4.1. A Widening Information Gap?

First of all, it is possible that consumer agencies and organizations will refrain from investing more money and efforts in the development of information systems for the new media because they fear that through these, they will not reach those consumers most in need of information. The information gap between the 'haves' and the 'have nots' may actually increase if the electronic data media take over some of the information formally transmitted in print. There are few signs that new groups of consumers, i.e., groups which are not already 'information seekers,' are reached by the media. Considerations of this sort will obviously be an important supply side factor. So too will cost development in general and the financial means available to agencies and organizations for the transmission of information.

It is possible, of course, that in the future neutral consumer information will be available only if the consumer is willing to pay a fee. The big question is: Will consumers be willing to pay a sufficiently large fee to make neutral information self-sustaining? The willingness to pay will no doubt be dependent on the information content and on the fee structure. A subscription system whose fixed fee varies only little or not at all, according to the amount of actual use, may be more attractive to a broad segment of consumers than the present fee systems used for example with videotex where the user pays per unit of time or per page inspected. Many consumers may need to look at many pages and to use much time before they find what they are after, and they should not be discouraged from exploring the system at their own pace (Jones, 1982). To some extent, such measures might counteract the tendency of a new medium to increase the information gap.

4.2. A Strong Feature: Voluntary Exposure

The individual consumer's interest in, and use of, neutral consumer information in the electronic data media are influenced by a number of characteristics of both the medium per se and the information it contains. One obvious strength is that the electronic data media basically provides you, the user, only with information that you yourself have sought out. With the exception of cycling pages on teletext or cabletext, the electronic data media all make it possible to selectively choose that particular piece of information needed by a consumer at a given moment. Of course the consumer will not always get hold of the information he or she was looking for. The way the system is built up will have an enormous impact. It must be easy to find the desired information, and - equally important - one must be able to learn quickly if a given piece of information does not exist in the system. One should not be side-tracked to other pages with an irrelevant content, etc. For existing videotex systems, many critics have pointed out that these conditions are very often not fulfilled.

Nevertheless, it is important to keep the common feature of these media in mind, i.e., they build upon 'voluntary exposure.' Not only is this a redeeming feature from a policy perspective, in most situations it is also reasonable to assume that the user is more likely to retain information retrieved in this active way than that acquired through more passive, non-voluntary exposure.

4.3. Immediate and Delayed Utility

The theoretical framework (cf. Sepstrup, 1980; Sepstrup & Ölander, 1986) distinguishes not only between 'active' and 'passive' exposure but also between the 'immediate' and the 'delayed' utility of the information to which the receiver is exposed. The immediate utility is determined by the positive and negative experiences that are coupled with the sheer exposure to information, i.e., with the media use itself. The delayed utility is that utility which the information brings about in the long run (as the receiver perceives it).

For both neutral consumer information and advertising, maximizing the delayed utility is the ultimate goal. The immediate utility is, however, not without importance. If there are immediate negative experiences (irritating or boring presentation, for example) which exceed the positive aspects of the exposure situation and the expected delayed utility, then the receiver loses interest and moves his/her attention to other matters.

Usually, advertisers make a lot of effort to provide positive immediate utility (eye-catching pictures, surprises, humour, etc.) whereas neutral consumer information to a larger extent hopes that delayed utility will be sufficient motive for persons to avail themselves of the information, thus putting less emphasis on immediate utility. This may often make neutral consumer information boring in the eyes of many consumers and thus insufficiently attractive unless the delayed utility is perceived to be extremely high.

Perhaps the electronic data media as such suffer from the same intrinsic weakness. That is, it may be difficult to make the immediate experience sufficiently enjoyable for consumers to invest time and money in using the media for the acquisition of information (even if it has a high delayed utility). Most media use in the home may be, as Sigel (1983) has pointed out, first and foremost a recreational activity. "No one would read the daily paper, Newsweek magazine or a non-fiction book ... unless they conveyed information in an entertaining manner. But delivering information over a terminal is anything but entertaining. Screens are meant for retrieving a desired fact or number and then going on to something else. They do not encourage the reader to linger over his favorite data base, or to share an amusing anecdote with spouse or family" (p. 163).

One sometimes comes across the opinion that the lack of success of electronic data media in the households is due to the fact that most people do not experience any need for factual information (be it about goods and services or any other aspect of society) and that entertainment is the only thing people look for in the media. I am not convinced that this is so, but such general hypotheses are of course difficult to disprove (or verify). A more testable hypothesis may be that the electronic data media - after a short period of fascination at the first encounter - do not provide sufficient immediate utility (cf. Sigel's remarks). In that case it does not matter very much whether the individual thinks that the information is useful - provides delayed utility - or not; without a certain amount of immediate utility there is simply no prolonged exposure to the medium.

Since it is rather difficult to think of ways in which the electronic data media can be made more permanently entertaining and attractive, this may be one of the reasons why there is not likely to be a fast or very substantial increase of household use of these media.

Some of the clearly negative aspects of the exposure situation, such as having to utilize a clumsy and bothersome search system (often a tree structure), difficulty in reading the characters used by the system, unsophisticated graphics, the time lapse before a page appears on the screen, etc., will probably soon be largely overcome by technological and psychological research. The question still remains, however, whether the positive, pleasurable aspects of the use of the electronic data media will be sufficiently great.

4.4. Not a Part of Everyday Media Consumption

Other things being equal, the cost of acquiring information is lower if the information is a constitutive part of those media the consumer normally seeks out. This, too, is probably a fact which will hamper the development of the electronic data media. As long as the use of these media is not an integrated and often recurring activity in people's everyday life, the perceived costs of using such media will be much higher than the costs associated with media which are used all the time (newspapers and magazines, radio and television, etc.). Consumer educators must hope that the electronic data media will blend into the everyday media environment of ordinary people for reasons other than its consumer information content. The electronic data medium most likely to succeed in this fairly soon is no doubt teletext.

4.5. Non-Comprehensiveness - A Major Problem

An ideal information system makes it possible for consumers to extract much information or little. It should be possible to find the information which one needs, without being loaded with lots of other information at the same time. If a system lives up to these demands, it must be in the consumers' interest that the database is as comprehensive as possible.

Some observers, such as Grunert (1984, 1985), have heavily criticized institutions which provide videotex systems with neutral consumer information for neglecting the need for comprehensiveness. Because of the very limited amount of information that can be included on one videotex page and the very large number of pages needed for providing comprehensive information about all the characteristics of a product, most systems have reduced the amount of information to a minimum, e.g., a very short summary of the results of a comparative product test. By doing so, according to the critics, full use is not made of the medium in those situations where it really could have an advantage over printed media: for products with many characteristics, many varieties, and frequent model changes. In experimental work with the West German videotex system, Grunert (1984) has tried to show that also in a rather inflexible videotex system, it is possible to organize the information so that it (a) contains large amounts of information and (b) makes it possible for the consumer to select those parts of the information which he or she has a special need for. Similar attempts have also been made in the U.K. (Sandringham, 1981). In more elaborate videotex systems which allow for an external computer to be connected to the information provider side, and/or access by means of a personal computer on the user side, it will of course be possible to an even larger extent to satisfy simultaneously the demands for huge amounts of data and selective retrieval. Dialogue programmes (questions and answers) will make such retrieval even simpler for the user. In future videotex systems, it is probably not the difficulties of storing and retrieving comprehensive information that will be the major crux.

Teletext is of course in its present forms much more restricted with respect to the amount of data (number of pages) accessible. In its known forms, teletext can hardly be used for detailed information about products and services in the form of product tests, market surveys, and the like. One has to rest content with providing short summaries and references to other media where more extended information is provided. This does not make teletext uninteresting, however. This use is successful in West Germany, and it is clear that for example informative labelling (based as it is on standardized, compressed labels) can be made to fit the medium very well. If such labels were obtainable on teletext, the consumer could study them in the home before visiting the store. If and when teletext takes the form of cabletext, using one or more channels, then obviously many more possibilities emerge.

In the previous paragraphs, I discussed comprehensiveness in terms of how much information is provided about a given product or service (how many varieties and brands are described, how many characteristics are dealt with, etc.). But comprehensiveness can of course also refer to the number of areas (different categories of products and services) that are covered by the consumer information contained in the medium. In order to make neutral consumer information an attractive constituent of the medium, thereby perhaps contributing to an increase in the number of subscribers, and in order to make consumers inclined to seek out the medium when they need consumer information, it is absolutely necessary that the information deals with many product areas. Unfortunately, here lies the major Achilles heel of existing electronic data systems (Maynes, 1982).

In the first instance, the problem is not the cost of transferring existing information to the format of the electronic medium (even though this may be very costly). The major problem is the cost of generating and continuously updating information about goods and services in a large number of areas. Without a dramatic increase in the economic resources at the disposal of those institutions (public agencies, voluntary organizations) which are responsible for comparative product testing and consumer information, it appears inconceivable that electronic data media will ever have an information content which meets consumers' expectations and demands for having the most important product and service areas covered. If, in addition, one maintains (as does Maynes) that the system must also contain local information (list of stores, their assortment and prices) then the possibility of getting even close to comprehensiveness becomes totally imaginary.

The technical ease with which information can be changed and updated in an electronic data medium actually creates an additional and somewhat paradoxical problem. Many of the experts responsible for existing consumer information systems are of the opinion that consumers put higher demands on the information being up-to-the-minute when it appears in the electronic media than when it appears in print. It appears as if the technical feasibility leads consumers into believing that it is also practically and financially possible for the information to be continuously updated. Of course, in such a medium it is always necessary to provide the date of collection for the information. But that does not solve the problem if consumers are unable to assess the rate at which information gets obsolete and thereby unnecessarily discard or become dissatisfied with information that they perceive as obsolete.

5. CONCLUSIONS

As should be apparent from the preceding pages, many factors seem to work counter to the dissemination of neutral consumer information through the electronic data media.

The presence of consumer information in these media is dependent on supply as well as demand. In the case of videotex, in the starting phase system operators have been interested in attracting some non-commercial information and have therefore often offered space to consumer organizations and agencies free of charge or at a reduced rate. In the longer perspective, however, there seem to be few signs that the operators will be willing to take the responsibility for seeing to it that the media continue to have an all-round, non-commercial content. Among other things, this has to do with the fact that most of the videotex systems are not run by operators who see them as public service media and with the - not unrelated - fact that most users today are found in business, not in private homes.

The presence of neutral consumer information in videotex systems therefore becomes totally dependent on there being either a sufficiently large number of households willing to bear the full cost of generating and distributing the information, or public agencies which are prepared to bear the costs so that the information can be offered free of charge or at a subsidized rate. In the information collected for this report, there are few signs that either of these conditions is met. Whether free or highly subsidized neutral consumer information forms a part of future videotex systems will of course in the last instance depend on decisions made in the political system. But since it will presumably be a long time before this becomes the most economical way of distributing consumer information, it is likely that public funds available for consumer information will continue to be channelled to other media.

When it comes to the data medium with the largest diffusion today, i.e., teletext, the degree to which it will contain neutral consumer information will be less dependent on the demand and willingness of individual consumers to pay. For teletext (and cabletext), consumer information will be part of a bigger package which the consumer can choose to receive or not. The system operators in this case are usually public broadcasting companies with traditional obligations to provide certain public services. The decisions with respect to content are mainly taken in the teletext editors' offices. However, it has not been possible in this survey to find any country in which neutral consumer information appears to be given high priority by these editors. Thus, whereas in principle teletext is a medium very well suited for (certain forms of) neutral consumer information, there is no reason to predict a rapid growth in this particular electronic medium either.

From the first part of this paper it should be apparent that the future of at least some of the electronic data media is very uncertain indeed, as far as diffusion among households is concerned. To the extent, however, that households will become subscribers to, and users of, these media, it is clear that neutral consumer information will maximally constitute a very minor part of the whole supply of information, and that the totally predominating part of consumer information will take the form of advertising and sales promotion. At best, neutral consumer information can have a corrective function. The overruling conclusion should be fairly obvious: It is on the formulation of demands, limitations, and rules with respect to commercial consumer information that consumer organizations and public policymakers should concentrate their efforts in the foreseeable future.

Accordingly, most of the recommendations made to the Nordic governments in the report upon which this paper is based have in fact to do with the monitoring and regulation of advertising and sales through the electronic data media.

In addition, the full report deals with some of the newer electronic visual media and their use for advertising and selling purposes. It is rather obvious that the effect of information technology on commercial consumer information will be faster and will have greater impact through the visual media than through the data media. Examples of new visual media are 'direct response television' (direct selling via television) and 'electronic shopping machines' usually situated in stores. There is definitely a need for consumer agencies and organizations to keep a close watch on these developments and to formulate minimum requirements for the commercial use of the new visual media while at the same time exploring the possibilities of using these media for neutral information and other non-commercial purposes.

REFERENCES

Goldberg, L. (1986 a). L.A. videotex outlet not profitable enough. Electronic Media, March 10, p. 26.

Goldberg, L. (1986 b). Videotex fortunes. Electronic Media, March 24, p. 3.

Grunert, K.G. (1984). Verbraucherinformation in Bildschirmtext: Möglichkeiten und Grenzen. Gröbenzell: Verlag Reinhard Fischer.

Grunert, K.G. (1985). Verbraucherberatung mit Bildschirmtext. Hauswirtschaft und Wissenschaft, 33, 254-264.

Jones, M.G. (1982). The need for consumer information networks. Remarks presented at the World Future Society, Washington D.C., July 20. Manuscript.

Mayer, R.N. (1986). Videotex in France: The Other French Revolution. Salt Lake City: University of Utah, Division of Social Science Research, Center for Public Affairs & Administration. Working Paper 86-5.

Maynes, E.S. (1982). Prestel in Use. London: National Consumer Council.

McIntyre, C. (1984). The cheapest TV in the world. Cable & Satellite Europe, No. 4, pp. 67-68.

Nahon, G. (1985). The growth of videotex in France beyond the forecasts. Proceedings of Videotex International, pp. 1-10. Pinner, UK: Online Publications.

Sandringham, S.J. (1981). The Telewhich? experience. Paper presented at Seminar on New Media - The Future of Consumer Information, Berlin, January. London: Consumers' Association.

Sepstrup, P., & Ölander, F. (1986 a). Consumer Information in the Electronic Media: Neutral Information, Advertising, Selling. Aarhus: Aarhus School of Business Administration and Economics, Department of Marketing. Working Paper No. 5.

Sepstrup, P., & Ölander, F. (1986 b). Forbrugerinformation i de elektroniske medier: Forbrugeroplysning, reklame, salg. Copenhagen: Nordic Council of Ministers.

Sigel, E. (1983). Conclusions. In: E. Sigel et al.: The Future of Videotex, pp. 161-172. White Plains, NY: Knowledge Publications.

AGGREGATE SAVING AND THE SAVING BEHAVIOR OF SAVER GROUPS IN SWEDEN ACCOMPANYING A TAX REFORM

Richard WAHLUND and Karl-Erik WÄRNERYD

The Economic Research Institute at
the Stockholm School of Economics
Department of Economic Psychology
Box 6501, S-113 83 Stockholm, Sweden

Between 1983 and 1985, a Swedish income tax reform was effected in three steps. One of its purposes was to stimulate household saving and decrease household indebtedness. The paper presents some aggregate data on household saving in Sweden during the last two decades and raises some questions about the development of the saving ratios. Most of the forms of saving that are covered by the statistics on saving ratios seem to develop in an opposite direction to what was intended with the tax reform. In order to try to find a way to study saving behavior which can help explain actual saving behavior, the authors performed a cluster analysis on interview data from a representative sample of Swedish males. The cluster analysis is based on the hypothesis that there are four groups of savers in society, differing with respect to their motives for saving: wealth managers, goal savers, buffer savers, and cash managers. These four clusters were found and each showed a very distinct behavior. According to this analysis, only the cash managers had acted against the intentions of the income tax reform. The others may have experienced a money illusion, not being aware that they decreased their saving in real terms although they increased it in nominal terms.

1. GENERAL BACKGROUND AND THE PURPOSE OF THE PAPER

There is and has long been a widespread opinion among politicians and top-level decision makers in government and business, among economists and other social scientists that there are many ill effects of high marginal income tax rates. Among other things, it is assumed that high tax rates discourage people from working in the official economy and encourage tax planning and tax evasion, that they hamper people's willingness to save and encourage people to speculate and to borrow for consumption, which in turn speeds up inflation.

In 1982, in order to give the taxation policy such a form that it "encourages work, productive efforts, and saving, and fights inflation, speculation, and tax frauds" (Wärneryd, 1983a), the Swedish Parliament decided to reform the Swedish income taxation laws (hence called "the tax reform"). Beginning in 1983 (on incomes earned in 1983 and declared in 1984), the marginal income tax rates, as well as the tax reducing value of deductions, were gradually lowered. The goal was stated as a maximal marginal rate of taxation of about fifty per cent "for a majority of all full-time working taxpayers" on incomes earned in 1985 and declared in 1986. The income brackets, for each of which a certain marginal tax rate is determined, were to be adjusted upwards by 5.5% annually - as predetermined in the bill to the Parliament - to compensate for (the expected) inflation. See Appendix for a more detailed description of household taxation regulations in Sweden in 1986, i.e. after the completion of the tax reform.

One of the intentions behind the tax reform was to stimulate household saving. In 1980, two years before the tax reform was decided and three years before the tax reform could have any direct effect on the households' income taxes, the saving ratio in Sweden was 5.0%. This level was considered too low. In 1984, when the tax reform had been in effect for two years, the saving ratio was 0.4%, and in 1985 it fell below 0%. Does this mean that the tax reform has been a complete failure when it comes to saving? Are these macro-level statistics really compatible with micro-level data, i.e. have the households really decreased their saving? And if not, what may then have caused the drop in the saving ratio? Or may the tax reform have affected different groups of savers differently, so that some groups may not have acted contrary to the intention of the tax reform, although the sum of all groups' behavior has resulted in a decreased aggregate saving contrary to the intention? The latter presupposes that there exist different groups of savers, but to our knowledge, there is so far no study in Sweden that has succeeded in defining such groups.

1.1. The purpose of this paper

The purpose of this paper is to make an attempt to **define groups of savers** by doing a cluster analysis on individual household data from a research project aiming at following up the income tax reform. The variables used concern how the income tax reform is perceived, what motives there may be for saving in bank accounts, as well as variables measuring financial situation, financial savings, indebtedness, and saving behavior. First, a short summary of the development of Swedish household saving up to the introductory stage of the Swedish tax reform will be presented.

2. THE DEVELOPMENT OF HOUSEHOLD SAVING IN SWEDEN

Berg (1983), who analysed the macro-economic determinants of consumption and saving of Swedish households between 1953 and 1979, found that there were three different versions of the national accounts, each showing a different development of the saving ratio. Among other things, he found that this had been "the decisive factor for whether the rate of inflation will have independent and negative effect on consumption expenditures in various studies" performed by Lundberg (1969), Wikner (1985), Ettlin (1976), Markowski and Palmer (1977), Lybeck (1978), Bentzel and Berg (1980), Berg et al (1981), and Palmer (1981), among others. The national accounts were finally officially revised in 1980, and it is the latest version that is used by (and for earlier years also revised by) Berg (1983) and is used here.

Figure 1 shows how the Swedish saving ratio - i.e. household saving in per cent of disposable income - has developed during the last 20 years. According to Berg (1983, p.17), the saving ratio had been fluctuating between 4% in 1950, 1959, and 1969 and about 8% in 1955 and 1964. Between 1970 and 1981, as shown in figure 1, the saving ratio was fluctuating between 2.3% (in 1972) and 5.0% (in 1974 and 1980), averaging 3.9%. Then, in 1982, in the year preceding the start of the reform, it suddenly fell to 0.5%. During the tax reform it continued to fall and ended up below 0% in 1985 as well as in 1986.

The saving ratio is the sum of two somewhat different saving ratios, the financial saving ratio and the real saving ratio. Households' financial saving comprises net saving in cash money, bank deposits, bonds, shares, loans (claims), and other financial assets minus loans taken (less amortizations and installment payments) and other liabilities. Real saving comprises households' investments in private homes and summer cottages, net investment in real estate, and investments made by self-employed. Figure 1 also shows the development of these two ratios during the last 20 years.

In the mid-1960's, both ratios were fluctuating somewhat around 3%. Then, in 1967, the financial saving ratio began to drop and the real saving ratio began to rise. During most of the 1970's, the financial saving ratio was oscillating between 0% and -3% while the real saving ratio was rather stable around 5%. At the beginning of the 1980's, the former began to increase and went up to as much as 1.9% in 1981, but only to drop to less than 1% in the following years, while the latter began to drop in 1981 and has continued to drop to 0% in 1984 and below zero in 1985 and 1986. All three saving ratios, including the total saving ratio, were thus about zero per cent in 1984, i.e. they were lower when the tax reform had been in effect during two years than they were before the start of the tax reform. Over the whole of the last 10 year period, though, the tendency is a slightly increasing financial saving ratio and a decreasing real saving ratio.

Considering the years 1953 - 1979, Berg (1983, p.180) concluded that "when expenditures for durable consumption goods are considered as investments, household saving to a large extent has not declined in relation to household disposable income. What has occurred is that the form of household saving has changed drastically so that real saving, rather than financial saving, has increased." As to later years, we have no figures showing whether this is still true or not, but, according to figure 1, the opposite seems to be prevailing now.

Berg (op cit) estimated a consumption function - using expected disposable income, net wealth, access to credit, pension wealth, demographic changes and relative unemployment as explanatory variables - and used it to simulate the effects of the development of the social security system on saving and capital formation. His results show that the basic old age pension, the supplementary pension scheme (ATP), and the collectively contracted union pension schemes, "on the average, have decreased household savings by four percent of GNP for the period studied. This drastic decline in household saving has not, however, brought about a corresponding decline in total net savings in the economy." During the 1970s, the actual and the simulated net saving coincided, i.e. "the household saving was outweighed by the funding of the ATP and the collectively contracted union pension schemes." This should not be forgotten when the present low saving ratio is labelled as a "crisis".

Figure 1: The saving ratio, the financial saving ratio, and the real saving ratio in Sweden, 1963 - 1985

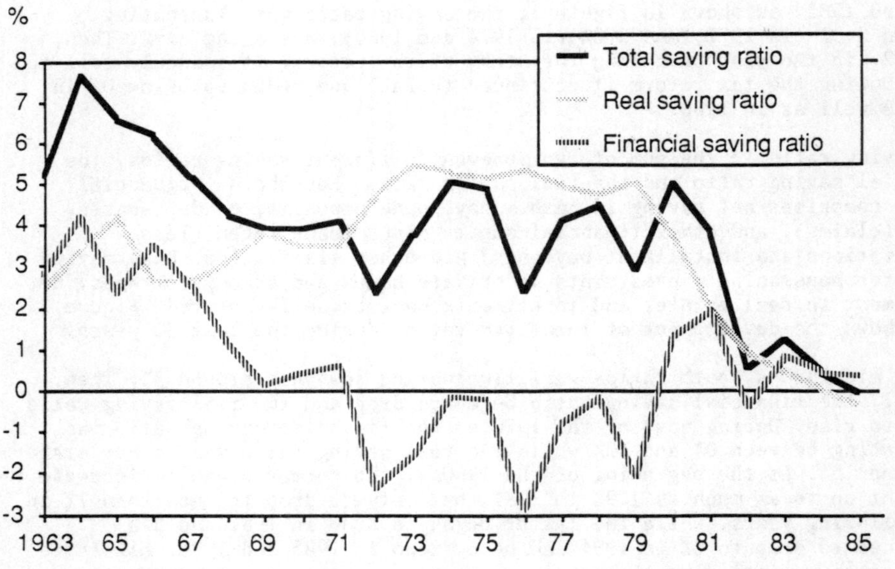

Source: Computed from the Swedish Financial and National accounts.

2.1. Disposable income, consumption, and saving

John Maynard Keynes (1936, p.210) indirectly defined saving when writing "An act of individual saving means - so to speak - a decision not to have dinner to-day. But it does **not** necessitate a decision to have dinner or to buy a pair of boots a week hence or a year hence or to consume any specified thing at any specified date." Behind Keynes's and most other definitions of saving is the idea that saving means postponing or refraining from consumption. Saving is hence seen as the result of a decision concerning consumption, or, in other words, the residual of disposable income when consumption has been paid for. In figure 2., real disposable income and real private consumption (1980 = 100) 1974 - 1984 is shown. Real disposable income was steadily increasing (except in 1978) until 1980 when it suddenly began to drop and it continued to drop to just above 95 in 1983 and 1984. Real private consumption increased sharply between 1974 and 1976. Since then it has fluctuated at about the same level.

Comparing the development of the saving ratios as shown in figure 1 and real disposable income and private consumption as shown in figure 2, it looks as if people have tried to maintain their living standard - in terms of real consumption - at the expense of their saving since the drop in real disposable income began in 1980, i.e. favoring consumption before saving when disposable income is decreasing. This is in agreement with the relative income hypothesis (Duesenberry, 1949), the life-cycle hypothesis (Modigliani-Blumberg, 1954), as well as the permanent income hypothesis (Friedman, 1957) when and if the decline is perceived as temporary. These indications are further supported by the fact that it is the financial saving ratio and not the real saving ratio which has fluctuated in directly opposite direction to real private consumption. It is of course impossible to conclude from this observation the causal direction between saving and consumption.

Figure 2: Real disposable income and real private consumption in Sweden, 1974 - 1984 (1980 = 100)

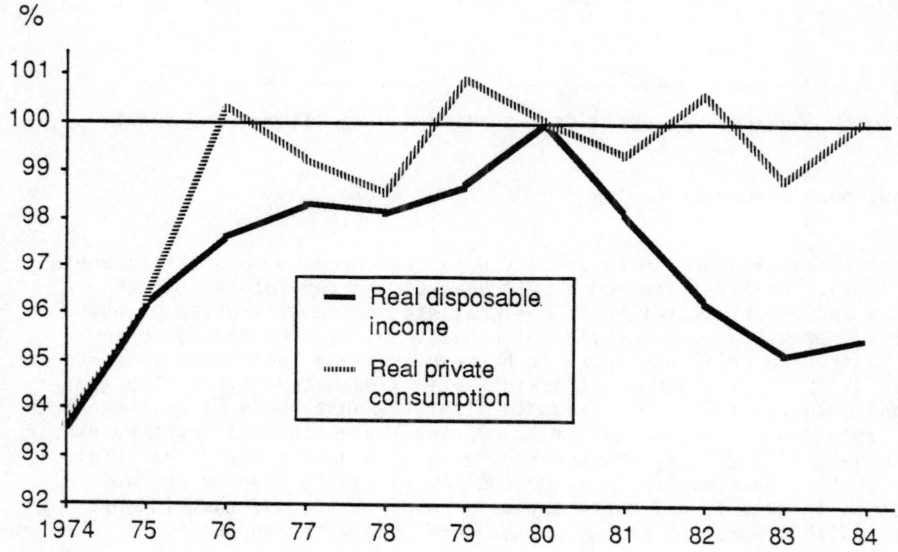

Source: Computed from National accounts Quarterly Reports (1975:1 - 1985:3)

2.2. International Comparison

The saving ratio has decreased in many other countries as well (Great Britain being an exception), but the level to which it has decreased in these countries is not as depressed as the Swedish one (table 1). Of course, international comparisons must be used with some circumspection. Among other things, there are differences between countries - and also within countries, over time and between sources, as Berg (1983) has pointed out - in how the saving ratio is calculated and there are differences in social security systems. The former makes comparisons uncertain, and the latter makes comparisons somewhat unjust (consider for example the effects on saving of the introduction of the pension schemes in Sweden, as mentioned earlier above). There is, however, no doubt that the Swedish saving ratio has by comparison fallen to a disquietingly low level.

Table 1: The saving ratio in some countries 1970 - 1984

Country	1970	1975	1980	1982	1984
Sweden	3.9	4.8	5.0	0.5	0.4
West Germany	17.9	15.2	12.8	13.1	11.5
Great Britain	5.7	10.5	14.8	10.8	11.5
USA	8.2	8.4	6.2	5.9	6.2
Japan	18.2	22.5	19.2	17.7	17.6

Source: OECD, National accounts (the Swedish Saving Delegation, 1986).

2.3. Household Financial Saving

The cluster analysis presented in this paper concerns households' **financial** saving during the first one and a half year of the tax reform. Let us therefore end our presentation of National statistics by looking at how different components of households' financial saving contributed to the change in the financial saving ratio between 1981 and 1984. This is shown in table 2. First, the financial saving ratio fluctuated between 1.9 (in 1981) and -0.4 (in 1982), but seems to stabilize just above 0% at the end of the last step in the tax reform. Comparing the nominal saving figures with the data of figure 2, the households seem to have tried to at least keep up their financial saving in nominal terms, while keeping up their consumption in real terms. There may be a "money illusion" that is more prevalent with respect to saving and savings than with respect to consumption!

The saving types that served to depress the saving ratio were "regular bank saving" and "other assets" (except for 1982); the latter includes discrepancies in estimates. Net loans taken increased between 1981 and 1982, but then decreased to just above 10% of disposable income in 1983 and 1984. Saving which increased during these years includes tax incentive bank saving, i.e. saving in bank accounts, the interest of which is tax exempt; bonds, including government lottery bonds; private life and pension insurances; and stock. The only things which did not change much over the years were the amount saved - or kept - as cash and "tax incentive stock saving", i.e. saving in stock for which gains and dividends are exempt from tax. Tax exempt interest from bank savings seems to have become more and more attractive to people, despite the fact that the marginal tax rates on income have been lowered through the tax reform, making regular bank saving more profitable now than earlier. At the same time, tax incentive stock saving does not appear to have increased its attraction, while shares in general came more into demand!

Life and pension insurances, which are deductible to a smaller extent after 1982, also became more popular, despite the comprehensive Swedish old-age pension and social security system and despite the tax reform. Saving in bonds more than tripled between 1981 and 1984. Lottery bonds have a comparatively low proportional tax levied on the winnings, but for other bonds regular income tax must be paid on the interest. The tax reform has in relative terms made the former less profitable and the latter more profitable. Indebtedness increased, although the tax reform was expected to discourage it. What "other assets" comprise and what makes them decrease is unknown to us. There are many question marks with respect to saving and they cannot be removed by the statistics collected from Financial and National accounts.

Table 2: The Swedish households' financial saving ratios 1981 - 1984

Year	Cash	Bank saving	Tax incent banks.	Bonds etc.	Life in-sur.	Regu-lar shares	Tax incent stock	Other assets	Indeb-ted-ness	Finan. saving ratio
1981	0.7	6.8	0.8	0.7	1.3	-1.2	0.4	2.1	9.8	1.9
1982	0.6	4.3	0.9	1.4	1.5	-0.7	0.6	3.0	11.9	-0.4
1983	0.6	2.9	0.8	2.3	2.5	-0.6	0.6	1.8	10.1	0.8
1984	0.8	2.9	2.0	2.2	2.7	-0.1	0.5	-0.5	10.2	0.4

Source: Computed from the Swedish Financial and National accounts.

3. METHOD

The empirical data used for this paper came from the last three out of four surveys carried out within a research project that was begun in 1982 in order to follow up the tax reform by measuring household economic behavior at four different points in time. The first survey was carried out in November/December 1982, just before the start of the tax reform. It was followed by a second in May/June 1983, a third in November/December 1983, and the fourth and last in May/June 1984. The project is primarily a continuation of surveys on tax behavior carried out by Wärneryd and Walerud (1981, 1982), but it also encompasses many other aspects of household economic behavior, such as saving behavior (see Wärneryd, 1983a, and Wahlund, 1985).

A total number of 1752 (72.4%) men out of a total sample of 2421 Swedish male citizens, 20 - 65 years of age, were interviewed by telephone. The interview time averaged 35 minutes. In order to collect some additional information, such as attitudes to Swedish taxes and to tax crime severity, perceived and expected rates of inflation, reasons for saving, as well as more exact figures for saving and savings, interest received and paid, indebtedness, etc., an additional mail questionnaire was sent to all respondents. This was answered by 1427 (81.4%) out of the 1752 interviewed. Table 3. summarizes the response and non-response rates for the different surveys, and in table 4. the non-response is elaborated.

Table 3: The response and non-response rates

Survey	No	Frequency	Percent	Valid Percent	Cum Percent
Nov-Dec 1982	S1	438	18.1	25.0	25.0
May-June 1983	S2	399	16.5	22.8	47.8
Nov-Dec 1983	S3	462	19.1	26.4	74.1
May-June 1984	S4	453	18.7	25.9	100.0
Total response		1752	72.4	100.0	
Non-response S1-1982 Nov-Dec	S1	154	6.4		
Non-response S2-1983 May-June	S2	180	7.4		
Non-response S3-1983 Nov-Dec	S3	163	6.7		
Non-response S4-1984 May-June	S4	172	7.1		
Total non-response		669	27.6		
TOTAL		2421	100.0		

Table 4: Reasons for non-response

Reason	Total sample No	Total sample %	S1 No	S1 %	S2 No	S2 %	S3 No	S3 %	S4 No	S4 %
Refusal	226	9.3	44	7.4	59	10.2	61	9.8	62	9.9
Ill	30	1.2	10	1.7	8	1.4	7	1.1	5	.8
Not at home	36	1.5	15	2.5	11	1.9	6	1.0	4	.6
Dead	7	.3	1	.2	3	.5	0	.0	3	.5
Secret telephone	42	1.7	12	2.0	10	1.7	9	1.4	11	1.8
Telephone unknown	217	9.0	51	8.6	53	9.2	61	9.8	52	8.3
Telephone and address unknown	44	1.8	9	1.5	13	2.2	4	.6	18	2.9
No answering	67	2.8	12	2.0	23	4.0	15	2.4	17	2.7
Total non-response	669	27.6	154	26.0	180	31.1	163	26.1	172	27.5
Interviewed	1752	72.4	438	74.0	399	68.9	462	73.9	453	72.5
Total sample	2421	100.0	592	100.0	579	100.0	625	100.0	625	100.0

It is important to point out the fact that old-age pensioner households as well as households consisting of a single female or of only teen-agers have been excluded in the surveys. At least old-age pensioner households have shown different saving behavior than other households (Lindqvist, 1981, 1983), and more than 20% of all households - about 17% of the population - are old-age pensioner households (Statistics Sweden, 1985). The reason for not including old-age pensioners in the sample was that their differing economic behavior would necessitate a larger sample. This is also partly the reason for excluding women, but the main reason here is that it would be very difficult to get the telephone numbers of female respondents due to the fact that men are still dominating in the telephone directories.

4. SAVING MOTIVES AND SAVER TYPES

From a behavioral vantage point it seems appropriate to disaggregate total household savings and use categories based on types of saving behavior. This way it may become possible to study the potentially different effects of saving stimulation measures on groups of savers characterized by different saving behavior and saving motives.

4.1. Types of saving

There are a few attempts to categorize saving behavior or even saving motives. The best known is probably that suggested by Katona (1975), who distinguished three types of saving on the basis of empirical research:

1. Contractual saving
2. Discretionary saving
3. Residual saving

Katona noted that **contractual saving**, which usually means repayment of debts or payments of life insurance or pension plans, is usually not seen as saving by the general public. Still, it is an important part of saving although it seems to follow rules that are somewhat different from what characterizes other types of saving. The **discretionary saving** is what the individual decides to save. This type of saving comes closest to the common-sense meaning of saving. The **residual saving** is money that the owner failed to spend and therefore has available, often in a bank account, as a temporary depository of funds.

4.2. Saving needs and saver types

Another categorization was presented by Lindqvist (1981), who, inspired by Ferber (1973), suggested that the reasons for saving can be classified in four hierarchical categories, expressing needs at different levels (figure 3). This idea was further elaborated by Wärneryd (1983b). At the bottom of the hierarchy is found the need for cash management, i.e. temporary deposits for money that has not (yet) been spent. This is the most basic need, common to all income earners since incomes and expenditures are not perfectly synchronized in time and place. Then there is a need for having some reserve to take care of possible irregularities: a buffer which protects against economic emergencies or serves the purpose of giving a chance to use opportunities for profitable buying.

The third type of need is to have capital to take care of planned irregularities, such as purchases of capital goods or real estate. It is referred to as goal-directed saving. Individuals and households may save in order to arrive at enough money to be able to pay for something costly that they really want to buy and it may be necessary to save for a down payment on a car or a home. It may also be necessary to show ability to save in order to get a loan. The fourth and highest category is wealth management. Ferber (1973) called this category "asset management". People characterized by this need do not increase their wealth through saving in the usual sense since they have better means, or think they have better means, of accomplishing wealth increases than saving from income: they invest their money. The tapering off of the hierarchy, making it look like a pyramid, means that the frequencies of people (savers) involved become smaller as one goes up the hierarchy.

Wärneryd (1983b) suggested that there may be distinct "saver types" or groups of savers formed on the basis of the hierarchy of saving needs - or motives - (figure 3), but so far there is no firm empirical support for this assumption, although there is some indication that different groups are characterized by predominant saving motives (cf. Babeau, 1981).

Figure 3: A hierarchy of saving needs <---> A hierarchy of saver types

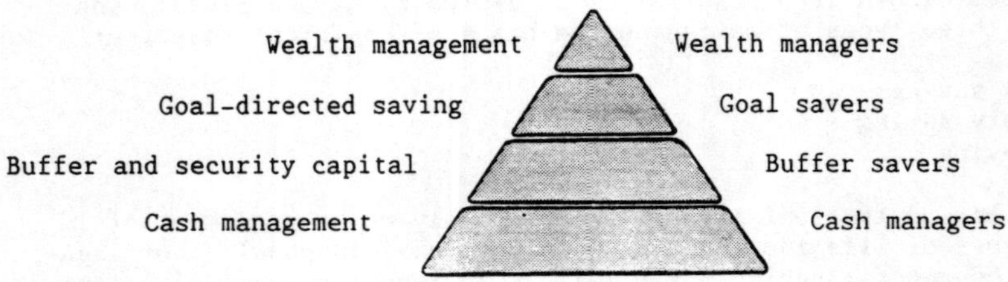

At this stage, two questions arise: What are the main characteristics of the four presumed groups of savers and how will the different groups be affected by the tax reform? Our expectations or working hypotheses are the following.

4.2.1. Wealth managers

Starting from the top, the wealth managers are expected to be high-income earners who have more wealth than any other group of savers. Their financial savings are expected to be greater than those of the other groups, especially savings in stock. The motives for saving on bank accounts are expected to be primarily for cash management and to have a buffer for using profitable buying opportunities. They are expected to use tax incentive saving to the full; to be active in buying and selling stock and bonds, the capital gains of which are subject to a reduced tax rate when sold after more than two years, and to make other investments with the possibility of making capital gains which are tax exempt as for example gains from the sale of art, gold and jewelry, and antiquities, or which is partly tax exempt such as ownership of condominiums.

It is likely that wealth managers will be both positively and adversely affected by the tax reform. A somewhat decreased maximum marginal income tax rate (from 85% to 80%) makes interests received and capital gains slightly more attractive. Considering the level of inflation 1982 - 1984, the perception of which has been investigated in our surveys (see Wärneryd and Wahlund, 1985), and the nominal interest rates, the real value of interests received on an investment is still negative, although a little less negative than earlier. Saving in bank accounts should thus become a little less discouraging than previously. At the same time, the new ceiling set for the deduction of paid interests (by 1985 making the minimum after tax cost about 50% of the interest paid as compared to as little as 15% earlier) will make loans much more expensive and thus loan financing less attractive. Wealth managers who have income from interest on capital can still profit from loan financing since paid and received interests can be offset within the same source of revenue, but only as long as paid interest is equal to or less than received interest. In general, since we expect the wealth managers to pay more interest than they receive, we expect them to decrease their investments in order to decrease their indebtedness.

4.2.2. Goal savers

Goal-savers have mostly, especially by banks, been thought to be young and saving in order to be able to buy an apartment or house or something else they want to have. Their most important saving motives should therefore be "to buy something" and "to get interest". Since this group of savers is expected to consist mostly of low- or middle-income earners, they are supposed to find it more profitable than before to save money in bank accounts, but for some savers with long-term saving goals the effect of a negative real interest rate may still be a deterrent. At the same time, lower marginal tax rates and the ceiling set for allowable interest deductions should discourage from instalment buying and other uses of credit, although most of the goal-savers are expected to have an income below the income that is affected by the ceiling set for deductions. The original aim of the tax reform was that 90% of all full-time working tax payers should have a marginal tax rate of 50% at the most by 1985. The ceiling effect on credit taken for this group would thus be expected to be insignificant. In general, increased saving and decreased indebtedness is expected from the goal-savers. At the same time, the low liquidity of earlier tax incentive saving schemes would tend to make short-term goal-savers less inclined to indulge in such saving. Long-term goal savers would be expected to display such saving only if the time constraints fitted in with their own goal horizons.

4.2.3. Buffer savers

The buffer savers would at first sight not be expected to be affected by the tax reform. This group of savers seems on the whole to have well-established saving habits which do not change appreciably over long periods of time. This suggests that they continue to save rather independently of outward circumstances. In general, this group is believed to consist of elderly people who just tend to put their savings on bank accounts and are shy of investing in stock or assets with low liquidity. The buffer savers may continue to save in order to reach a more satisfactory level for their buffer capital or they may add to the capital so that its real value at least remains constant. In both cases, with lower marginal tax rates on the interest, these goals can be attained more easily, and thus their discretionary saving should decrease. On the other hand, with more money to save after tax - due to the tax reform - they may increase their saving temporarily to reach the satisfactory size of their buffer sooner. Some of the buffer savers may also stop saving and just refrain from dissaving when the capital has reached a satisfactory nominal level. The tax incentive saving was up to and including the first quarter of 1984 characterized by low liquidity. The buffer savers would therefore be expected to indulge in such saving only when they had satisfactory buffers. The new tax incentive saving has a high degree of liquidity, although there is a fee for early withdrawal. The new saving scheme would thus be expected to attract buffer savers.

4.2.4. Cash managers

The cash managers save on bank accounts more or less by default or failure to spend. They keep their money on bank accounts to have it easily available for expenditures. If the tax reform means that this category of savers, who usually have little capital, receive more cash, there should be some increase in both the stock and the flow of their saving. On the other hand, those who own a house and therefore are expected to be in debt, will incur higher after tax interest costs as a result of the tax reform, and should therefore be expected to want to decrease their saving, or to dissave, in order to cover the higher interest costs. In addition, they may also try to decrease their indebtedness by decreasing their saving, or by dissaving. These savers would not be attracted at all by the earlier type of tax incentive saving and only slightly more interested in the present type of tax incentive saving.

5. RESULT OF THE CLUSTER ANALYSIS

The clustering method used is Howard-type clustering, programmed by Wordley and modified by Carmone (Howard & Harris, 1966). Standardized data have been used as well as equal weight for each variable. After list-wise deletion of cases due to missing observations had been executed, 948 respondents (72%) out of 1314 remained. The pooled within group variance decreased from 23700.0 to 21691.6 in the first split, to 20444.9 in the second split, and to 19762.5 in split number three. A fourth split would have given 19228.6.

5.1. Saving motives and the effects of the tax reform

The by far most important stated motive for bank saving is saving for having a buffer. This is the most important motive for each cluster - hence referred to as saver **groups** - and the importance is about the same for all groups. The second most important saving motive is liquidity, "to pay for bills etc.", i.e. cash management. In the third place is found "to buy something", i.e. goal-directed saving, and the least important motive is to receive interest. All these saving motives vary between the groups in importance. For one group also the order of the motives as to importance differs from those of the other groups. Two of the groups - group 1 and group 4, hence referred to as "wealth managers" and "cash managers" - are inclined to view the tax reform more negatively than the other two: group 2 and group 3, hence referred to as "goal savers" and "buffer savers". Goal-directed saving and saving to get interest are both somewhat more important for wealth managers than for cash managers while the opposite is found for saving in the form of cash management. For both groups, saving for cash management purposes is more important and goal-directed saving is less important than for the remaining two groups. The group most positive to the tax reform - the goal savers - view goal-directed saving as the next most important saving motive and to get the interest as much more important than the other groups, even though it is still the least important saving motive for all groups. On the whole, this is in accordance with our hypotheses.

5.2. The groups of savers

What, then, are the other characteristics of the groups, making it possible to define saver types, and how do the groups respond to the tax reform?

5.2.1. Wealth managers

Group 1, which is one of the two groups that are negative to the tax reform and the group which apparently knows more about tax regulations and thus possibly also more about the effects of the tax reform than any other group, has the highest taxed income in 1980 or 1981 as well as the highest tax deductions that year. In this group, the burden of supporting the family, i.e. the per cent of the household not contributing to the support of the household, is the next highest, but this does not seem to affect the living standard of the group members. The group members' perception of their financial standard is more favorable than that of any other group. The fact that their bank savings, their savings in stock as well as their saving on the tax incentive accounts all are greater than for the other groups, probably explains this. This leads us to consider group 1 as consisting of wealth managers who save on bank accounts to pay for loans taken for investments or tax planning and to have cash ready for possible investment opportunities, in addition to paying ordinary bills and interest on loans.

The average age of the wealth managers is 45 years, i.e. people in the middle of a rather successful - or at least profitable - career. They have perceived an increase in their financial standard, maybe due to wise investments in shares or in tax incentive accounts, using the up to now rather profitable effects of deductions. The reason for expecting a decrease in the financial standard may be that deductions are becoming less profitable due to the tax reform, i.e. interest paid is greater than interest received and thus cannot be completely offset within the same source of income. The wealth managers now have more in bank accounts and in shares than twelve months ago, but expect a less positive development in the year ahead. The group is the only one which has been able to increase its consumption during the last year, at the same time as its discretionary saving has increased to a larger extent than that of the other groups. Discretionary saving is expected to decrease during the next twelve months. The group has lowered its debts during the preceding year and plans to lower the debt burden even more in the following year. This is completely in agreement with what should be expected from a wealth manager unfavorably affected by the tax reform. It is the smallest group - only 15.5% of the respondents belong to this group - and this agrees well with the pyramid idea of Lindqvist and the estimates made by Babeau (1981).

5.2.2. Goal savers

The group most positive to the tax reform, at the same time being the next most knowledgable about taxation rules, is group 2. This group considers bank saving in order to get interest more important than any other group and is the only group that considers goal-directed saving to be the next most important bank saving motive, which leads us to consider the group as consisting of goal savers. The goal savers average above 50 in age, i.e. older people, which is the opposite of what we expected. Their support burden is the lowest of all groups. They have left family responsibility behind and can now afford a rather high living standard, despite having a taxed income of only average size.

The goal savers consider their financial standard to be high, almost as high as the wealth managers, but they have neither experienced, nor expect any great change in their financial standard. They have almost as much money in bank accounts as wealth managers and about twice as much saved in shares, bonds, etc compared to the remaining two groups. They have been able to increase their bank savings during the last year but do not expect to increase either bank or stock savings to any great extent in the following twelve months. Instead, they try to reduce their debts even more than they have done during the last year. As mentioned earlier: they seem to be aware of the negative effects of the tax reform on deductions. The goal savers have also decreased their consumption during the last year, at the same time as they have increased their discretionary saving, possibly in order to be able to buy something desired later on. On the whole, this group behaves as expected, but for quite other reasons than expected. Twenty-five per cent of the respondents belong to the group, which is slighly more than expected.

5.2.3. Buffer savers

Group 3 is almost as positive to the tax reform as the goal savers, but its knowledge about taxation rules is less than for any other group. "To have a buffer" is considered slightly more important by this group than by the other groups, and we consider group 3 to consist of buffer savers. Contrary to what we expected, this is the youngest group, with a comparatively light support burden. Presumably, this group consists of people in the beginning of their careers, before having begun to earn a lot of money and before getting a sizable family. The respondents' average taxed income in 1980 or 1981 is lower than for all other groups and approved deductions are almost as low as those of the goal savers. The group considers its living standard to be less favorable than what the wealth managers and goal-directed savers do, but it is still considered to be rather good. The living standard is perceived to have increased in the last twelve months, and is expected to increase even more in the coming year. These are the charateristics that we expected of the goal savers.

The buffer savers have not yet succeeded in building up a great buffer. Their bank savings and savings in shares etc. are only slightly surpassing those of group 4, which will be defined as consisting of cash managers. On the other hand, the group expects to increase its savings both in bank accounts and in shares and similar assets. The buffer savers have already increased their discretionary saving but intend to increase this kind of saving even more in the following year. Although not very knowledgable about taxation rules, they intend to lower their debts. At the same time they save rather little on tax incentive accounts. They clearly hope to increase their savings in order to arrive at a greater buffer. The members of the group have decreased their consumption less than both the goal savers and the cash managers, despite having been able at the same time to increase their saving and savings. This group consists of 29.5% of the respondents, which means that it is almost as large as the largest group. This is also slightly more than expected.

5.2.4. Cash managers

Group 4 is the group which is most negative to the tax reform. As to its attitude toward the tax reform and to the importance of bank saving motives, the group resembles that of wealth managers, but far from consists of wealth managers. First, its knowledge about taxation rules is much less. Second, its financial standard is the lowest of all groups, which is possibly caused by a high support burden (the highest of all groups) combined with a meager average income and lack of sufficient knowledge to manage this income as profitably as possible. The head of the household is younger than the wealth managers and has not yet accomplished a profitable career. Although the deductions in this group are much lower than those of the wealth managers, they are higher than those of the remaining two groups. The reason appears to be that the group consists of families with children, living in a house bought with borrowed money, and/or with household goods bought on instalment credits. The group has perceived a negative change in their financial standard and expects it to continue to get worse. One reason may be the expected negative effects of the tax reform on deductions made. We consider this group to consist of cash managers.

The cash managers' bank savings, savings in shares, bonds, etc as well as monthly saving in tax incentive accounts are all lower than for the other groups. At the same time, they are dissaving from bank accounts and expect to continue to dissave, maybe to compensate for higher costs of living because of higher interest costs for loans and higher taxes on real estate. In addition, the cash managers have increased their debts, despite the possible negative effects of the tax reform. This means that they may have entered a negative spiral, making their financial situation increasingly more difficult. It is the only group that expects its indebtedness to increase, but not to the extent that it already has increased. This is contrary both to what we expected from this group and to the intention of the tax reform. It has not changed its savings in stock and does not plan to. The group has also decreased its consumption as well as its discretionary saving more than any other group, and expects to save even less in the coming twelve months. This is what we expected, but for different reasons. The group saves mainly to pay for bills and to take care of eventualities. It cannot afford to save for any other purpose. The group accounts for 30.0% of the respondents, which is less than expected.

Table 5 on the next page shows the means for all variables mentioned above, for each group of savers.

Table 5: The resulting means for four groups from the cluster analysis

	WEALTH MANAGERS	GOAL SAVERS	BUFFER SAVERS	CASH MANAGERS	TOTAL SAMPLE
Taxation and the tax reform					
Tax reform effect	-0.03	0.17	0.15	-0.06	0.06
Tax knowledge	4.22	3.36	2.61	2.66	3.06
Age and financial situation					
Age	44.76	52.96	33.01	39.04	41.62
Taxed income 1980/81	117.17	74.21	55.27	69.17	73.76
Deductions made 1980/81	24.43	4.53	5.78	8.09	9.05
Support burden	0.36	0.14	0.23	0.41	0.28
Financial standard	1.38	1.34	1.04	0.35	0.96
Perceived change last year	0.17	0.06	0.26	-0.52	-0.04
Expected change next year	-0.08	-0.10	0.35	-0.23	-0.00
Bank saving motives					
To pay for bills etc.	2.57	2.05	2.19	2.62	2.34
To get the interest	0.80	1.30	0.61	0.67	0.83
To buy something	1.69	2.17	2.02	1.51	1.85
As a buffer	2.95	2.88	3.02	2.93	2.95
Wealth					
Bank savings	68.66	61.92	17.43	14.97	35.76
Change in bank savings	0.35	0.39	0.16	-0.55	0.03
Expected change	0.07	0.05	0.41	-0.30	0.05
Stock savings	33.50	10.26	5.60	5.58	11.09
Change in stock	0.51	-0.03	0.03	0.04	0.09
Expected change	0.27	0.02	0.14	0.01	0.09
Saving behavior					
Changed consumption	0.08	-0.21	-0.02	-1.60	-0.53
Changed discretionary saving	0.19	0.06	0.18	-0.46	-0.04
Expected change next year	-0.17	-0.17	0.26	-0.41	-0.11
Changed indebtedness	-0.14	-0.23	0.05	0.17	-0.01
Expected change next year	-0.36	-0.39	-0.39	0.03	-0.26
Tax exempt saving	476.05	199.47	62.68	38.03	153.59
Number of respondents	147 (15.5%)	237 (25.0%)	280 (29.5%)	284 (30.0%)	948

POOLED WITHIN GROUP VARIANCE BY SPLIT (the starting variance is 23700.0):
1: 21691.6 2: 20444.9 3: 19762.5 (4: 19228.6)

5.3. The variables used in the cluster analysis

The variables used in the cluster analysis are measured in the following way:

The tax reform effect measures the respondents' opinion about the general effect of the tax reform on the financial situation of the respondents' household. The answer "get worse" was coded -1, "be unaffected" as well as "don't know" were coded 0, and "will improve" was coded 1.

Tax knowledge is measured through six questions relating to taxation rules and an index is computed running from 0 to 7. A reliability test resulated in a Chronbach's alpha coefficient of 0.53.

Taxed income and **deductions** are the income actually taxed and deductions actually allowed for 1980 (survey two) or for 1981 (survey three and four). Both variables are in 1,000 SEK, deflated by the rate of inflation with 1980 as a baseline.

Support burden is the per cent of the household members not contributing to the support of the household.

Financial standard as rated by the respondents on a scale from -3 (very bad) to 3 (very good).

Perceived and expected change in financial standard are measured by asking the respondents if they think that their household's financial standard **has** decreased, not changed, or increased during the last twelve months, as well as it they think it **will** decrease, remain unchanged, or increase in the next twelve months. The answer "decrease" was coded -1, "remain unchanged" was coded 0, and "increase" was coded 1.

The importance of bank saving motives as rated by the respondents and weihgted by the importance rank, resulting in an index running from 0 to 4.

Bank savings are how much money, in total, the respondents think they have on all their bank accounts "today". The savings are measured on an interval scale: 0 SEK, 1 to 5,000 SEK, 5,000 to 10,000 SEK, 10,000 to 20,000 SEK, 20,000 to 50,000 SEK, and "more than 50,000". The values assigned to the intervals are 0, 2.5, 7.5, 15.0, 35.0, and 100.0, respectively, i.e. in 1,000 SEK.

Stock savings are how much money the respondents think they could get for their stock investments if these were disposed of "today". The savings are measured on an interval scale: 0 SEK, 1 to 3,000 SEK, 3,000 to 10,000 SEK, 10,000 to 25,000 SEK, and "more than 25,000 SEK". The values assigned to the intervals are 0, 1.5, 6.5, 17.5, and 45.0, respectively, i.e. in 1,000 SEK.

(Experienced) change and expected change in bank as well as in stock savings are all measured as is change in household financial standard (see above).

Changed consumption is measured through an index based on the respondents' stated changes in the consumption of four product groups and running from -4 (decreased consumption of all four product categories asked about) to 4 (increased consumption of all four product categories). A reliability test resulated in a Chronbach's alpha coefficient of 0.61.

Changed and expected change in discretionary saving as well as in household indebtedness are all measured as is change in household financial standard (see above).

Tax exempt saving is the amount that the households save each months on tax exempt saving accounts. It is in SEK, deflated by the rate of inflation with 1980 as a baseline.

6. CONCLUSIONS

With respect to saving, the aim of the tax reform was to stimulate saving and to discourage households from incurring debts. At the beginning of this paper it was shown that at the aggregate level the saving ratio has not increased since the beginning of the tax reform. Instead it has gone down slightly. Real saving accounts for most of the decrease in saving. Financial saving began to increase in the mid-70's, but the development has stagnated since the beginning of the 1980's and during the introductory stage of the tax reform.

Decreased real disposable income seems to have caused the general decline in saving. People have maintained their consumption level in real terms, which means that they have favored consumption before saving during this period, despite the income tax reform. At the same time, people have slightly increased their financial saving in nominal terms, which supports the idea that the stagnated financial saving ratio may have been caused by a money illusion. People may have expected a greater positive effect of the tax reform than actually accrued, which made the tax reform stimulate consumption instead of saving. Although the financial saving ratio has stagnated, there has been a change in the forms of financial saving. The changes are in most cases directly opposite to what would be expected from the intentions of the tax reform. It is impossible to conclude from the aggregate statistics why saving is not changing as expected. Does the cluster analysis of interview data reported here make it possible better to understand the development of saving behavior in Sweden?

The cluster analysis revealed four types of savers as hypothesized: one group of wealth managers, another group of goal savers, a third group consisting of buffer savers, and a fourth group consisting of cash managers. Two of the groups, the wealth managers and the cash managers, exhibit most of the characteristics expected. The wealth managers are well-off, financially active and somewhat negative to the tax reform and the cash managers are financially burdened, have difficulties in making both ends meet, and are also negative to the tax reform. For the remaining two saver groups, the findings were contrary to our expectations. The goal savers were expected to be primarily younger persons and the buffer savers to be elderly people, but the opposite was found. The goal savers are older than any other group of savers, comparatively well-off despite a rather modest income, financially active and positive to the tax reform. The buffer savers are younger than the other groups of savers, about as little well-off as the cash managers, and positive to the tax reform.

The only group acting against the intentions of the tax reform were the cash managers. The cash managers have both decreased their discretionary saving and increased their indebtedness and they have also, in fact, dissaved from their bank savings. They also expect to continue to decrease their discretionary saving, increase their debts and dissave from their bank accounts, although not to the same extent as during the last twelve months. Similarly, the buffer savers have increased their indebtedness, but to a very limited extent, which is far outweighed by an increase in their discretionary saving. The wealth managers and the goal savers both expect to decrease their discretionary saving, but this is more than offset by an expected decrease in indebtedness. Both of these two groups expect their savings as well as stock ownership to increase in the next twelve months, although to a lesser extent than during the preceding year.

Considering the cash managers' total savings, they must have been saving comparatively little already before beginning to reduce their discretionary saving or to dissave. Since the group size is only slightly larger than that of two other groups, the group's changes in saving behavior contributes comparatively little to changes in aggregate saving. In addition, no other group has reduced its consumption as much as this group, which means that the cash managers' dissaving is most likely not caused by a willingness to maintain their real consumption level at the expense of saving, but by too little ability to save. The fact that the saving ratio has not increased during the 1980's while the three remaining groups in our survey report that they have increased their saving flow as well as savings means that there is **either** a money illusion present **or** that people have begun to save in forms not covered by the different saving ratios **or** that households not included in the surveys, i.e. female and pensioner households, or the non-household part of aggregate "household" saving in the national accounts, are causing the change in the saving ratios **or** that either our figures, those in the national accounts or both are erring **or** a combination of these explanations. Also, a different pattern may show up if a cluster analysis is run on each survey or for each year separately.

The cluster analysis performed supports the pyramid idea of Lindqvist (1981), although there is not a complete conformity as to the relative size of the different groups. Group 2, consisting of goal savers, was expected to be smaller and group 4 - the cash managers - to be somewhat larger than was found. The findings from this cluster analysis will be followed by further analyses where changes over time and the unexpected relative sizes of the groups will be especially analyzed. This way of analyzing the interview data seems quite promising since it provides a mean to find out something about what goes on under the aggregate phenomenon covered by official statistics.

REFERENCES

Babeau, A. (1981). Diversité des motivations et évolution des comportements d'épargne. Audition devant la Commission de l'Epargne. Centre de Recherche Economique sur l'Epargne (CREP).

Bentzel, R. & Berg, L. (1983). "The role of demographic factors as a determinant of savings" in Modigliani, F. & Hemming, R. (red.), The determinants of national savings and wealth, Mcmillan, London.

Berg, L. (1983). Konsumtion och Sparande - en studie av hushållens beteende (Consumption and Savings - a study of household behavior). Acta Univ. Ups. Studia Oeconomica 8, Uppsala.

Berg, L., Bergström, R., Bergström, V. & Nilsson, C. (1981). Svenska modellen (The Swedish Model). Liber, Stockholm.

Duesenberry, J.S. (1949). Income savings and the theory of consumer. Harward University Press, Cambridge, Mass.

Ettlin, F. (1976). "Hushållens konsumtion och sparande i Sverige under två decennier" ("Household consumption and saving in Sweden during two decades) in Skandinaviska Enskilda Bankens Kvartalstidskrift, No 3-4.

Ferber, R.A. (1973). "Family Decision Making and Economic Behavior" in Sheldon, E.B. (ed.) Family Economic Behavior: Problems and Prospects, p. 29-61. Lippincott, Philadelpia.

The Financial and National accounts of Sweden (1975 - 1986). Various reports from Sweden Statistics and the International Institute of Economic Research, Stockholm.

Friedman, M. (1957). A theory of the consumption function. NBER, Princeton.

Howard, N. & Harris, B. (1966). A Hierarchical Grouping Routine, IBM 360/65 FORTRAN IV Program. University of Pennsylvania Computer Center.

Katona, G. (1975). Psychological Economics. Elsevier, New York.

Keynes, J.M. (1936). The General Theory of Employment, Interest and Money. The Mcmillan Press Ltd, London.

Lindqvist, A. (1981). Hushållens sparande - beteendevetenskapliga mätningar av hushållens sparbeteende (Household saving - behavioral scientific measurements of household saving behavior). The Economic Research Institute at the Stockholm School of Economics, Stockholm.

Lindqvist, A. (1983). Hushållens skuldsättning (Household indebtedness). Studies in Economic Psychology: 118, The Economic Research Institute at the Stockholm School of Economics, Stockholm.

Lundberg, L. (1969). Kapitalbildningen i Sverige 1861-1965 (Capital accumulation in Sweden 1861-1965). IUI/Almqvist & Wicksell, Stockholm.

Lybeck, J.A. (1978). Konjunkturer och svensk ekonomisk politik (Business cycles and Swedish economic policy). Nacka.

Markowski, A. & Palmer, E.E. (1977). Fluctuations in the consumption ratio in Sweden. International Institute of Economic Research, Stockholm.

Modigliani, F. & Brumberg, R. (1954). "Utility analysis and the consumption function: an interpretation of cross-section data" in Kurihara, K.K. (red.). Post Keynesian Economics, Rutger University Press.

National accounts. See (The) Financial and National accounts above.

Palmer, E.E. (1981). Determination of personal consumption. International Institute of Economic Research, Stockholm.

Reformerad inkomstbeskattning (Reformed income taxation), (1982). The government's bill 1981/82:197 to the Parliament, Stockholm.

Statistics Sweden (1985). SCB: Statistics Sweden, Stockholm.

Svenska ekonomins sparande 1970-1985 (the saving of the Swedish economy 1970-1985), (1986). The Swedish Saving Delegation, Stockholm.

Taxes in Sweden, (1986). Fact Sheet on Sweden, FS 35 r Qaf, The Swedish Institute, Stockholm.

Wahlund, R. (1985). Hushållens ekonomiska beteenden - datarapport nr 1, 2, 3 och 4 (The Economic Behavior of Households - Data Reports no 1, 2, 3 and 4). The Economic Research Institute at the Stockholm School of Economics, Stockholm.

Wikner, G. (1975). Hushållens sparande och samhället (Household saving and the society). Sparfrämjandet, Borås.

Wärneryd, K-E, (1983a). Taxes and Economic Behavior: The Swedish Tax-Payers Facing a Tax System Change. Paper presented at IAREP:s 8th Annual Colloquium in Economic Psychology, Bologna.

Wärneryd, K-E, (1983b). The saving behavior of households. Paper presented at the conference "Saving in a Time of Economic Stagnation", arranged by Groupement International pour l'Etude des Problémes de l'Epargne, Scheveningen, June 9-11.

Wärneryd, K-E. & Wahlund, R. (1985). "Inflationary Expectations" in Brandstätter, H. & Kirchler, E. (eds.), Economic Psychology - Proceedings of the 10th IAREP Annual Colloquium, Linz.

Wärneryd, K-E. & Walerud, B. (1981). Skatter och ekonomiskt beteende 1 (Taxes and economic behavior 1). Studies in Economic Psychology: 114, The Economic Research Institute at the Stockholm School of Economics, Stockholm.

Wärneryd, K-E. & Walerud, B. (1982). Taxes and economic behavior: some interview data on tax evasion behavior in Sweden. Journal of Economic Psychology, 1982:3.

APPENDIX

Household Taxes in Sweden by the End of the Tax Reform
(Reprinted from "Taxes in Sweden", 1986)

The Swedish tax system includes numerous direct and indirect taxes and fees. The most important direct levies are the national and local income taxes and the national tax on property. Inheritance taxes (succession duties) and the gift tax are also direct. Aside from taxes, there is an extensive system of employer contributions (social security fees) which cover pensions, health benefits and other social insurance.

Revenues from indirect taxes, virtually all of which go to the State, stem from two main sources: the value-added tax and excises on selected commodities.

The Swedish Parliament, or *Riksdag*, has the power to determine both national and local taxes. However, the local authorities are free to set the tax rates in their respective municipalities and county council districts.

Sweden has concluded conventions with about 50 other countries for the avoidance of double taxation on income and capital.

Direct taxation

Physical persons pay income tax to both national and local governments whereas *legal persons* (except domestic estates of deceased persons) are liable only for payment of national income tax as of the income year 1986. To compensate for the loss of local income tax from legal persons, the rate of national income tax has been raised to 52% for corporations and economic associations (mainly cooperatives) and to 40% for other legal persons.

For *physical persons* the national income tax is progressive and in 1986 ranges from 4% up to 50% in the highest brackets. On the other hand the local income tax is proportional. Once a year each local government decides what percentage of taxable income is payable. In 1986 the average local income tax rate is about 30%. There are certain tax ceilings that make it impossible for national plus local income taxes to exceed 80% in any bracket.

Qualified foreign researchers working temporarily for Swedish institutions and companies, however, are only taxed for 70% of their pay for an assignment, while certain types of compensation for extra expenses attributable to their stay in Sweden are tax-exempt.

National income tax on physical persons is divided into two parts, a *basic amount* and a *supplementary amount*. This division is carried out in order to lower marginal tax rates (i.e. the sum of national and local income taxes payable on any additional income) and to limit the tax impact of deductions for deficits in sources of income (see below).

In the national income tax table, taxable income is expressed in so-called base units. A base unit is equivalent to a particular amount. The base unit for 1986 has been fixed at SEK 7,800.

The *basic amount* is calculated using taxable income, i.e. income after deductions for deficits in sources of income. The national tax rate for the basic amount is 20% in the highest bracket in 1986. Persons with incomes exceeding 16 base units, the so-called breakpoint, must also pay a *supplementary amount*. The latter is calculated using an income figure from which no deductions have been made for deficits in sources of income. The supplementary tax rate is zero on incomes up to breakpoint. As of the income year 1986, the supplementary rate ranges from 5% to 30% depending on income.

There are two ceilings designed to guarantee that a taxpayer may keep a certain minimum percentage of his or her income after tax. One is the *marginal tax ceiling*, which entails that as a rule, a person may keep at least about 20% of any increase in income. Another ceiling is provided by the so-called *limitation rule*, which means that a person should normally retain at least about 20% of his income after paying income and property taxes.

Main features of taxes on physical persons

Taxable income and deductible expenses are calculated separately for each source of income. There are certain standard deductions for some sources of income. *Employees* are entitled to a standard deduction of at least SEK 3,000.

Aside from the deductions that may be made in the various sources of income, there are so-called *general deductions*. Among these are deductions for deficits in sources of income. As mentioned above, limits have been placed on the tax impact of this deduction entitlement. This limitation is linked with the reduction in marginal tax rates which started in 1983. The purpose of the limitation is to restrict the value of deductions in sources of income for tax purposes to a maximum of 50%. There are certain exceptions, however, in the form of special offsetting rules.

In addition, there are certain general deductions justified mainly for social welfare reasons. This applies to the deductions for *regular maintenance* to a former spouse and to children not living at home (the latter only up to SEK 3,000 per child).

In the assessment of local income taxes, a *special basic deduction* (exemption) of SEK 7,500 is allowed. In some cases an extra deduction may be allowed if a person's ability to pay taxes has been significantly reduced on account of prolonged illness, accident, old age or the like. Retired people whose main source of income is the national basic pension have long enjoyed such an *extra deduction for reduced ability to pay taxes.* A person who receives only a basic pension is entitled to such large deductions that he or she will not be liable for any income tax. The extra deduction is phased out as the person's income apart from the basic pension increases. There are additional rules on deductions in cases where income after taxes is below subsistence level, i.e. the minimum amount needed to support the taxpayer, his or her spouse and any dependent children.

National income tax rates for 1986
(Base unit = SEK 7,800)

Taxable income in base units	Taxable income in SEK	National income tax at the lower end of each bracket, SEK	National income tax rates on excess, %
A. Basic amount			
0—1	—7,799	0	0
1—9	7,800—70,199	0	4
9—10	70,200—77,999	2,496	15
10—18	78,000—140,399	3,666	20
18—21	140,400—163,799	16,146	24
21—	163,800—	21,762	20
B. Supplementary amount			
16—19	124,800—148,199	0	5
19—21	148,200—163,799	1,170	10
21—23	163,800—179,399	2,730	15
23—26	179,400—202,799	5,070	20
26—45	202,800—350,999	9,750	25
45—	351,000—	46,800	30

SEK 1 (Swedish krona) = USD 0.13 or GBP 0.09 (approximately)

Tax exemptions on certain savings
Money earned on accounts totaling up to SEK 35,000 in the so-called national savings system *(allemanssparandet)* are tax-exempt. The system went into effect on April 1, 1984.

Tax reductions
Certain credits may be subtracted directly from a person's total tax bill. A married person with a spouse at home or a single person with a child under age 18 is entitled to a *tax reduction of up to SEK 1,800 per year.*

There is also a *tax reduction for trade union dues.* The maximum credit is SEK 480.

Special regulations for taxation of spouses
Income from work is called "A"-income while income from capital and similar sources is referred to as "B"-income. A-income is taxed individually. For spouses, there are regulations which entail that their B-incomes are combined and taxed jointly. Effective from 1985, joint taxation is limited to supplementary amounts. The first SEK 5,000 in B-income for each spouse is being treated as A-income.

Taxation of housing
A person who owns a *house or leisure property* is required to list a certain percentage of the property's assessed value as presumed income, according to a scale which starts at 2% and rises to 8% as the value increases. In principle, deductions are allowed only for interest expenses (standard method).

As for multifamily dwellings owned by non-profit housing companies or housing cooperatives, taxation also follows a standard method. In this case, 3% of the assessed value of the property is listed as income, while deductions are allowed mainly for interest expenses only.

Other owners of multifamily dwellings than those mentioned above are taxed according to the so-called conventional method, which is applied when all revenues from the property are reported and deductions are made for interest payments, operating and maintenance expenses etc. The conventional method is also applied, with some exceptions, in cases where tenants own the property (condominiums). In addition to the above-mentioned standard tax assessment of housing cooperatives, the *members of the cooperative are subject to individualized income taxation.* If the value of a share in the housing cooperative exceeds SEK 50,000 the members are supposed to list 3% of the excess value as income.

Assessment of property value
The assessed value of real estate provides a basis for calculating the municipal guarantee amount (estimated revenue) and the standard income from other real property. In principle, assessed value is determined every five years by a public assessment process. The authorities decide at that time which properties are liable to taxation, what assessed value should be assigned to each property and whether a piece of real estate should be regarded as an agricultural property or as other real property.

Capital gains tax
Capital gains connected with the non-business sale of fixed or personal property are taxed as income from casual economic activity. Capital gains tax is part of ordinary income tax. In other words, these gains are added to the taxpayer's other income for taxation purposes. Capital losses may be subtracted from capital gains.

Capital gains are taxed according to three different systems, depending on what kind of property is sold. Gains arising from the sale of *real estate* are taxable regardless of how long a person owned the property. The owner is, however, allowed to add to the purchase price a conversion figure based on the consumer price index. This indexation system is not applicable, in principle, during the first four years of ownership. Capital gains tax on the sale of a primary residence may be postponed.

Any capital gain from selling a *share in a cooperative housing* (tenant-owner) association is taxed regardless of the period the share is held, according to a sliding scale beginning at 100% of the gain and falling to 25%. In calculating the taxable gain, exemptions are allowed for the acquisition price, costs of improvement and certain capital contributions.

Capital gains from the sale of *shares and certain participations* are taxable regardless of how long they were held. The length of ownership is, however, taken into account in calculating the gains. If the shares have been held for less than two years, the entire gain is taxable. Only 40% of the capital gains on shares owned for longer than two years are taxable. Late in 1983, however, there was an increase in taxation of capital gains from the sale of shares in companies listed on the Stockholm Stock Exchange or other exchanges which are sold after being held for two years. This was achieved by changing some of the rules for calculating the amount subject to tax.

Capital gains arising from the sale of *other personal property* than the above-mentioned are taxed only if the period of ownership was less than five years. During the five-year period, the taxable portion of the capital gains is determined by a scale that declines from 100% to 25%.

Other taxes

Property tax is payable mainly by physical persons. Corporations and most economic associations do not normally pay property tax.

The property subject to taxation consists of the value of certain assets owned by the taxpayer, after deducting his or her liabilities. These taxable assets include real estate, certain personal property used in a business or intended for personal use, bank assets, bonds and shares. Special tax relief rules apply to shares in companies not listed on stock exchanges.

Property tax is payable on taxable assets exceeding SEK 400,000. The tax is progressive. On assets of up to SEK 600,000, it totals 1.5% of the amount exceeding SEK 400,000. The highest rate, 3%, applies to assets of more than SEK 1,800,000. In the case of spouses and their children under age 18 living at home, property tax is based on their combined assets.

Beginning in 1985, a national tax on real estate is levied on tenement houses, office buildings, smaller houses (including both permanent dwellings and leisure properties) and dwellings on agricultural properties. The assessed value of the estate provides the basis of the tax except in the case of smaller houses where the basis is maximized at a third of the assessed value. The rate of the tax—presently ranging from 1% to 2%—differs depending both on whether the estate is a tenement house or a smaller house and whether its taxation follows the standard or the conventional methods (see "Taxation of housing" above). For conventionally taxed properties the tax is deductable as working costs.

Sweden's *inheritance tax* (succession duty) is a tax on the added property received by an heir in connection with another person's death. The tax is based on the amount received.

The inheritance tax is progressive. The rate thus rises as the amount inherited becomes larger. In addition, different tax tables are used depending, among other things, on the relationship between the heir and the deceased. There are lower tax rates on inheritances paid to the closest relatives, who are also favored by the fact that the tax-free basic amount that may be subtracted from their inheritance is higher in their case. As an example, the tax on an inheritance of SEK 200,000 left to a surviving spouse is SEK 18,000 while it is SEK 75,350 if the recipient is a more distant relative.

Gift tax is a supplement to inheritance tax and is calculated, in principle, according to the same rules. Just as in the case of property tax, special relief is granted in calculating inheritance tax on assets in unlisted companies. Certain non-profit organizations are exempt from inheritance or gift tax.

Effective from January 1, 1984 there is a new sales tax on stocks and certain other securities. The tax amounts to 0.5% of the purchase price and is levied on both seller and buyer. The tax on given transaction thus totals 1%. Securities brokers are responsible for the tax on transactions in which they take part. Those who take part in large-scale securities transactions—amounting to SEK 500,000 or more per year—even without being brokers are likewise responsible for ensuring that the tax is paid.

For further information please contact:
The Swedish Embassy or **Consulate**
in your country (in the U.S.:
The Swedish Information Service,
825, Third Ave., New York, N.Y. 10022)
The Swedish Institute
Mailing address: Box 7434, S-103 91 Stockholm, Sweden
Office: Sverigehuset (Sweden House), Kungsträdgården, Stockholm

This fact sheet is produced as part of the Swedish information service abroad, and is intended to be used for reference purposes. It may be freely used in preparing articles, speeches, broadcasts, etc. No acknowledgment is necessary. Please note the date of publication.

LiberKartor Stockholm NORDISKA TRYCKERI AB

LEVEL OF OWN CONTRIBUTION TOWARDS A PUBLIC SERVICE AS AN INDICATOR FOR CONSUMER APPRAISAL

Dick Francken
Ton Kuylen

mailing address:

SWOKA
Koningin Emmakade 192-195
2518 JP THE HAGUE
The Netherlands

1. INTRODUCTION

This study deals with consumers' appraisal of quasi public supply. Quasi public supply is the supply of goods and services which is subsidised by the government and is provided for (individual) end-users. The quasi public supply can be differentiated on the one hand from the public supply (e.g. defence, judicial infrastructure) by the individual basis on which it can be used, and on the other hand from the private supply in the sense that the government objectives are incorporated in the decisions prior to production and supply. In order to achieve these objectives, the government supplies many quasi public goods and services below cost price. The motives on which this type of government policy may be based are described by Van 't Eind & De Kam (1982) as follows:

- the underestimation motive: the government believes that (potential) users underestimate the value of facilities. In this context reference is made in the literature to 'merit goods';
- the development motive: the government considers that certain (desirable) services are viable, but that it will not be possible for their development to take place in line with natural market forces;
- the justice motive: in the government's opinion there are certain services to which everyone in a particular situation is entitled, but for which the commercial economic price would demand so much of the consumer's disposable income, that in practice use of such a service would hardly be feasible without subsidisation;
- the external effects motive: in the government's opinion positive effects may be derived from certain households behaving in line with natural market forces, without these being calculated in market prices.

A result of the subsidisation of services by the government is that the indications, as derived from the normal market mechanism for consumers' appraisal of goods and services, are less appropriate or even completely irrelevant for the provision of public supply.
The contribution that consumers have to pay themselves for a quasi public service therefore cannot be seen as a completely adequate indicator of consumer appraisal. (In theory the consumer's own contribution should equate to the utility that the consumer has from the marginal consumed unit of such a service.)
In order to be able to justify its motives for the subsidisation of quasi public services and to ensure that effective guidelines can be given for the use of these services, it is important for the government to be aware of the extent to which variations in the level of the contribution from (specific groups of) consumers result in changes in the use of a service.

The question directly involved here can be defined as follows:

given an actual usage level, to what extent is the level of the consumer's own contribution towards a public service a good indicator for his/her appraisal of that service.

This is the subject of the study reported here. On the basis of a question format specifically developed for this study we have endeavoured to provide an answer to the question outlined above, for 14 different public services.

The contents of this paper in a nutshell. First a short and more general description is given of the methods and techniques used in literature to study consumer appraisal of public services. After this a newly developed measurement device - the equivalence method - is described (paragraph 3).

In paragraph 4 the results are given, using the equivalence method, of a large survey, which is representative for the Dutch population. A cross-tabulation of the data in paragraph 4.1. to 4.2. is used to indicate the extent to which a consumer's own contribution toward a facility is a good indicator for his/her appraisal of that facility. After this in paragraph 4.4. HOMALS analysis is used for a better statistical foundation of the equivalence method and for a better understanding of the underlying structure in the data. Finally, in paragraph 4.5. canonical discriminant analysis is used to interpret the differences in characteristics of groups of persons in their use and appraisal of public service.

2. CONSUMER APPRAISAL

Two different approaches can be identified in the literature about methods and techniques available for studying consumer appraisal of quasi public supply. In one approach it is the actual observed behaviour that forms the basis for the measurement of individual appraisal. Where the other approach is concerned, the consumers' individual appraisal is not derived from actual observed behaviour, but from what the consumer him/herself (verbally) identifies as his/her preferences (i.e. appraisal). The first of these approaches is described in the literature as the 'revealed preferences' method. The second approach is known as the 'stated preferences' method.

2.2. Revealed preferences

Consumers' revealed preferences can relate to various different forms of behaviour: purchase behaviour, usage behaviour and voting behaviour. An important stipulation for the validity of the results from this method is that the assumptions of the normal market model are satisfied (i.e. completely free competition, fully informed consumers, etc.). For more detailed discussion and evaluation of the revealed preferences method, reference should be made to a literature review, by Wilms (1984). The subject of revealed preferences amongst consumers for quasi public services will not be discussed further in this report.
The method adopted in this study for the measurement of consumer appraisal comprises the interview method based on a kind of stated preferences.

2.2. Stated preferences

As a method for determining consumer appraisal of quasi public services, the measurement of stated preferences is based on interviews conducted with individual consumers. The respondent is asked to evaluate the different services in the context of the other services. The exact method with which this is achieved may vary and may involve different circumstances (Bohm, 1972, 1979; Ferris, 1983; Maital, 1979).
In the following paragraph an outline is given of the method developed for this study to identify consumers' stated preferences for subsidised services.

3. THE EQUIVALENCE METHOD

3.1. Introduction

In order to relate the consumer's appraisal of a quasi public service to the level of his/her own financial contribution the equivalence method has been used.
The essence of this method is that a relationship is assumed between the extent to which a consumer considers (in terms of what personally affects him or her) that:

- he/she could do without a public service (= subjective necessity), and the extent to which:
- a public service is considered either more (sooner) or less (later) appropriate for a price increase (= subjective price), in comparison with other services.

So, it is assumed that the higher the need of a public service, the less acceptable a price increase will be. This will especially be true when there are no substitutes and/or real possibilities to reduce the use of a particular service. In other words, a price increase (= a higher own financial contribution) will be considered less acceptable by consumers, when financial consequences are less 'escapable', and thus will have a more direct effect on the amount of a consumer's disposable income.
This assumption seems to contradict the axiom in economic theory, that a higher need of a good will imply a willingness to pay a higher price. This 'contradiction' may exist by the fact that with stated preferences on public services, the rol of a price-mediating agent (the government) is implicitly given. In the market mechanism this agent is absent.

The relationship (correlation) between subjective price and subjective necessity - as defined above - may be used as a yardstick for the degree in which the price (= level of own financial contribution) of a public service is a good indicator for consumer appraisal.
The stronger this (positive) relationship, the better the level of the consumer's own contribution towards a service will be as an indicator for consumer appraisal, and the weaker (or more negative) this relationship is, the poorer the consumer's own contribution will be as an indicator for consumer appraisal.

3.2. Conceptual model

On a ratio-measurement level the subjective necessity of a public service and the acceptability ('appropriateness') of a price increase can be represented as in figure 1. A change in one variable (= subjective price) is related to a proportional change in the other variable (= subjective necessity).

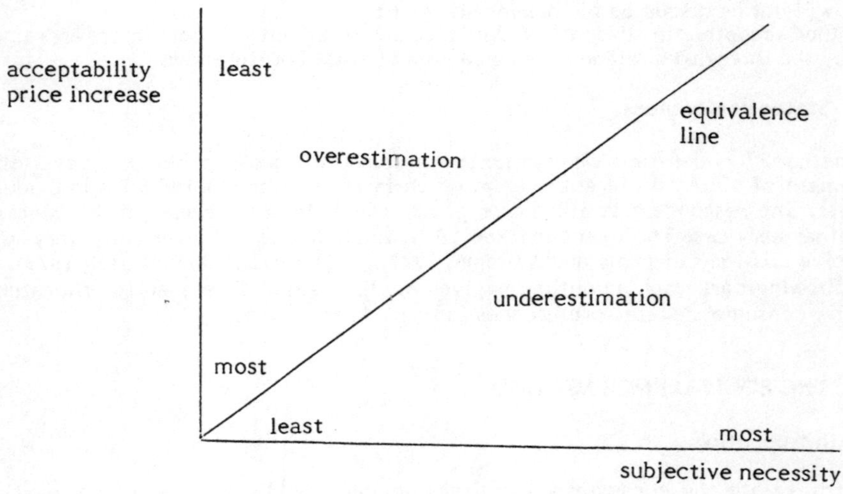

Figure 1 Graphic representation of the equivalence method

The closer the relative position of a public service in figure 1 is to the equivalence line, then the closer the ratio of the subjective price and the subjective necessity of a particular service will be to the value 1, i.e. in such cases the price (= level of own contribution) will be a more realistic indicator for consumer appraisal of a particular public service. If the relative position of a service in figur 1 is further away from the equivalence line O-E, then the price (= own contribution) will be a poorer indicator for consumer appraisal. It is for instance possible that the price is an overestimation of consumer appraisal, in which case the relative position of a particular service, in figure 1 will lie above the equivalence line. However, the price may also be an underestimation of a particular service lying below the equivalence line. In the first of these cases, the ratio between subjective price and subjective necessity is greater than 1 and in the second case it is less than 1.
In this way it would be theoretically possible to identify for a public service the degree in which the level of the consumer's own contribution is a good (or bad) indicator for individual consumer appraisal.

3.3. Answer combinations

The interpretation, given above, of figure 1 is based on ratio data. However, the question format used in this study (see: appendix I) is based on ordinal data. This necessitates a slightly different interpretation of the data.
The three groups of services that are distinguished in both the questions over the subjective necessity (Q 172) and those over the acceptability of price increases (Q 173/174) can be identified in scheme 1.

	can possibly do without (B)	can definitely not do without (C)
first/most appropriate for a price increase (E)	BE equivalence	CE under-estimation
Not endorsed (N)	BN	CN
last/least appropriate for a price increase (L)	BL over-estimation	CL equivalence

Scheme 1 Interpretation of answer combinations in question format (see: Appendix)

In answering the questions about the three (from the total fourteen) services which would be considered most and least appropriate respectively for a price increase, the services which had been allocated to the category 'could easily do without' (= column A) were excluded*.

* One might expect that services identified as 'can easily do without' would be the ones to be considered most often (first of all) appropriate for a price increase. One result of this would be poorer differentation in terms of 'considered most (first) appropriate for price increase' between the services identified in columns B and C.

In scheme 1 this means that it is impossible for the combinations A-E, A-N and A-L, to occur; the combinations that can arise are B-E, B-N, B-L, C-E and C-L.

3.4. Group sizes

The size of the six groups for each of the services provides a yardstick for the extent to which the price (= the level of consumer's own contribution) for a service is a good indicator for consumer appraisal. The more that a large proportion of respondents fall into groups BE/BN and CL, the better the price is as an indicator for consumer appraisal. There is then evidence of price-appraisal equilibrium for the service concerned. Since where CL is concerned, both the subjective price and the subjective necessity are relatively high, and for BE/BN both are relatively low (or 'middling'). On the other hand, the larger the proportion of respondents found in groups BL and CE, the weaker the price-appraisal equilibrium, i.e. the greater the disturbance of the price-appraisal equilibrium. In group BL are the respondents who consider, for a particular service, that it may be possible to do without the service, but who also regard the service as the least appropriate for a price increase. With the BL group therefore, the price of the service concerned is relatively higher than their appraisal of the service, i.e. they consider the service relatively expensive. For the CE-group the converse applies. For these respondents the price of the service concerned is lower than their appraisal, i.e. they consider the service relatively cheap.
Finally the CN-group comprises the people who regard a certain service as completely indispensable and who are more or less neutral toward a price increase. In their view the service concerned will not be considered appropriate for a price increase either first or last. This implies that the CN-group regards the service as relatively cheap in comparison with the CL-group, and in comparison with the CE-group as relatively more expensive.

4. RESULTS

A total of 12,150 persons aged 15 years or older, living in 5,982 households, answered the questions shown in Appendix I. These questions formed part of a larger survey on the use of quasi public services in the Netherlands. The study took the form of a postal survey. The sample of respondents taking part is representative for the population of the Netherlands

4.1. Dispensibility of services (= subjective necessity)

In Table 1 the frequencies and percentages are presented showing the extent to which respondents feel that they could do without fourteen quasi public services.
The service identified by the highest number of people as the one they could definitely not do without is that of the home help service: 7,697 (= 63%) respondents say that they definitely could not do without this service. After this service come: old people's centres, library and indoor or outdoor swimming pool, legal aid centre, baby and toddler advisory centre, etc. The service identified by the highest number of people as one that they could easily do without is paid football, followed by radio/television educational course material (Teleac), creche/play group/child day-care centre, music school/ballet school/creativity centre, etc.

Table 1 The extent to which fourteen quasi public services are considered to be dispensable by the respondents (N = 12.150)

	can easily do without (A)		can possibly do without (B)	can definitely not do without (C)		don't know
services	%	ranking	%	%	ranking	%
1. music/ballet school	42	4	28	21	12	9
2. legal aid centre	25	9	22	45	4	8
3. creche/toddlers' play group	43	3	22	26	11	9
4. paid football	55	1	23	13	13	9
5. radio/TV course	45	2	34	11	14	10
6. theatre	29	7	32	30	8	9
7. home help service	16	14	13	63	1	8
8. zoo	25	10	37	28	10	10
9. neighbourhood centre	26	8	28	37	7	9
10. old people's centre	24	11	14	54	2	8
11. library	17	13	23	52	3	8
12. museum	30	6	31	29	9	10
13. baby advisory centre	32	5	10	43	5	9
14. swimming pool	17	12	23	43	6	8

The percentages and rankings shown in Table 1 relate to the total group of respondents. The extent to which the services are considered to be dispensable may of course vary very markedly between individuals. The same applies to the results for the rejection of price increases, shown in Table 2 and discussed below. In paragraph 4.5 further attention will be paid to these individual differences.

4.2. **Rejection of price increases** (= subjective price)

Table 2 shows the frequencies with which each of the fourteen services is mentioned by the respondents as one of the three services that would be most and least likely respectively to be considered appropriate for a price increase.
The service that is mentioned most often as appropriate for a price increase is museums. Museums are mentioned by 3,240 people as one of the three (of the fourteen) services which is most (first) considered appropriate for a price increase. Following museums are: theatre, library, zoo, paid football, etc.
The service which is considered by respondents as the least (last) appropriate is that of the home help service, followed by old people's centres, legal aid centres, swimming pools, libraries, etc.

Table 2 The frequencies with which fourteen services are mentioned by respondents as one of the three facilities considered most or least appropriate for a price increase (see Appendix 1, Q 173 and Q 174)

	Most appropriate for a price increase (E)		**Least** appropriate for a price increase (L)	
services	N	ranking	N	ranking
1. music/ballet school	1837	6	917	12
2. legal aid centre	1813	7	2925	3
3. creche/toddlers' play group	1441	10	1251	9
4. paid football	1842	5	827	13
5. radio/TV course	1729	9	511	14
6. theatre	2731	2	1440	8
7. home help service	993	12	5448	1
8. zoo	2208	4	1048	10
9. neighbourhood centre	1317	11	1547	7
10. old people's centre	680	13	3680	2
11. library	2607	3	2543	5
12. museum	3240	1	936	11
13. baby advisory centre	612	14	2402	6
14. swimming pool	1802	8	2751	4

In Table 1 it is indicated that 8-10% of respondents is unable to specify the extent to which they consider the fourteen services could be dispensable. The question about the services which would be considered most (first) and least (last) appropriate for a price increase is not answered by 22% and 14% of respondents respectively.

4.3. Answer combinations

In paragraph 3.4. an explanation is given of how the six groups (BE, BN, BL, CE, CN and CL) can be interpreted as a yardstick of the extent to which the price of a service may be a good indicator for consumer appraisal.
The higher the proportion of respondents falling into groups BE/BN and CL, the more the price (= level of consumer's own contribution) can be regarded as a better indicator for consumer appraisal. In this case there is evidence of greater price-appraisal equilibrium for the service concerned. Conversely, the higher the proportion of respondents falling into groups BL and CE, the greater is the extent to which the price-appraisal equilibrium is reduced, such that there is more 'disturbance'.

Tables 3a and 3b present the percentages for each of the six groups (BE, BN, BL, CE, CN and CL) per service, differentiating the users and non-users for each service.
It can be seen (Table 3a) that among the users of a service the least 'price-appraisal disturbance' is evident for services 2, 3, 7, 9, 10 and 13, mainly 'care' services, and for active leisure services (= service 1, 8, 14). The groups BL and CE are smallest for these services, together accounting for no more than 15% of the respondents. Evidence of disturbance is greatest for several 'cultural' services (6, 11 and 12). For these three services groups BL and CE account for 19-26% of respondents. For these three cultural services the CE-group is also far larger than the BL group. This

Table 3a Sub-group sizes per service for each answer combination (Q 172 with 173/174), based on users.

	1 mus./blt school	2 legal aid	3 creche	4 paid footb.	5 r/tv course	6 theatre	7 home help	8 zoo	9 neighb. centra	10 old p. centre	11 libr.	12 museum	13 baby adv. c.	14 swimm. pool
sub-group size (%)														
B-E	16	4	8	15	18	15	1	15	7	-	5	20	3	6
B-N	17	5	13	20	32	16	2	30	22	3	5	15	7	10
B-L	4	2	9	7	7	5	2	6	5	4	3	4	3	4
C-E	7	13	6	11	10	14	8	8	8	11	23	20	9	9
C-N	35	26	25	26	23	30	17	32	39	26	29	29	36	36
C-L	21	50	38	21	10	20	70	9	19	56	35	12	42	35
total persons	748	531	565	693	267	2.575	276	3.929	2.406	238	3.259	3.080	1.451	2.083

Table 3b Sub-group sizes per service for each answer combination (Q 172 with 173/174), based on non-users.

	1 mus./blt school	2 legal aid	3 creche	4 paid footb.	5 r/tv course	6 theatre	7 home help	8 zoo	9 neighb. centra	10 old p. centre	11 libr.	12 museum	13 baby adv. c.	14 swimm. pool
sub-group size (%)														
B-E	20	11	15	27	24	26	2	20	11	2	14	29	2	10
B-N	35	16	26	35	46	28	8	34	31	13	22	28	13	19
B-L	5	6	5	7	5	6	7	6	5	5	6	4	3	5
C-E	8	10	7	7	4	10	8	8	5	6	13	12	5	10
C-N	25	29	34	19	18	23	23	28	38	36	34	23	50	37
C-L	7	28	13	5	3	7	52	4	10	38	11	8	27	19
total persons	4.479	6.713	4.633	3.198	4.670	4.159	8.104	3.193	4.624	7.218	4.763	3.564	4.964	5.880

indicates that these three cultural services are relatively more frequently considered cheap 'for the price' compared to other services. Service 3 (creche, etc.) is the only service for which CE is smaller than group BL, indicating that this service is regarded by a relatively high proportion of people as being expensive 'for the price'.
It is also evident that for service 2 (= legal aid centra) and for the services 7, 10 and 13 (three 'care' services) the BE/BN group is relatively small and the CL group relatively large, whilst for services 5, 8 and 12 the opposite is the case. It is true that in these groups (BE/BN and CL) there is still evidence of price-appraisal equilibrium, but for services 7, 10 and 13 this equilibrium is evident at a higher price-appraisal level than for services 5, 8 and 12.

On comparison of users and non-users of the various services (compare Table 3a with 3b), it appears that the percentage of respondents considering that a service can definitely not be dispensed with (the three 'C'-categories), is consistently 20-25% higher for users than for non-users. It also appears that among non-users the BE/BN-group is always relatively large, whilst the CL-group is relatively small. This indicates that the non-users not only have a relatively low appraisal of the services concerned compared to users, but they also consider these services appropriate for an increase in the level of the consumer's own contribution. However, there are also some similarities between users and non-users. Both groups regard the cultural services: theatre (6), library (11) and musuem (12) as relatively cheap for the price (CE group relatively large compared to the BL-group). And for both users and non-users the BN-group is relatively small for service 2 (legal aid centre) and services 7, 10 and 13 (three 'care' services), whilst the CL-group is relatively large. For these four services it therefore appears that the price-appraisal equilibrium is at a higher level than is the case for the other services, such as 1, 4, 5, 6, 8 and 12 (see Table 3b).

4.4. **Inter-relationship between the answer categories**

In order to investigate the extent to which the answer categories (BE, BN, BL, CE, CN and CL) are inter-related, a HOMALS analysis was carried out. The resulting plot from this analysis is illustrated in figure 2.
For further information on the theory on which this technique is based, reference should be made to Gifi (1982). It is not considered necessary to provide a detailed description of the HOMALS technique here since an overall idea of the answers given is considered sufficient.
The following guidelines are relevant to the interpretation of figure 2.
The distances between points in the diagram indicate which answers are given together. The closer together two or more points lie, the more frequently these answers are given together, and this accounts more the greater the distance to the origin. Similarly, the more centrally (= closer to the origin) certain answer combinations lie, the more these answer combinations go together with various other answers combinations. In this way reflecting heterogeneity.

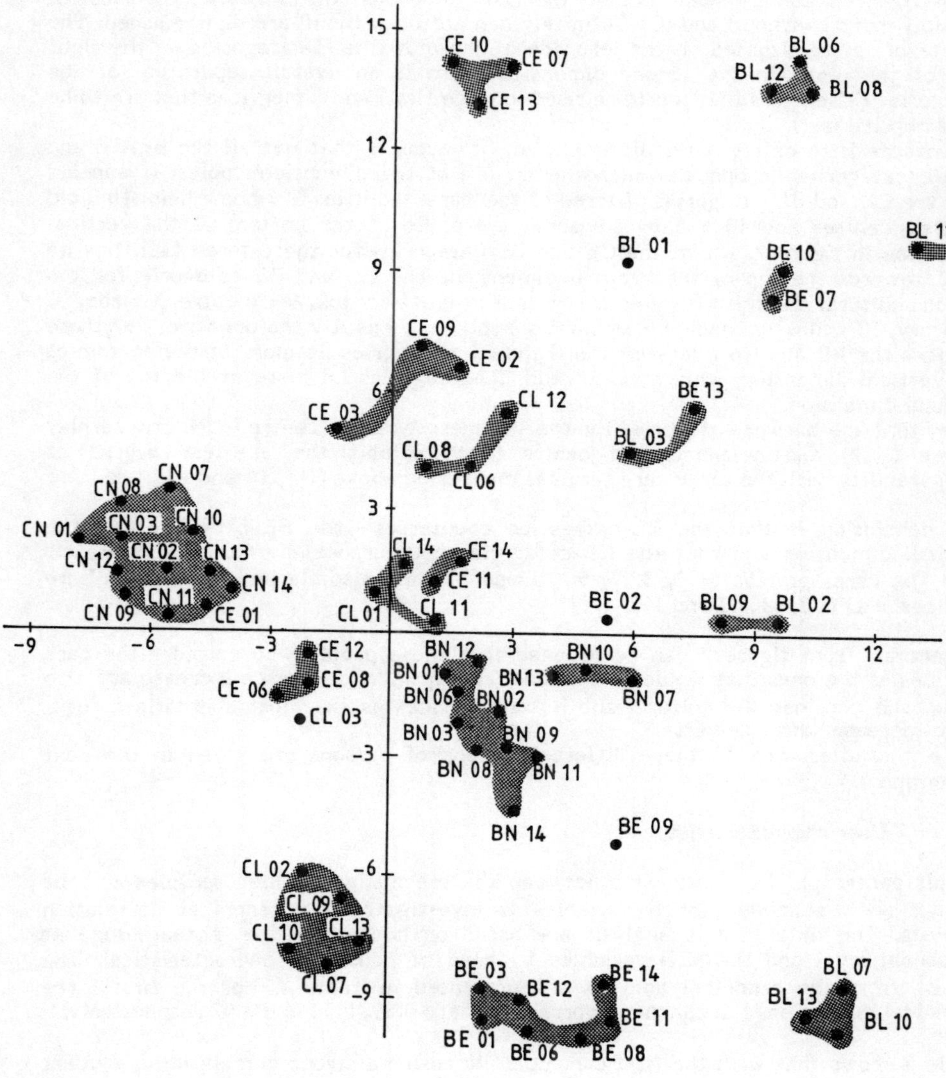

Figure 2 Homals analysis of answer combinations (Q 172 with Q 173/174, see: appendix) with twelve public services

(Note: paid football (04) and radio/tv courses (05) are not included in this analysis)

From figure 2 can be seen that on the first dimension the answer categories (B) 'possibly can do without' and (C) 'definitely can not do without' are distinguished. The B-categories are situated on the left side of the plot, the C-categories on the right side of the plot. On the second dimension there is an overall separation of the categories E (services that are to be rised in price first) and L (services that are to be rised in price last).
A characteristic of the vertical dimension, however, is that not all the BE/CE and BL/CL categories lie opposite eachother at one of the dimension's poles. It appears that the CL and BL categories of three of the 'care' facilities (7 = home help, 10 = old people's centres and 13 = baby advisory centre) lie at the bottom of the vertical dimension in figure 2, whilst the CE and BE-categories for these three facilities lie more towards the top of the vertical dimension. The CL and BL-categorie for the various cultural and leisure services (1 = music/ballet schook, 6 = theatre, 8 = zoo, 11 = library, 12 = museum and 14 = swimming pool) show exactly the opposite. For these services the BE and (to a lesser extent) the CL categories lie more at the bottom of the vertical dimension, whilst the BL and CL-categories lie more at the top of the vertical dimension.
Note, that the answer categories for the services: legal aid centre (= 2), creche/play centre (= 3) and neighbourhood centre (= 9) exhibit the greatest degree of comparability with the three care services mentioned above (= 7, 10 and 13).

The conclusion is that the BL-categories counterpose the BE-categories on the vertical dimension and that the CE-categories counterpose the CL-categories, for both the care services (= 2, 3, 7, 9, 10 and 13) and also the cultural and leisure services (= 1, 6, 8, 11, 12 and 14).

In general, from figure 2 can be deduced that those people who consider the care services as the ones that would be the least appropriate for a price increase are also those who consider the cultural and leisure services as the most appropriate for a price-increase, and vice versa.
Some characteristics of these different groups of persons are given in the next paragraph 4.5.

4.5. User characteristics

In this paragraph the relationship between the use made of public services and the various socio-economic (SED) variables is investigated via canonical correlation analysis. The data in this analysis are based on households (i.e. actual usage at household level and the SED variables by head of household characteristics). The results from the canonical analysis are presented in Table 4. For the first three canonical dimensions the canonical correlations are 0.89, 0.56 and 0.42 respectively.

Table 4 shows that with the first canonical dimension a strong correlation is evident for the use of service 3 (= creche/play group/child day-care centre) and of service 13 (advisory centre for babies/children). This canonical dimension could therefore be described as 'care' services for households with children. It also appears that from the predictor variables: household size and life cycle stage 3 (= co-habitating or married/divorced/separated, 35 years old with 1 or more children aged 4 years) are highly correlated with the first canonical dimension.
The usage variables correlating most strongly with the second canonical dimension are the 'cultural' services 6 (= theatre), 11 (library) and 12 (= museum). The 'active leisure' services 1 (= music school, etc.), 8 (= zoo) and 14 (= swimming pool) also correlate relatively strongly.

Table 4 Correlations of usage variables (at household level) and SED-variables (head of household) with the canonical variables of the criterion set

	correlations with the canonical variables of the criterion set		
	V1	V2	V3
Usage variables (= criterion)*			
G01	-0.02	**0.31**	0.17
G02	0.04	0.27	-0.06
G03	**0.67**	0.00	0.10
G06	-0.10	**0.58**	0.48
G07	0.00	-0.30	**0.42**
G08	0.24	**0.38**	-0.39
G09	0.01	0.27	0.09
G10	-0.10	-0.33	**0.54**
G11	0.02	**0.47**	0.28
G12	-0.05	**0.72**	0.31
G13	**0.96**	-0.02	0.02
G14	0.10	**0.41**	-0.20
SED-variables (= predictor)			
Household size	**0.37**	-0.00	-0.17
One person households	-0.22	0.03	**0.21**
Life cycle stage 2	-0.13	0.12	-0.13
" stage 3	**0.88**	-0.01	0.02
" stage 4	-0.05	0.07	-0.17
" stage 5	-0.15	0.00	-0.06
" stage 6	-0.11	-0.06	-0.02
" stage 7	-0.17	-0.00	0.00
" stage 8	-0.21	**-0.28**	**0.28**
Length of residence	-0.19	**-0.27**	0.01
Employment	0.22	0.13	-0.18
Education to HMBO level	0.06	**0.27**	0.06
Education to HMAVO level	0.02	**0.35**	0.13
Widowed	-0.14	-0.20	**0.20**
Unmarried	-0.15	**0.27**	0.03
Income	0.09	0.17	-0.08
Urbanisation	-0.10	0.08	0.05
Canonical correlations	0.89	0.56	0.42

* Paid football (4) and radio/television courses (5) are not included in this analysis.

The SED-variables associated with the second canonical dimension are education and marital state. People with a higher level of education and single people make more frequent use of the services mentioned. A negative relationship is identified for residental stability and life-cycle stage. Older people in a later life-cycle stage, who have usually been living for a relatively long time in the same place, tend to make comparatively less use of the 'cultural' and 'active leisure' services mentioned.
Finally for the third canonical dimension, it is the service 10 (= old people's centres) and 7 (= home help service) that show the strongest correlations. This canonical dimension can be described as 'care' services for 'older' households (to be differentiated from canonical dimension 1 that can be described as 'care' services for 'younger' households). The predictor variables associated most strongly with this third canonical dimension are: life-cycle stage 8 (= people aged 65+ years), people living alone and widows/widowers.

4.6. Discussion

In order to relate a consumer's appraisal of a public service to the level of his/her own financial contribution, it is assumed that the higher the need of a public service, the less acceptable a price increase will be. The stronger this (positive) relationship, the better the level of a consumer's own contribution towards a service will be as an indicator for consumer appraisal, and vice versa. This is the essence of the equivalence method that has been used in this study.

In total fourteen quasi public services have been evaluated by a representative sample of the Dutch population. A homogeneity analysis on the evaluation of the fourteen services did support a distinction of the services on a subjective necessity dimension and an acceptability of price increase ('subjective price') dimension, as is essential in the equivalence method.
A canonical discriminant analysis reveals three main categories of services: the 'care' services for households with children (creche, advisory centre for babies), the 'cultural' and 'active leisure' services (museum, library, theatre and music school, zoo, swimming pool), and finally, the 'care' services for 'older' households (old people's centre, home help service).

The most important factor in this study for the appraisal of services is frequency of use. Life-cycle variables strongly relate to the evaluation of 'care' services, while social status variables (income, education) more relate to the evaluation of 'cultural/leisure' services. These findings may explain why in the homogeneity analysis the 'care' services and 'cultural/leisure' services oppose each other: those people who consider the care services as indispensable and least appropriate for a price increase, consider the 'cultural/leisure' services as less indispensable and more appropriate for a price increase, and vice versa.

Within the consumer research field methods and techniques to study consumer's appraisal of public services are still poorly developed. Although the results indicate that the measurement device used in this study may be helpfull, several restrictions can be mentioned. Firstly, use is made of a forced choice format. On the one hand this may result in more relevant answers, but on the other hand the answers will be influenced by the services that are (not) included. By this the results of the equivalence method are strongly dependent on the public services involved. A second restriction concerns the public services that can be included. Public services for which an official indication for use (a referral) is needed (e.g. hospitals) are less suitable. Services with a voluntary use imply more realistic choice possibilities. A third restriction refers to the discrepancy that may exist between stated preferences and actual behavior. It is not an automatic given that people will behave as they say, they would prefer.

A final restriction with regard to this study has to do with the (independent) variables used to explain consumer's appraisal. Results indicate that actual use of a service is an important factor for the explanation of consumer's appraisal. This calls for a refinement of the measurement of usage variables, not only a refinement of actual use, but also of potential use, and even of (actual and/or potential) use made by relevant others. Besides this, more attention to political affiliation variables (Francken, 1986) and to 'informal economy' variables may be needed to explain consumer's appraisal of public services.

Literature

Bohm, P. (1972)
Estimating Demand for public Goods - An Experiment, European Economic Review, 3.

Bohm, P. (1979)
Estimating willingness to pay: why and how?, Scandinavian Journal of Economics.

Eind, C.J. van 't en C.A. de Kam (1982)
Heroverwegingen van bezuinigingen op publieke uitgaven, Economisch Statistische Berichten, 67, 24 maart.

Ferris, J. (1983)
Demands for public spending: an attitudinal approach, Public Choice, 40, 2.

Francken, D.A. (1986)
Consumer perceptions and preferences for public expenditure, Journal of Economic Psychology, 7, June.

Maital, S. (1979)
Measurement of net benefits from public goods: a new approach using survey data, Public Finance, nr. 1.

Wilms, P.J.M. (1984)
Op waarde geschat, Instituut voor Onderzoek van Overheidsuitgaven, Onderzoeksreeks nr. 11, Den Haag.

Appendix: Question format

Consumer preferences

Q 172 The various public services that are subsidised by the government, are not as relevant to some people as to others. For some people, a particular service may be unimportant because they do not/will not make use of it either now or in the future. Other services, however, may be very important to these people.

Listed below are fourteen services. We should like to know how important each of these services is for you personally. We are not therefore concerned here with the extent to which you think that a particular service is important to other people.

a. First, please place a cross under column A against each service that is so unimportant to you, that you consider you could easily do without it.

b. Then, please place a cross under column B against each service that you personally feel you could possibly do without, even if it is a service that might be important to you.

c. Finally, please place a cross under column C against each service that is so important to yourself that you could definitely not do without it.

Q 173 In the previous question you have placed a cross under columns B and C against certain services.
From these services please select the three that you consider are **first (most) appropriate** for a price increase for the user (i.e. consumer).

Please note: You should base this selection on your own situation and not on that of other people.

Please do not include any service against which you have just placed a cross under column A.

Q 174 From the services against which you places a cross in column B or C, would you now please select the three that you consider to be the **last (least) appropriate** for a price increase for the user (i.e. consumer)

A PSYCHOLOGICAL OPPONENT PROCESSES THEORY OF CONSUMPTION*

by

FERNANDO B. SALDANHA

University of Arizona

and

PIERRE-JEAN LANCRY

Université Paris XII - Val-de-Marne

* We are thankful to Lester Taylor for discussions and inspiration.

1. INTRODUCTION.

More than a decade ago, Tibor Scitovski published "**The Joyless Economy,**" [6], a pioneering work in which the motivations and behavior of a consumer are explained with basis on the experimental findings of psychologists, and on the theories built upon these findings. Unfortunately, the ideas contained in this important book had only a reduced impact on the economic profession. Very few of the research paths suggested by Scitovski were explored. The present paper consists in one such exploration.

We construct a model of consumption behavior based on psychological opponent processes theory (POPT). Scitovski argued that the largest part of consumption behavior resembles addictive behavior, whose most convincing explanation would be POPT. This theory, which was developed by R. L. Solomon and his associates at the University of Pennsylvania, departs from the observation that hedonic sensations are often followed by a posterior effect of an opposite character. Thus, for example, the anxiety experienced during a parachute jump gives rise to a feeling of exhilaration, and sexual stimulation is often followed by irritation or depression. The theory itself consists in the statement that a stimulus, besides causing a primary reaction, called the A-process, also generates a secondary process, called the B-process. The B-process has a hedonic sign that is opposite to that of the primary process, and is thus referred to as an opponent process. An important characteristic of the B-process is its sluggishness. That is, "it has a relatively long latency, recruits slowly, and dies slowly." ([7], p. 125) The typical response to a pleasurable stimulus would then be as depicted in Figure 1.

Figure 1

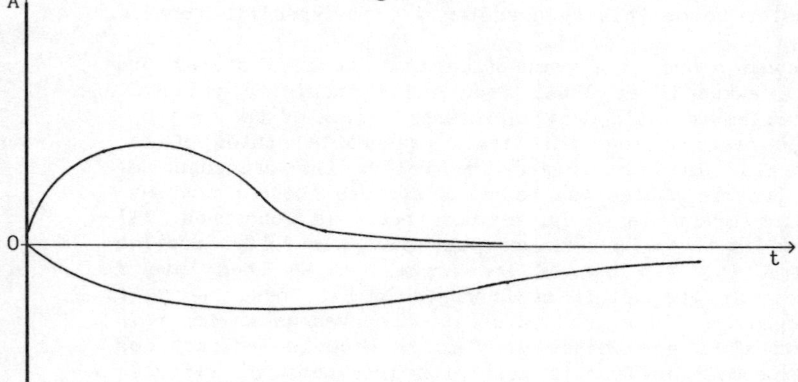

Assuming that the algebraic addition of the A and B processes is meaningful, and defining $X \equiv A - B$, the net result is as shown in Figure 2.

Figure 2

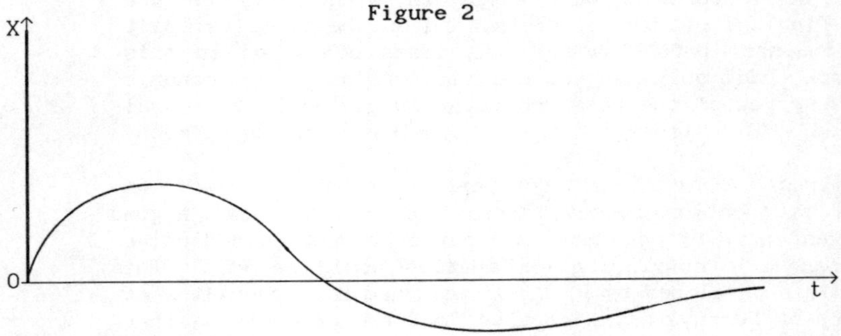

An initial pleasurable period is followed by a longer period of pain or suffering. If the stimulus is repeated many times, then the pleasure felt at each peak decreases in intensity, and the pain felt after stimulation stops becomes more severe.

Perhaps due to the apparent requirement that hedonic states be measurable, not much attention was given to this model by economists. Taylor [8] developed a theory of rational consumer behavior based on POPT. His pioneering work was for us a source of inspiration, even though in our model the consumer is myopic. The work of Coursey [1] must also be mentioned.

We postulate the existence of two basic behavioral modes, called **myopic behavior** and **abstinence**, and define the conditions under which each one of these modes prevails. Rational optimizing is excluded *a priori*. Of course, such an exclusion is not motivated by the belief that behavior can never be rational. Our objective is to study irrational behavior in the context of POPT, and it is easier to do this by assuming a pure, specific form of irrationality.

As observed above, the assumption that hedonic states are measurable is awkward, at least from the economist's point of view. This problem is avoided by an interpretation of the $X \equiv A - B$ process as representing objectively measurable states of the consumer's brain. In this regard, we follow the precedent of Wichers [9]. Hedonic states may be associated to these processes, but this is irrelevant in so far as the theory is concerned. All that is needed is that the consumer must have a utility function having $X \equiv A - B$ as one of its arguments. We then have a two-tier model, in the spirit of Lancaster's [4] "new theory of consumption behavior." The good in question serves as an input in the production of X, and the demand for the good is indirect, or derived. The production function exhibits intertemporal effects, formally analogous to those postulated in POPT.

Of the two basic behavioral modes, myopia and abstinence, the first consists simply in the maximization of current period's utility, while abstinence means, of course, no consumption. Following the "evolutionary approach" of Nelson and Winter [5], we assume that the strategy of behaving myopically prevails until it proves to be inefficient, in which case the consumer attempts to abstain from consumption. However, there is a threshold of pain beyond which the consumer becomes irrational, and reverts to myopic behavior. Thus, if an attempt to withdraw results in excessive pain, then it is unsuccessfull.

The role of POPT in the context of our model is to provide the link between present consumption and future hedonic effects. Several patterns of dynamic behavior appear to be possible. Some stylized facts, like the decrease in pleasure after repeated exposure to stimuli, the pain of withdrawal, or the persistence of consuming harmful commodities are explained. An interesting result is that those commodities whose consumption tends to increase until they absorb all of the consumer's income are in reality "bads." That is, for thes commodities, in a steady state the B-process overcomes the A-process, with the net result being a painful hedonic state.

As a side remark, we observe that the framework of our model can be used to analyze the question of which commodities will in general be consumed according to rational, optimizing, policies, and which ones will be myopically consumed. We suggest that those goods that generate opponent processes that i) are not very sluggish, and ii) have very distinctive features are, other things being equal, more likely to be rationally consumed. Thus, if somebody always develops a rash immediately after eating pineapples, then he or she is likely to avoid them. On the other hand, some of the most unpleasant effects of certain drugs may manifest themselves only after a relatively long period of use, and are quite similar to organic and psychological troubles that could have other causes. In cases like the latter the consumer may be unable to identify the true model that generates his hedonic states. In particular, he may remain unaware of the existence of a B-process.

The remainder of the paper is as follows. In Section 2 the basic model is presented. Section 3 contains an analysis of myopic behavior, and deals with the problems of stability, comparative statics, and welfare analysis. Abstinence is studied in Section 4. In Section 5 we analyze a mixed form of behavior: oscillations between myopia and abstinence. Section 6 contains an analysis of the possible types of dynamic evolution of behavior. Finally, Section 7 contains our conclusions, and indicates some directions for further research.

2. The Model.

Consider a consumer that can spend his income in two alternative ways. He can buy a commodity Y whose consumption directly enters his utility function, or another commodity A that serves as an input for an "internal" production processs whose whose output X enters his utility function. The consumer is assumed to have a constant income flow I. No lending or borrowing are allowed. His utility function is taken to be intertemporally separable, of the form

$$(1) \qquad \mathcal{U}(X(.),Y(.)) = \sum_{t=0}^{\infty} U(X(t),Y(t))\delta^t$$

where

$$U(X,Y) = V(X) + W(Y)$$

$$V(X) = \frac{1}{2} v_0 X^2 + v_1 X \qquad v_0 < 0,\ v_1 > 0$$

$$W(Y) = wY \qquad w > 0$$

$$0 \le \delta < 1.$$

The value of X(t) is determined by the equations

$$(2) \qquad X(t) = A(t) - B(t)$$

$$(3) \qquad B(t) = (1-b_1)B(t-1) + b_2 A(t),$$

where $0 < b_1 < 1$ and $0 < b_2 < 1$. Given initial conditions B(-1), equations (2) and (3) are a representation of an "internal" production function that maps (A(0),A(1),...,A(t)) into X(t). The inequality $b_2 < 1$ means that consuming A in period t has a positive effect in utility **in that period**, since the marginal (one-period) utility of current consumption is $(1-b_2)V'(X)$.

Equations (2) and (3) define a linear system whose unit impulse response is qualitatively similar to the one postulated by Solomon and Corbit. For example, if B(-1) = 0, A(0) = 1, and A(t) = 0 for t ≥ 1, then

$$X(0) = (1-b_2)$$

$$X(t) = -b_2(1-b_1)^t \qquad (t \ge 1).$$

In Figure 3 the unit impulse response of the system is depicted. There is a positive effect on utility in period 0, and then a long lasting negative reaction, which decays geometrically.

Figure 3

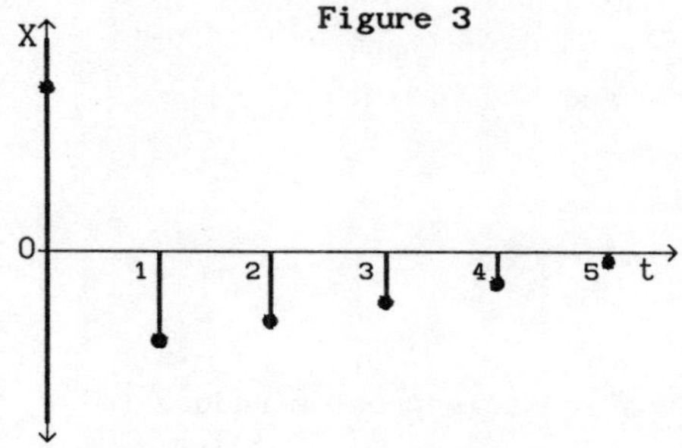

We assume that the consumer has two basic behavioral modes. He can maximize his current utility, and disregard the future effects of consumption on his utility, being unaware of the existence of the B-process. In this case we say that he displays **myopic behavior**, and write $\beta(t) = 1$. He can also decide that consuming good A is not advantageous to him, and abstain from buying it. We call this form of behavior **abstinence**, and write $\beta(t) = 0$ to denote it.

At each moment of time the consumer's behavioral mode is determined by the following rules:

BM) There are scalars U^+, U^- such that $U^- < U^+ \leq wI$, and

BM1) $U(t) < U^- \Rightarrow \beta(t+1) = 1$

BM2) $\beta(t) = 1$ and $U(t) > U^+ \Rightarrow \beta(t+1) = 1$

BM3) $\beta(t) = 1$ and $U^- \leq U(t) < U^+ \Rightarrow \beta(t+1) = 0$

The interpretation of these rules is as follows. U^- is a lower bound below which there is excessive "suffering" that causes irrational, myopic, behavior. U^+ is a threshold for the perception that consumer's surplus is negative. The most natural value for U^+ is $U^+ = wI$, but in what follows we only impose $U^+ \leq wI$. Given this interpretation of U^+ and U^- the meaning of BM1-BM3 should be clear. BM1 states that excessive "suffering" causes irrational behavior. If the consumer behaves myopically in period t then he will also do so in period t+1, unless a low utility level leads him to the perception that consumption of the good results in a negative consumer's surplus. This is expressed by BM2 and BM3.

We show below that, under certain conditions, the rule BM may determine a mixed pattern of behavior: oscillation between myopia and abstinence. In the next three sections we study the three possible forms of behavior.

3. Myopic behavior.

Since the myopic consumer does not take into account the future effects of consumption, his behavior in the current period t is given by the solution of the following maximization problem:

$$\max \quad V(X(t)) + wY(t)$$

subject to (2), (3), and

$$\text{(4)} \qquad pA(t) + Y(t) \leq I$$

$$A(t) \geq 0, \qquad Y(t) \geq 0.$$

The Kuhn-Tucker conditions for this problem reduce to

$$\text{(5-a)} \qquad \frac{1-b_2}{p} = \frac{w}{V'(X(t))} \qquad \text{if} \quad 0 < A(t) < \frac{I}{p}$$

$$\text{(5-b)} \qquad \frac{1-b_2}{p} < \frac{w}{V'(X(t))} \qquad \text{if} \quad A(t) = 0$$

$$\text{(5-c)} \qquad \frac{1-b_2}{p} > \frac{w}{V'(X(t))} \qquad \text{if} \quad A(t) = \frac{I}{p},$$

together with (2), (3), and (4).

In the case of an interior solution (5-a) is the relevant condition. The consumer equates the trade-off rate between X and Y to his marginal rate of substitution between these "commodities." Notice that the trade-off rate $(1-b_2)/p$ refers only to the current effects of consumption.

Solving (5-a) for A(t), we obtain

$$\text{(6)} \qquad A(t) = \bar{A} + \frac{1-b_1}{1-b_2} B(t-1) ,$$

where $\bar{A}$ is defined by

$$\text{(7)} \qquad \bar{A} = \left[\frac{-1}{(1-b_2)v_0}\right]\left[v_1 - \frac{wp}{1-b_2}\right].$$

In what follows we assume

$$\text{(8)} \qquad 0 < \bar{A}.$$

This assumption eliminates the uninteresting case in which the consumer never buys the good.

Using (2), (3), and (6), we find

$$\text{(9-a)} \qquad X(t) = \bar{A}(1-b_2) \qquad \text{if} \quad 0 < A(t) < I/p,$$

which means the consumer keeps X fixed at $X = \bar{A}(1-b_2)$ as long as this is budget feasible. We also have

$$X(t) = -(1-b_1)B(t-1) \qquad \text{if } A(t) = 0, \tag{9-b}$$

$$X(t) = (1-b_2)\frac{I}{p} - (1-b_1)B(t-1) \qquad \text{if } A(t) = \frac{I}{p}. \tag{9-c}$$

Now, it follows from (6) that A(t) varies from 0 to I/p as $-(1-b_1)B(t-1)$ varies from $(1-b_2)\bar{A}$ to $(1-b_2)(\bar{A}-(I/p))$. When B(t-1) is large the consumer spends all his money on the good, but still does not manage to raise X to $(1-b_2)\bar{A}$. As B(t-1) decreases, so does the consumption of A, and X increases, up to the level $(1-b_2)\bar{A}$. Any further decrease of B(t-1) does not lead to a change in X.

In general, we conclude that:

i) (5-a) and (9-a) determine A(t) and X(t) if

$$\left[\frac{1-b_2}{1-b_1}\right]\bar{A} < B(t-1) < \left[\frac{1-b_2}{1-b_1}\right]\left[\frac{I}{p} - \bar{A}\right] \tag{10-a}$$

ii) (5-b) and (9-b) determine A(t) and X(t) if

$$B(t-1) \le -\left[\frac{1-b_2}{1-b_1}\right]\bar{A} \tag{10-b}$$

iii) (5-c) and (9-c) determine A(t) and X(t) if

$$B(t-1) \ge \left[\frac{1-b_2}{1-b_1}\right]\left[\frac{I}{p} - \bar{A}\right] . \tag{10-c}$$

Case ii) turns out to be irrelevant since obviously $B(t) \ge 0$ for all t, as long as $b_1 \le 1$. In cases i) and iii) the consumer spends respectively a portion or all of his income on good A.

3.1. Stability of steady states.

We now investigate the dynamics of myopic behavior. Using (3) and (6), we obtain

$$B(t) = \lambda B(t-1) + b_2\bar{A} , \tag{11}$$

where $\lambda = (1-b_1)/(1-b_2)$.

The condition for the stability of the first-order linear difference equation (11) is $|\lambda| \leq 1$ (cf. [3], p. 16). Equivalently, (11) is stable if and only if

$$\text{(S)} \qquad b_2 < b_1 .$$

Then (11) is stable if and only if a positive steady state value of A determines a positive steady state value of X. Indeed, letting a hat denote a steady state value of a variable, we have, from (3), $b_1\hat{B} = b_2\hat{A}$, and hence (2) implies that

$$\text{(12)} \qquad \hat{X} = \left[1 - \frac{b_2}{b_1}\right] \hat{A}.$$

This shows:

Proposition 1: The following two conditions are equivalent:

i) The commodity is a "bad," in the sense that any steady state level of consumption has an adverse effect on the consumer's welfare.

ii) For any income level I, consumption of the commodity increases until it absorbs all of the consumer's income.

If (S) holds, and assuming that the value of A(t) given by (6) and (7) remains budget feasible, then B converges monotonically to the steady-state value

$$\text{(13)} \qquad B^* = \frac{(1-b_2)b_2}{(b_1-b_2)} \bar{A} ,$$

and hence, from (6), A converges monotonically to

$$\text{(14)} \qquad A^* = \frac{(1-b_2)b_1}{(b_1-b_2)} \bar{A} .$$

The value of X does not vary. It remains constant at

$$\text{(15)} \qquad X^* = (1-b_2)\bar{A} .$$

We assume that the myopic consumer's steady state consumption of good A does not absorb all of his income:

$$\text{(A)} \qquad A^* < \frac{I}{p} .$$

Given this assumption, the monotonic convergence of A implies that if the value of A(t) determined by (6) and (7) is budget feasible, then the same is true of $A(t+\tau)$, for $\tau > 0$. Now, from

(6), if

$$(16) \qquad B(-1) < \left[\frac{1-b_2}{1-b_1}\right]\left[\frac{I}{p} - \bar{A}\right],$$

then $A(0) < I/p$. We conclude that if (S) and (16) hold then the evolution of the system is governed by equation (11), and A, B, Y, and U converge monotonically to their steady state values. More specifically, we can solve (11), to find

$$(17) \qquad B(t) = B^* + (B(-1) - B^*)\lambda^{t+1},$$

and then use (9-a) and (15) to obtain

$$(18) \qquad A(t) = A^* + (B(-1) - B^*)\lambda^{t+1}.$$

From (4) and (18) we conclude that

$$Y^* = I - pA^*$$

$$Y(t) = Y^* - p(B(-1) - B^*)\lambda^{t+1}.$$

Using this last relation and (9-a) we finally find

$$(19) \qquad U(t) = U^* - wp(B(-1) - B^*)\lambda^{t+1},$$

where

$$U^* = V(X^*) + wY^* .$$

3.2. Comparative Statics: Myopic behavior.

In both this and in the next subsection we assume that the relations (S) and (16) are satisfied, so that the evolution of the A and B processes is governed by equation (11), which then satisfies the condition for stability. The steady state values A^*, B^*, and X^* are then respectively given by (14), (13), and (15).

From (7), we have

$$\frac{\partial \bar{A}}{\partial I} = 0$$

$$\frac{\partial \bar{A}}{\partial p} = \frac{w}{(1-b_2)^2 v_0},$$

and it follows that

$$\frac{\partial A^*}{\partial I} = \frac{\partial B^*}{\partial I} = \frac{\partial X^*}{\partial I} = 0$$

$$\frac{\partial A^*}{\partial p} = \frac{wb_1}{(1-b_2)(b_1-b_2)v_0} < 0$$

$$\frac{\partial B^*}{\partial p} = \frac{wb_2}{(1-b_2)(b_1-b_2)v_0} < 0$$

$$\frac{\partial X^*}{\partial p} = \frac{w}{(1-b_2)v_0} < 0.$$

The income elasticity of X is zero since the utility function is quasilinear. The demand curves for A and X are downward sloping. Clearly, we also have

$$\frac{\partial Y^*}{\partial I} = 1 .$$

3.3. Welfare analysis: Myopic Behavior.

Given a constant consumption level $\hat{A}$, the consumer's steady state utility is given by

$$\hat{U} = \frac{1}{2} v_0 \hat{X}^2 + v_1 \hat{X} + w(I - p\hat{A}) , \tag{20}$$

where X and A are related as in (12). It follows that

$$\hat{U} = wI + \frac{1}{2} v_0 \hat{X}^2 + \left[v_1 - \frac{wpb_1}{b_1-b_2}\right] \hat{X} . \tag{21}$$

We want to compare the steady state utilities U^* and U^{**} that correspond respectively to myopic and rational behavior. From (21), we have

$$U^{**} - U^* = \frac{1}{2} v_0 \left[X^{**2} - X^{*2}\right] + \left[v_1 - \frac{wpb_1}{b_1-b_2}\right](X^{**} - X^*) = \tag{22}$$

$$= -v_0(X^{**} - X^*)\left\{\frac{-1}{v_0}\left[v_1 - \frac{wpb_1}{b_1-b_2}\right] - \frac{1}{2}(X^{**} + X^*)\right\} ,$$

and since the value of X^* is given by (15), it remains to calculate the value of X^{**}.

The optimal steady state values of A, X, and Y are given by the solution of the following optimization problem:

$$\max \ V(X) + wY$$

subject to

$$X = \left[1 - \frac{b_2}{b_1}\right] A$$

$$pA + Y \le I$$

$$A \ge 0, \qquad Y \ge 0 .$$

The Kuhn-Tucker conditions for this problem reduce to

$$\text{(23-a)} \quad p^{-1}\left[1 - \frac{b_2}{b_1}\right] = \frac{w}{V'(X^{**})} \qquad \text{if } 0 < A^{**} < \frac{I}{p}$$

$$\text{(23-b)} \quad p^{-1}\left[1 - \frac{b_2}{b_1}\right] < \frac{w}{V'(X^{**})} \qquad \text{if } A^{**} = 0$$

$$\text{(23-c)} \quad p^{-1}\left[1 - \frac{b_2}{b_1}\right] > \frac{w}{V'(X^{**})} \qquad \text{if } A^{**} = \frac{I}{p},$$

together with the budget constraint (4), with (12), and with the nonnegativity constraints.

The conditions (23) are similar to the conditions (5) derived for the optimization problem of a consumer displaying myopic behavior. The difference is that in (23) the trade-off rate between X and Y is the one that truly holds in the long run, namely $(1-(b_2/b_1))/p$, and not the rate $(1-b_2)/p$ mistakenly perceived by a myopic consumer.

Solving (23-a) for A^{**} and X^{**} we obtain

$$\text{(24)} \quad A^{**} = \frac{-1}{v_0\left[1 - \frac{b_2}{b_1}\right]}\left[v_1 - \frac{wpb_1}{b_1 - b_2}\right]$$

$$\text{(25)} \quad X^{**} = \frac{-1}{v_0}\left[v_1 - \frac{wpb_1}{b_1 - b_2}\right] .$$

From (7), (15), and (25), we obtain

$$\text{(26)} \quad X^{**} - X^{*} = \frac{-wp}{v_0}\left[\frac{1}{1-b_2} - \frac{b_1}{b_1 - b_2}\right] = \frac{-wp}{v_0}\,\frac{(b_1 - 1)b_2}{(1-b_2)(b_1 - b_2)} < 0 ,$$

and conclude that overconsumption is the rule.

Using again (7), (15), and (25) to calculate $X^{*} + X^{**}$, we can substitute in (22) to find

$$(27) \qquad U^{**} - U^{*} = - \frac{w^2(1-b_1)b_2}{2(1-b_2)^2(b_1-b_2)^2 v_0} p^2 .$$

The higher the price of the good the larger the welfare loss due to myopic behavior. It is also easy to see that the welfare loss decreases with b_1 and increases with b_2. This is quite intuitive. When b_1 is close to unity the B-process decays rapidly, and disregarding the future has little importance. And a high value of b_2 means that the future effects of consumption are strong.

4. Abstinence.

Suppose that the consumer abstains from the good from period $\bar{t}$ on. Then, for $\tau = 0,1,2,\ldots,$ the following relations hold.

$$A(\bar{t}+\tau) = 0$$

$$B(\bar{t}+\tau) = (1-b\ )B(\bar{t})$$

$$X(\bar{t}+\tau) = -B(\bar{t}+\tau)$$

$$Y(\bar{t}+\tau) = I$$

$$U(\bar{t}+\tau) = wI + \frac{1}{2} v_0 B(\bar{t}+\tau)^2 - v_1 B(\bar{t}+\tau) .$$

B decreases geometrically with time, and U converges to wI.

5. Oscillatory behavior.

In this section we study only the simplest type of oscillations, namely the case where the consumer alternates *ad infinitum* between a single period of myopia and another single period of abstinence. We argue below that this is, in the context of our model, the only possible type of oscillatory behavior.

Suppose that, for some $\bar{t} \geq 0$, and for $\tau = 0,1,2,\ldots,$ the following relations hold.

$$A(\bar{t}+2\tau) = 0$$

$$A(\bar{t}+2\tau+1) = \bar{A} + \frac{1-b_1}{1-b_2} B(\bar{t}+2\tau)$$

$$X(\bar{t}+2\tau+1) = X^{*} .$$

We then have, from (3),

$$B(\bar{t}+2\tau 1) \;=\; b_2\bar{A} + \frac{1-b_1}{1-b_2}\,B(\bar{t}+2\tau)$$

and hence

$$(30) \qquad B(\bar{t}+2\tau+2) = (1-b_1)\bar{B}(t+2\tau+1) = (1-b_1)b_2\bar{A} + \frac{(1-b_1)^2}{1-b_2}\,B(\bar{t}+2\tau)\,.$$

This is a difference equation describing the evolution of $B(\bar{t}+2\tau)$. If $(1-b_1)^2 < (1-b_2)$ (which is always the case if (S) is satisfied) then (30) is stable, and $B(\bar{t}+2\tau)$ and $U(\bar{t}+2\tau)$ converge respectively to

$$(31) \qquad \tilde{B} \;=\; \frac{(1-b_1)(1-b_2)b_2\bar{A}}{b_1(2-b_1)-b_2}$$

$$(32) \qquad \tilde{U} \;=\; wI + \frac{1}{2}\,v_0\,\tilde{B}^2 - v_1\tilde{B}\,.$$

We also have

$$(33) \qquad \hat{U} \;\equiv\; \lim_{\tau\to\infty} U(\bar{t}+2\tau+1) \;=\; U^* + \lambda wp(B^*-\tilde{B})\,.$$

Indeed, defining $\hat{X}$ and $\hat{Y}$ in the obvious way, $\hat{X} = X^*$ implies that

$$\hat{U} - U^* \;=\; w(\hat{Y} - Y^*)\,.$$

From (4) and (6),

$$Y^* \;=\; I - p\bar{A} - \lambda pB(\bar{t}+2\tau)\,,$$

and hence the convergence of $B(\bar{t}+2\tau)$ to $\tilde{B}$ implies (33).

Notice also that $\hat{U} > \tilde{U}$ and that the amplitude of the oscillations increases with time

$$A(\bar{t}+1) < A(\bar{t}+3) < \ldots$$

$$U(\bar{t}) > U(\bar{t}+2) > \ldots$$

$$U(\bar{t}+1) > U(\bar{t}+3) > \ldots$$

if $U(\bar{t}) > \tilde{U}$, while it decreases with time if $U(\bar{t}) < \tilde{U}$.

6. Dynamic evolution of behavior.

In this section we classify the different types of dynamic behavior that our model can generate, and specify the conditions under which the consumer displays these forms of behavior. We assume (S), (A), $B(-1) = 0$, and $\beta(0) = 1$.

M) Persistent myopic behavior.

The consumer displays the kind of behavior described in Section 3. In the long run he overconsumes the good, and therefore ends up with a consumer's surplus that is too small, and may even be negative. The condition for this type of behavior is

$$U^+ \le U^* . \tag{35}$$

MA) Permanent abstinence after myopic behavior.

The consumer behaves myopically, as described in Section 3, from period 0 to some period $\bar{t}$, and thereafter abstains from consuming the good. In the long run his utility converges to wI. This case obtains when (35) is not satisfied and

$$U^- \le wI + V\left\{(1-b_1)\left[X^* + \frac{U^+ - wI - V^*}{wp}\right]\right\} \tag{36}$$

MO) Persistent oscillations after myopic behavior.

The consumer behaves myopically from period 0 to some period $\bar{t}-1$. Thereafter he oscillates between myopia and abstinence in the following way. For $t = \bar{t}+2\tau$, $\tau=0,1,2,\ldots$, he abstains, and for $t = \bar{t}+2\tau+1$, $\tau=0,1,2,\ldots$, he behaves myopically.

This case occurs when neither of the relations (35) and (36) is satisfied and $\hat{U} \ge U^- \ge \tilde{U}$.

MOA) Myopic behavior followed by oscillations of decreasing amplitude and finally by abstinence.

There are $\bar{t}$ and t', with $0 < \bar{t} < t'$, such that the consumer behaves myopically in periods $0,1,\ldots,\bar{t}-1$, then oscillates between abstinence and myopia in periods $\bar{t},\bar{t}+1,\bar{t}+2,\ldots,t'$, and abstains from consuming the good thereafter. The oscillations in the intermediate period are of decreasing amplitude. In the long run the consumer's utility approaches wI.

The consumer displays this type of behavior when $\tilde{U} > U^-$ and neither of the inequalities (35) and (36) holds.

MOM) Myopic behavior followed by oscillations and finally by persistent myopic behavior.

There are $\bar{t}$ and t', with $0 < \bar{t} < t'$, such that the consumer behaves myopically in periods $0,1,\ldots,\bar{t}-1$, then oscillates between abstinence and myopia in periods $\bar{t}, \bar{t}+1, \bar{t}+2, \ldots, t'$, and behaves myopically thereafter. In the long run the consumer's utility approaches wI.

The consumer displays this type of behavior when neither of the inequalities (35) and (36) holds, and $\hat{U} < U^{-}$.

We now discuss the conditions under which each one of the above forms of behavior takes place.

It is assumed that the consumer behaves myopically in period zero. That is, he starts to consume the good without previous knowledge of its characteristics, and consumes it up to the point where the marginal utility of the dollar spent on the good equals his marginal utility of income. Since he is not aware of any future effects of consumption on his welfare, this marginal utility refers to his one-period utility U and not to his long-run utility function $\mathcal{U}$.

As long as the consumer's behavior remains myopic his one-period utility function U decreases monotonically, and approaches U^{*} from above. It follows immediately that if $U^{+} \leq U^{*}$, then $U(t) > U^{+}$ for all t. Here rule BM2 is the relevant one. The consumer never perceives that it is better not to consume the good, either because the consumer's surplus remains positive ($U^{*} >$ wI), or because his threshold of perception is too low (wI $\geq U^{*} > U^{+}$). This is case M.

A consumer who becomes abstinent so remains in the future unless his utility eventually falls below the threshold of pain U^{-}. From Section 4, we know that the utility of an abstinent individual is monotonically increasing with time. It follows that if the consumer becomes abstinent at $\bar{t}$ and $U(\bar{t}) \geq U^{-}$, then he remains abstinent forever. We then have case MA. In the Appendix we show that (36) is equivalent to $U(\bar{t}) \geq U^{-}$.

It may also happen that as the consumer becomes abstinent at $\bar{t}$, $U(\bar{t}) < U^{-}$. Then he returns to his original myopic behavior at time $\bar{t}+1$, but not due to a lack of awareness of the negative consumer's surplus that results from such behavior, but rather because he is unable to behave rationally in a situation of intense pain. It is shown in the Appendix that consumption will always raise the consumer's utility in period $\bar{t}+1$ above the threshold of perception $U^{+} > U^{-}$. Then the consumer abstains again in period $\bar{t}+2$. He continues to oscillate between abstinence and myopia until one of two possible events occurs:

1. For some $t' > \bar{t}$ he abstains but his utility $U(t')$ remains above U^{-}.

2. For some $t' > \bar{t}+1$ he behaves myopically but his utility $U(t')$ remains strictly below U^{-}.

In Section 5 it was shown that oscillatory behavior determines monotonic convergence of the consumer's utility in periods of abstinence to $\tilde{U}$, and of his utility in periods of myopia to U. Consider then the following possibilities:

i) $U^- < \tilde{U}$. Then $U(\bar{t}) < U^- < \tilde{U} < \hat{U}$, hence event 2. can never occur, oscillations are decreasing in amplitude, and event 1. sooner or later takes place. Indeed, as shown in the Appendix, $U(\bar{t}+1) > U^-$, and $U(\bar{t}+2\tau+1)$ converges monotonically to $U > U^-$, hence $U(\bar{t}+2\tau+1)$ can never fall below U^-. Oscillations are decreasing in amplitude because $U(\bar{t}) < \tilde{U}$. And $U(\bar{t}+2\tau)$ converges monotonically to $\tilde{U} < U^-$, hence sooner or later $U(\bar{t}+2\tau)$ becomes smaller than U^-, and the consumer becomes then permanently abstinent. This is case MOA.

ii) $\tilde{U} \le U^- \le \hat{U}$. A similar reasoning shows that neither event 1. nor event 2. can ever occur, and the oscillations persist forever. This is case MO.

iii) $U^- > \hat{U}$. Then also $U^- > \tilde{U}$, hence event 1. can never occur. Event 2. sooner or later takes place, and the consumer finally becomes permanently myopic. This is case MOM.

Figure 4 shows the regions in (U^+, U^-)-space where the different patterns of behavior take place.

Figure 4

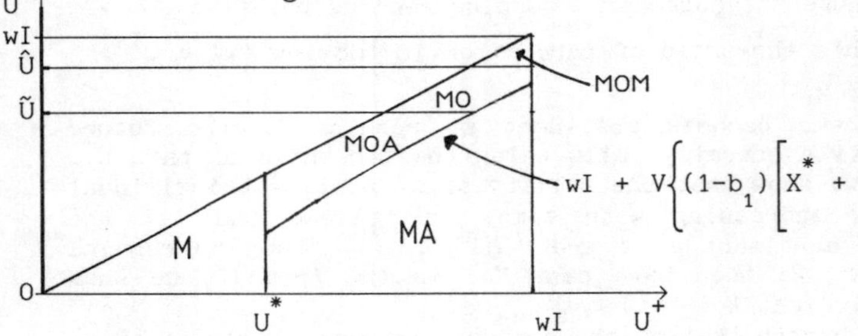

7. Conclusions.

If POPT appropriately describes the effects of consuming a given commodity, and myopia and abstinence are the possible basic modes of behavior then several pathological dynamic behavioral patterns may result. The best of these seems to be steady state overconsumption with positive consumer's surplus and abstinence. Other outcomes of a more undesirable charater are possible. Steady state overconsumption with a negative consumer's surplus cannot be ruled out, if the consumer is not very perceptive, or if he is unable to withstand the pain from withdrawal and finally becomes irrational due to an excess of pain. Such a state of affairs probably consists in the phenomenon that is usually called "addiction." Losses due to underconsumption are also possible. The consumer may end up abstaining even though the optimal consumption policy would generate a positive consumer's surplus. Thus, there is the paradoxical possibility that optimal taxation would increase the consumption of a potentially addictive commodity. Notice also that the "worst" combination of characteristics (low U^+, high U^-) does not lead to particularly high welfare losses. In terms of welfare the worst case seems to be MOM, in which the consumer repeatedly goes through the pains of withdrawal. And this case happens when both U^+ and U^- are relatively high: the consumer perceives that consuming the good has a negative effect on his welfare, but does not have the necessary will power to abstain from its consumption..

Our model does not allow for gradual withdrawal. This has a certain element of realism, but still needs justification. If $b_1 > b_2$ and $U^* < wI$, then there is a path towards abstinence in which $U(t) > U^*$ for all t. Then if $U^* > U^-$, gradual withdrawal is, at least in principle, possible. However, in practice such a strategy seldom works. As the levels of the A and B processes approach zero during gradual withdrawal the maximum possible one-period consumer's surplus steadily increases. This is due to the concavity of U. Meanwhile, the previous experience of a negative consumer's surplus recedes into the past. The consumer may then end up returning to myopic behavior. The important difference from abrupt withdrawal is that during gradual withdrawal consumption is a constant reminder of the possibility of a short-run increase in utility if consumption is increased. For similar reasons the optimal consumption level A^{**} may be unstable. At this steady state consumption level there is persistent evidence that a higher consumption level would increase utility in the short run, since $A^* > A^{**}$. Thus, escaping from addiction may be difficult for the same reasons why myopic behavior arises in the first place.

The discussion in the previous paragraph suggests several topics that deserve further research. In order to formalize this discussion we would need models in which the consumer's memories "depreciate" and in which the "anchoring" role of consumption is made explicit. Another area of research would deal with the strategic problem of a consumer who is aware that his probability of becoming irrational in the future depends on his present level of consumption. On this topic, see Elster [2].

APPENDIX

We assume that $U(\bar{t}-1) = U^+$, which is a reasonable approximation if b_1 and b_2 are small, and prove the following two facts:

A.1 $\quad U(\bar{t}) \geq U^- \quad \Leftrightarrow \quad (36)$

A.2 $\quad U(\bar{t}+1) > U^+$,

where $\bar{t}$ is the period in which behavior first switches from myopia to abstinence ($\beta(t) = 1$ for $t < \bar{t}$, $\beta(\bar{t}) = 0$).

A.1 Let $V^* = V(X^*)$, where $X^* = \bar{A}(1-b_2)$. We have $U^+ = U(\bar{t}-1) = V^* + w(I - pA(\bar{t}-1))$, whence

$$A(\bar{t}-1) = \frac{V^*+wI-U^+}{wp}$$

$$(*) \qquad B(\bar{t}-1) = A(\bar{t}-1) - X^* = \frac{V^*+wI-U^+}{wp} - X^*.$$

Since $A(\bar{t}) = 0$, $B(\bar{t}) = (1-b_1)B(\bar{t}-1)$, and

$$U(\bar{t}) = wI + V(-B(\bar{t})) = wI + V\left\{(1-b_1)\left[X^* - \frac{V^*+wI-U^+}{wp}\right]\right\},$$

the equivalence A.1 follows immediately.

A.2 For all t, $X(t) = X^*$, and hence

$$U(t) = V^* + wI - wpA(t),$$

and therefore

$$U(\bar{t}+1) - U^+ = U(\bar{t}+1) - U(\bar{t}-1) = wp[A(\bar{t}-1) - A(\bar{t}+1)] .$$

Then, from (8), $U(\bar{t}+1) > U^+ \Leftrightarrow B(\bar{t}) < B(\bar{t}-2)$.

Since consumption of the good is zero at $\bar{t}$, (11) implies that

$$B(\bar{t}) = (1-b_1)B(\bar{t}-1) = \frac{(1-b_1)^2}{(1-b_2)} B(\bar{t}-2) + (1-b_1)b_2\bar{A} .$$

From this, (10-a), and (S), we easily obtain

$$B(\bar{t}) < \left[\frac{(1-b_1)}{(1-b_2)}\right]^2 (1-b_2)^2 B(\bar{t}-2) < B(\bar{t}-2) .$$

REFERENCES

[1] Coursey, D., "Hierarchical Preferences and Consumer Choice," unpublished Ph.D. dissertation, Department of Economics, University of Arizona, 1982.

[2] Elster, J., **Ulysses and the Sirens: studies in rationality and irrationality**, Cambridge University Press, 1979.

[3] Gandolfo, G., **Economic Dynamics: Methods and Models**, North Holland, Amsterdam, 1980.

[4] Lancaster, K., "A New Approach to Consumer Theory," **Journal of Political Economy**, 1966, vol. 74, 132-155.

[5] Nelson, R., and S. Winter, **An Evolutionary Theory of Economic Behavior**, Harvard University Press, 1985.

[6] Scitovski, T., **The Joyless Economy**, Oxford University Press, 1976.

[7] Solomon, R., and J. Corbit, "An Opponent-Process Theory of Motivation: I. Temporal Dynamics and Affect," **Psychological Review**, 1974, vol. 81, 2, 119-145.

[8] Taylor, L., "Opponent Processes and the Dynamics of Consumption," in **Economic Psychology: Intersections in Theory and Application**, A. MacFadyen and H. MacFadyen (eds.), North Holland, Amsterdam, 1986.

[9] Wichers, C., "A Mechanistic Theory of Individual Behavior," Ph.D. dissertation, University of Amsterdam, 1968.

Part Two
Consumer Choice and Marketing: Quality, Novelty and Learning

AN ASSOCIATIVE MODEL OF THE EFFECTS OF INFORMATION FRAME ON CONSUMER BEHAVIOR

Irwin P. Levin*

1. INTRODUCTION

This paper will summarize our program of research on framing effects in judgment and decision making, describe a model to explain these effects, and present data to test this model in the area of consumer behavior.

1.1. Background: Research by Tversky and Kahneman

Judgments and decisions can be influenced greatly by the way information is presented or framed. In a classic study of this type Tversky and Kahneman (1981) examined choices between two intervention programs for dealing with an emergency situation in which a fixed number (600) of lives would be lost unless one of the programs was adopted. Some respondents were asked to choose between the following two programs: If Program A is adopted, 200 people will be saved. If Program B is adopted, there is a one-third probability that 600 people will be saved and a two-thirds probability that no people will be saved. The majority (72%) of the respondents chose Program A, preferring a sure savings of 200 lives over a gamble that offers a one-third chance of saving 600 lives. Other respondents were given the following choice: If Program C is adopted, 400 people will die. If Program D is adopted, there is a one-third probability that nobody will die and a two-thirds probability that 600 will die. Here, the majority (78%) chose Program D, indicating a risk seeking preference for the gamble over the sure loss of 400 lives. Thus, even though Programs A and C are formally equivalent and Programs B and D are formally equivalent, the choice between A and B turned out differently than the choice between C and D. In other words, choices differed depending on whether the information describing the programs was framed in terms of gains or losses.

*Professor of Psychology, The University of Iowa, Iowa City, Iowa 52242, USA

Prospect theory (Kahneman & Tversky, 1979) was used to explain these results by pointing to an asymmetry between the effects of gains and losses. According to this theory, outcomes are conceptualized as gains or losses from a subjectively neutral reference point. The value function describing the subjective worth of possible outcomes of a gamble or prospect is assumed to be concave in the domain of gains and convex in the domain of losses, and to be steeper for losses than for gains. These differing properties of the value functions for gains and for losses explain the above results, as well as other phenomena associated with risky choice and gambling.

As attractive as prospect theory is as an alternative to standard utility theory for explaining risky decision making, it does not apply directly to a fundamental question in the study of consumer behavior: How does the attractiveness of a single purchase vary as a function of the way in which its key attributes are framed? Research in our laboratory addresses this question.

1.2. Research at The University of Iowa

In our initial study of framing effects (Levin, Johnson, Russo, & Deldin, 1985), respondents were asked to make evaluations in each of three tasks - a consumer judgment task, a gambling or risk-taking task, and a student evaluation task. Each task involved two important attributes, at least one of which could be labeled or framed in alternative ways. In the consumer judgment task respondents were asked to rate their personal satisfaction with various purchases of ground beef based on varying combinations of the price of meat and its quality. For half the respondents, quality was expressed in terms of percent lean (the positive condition) and for the other half quality was expressed in terms of percent fat (the negative condition). For example, the purchase \$1.50/lb.-80% lean in the positive condition was represented in the negative condition as \$1.50/lb.-20% fat. Satisfaction ratings were significantly higher in the positive condition than in the negative condition, both when respondents evaluated purchases described by price-quality combinations and when they evaluated purchases described by quality alone. This is illustrated in Figure 1. (Analogous results were obtained in the gambling task where respondents indicated higher likelihood of taking gambles when the gambles were described in terms of probability of winning rather than probability of losing, and in the student evaluation task where respondents gave higher ratings when students' test scores were presented in terms of percentage correct rather than percentage incorrect.)

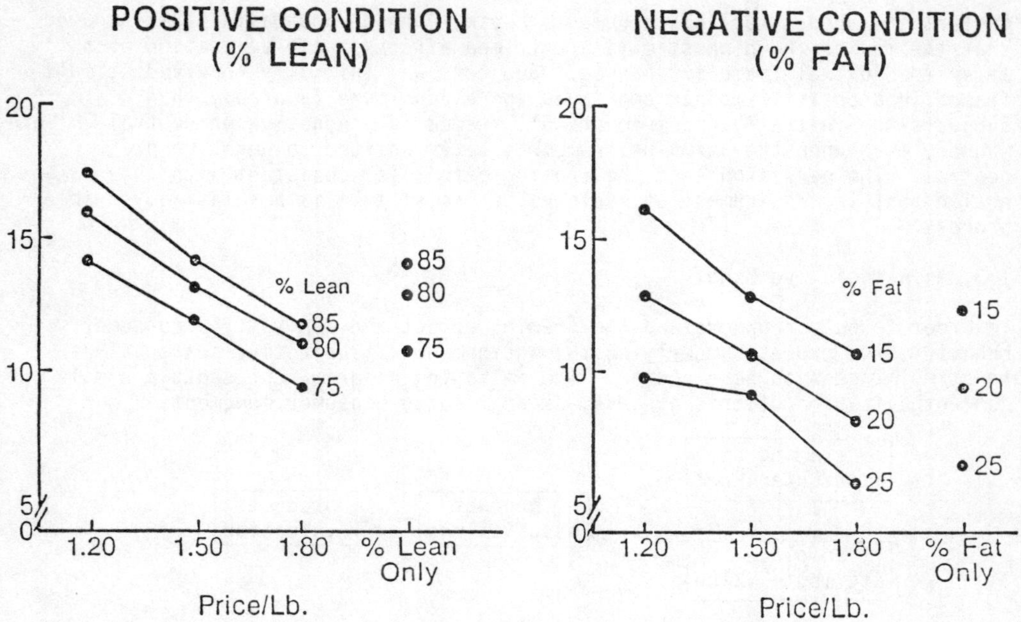

Figure 1. Framing effects in a consumer judgment task: Mean rated satisfaction with purchases of ground beef as a function of the way in which quality is labeled. (from Levin, et al., 1985).

A followup study by Levin, Johnson, Deldin, Carstens, Cressey, and Davis (1986) helped clarify the locus of the framing effect in evaluating choice options. The basic question here is which component of the information integration process is affected by information frame: the evaluation of stimuli or the elicitation of responses (Anderson, 1981; Mellers & Birnbaum, 1982). It could be that positively framed stimuli are perceived more favorably than negatively framed stimuli even when the objective stimulus values are equivalent. Alternatively, the stimuli may be perceived the same in each condition but the positive framing condition may tend to elicit a bias to respond favorably while the negative framing condition may tend to elicit a bias to respond unfavorably. Levin et al. (1986) were able to support the former interpretation over the latter by showing that reversals in preference for choice options across framing conditions are predictable from the rating of individual options in each condition and that the framing effect does not generalize to neutral stimuli imbedded in positively or negatively framed stimuli. The authors thus concluded that the way stimuli are framed appears to affect their subjective scale values and this determines both how they are responded to in an absolute sense and how they are compared to other stimuli.

As further support for this argument, Levin, Johnson and Davis (1987) showed that the manner in which stimuli are framed affects their evaluation even after the initial frame is changed. Subjects who initially received stimuli framed in a positive manner continued to respond more favorably than subjects who initially received stimuli framed in a negative or neutral manner, even when the stimulus frame was later shifted to negative or neutral. The persistence of the framing effect is consistent with the notion that the assignment of scale values to stimuli is a relatively stable process.

1.3. An Associative Model

In order to better understand the framing effect and apply it to consumer behavior, the process underlying the assignment of subjective scale values to stimuli needs to be explored. The following diagram represents a simple conceptualization of this process, as applied to consumer judgments.

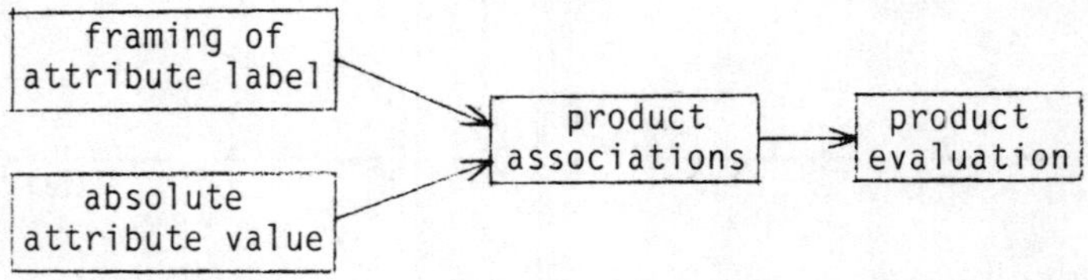

According to this model, both the absolute value of a product attribute and the manner in which that attribute is framed or labeled affect the consumer's network of associations to the product, which in turn affects the overall evaluation of the product. This model was tested in the following study.

2. TEST OF MODEL

The present study was designed to achieve increased understanding of the role of information frame on the evaluation of individual stimuli. The specific hypothesis under investigation is that framing a stimulus in positive terms is more likely to lead to favorable associations than framing the same stimulus in negative terms. The task requires respondents to indicate their associations to a meat purchase that is alternatively described as 75% lean or 25% fat. The use of the label "lean" is expected to produce more favorable associations than the use of the label "fat".

2.1. Method

Respondents were 102 students in introductory psychology classes at The University of Iowa who were completing part of a research participation requirement. The experimental material of present interest was printed on a single page of a larger booklet containing material for several short, unrelated experimental procedures. Different forms of the material were included in two different experimental conditions. Respondents in the positive framing condition (n=55) were instructed to consider a purchase of ground beef that is 75% lean. Respondents in the negative framing condition (n=47) were to consider a purchase of ground beef that is 25% fat.

The remainder of the instructions were as follows: "In this brief survey we want to know what associations or thoughts come to mind when making consumer purchases. We will present you with pairs of possible associates. In each pair we want you to indicate by filling in one of the squares which item in the pair you are most apt to associate with a purchase of 75% lean (25% fat) ground beef and the extent to which you associate the purchase with that item rather than the other item in the pair."

Printed below these instructions were four horizontal arrays of seven squares each, labeled as follows:

☐	☐	☐	☐	☐	☐	☐
good-tasting						**bad-tasting**
☐	☐	☐	☐	☐	☐	☐
greasy						**greaseless**
☐	☐	☐	☐	☐	☐	☐
high quality						**low quality**
☐	☐	☐	☐	☐	☐	☐
fat						**lean**

Responses were scored by converting to a scale of -3 to +3, with positive values representing the positive item in the pair (good-tasting, greaseless, high quality, lean) and conversely for negative values. Zero represents the mid-point of the scale.

2.2. Results and Discussion

In each item-pair responses were significantly higher (more favorable) in the positive framing condition than in the negative framing condition ($p < .01$ in each case). The largest difference was for the pair "lean-fat" where the means were +1.15 and -1.17, respectively, for the positive and negative conditions, $t(100) = 6.95$. For the pair "high quality-low quality" the means were +1.33 and -0.34, $t(100) = 5.17$; for the pair "greaseless-greasy" the means were +0.49 and -1.04, $t(100) = 4.77$; and for the pair "good tasting-bad tasting" the means were +1.69 and +0.43, $t(100) = 3.95$. These results are summarized in Figure 2.

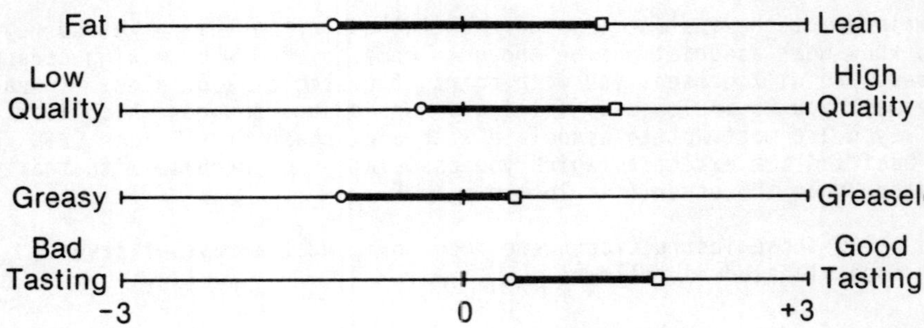

Figure 2. Mean response on each rating scale in positive condition (squares) and negative condition (circles).

The prediction that the "% lean" label would produce more favorable associations than the "% fat" label was supported. A purchase of ground beef that is said to be 75% lean is rated as leaner, of higher quality, less greasy, and better tasting than a purchase that is said to be 25% fat.

Now that we have shown that information frame affects both the associations to a stimulus and the overall evaluation of that stimulus (Levin, et al., 1985, 1986, 1987), it is of interest to consider which effect mediates the other. It is possible in the present case that the implicit formation of an overall impression of the meat purchase served as a mediator of responses to the specific rating scales. However, the task did not call for an overall evaluation of the meat purchase. Furthermore, both the absolute ratings and the differences in ratings between framing conditions varied across scaling dimensions. As can be seen in Figure 1, the greatest difference between conditions and the greatest degree of symmetry about the neutral point occurred along the lean-fat dimension. This is not surprising, given the compatability between the labeling of the stimulus object and the rating scale. By contrast, even though the difference between conditions was statistically significant, both the % lean and the % fat labels produced positive evaluations on the taste dimension. These results show that each response dimension was responded to separately, rather than being influenced solely by a generalized halo effect produced by the stimulus label.

The most parsimonious interpretation of the set of results obtained in the present study and its predecessors is that the stimulus label elicits associations which, in turn, affect the evaluation of the stimulus object. Framing the description of the stimulus object in positive terms leads to more favorable associations than framing the object in negative terms.

3. SUMMARY AND CONCLUSIONS

The effect of information frame on judgments and decisions has been demonstrated in several ways. The work in our laboratory has concentrated on the way in which the label attached to a stimulus affects its evaluation. Positive labels such as "percentage lean" of ground beef, "probability of winning" a gamble, and "percentage correct" on an exam produce more favorable evaluations than their negative counterparts.

It was proposed that different associations produced by alternative labels affect the evaluation of stimuli such as consumer products. In an experiment designed to test this model, the labeling of a ground beef purchase in terms of "percent lean" or "percent fat" affected a variety of associated dimensions such as quality, taste, and greasiness. The implications of these results for understanding consumer behavior and marketing practice are clear: Labeling product attributes in positive terms produces more favorable reactions than labeling attributes in neutral or negative terms.

References

Anderson, N.H. (1981), Foundations of information integration theory, New York: Academic Press.

Kahneman, D., & A. Tversky (1979), Prospect theory: An analysis of decision under risk. Econometrica 4, 362-377.

Levin, I.P., R.D. Johnson, P.J. Deldin, L.M. Carstens, L.J. Cressey, & C.R. Davis (1986), Framing effects in decisions with completely and incompletely described alternatives. Organization Behavior and Human Decision Processes 38, 48-64.

Levin, I.P., R.D. Johnson, C.P. Russo, & P.J. Deldin (1985), Framing effects in judgment tasks with varying amounts of information. Organizational Behavior and Human Decision Processes 37, 362-377.

Levin, I.P., R.D. Johnson, & M.L. Davis (1987), How information frame influences risky decisions: Between-subjects and within-subject comparisons. Journal of Economic Psychology, in press.

Mellers, B.A., & M.H. Birnbaum (1982), Loci of contextual effects in judgment. Journal of Experimental Psychology: Human Perception and Performance 8, 582-601.

Tversky, A., & D. Kahneman (1981), The framing of decisions and the psychology of choice. Science 211, 453-458.

A MODEL OF ADVERTISING AND LEARNING

Y. Kotowitz

Department of Economics, University of Toronto
150 St. George Street, Toronto, Ontario M5S1A1
Canada

Abstract

This paper describes and analyses a model which integrates some of the behavioral elements of psychological and marketing theories into an economic model of a rational, though ignorant, consumer. Rationality is interpreted here in a limited sense, to imply expected utility maximization given Baysian learning. Behavioral elements enter through the weight assigned to information received from advertising or experience, which depends on the nature of the information supplied.

1. INTRODUCTION

Economic analysis of advertising usually concentrates on market responses, on the assumption that advertising somehow affects consumer demand. While economists acknowledge that advertising may affect demand by affecting consumer tastes,[1] most of the economic literature assumes that advertising affects demand through the supply of information about product characteristics directly[2] or indirectly through advertising expenditure.[3] When direct information is provided, it is assumed to be truthful. However, casual observation, as well as a large number of court convictions for false advertising, suggest that such assumptions are not always justified. This information comes from a suspect source; consumers are aware of the producer's conflict of interest; the puzzle is why and how consumers take this into account in their consumption decisions.

---

* Comments of J. Carr and F. Mathewson are gratefully acknowledged. Financial assistance was provided by the Canada Department of Consumer and Corporate Affairs, and the Federal Trade Commission. The usual disclaimers apply.

Richard Schmalensee (1982) argues: "In order to analyze the effects of actual advertising on demand elasticities in a persuasive fashion, it would be necessary to employ a tractable, generally accepted micro-model of the effects of actual advertising on buyer behavior. No such model now exists, though the empirical literature on consumer behavior may be rich enough to permit its construction."

Unfortunately, there is a wide gap between the economic and behavioral approach to advertising. The economic approach is based on the assumption of consumer rationality, which translates into decision rules based on expected utility maximization. Information is assumed to be processed according to the Baysian update rule and information gathering is conducted so as to maximize expected utility, given Baysian learning. Information is thus collected until its expected value in terms of utility is equal to the marginal costs of obtaining it. These costs are mainly external and involve time and financial costs. To insure rationality, these rules of behavior are generally assumed to be consistent with the market outcomes based on them. This insures that consumers are following rules which are optimal in the light of market outcomes. The implication for advertising is that it must supply correct information, (though not necessarily error free), if it is to be believed and hence survive as a market instrument.

The behavioral approach is more inductive and experimental in nature, concentrating on internal processes associated with information acquisition. It argues that limits on ability of individuals to manipulate information, the psychic costs of sorting information and making decisions and psychological limitations on human learning bring into serious question the implied rationality and the associated expected utility calculus of economic theory. Moreover, it charges that economic theory fails to take account of human complexity and diversity and is therefore much too simplistic. Experimental and other evidence suggests that in many cases these criticisms are valid and that consumers will acquire less information than is optimal according to economic theory and therefore, make inappropriate decisions.

Behavioral approaches therefore assert that there is no presumption that market outcomes are consistent with consumer expectations. Some advertising may well supply misinformation and mislead consumers into making inappropriate purchases at prices which are too high relative to alternatives. There is a significant amount of evidence to suggest that for some products this is the case. Thus, for example, Scherer (1980) cites liquid bleach and aspirin where advertised brands, which are essentially identical to unadvertised brands, sell at a very substantial premium.

The purpose of this paper is to describe and analyse a model which integrates some of the behavioral elements of psychological and marketing theories into an economic model of a rational, though ignorant, consumer. Rationality is interpreted here in a limited sense to imply expected utility maximization given Baysian learning. Behavioral elements enter through the weight which is assigned to information received from advertising or experience, which depends on the nature of the information supplied. Our analysis concentrates on the direct rather than the indirect advertising effect, i.e., on the content rather than expenditure of advertising.

We restrict ourselves to the analysis of advertising which supplies information about product characteristics. We ignore the possible effects of advertising through "low involvement learning", without conscious effort (Bettman, 1979).

Section 2 presents the basic learning model, Section 3 adds advertising and Section 4 summarises the results and discusses some limitations and possible extensions.

2. EXPERIENCE ONLY, NO ADVERTISING

Consider the problem facing a consumer at each point of time in determining a budget allocation between the consumption of two brands of a specific product (brand 1 and brand 2) and a numeraire good Z composed of a bundle of all other commodities, where the consumer has a constant stream of income per period. In order to focus on the informational aspects of the problem, we assume that the marginal utility of the numeraire good is fixed and independent of the consumption of the specific product, so that income effects are ignored. As well, we assume that the two brands of the product are perfect substitutes, and have the same price per unit, so that the consumer purchases only one unit of this product per period. The qualities of good Z and of brand 1 are known with certainty and their utility indexes are set arbitrarily at 1. The quality of brand 2 is however uncertain. The consumer's expected utility in period t is defined by

$$\text{(1)} \qquad EU_t = EU(\gamma + a(i)q_t(1-\gamma))+Z_t$$

where $\alpha(i)$ measures the intensity of preference for brand 2 by consumer i, $\gamma = 1$ if the consumer buys brand 1 and 0 otherwise and $u'>0$, $U''<0$. Quality is measured as a bundle of characteristics $q = \sum_i x_i$ where the characteristics x_i are scaled so that the consumer production technology is linear in characteristics. The quality index is measured to reflect the subjective evaluation of the product by the consumer if all product characteristics were known. In most of the following we assume that q is comprised of only one characteristic in order to simplify the analysis. The results are insensitive to this assumption.

We assume that consumer knows that the distribution of quality of brand 2 (q) is normal with unknown mean (Q) and known variance (w). In addition, the consumer takes into consideration his ability to measure q by using the product; assume that the observed value of q is $y = q+\varepsilon$, where ε is a measurement error, distributed normally with mean 0 and fixed variance h. Thus the distribution of measured quality (y) is normal with $E(y) = Q$ and variance $var(y) \equiv w + 2p\ (wh)^{1/2} + h$, where ρ is the correlation coefficient between q and ε. Define s as the consumer's estimate of var(y). This estimate may not be accurate because it cannot be refuted by experience as the error is not observable. Thus s, even if it is erroneous, is fixed for each individual.

Given this specification, experience with brand 2 may be insufficient to evaluate its quality with certainty. This may be the result of objective factors stemming from the intrinsic variability in the quality of the brand in question, or subjective factors because of the consumer's inability to identify quality. Objective factors, measured by w are, for example, the frequency of repair of a durable good, the probability of complete product failure and variations in physical performance characteristics. These are dependent on the state of production technology and on the care and cost of manufacturing the product. Subjective factors, measured by h, are associated with limitations of the consumer in evaluating quality. This may flow from variability in the conditions of usage, which lead to possible variations in the evaluation of performance. Or the individual's mood and hence, own objective valuation, may vary from time to time yielding different evaluations of the same product. The distinction between objective and subjective variance is important because the first is a policy variable of the producer but the second is not. Also, they affect consumer decisions in different ways.

In order to make a decision about the product, the individual must form an opinion about the average quality of the uncertain product. This opinion may be gleaned by word of mouth from other consumers, from the news media, or from personal search. We assume that the individual formulates an opinion in the form of a Baysian prior probability distribution of the mean quality (Q). We assume this prior is normally distributed with mean μ and variance v, and that the consumer uses a Baysian update rule to modify beliefs through time in light of accumulated experience from the consumption of brand 2. A time (t+1), therefore, the posterior is also normally distributed with the mean and variance given by equations (2) and (3) respectively.

(2) $$\mu_{t+1} = [(s\mu+vy)/(v+s)]_t$$

(3) $$v_{t+1} = [sv/(v+s)]_t$$

or, in terms of changes in the prior mean and variance (ignoring time subscripts),

(4) $$\Delta\mu = m(y-\mu)$$

(5) $$\Delta v = -mv$$

where $m \equiv v/v+s$ is the speed of learning. Equations (1) to (5) assume that information does not depreciate.

The fact that information becomes dated or is forgotten does not change the consumer's prior conception of the average quality of brand 2; it does change the consumer's estimate of the <u>reliability</u> of his prior beliefs and modifies the estimate of the prior's variance. As the reliability of prior beliefs is likely to decline with the passage of time, the variance of the prior must rise with time. We shall assume this process occurs in a linear fashion so that equation (5) is modified to include a "coefficient of information depreciation" in the form:

(5a) $\Delta v = (-m + \delta)v$

The effect of "forgetting" is to counteract the effect of experience on the prior variance and to decrease the rate at which the prior variance is reduced with experience. Note that, as $t \to \infty$, v approaches a finite positive limit. This is because Δv approaches zero before v approaches zero. As the rate of reduction in uncertainty due to accumulated experience falls to the level of the rate of information depreciation, the level of uncertainty stabilizes at the steady state level $v^* = s/(1-\delta)$. In the steady state for v, equation (4) degenerates into the standard adaptive expectation equation $\Delta\mu = \delta(y-\mu)$. The "forgetting" coefficient is then a lower bound of the speed of learning when experience is accumulated.[4]

If the consumer attempts to maximize discounted expected utility over a given horizon, an optimal policy consists of choosing a reservation quality at each point of time R_t for the unknown brand, such that if $\mu_t > R_t$, the unknown brand is purchased at time t, i.e., if the consumer believes that the mean quality of brand 2 at time t exceeds this reservation level at time t, brand 2 is purchased. Otherwise brand 1 is bought. Note that once the individual buys brand 1, he always buys brand 1, unless some additional information from outside sources leads to a change in the prior in favor of 2 or unless the time horizon changes. If the individual buys brand 2, he revises his estimate about the prior mean and variance in the light of experience with the product, compares the new prior with his reservation value and proceeds as before.

3. EXPERIENCE AND ADVERTISING

We are now in position to incorporate advertising content into the model. Advertising expenditures determine the number of consumers and their attentiveness to advertising messages while content is assumed to affect their perception and their behaviour.

Advertising content has three functions--first to capture the consumer's attention, second to insure message retention and finally to transmit information about the product. In the language of communication experts, the first and second functions are to create an "interrupt" (Simon, 1957) in order to induce conscious consideration of the information supplied. (This is the role of the pretty girl/boy in the bikini which may not have anything to do with the information transmitted.) We ignore this component and concentrate here on the informational content of advertising. We ignore the possible effects of advertising through "low involvement learning" without conscious effort (Bettman, 1978).

Consider the message content of informative advertising. Such advertising is assumed to make claims about the quality of the characteristic relevant to the determination of quality. Define the advertising claim of quality measure as c. The consumer incorporates this information in the prior according to Bayes rule, weighing its value in inverse relation to his estimate of its reliability r, which may be interpreted as the consumer's estimate of the proportion of the variance of true mean quality (q), explained by the advertising message; i.e. r may be interpreted as the consumers unconditional estimate of the coefficient of variation between c and q. Upon receipt of the advertising message and assuming no passage of time to process the information, the revised prior mean (μ') and variance (v') become (again ignoring time subscripts)

(6) $$\mu' = [(r\mu+vc)/(r+v)]$$

(7) $$v' = [rv/(r+v) \leq v$$

Once the advertising message is received and incorporated in the consumer's posterior, there is no role for further advertising. There is no reason to believe that a consumer revises the prior again upon receipts of the same message from the same advertiser. Repetition in this context may be necessary to insure that the information is received by the consumer. But once received, there is no further effect unless the message changes, or the identity of the advertiser is disguised.

There is nothing in the Baysian learning process to determine the credence of the advertising message. There are two ways to proceed: We may assume rational expectations. That is, we may define a value of r which is consistent with equilibrium levels of c, assuming that such equilibrium levels exist. Because, in the absence of government regulations, there is no dollar cost to making exaggerated claims, there is no limit on such claims. Firms will thus make unlimited claims which are unrelated to the true quality of their product unless there is a market mechanism to discipline exaggerated claims, so that c will be correlated with true product quality.

In the absence of government regulations, the consumer model does not supply a penalty for false or exaggerated advertising. While the benefits to firms from exaggerated advertising rise with true product quality, they are always positive: If it pays to advertise at all it pays to exaggerate without limit because the marginal cost of exaggeration is zero.

As a consequence, in the absence of truth in advertising regulations, no correlation between advertising claims and true quality can be established and hence advertising claims contain no useful information. The content of advertising is therefore irrelevant and should not affect rational consumers. This is the position of those who cast advertising exclusively as a signal of quality (e.g. Nelson 1974, Klein and Leffler 1981).

A definite exaggeration level requires the imposition of additional structure. This defines the second way to proceed. The psychology and marketing literature dealing with cognitive processes suggests that credibility of information depends on its conformity with both general and particular preconceptions. Conformity with general preconceptions may be related to persuasiveness, in the sense that the information supplied does not contradict general knowledge. For example, the washing power of detergeants may be reasonably related to the presence of enzymes, automobile horsepower is related to acceleration, etc. Conformity to particular preconceptions must be related to the prior. The theory of cognitive dissonance states that people are uncomfortable in the presence of conflict. When information is received which contradicts accepted beliefs, a dissonance is created. To resolve the conflict, consumers may acquire additional information or re-evaluate the source of the conflicting information, possibly discarding some of it. In particular, when new information conflicts with prior decisions, it is likely to be ignored. In terms of our model, the theory suggests that the more likely is the information to conflict with the prior--"cognitive dissonance"--the less credible it is.

A convenient way of measuring such conformity, in terms of the probability that the information came from the prior, is to specify r as a function of the distance of the information from the prior mean, measured in terms of standard deviations. We may thus specify the following relationships for reliability:

(8) $$r = r(|c - r|/v), \quad \text{where} \quad r' > 0 \quad \text{and} \quad r'' > 0 .$$

Returning to equations (6) and (7), we see that the effects of advertising on μ' and v' rises with consumer's ignorance because when the prior is diffuse, consumers are more receptive to advertising ($\partial r/\partial v < 0$) and give low weight to their uncertain prejudices. As r rises, advertising is discounted, so that $r \to \infty$ leads to $\mu' \to \mu$ and $v' \to v$, the advertising is ignored and priors are not revised.

This specification of r yields a limit on the ability of advertising to affect consumer perceptions; as advertising claims are exaggerated, consumer confidence in them falls reducing the weight given to the advertising. This negative indirect effect, represented by the first term of equation (9), may offset the direct effect of increased c, represented by the second term.

(9) $$d\mu'/dc = r'(\mu-c)/(v+r)^2 + v/(v+r)$$

As $d^2\mu'/dc^2 = r''(\mu-c)/v < 0$, the marginal effects of advertising claims on consumer perceptions declines as c rises.

$d\mu'/dc = 0$, therefore defines the maximum influence which advertising may have on a consumer with initial perceptions of μ and v.

It therefore defines the optimal level of exaggeration for the firm. Note that the level of exaggeration is related to perceived product quality as well as the prior variance. Thus, it is lower for products the quality of which is relatively well known, than for products about which consumers know little (i.e. large v).

4. CONCLUSIONS AND QUALIFICATIONS

Within our economic model of consumer behavior, we investigated ways of incorporating elements of psychology and marketing theory in order to analyse advertising. This is a somewhat uneasy marriage, as the psychological theories contradict the basic tennents of consumer rationality: Baysian learning and optimization which underly the economic theory of consumer behavior.

Nonetheless, it appears to us that the model presented here is useful in suggesting a way to incorporate behavioral elements into economic analysis. While the behavioral evidence casts serious doubts on the strict Baysian model as a representation of consumer learning and behavior, it does not invalidate the model as an approximation, if modified properly. For example, the simple rules for learning, which were derived in the context of a simple baysian decision model, can be interpreted as reasonable rules of thumb for the updating of information. Product quality perceptions at any point in time are weighted averages of prior perception and new information. The relative weights of these depend on the degree of consumer confidence embodied in the variance of his prior and on the reliance placed on the new information measured by the sample variance. Such variance cannot be interpreted literally as the objective variance of product quality but rather as an estimate of the credence and importance which the consumer is willing to place on such information. This is embodied in our subjective variance measure (h). As well, the notion that consumers become more confident about the product and their evaluation of it with use is consistent with the behavioral evidence. The analysis of informative advertising is then a natural extension of the learning model.

However, we have dealt only with informative advertising--which transmits information intended to affect consumers in a conscious manner. We have not analysed advertising which relies on 'low involvement learning'. The 'rational' Baysian approach is less likely to be successful here. The effectiveness of such advertising is not clearly established, though casual observation suggests that it is very common. It's formal analysis remains on a future research agenda.

Footnotes

1. See, for example, Dixit and Norman (1978).
2. See, for example, Grossman and Shapiro (1982).
3. See, for example, Nelson (1974), Klein and Leffler (1980), Kihlstrom and Riordan (1983).
4. This is equivalent to the linear learning model commonly used in psychology.

References

Bettman, J. R. An Information Processing Theory of Consumer Choice, Reading, Mass., Addison-Wesley, 1979.

Cummings and Venktesan. 1976. "Cognitive Dissonants and Consumer Behavior--A Review of the Evidence", Journal of Marketing Research.

Festinger, L. 1957. A Theory of Cognitive Dissonance. Stanford, U.P.

_______. 1964. Conflict, Decision and Dissonance. Stanford, U.P.

Grossman, G. M., and Shapiro, C. 1982. "Informative Advertising with Differentiated Products", mimeo.

Klein, B. and Leffler, K. B. 1981. "The Role of Market Forces in Assuring Contractual Performance". Journal of Political Economy.

Kihlstrom, R. 1974. "A General Theory of Demand for Information About Product Quality" Journal of Economic Theory. 8(4)(August): 413-439.

Kihlstrom, R. E. and Riordan, M. A. 1983. "Advertising as a Signal." D.P. 150 Center for the Study of Organizational Innovation, University of Pennsylvania.

Kotowitz, Y. and F. Mathewson. 1979a. "Informative Advertising and Welfare", American Economic Review. Vol. 69, No. 3, June.

_______. 1979b. "Advertising, Consumer Information and Product Quality". Bell Journal of Economics. Vol. 10, No. 2.

Mitchel, A. et al. 1978. The Effects of Information on Consumers and Market Behavior. American Marketing Association.

Nelson, P. 1974. "Advertising as Information" Journal of Political Economy 82(4) (July/August): 729-754.

Scherer, F. 1980. Industrial Market Structure and Economic Performance, 2nd ed., Rand McNally.

Schmalensee, R. 1982. "Advertising and Market Structure," I.E.A. Conference on "New Developments in Market Structure".

Slovic, P., B. Fischoff, and S. Lichtenstein. 1977. "Behavioral Decision Theory," Ann. Rev. Psych. 28: 1-39.

AN ALTERNATIVE TO THE RANDOM UTILITY APPROACH IN MODELING THE PREFERENCE FOR VARIETY

ELLIOTT MIDDLETON

Department of Business Administration, College of St. Thomas, St. Paul, MN 55105 USA*

A preference for "variety" implies context-sensitive utility generation. When "physical" and "informational" elements interact in a general, context-sensitive utility formulation, utility maximization can determine a "random utility" choice parameter.

1. Introduction

The preference for variety is a widely-observed human characteristic. Scitovsky [1] devoted a book to reviewing the experimental evidence for such a preference. More recently, Machina [2] has introduced a random utility model to represent a certain type of preference for "variety." Random utility models in general deal with the case in which, when confronted with a choice between two alternatives, an individual chooses each alternative a positive proportion of the time. "It seems natural to suppose that this is because he or she 'preferred' each one to the other those same proportions of the time" (Machina, [2], p. 575). However, as Machina points out, the assumption of stochastic preferences to "explain" stochastic choice does not entirely satisfy. Machina constructs a model in which stochastic choice functions can be generated by deterministic preferences over lotteries. However, the lotteries approach is not well suited to a treatment of the mixture of characteristics in a market with differentiated commodities, i.e., how "product differentiation" may contribute to a commodity's utility. The experiments reported informally by Scitovsky [1] suggest an alternative formalization, however, which explicitly treats the relationship between alternatives within the subject's experience in terms of the "subjective novelty" of those alternatives. The present paper develops a model of "subjective novelty" in the case of product differentiation in a static framework; treatment of other aspects of this approach to modeling the preference for "variety" may be found in Middleton [3, 4].

The plan of the paper is as follows. Section 2 introduces the idea of context (in the sense of "subjective novelty") as a determinant of utility, and constructs a very simple model with some examples. Section 3 advances a distinction between "physical" and "informational" utility and demonstrates how their interaction can yield a "random utility" probability preference parameter or stochastic choice function as a result. Section 4 analyzes the major qualitative aspects of the present approach and compares this approach with the standard and random utility models. Section 5 concludes the paper.

2. Subjective Novelty and Framing

The experimental results suggest that the preference for "subjective novelty" or "variety" (here used interchangeable) is critically dependent on the way the subject "frames" an alternative in terms of other available alternatives (see Smith and Yu, [5], for a similar "prominence" theory of choice behavior; they point out, in particular, that the random utility models exhibit the regularity property that the number of alternatives can not affect the utility of any alternative).

Let a good x_i be defined by a "minimum specification" of characteristics C^x from a universe of characteristics appearing in m differentiated versions of the good x): $C^x = \{c_1, \ldots, c_n\}$. Let the (perfectly informed) consumer be sensitive to the degree to which a variant "varies" from the product "norm"; the experimental literature (Scitovsky, [1]) suggests that this preference structure will take a roughly parabolic form (the "Wundt curve"). For m differentiated versions of the good in the set X (the set of characteristics in each variant x_i drawn from C^x) let p_i be the probability of characteristic c_i's inclusion in a variant drawn at random from X; this is also the frequency withwhich c_i appears in all variants. If the "novelty" of a characteristic is inversely related to its probability, then we

---

*The author would like to thank Mark Machina for prompting an examination of the issues raised in this paper by pointing out salient differences between the present approach and the random utility approach with regard to product differentiation. All errors are my own.

can define some novelty or "surprise" function (assumed the same for all characteristics; i.e., the subject is not sensitive to any dependencies that may exist between the characteristics)

(1) $h_i = h(p_i)$ $h(1) = 0,\ h' \angle 0,\ h(0)$ not defined (or arbitrarily large; see [3])

Characteristics with unit probability (contained in the minimum specification) are clearly not "novel." Further, the function may require special definition for characteristics with zero probability; however, when a new characteristic with zero prior probability is added to the "repertoire" of the good it immediately assumes a positive probability with respect to the set of variants on the market.

In information-theoretic terms, of course, the novelty or "surprise" function would be represented by the entropy measure

(2) $h_i = \log 1/p_i$

which has been used "successfully" in the empirical literature, although its behavioral justification remains an open question.[1]

The experimental results suggest that for a variant including several characteristics outside the minimum specification C^x the amount of "subjective novelty" (defined in terms of the subject's experience of the good's currently available "repertoire") should increase monotonically with additional characteristics, so that we can define

(3) $H(x_j) \equiv H(q_j{:}p_j)$

where $H(x_j)$ is the "novelty" of variant j including the set q_j of characteristics appearing in xj, and pj is the set of "prior probabilities" associated with q_j. Now $H(x_j)$ will vary directly with the <u>number</u> of (non-ubiquitous) characteristics in the variant and, <u>ceteris paribus</u>, inversely with the probability of each characteristic.[2] We assume that the individual possesses a preference function V(x) (which for present expository simplicity is based on "novelty" alone[3]).

The model has some interesting properties arising from context-sensitivity. For example, consider the following products comprising the characteristics A, B, and C (where A constitutes the minimum specification):

x1	x2	x3
ABC	AB	A

Let $h(p_i) = 1/p_i$ and $H(x_j) = \sum_{i=1}^{n} h(p_i)$, summing over the n characteristics in the good variant j. Let (suppressing arguments) $V = -H^2 + 7H$. Then

$p_A = 1$ $p_B = 2/3$ $p_C = 1/3$

$H(x_1) = 4\ 1/5$ $V(x_1) = 11\ 1/4$

$H(x_2) = 1\ 1/2$ $V(x_2) = 8\ 1/4$

$H(x_3) = 0$ $V(x_3) = 0$

The consumer prefers x_1 to x_2. Assume a new good $x_4 = \{A,D,E\}$ is introduced so that now ("in context") we have

$pA = 1 \quad pB = 1/2 \quad pC = 1/4 \quad pD = 1/4 \quad pE = 1/4$

$H(x_1) = 6 \qquad V(x_1) = 6$

$H(x_2) = 2 \qquad V(x_2) = 10$

$H(x_3) = 0 \qquad V(x_3) = 0$

$H(x_4) = 8 \qquad V(x_4) = -8$

The introduction of good x_4 has caused a preference reversal between goods 1 and 2 even though no characteristics of those goods have changed, though only the context or "frame" in which they are perceived has changed! Such reversals may be pandemic in a dynamic market for differentiated commodities under the present utility specification.

3. Physical and Informational Utility

In some cases the random utility preference parameter or stochastic choice parameter may be derived as a special case of an extended context-sensitive model. This will be seen to be true when the information set available to the consumer includes past consumption decisions.

Let us introduce the distinction between "physical" or non-context-dependent and "informational" or context-dependent utility. The latter is given by V, while the former is a function of the intrinsic, "physical" characteristics n a good, and is formally identical to physical utility in the standard model (see [3,5]). Let total utility (for the purposes of exploring some implications of this relationship for the random utility models) be given by

(5) $U = U\{V[H(x_j)], P(x_j)\}$

where $P(x_j)$ is the physical utility sub-function; and physical and informational utility are assumed to be additively separable. A simple example of utility maximization using this function will demonstrate the capacity of the model to determine a "random" utility choice parameter.

Let there be two one-characteristic goods with the following properties: $P(x_i) = k$ per unit time and $P(x_j) = k/2$ per unit time. (This is not, technically speaking, a case of product differentiation, but of "spontaneous alternation"). Further assume that instead of attending (at all) to static "spatial" (contemporaneous market) context as in the product differentiation example above, the subject attends to his own consumption history as the relevant information set or context alone, with a memory length μ (Scitovsky, [1], pp. 37-38, cites evidence of "alternation experiments" supporting the application of the subjective novelty concept to this intertemporal type of context). Then if μ_i = the temporal measure of consumptions of x_i, and similarly for good j, we have that

(6) $p_i = \dfrac{\mu_i}{\mu},\ p_j = \dfrac{\mu_j}{\mu}\ [= 1 - p_i].$

If in this case $H(x_i) = 1/p_i$ (as each good has only one characteristic we may substitute its consumption frequency for the characteristic's) and (suppressing arguments) $V = -H^2 + bH$, then we may write the total utility function for the entire period of memory as

(7) $$U = p_i \{V[H(x_i)] + P(x_i)\} + (1 - p_j) \{V[H(x_j)] + P(x_j)\}$$

$$= p_i [- \frac{1}{p_i^2} + \frac{b}{p_i} + \mu k\} + (1 - p_i) \{- \frac{1}{(1-p_i)^2} + \frac{b}{(1-p_i)} + \frac{\mu k}{2}\}.$$

The consumer is assumed to maximize utility over the entire block of memory or gegenwartsdaurer (German for "duration of the present", technically short-term memory [1, p.50ff.]) without any other (intra-gegenwartsdauer) time preference. It can be seen from the first order conditions that utility maximization will occur when

$$(8) \quad \frac{2p_i - 1}{p_i^2 (1-p_i^2)} = \frac{3\mu k}{2}$$

The consumer will solve this expression for the value of p_i (and simultaneously of p_j) that meets the equality (or act as if she solves it). The consumer optimizes physical and informational utility intertemporally, balancing the taste for "variety" with stable "physical" preferences within the period of memory. The stochastic choice parameter is seen to be a result in the context of this optimization decision, given the physical preference parameters and the length of the consumer's time horizon for "variety."

4. Analysis

The simple examples above illustrate the major qualitative differences between the present approach and the random utility approach. These can be characterized as follows: (1) extreme path dependence; (2) possibly abundant preference reversals, i.e. transitivity only when all alternatives are held constant (non-regularity); (3) a somewhat different view of utilitarian "consistency" from the standard model or the random utility models; (4) another means of derivation of the stochastic choice function as a result.

In the first instance, "extreme path dependence" results from dependence of utility on the information set available to the agent. While assumed to represent the "market" in the first set of examples above, it is perhaps more accurate to case the example in terms of the subject's information regarding markets past and present, so that available alternatives may exist of which the subject is ignorant, and conversely, alternatives not currently available on the market but within the subject's experience may contribute to subjective novelty: and his preferences may change with increasing "knowledge". In this respect, the model captures some of the increasing sophistication of tastes with experience that the human capital approach deems the result of "investment" in the consumption activity (see Stigler and Becker, [6], for example). Simonton [7] has found empirical support for the present view regarding tastes in music, for example.

Second, in terms of the preference for "subjective novelty" it is clear that preference reversals may be commonplace dynamically, especially as "fashion" (contemporaneous context) and the distribution of characteristics represented in the marketplace change. The experimental and empirical studies in psychology appear to lend circumstantial confirmation to the marketing maxim that product innovations ought to be "new, but not too new" (see Rink and Swan, [8], for informal discussion of product innovation as means of extending a product's "life cycle").

Third, the present model "elevates" consistency to a relational level different from what is possible in either the standard model or the random utility models. When preferences are dependent on the context in which an alternative is perceived (in the non-regular sense developed here), transitivity assumes the rather fragile status described above However, the subject possesses an entirely consistent preference for (subjectively) "novel" experiences (which has its own arguable normative appeal; see [3] for motivation); hence rankings will vary with experience quite naturally and "consistently" in terms of the present model. In this sense, the model offers a theory of "informational" tastes. As new products are introduced which attempt to provide optimal levels of subjective novelty to the market, their very introduction will alter existing goods' utilities. To take an extreme example, if a novel characteristic is introduced which becomes ubiquitous (part of the minimum specification) it ceases to contribute to subjective novelty.

If the changes in characteristic-probabilities resulting from the introduction of new goods are interpreted as infinitesimal, then the necessary condition for a good x_i to maintain constant informational utility in the face of such a change is that $dH(x_i) = 0$. For a consumer to preserve an attitude of indifference between two alternative goods it is necessary that $dH(x_i) = dH(x_j)$. For two goods for which (suppressing arguments) $V = -H^2 + bH$ and $V_i > V_j$, for the preference ranking to be maintained it is necessary that $-2H_i dH_i + bdHi > -2H_j dH_j + bdH_j$, or more briefly, that $dVi > dVj$. In any event, these "partial equilibrium" conditions (because they do not deal with changes in ranking due to changes in the physical utility of goods) are rather restrictive, and unlikely to met under any but a very small subset of the possible changes of the characteristic-probabilities.

Fourth, when the distinction between physical and informational utility is made, the trade-off between these two types of utility is seen to provide a plausible determination of the "stochastic" choice function.

5. Conclusion

The psychology literature surveyed by Scitovsky [1] revealed a pervasive contextual element to preference formation, some aspects of which (i.e. the application to product differentiation) have been modeled here. Scitovsky suggested applying the model to job satisfaction and a number of other areas. Middleton [3,4] provides a formalization and suggests that subjective novelty may play an important role in "animal spirits"; as too much "change" in the economic environment may impair business and consumer confidence (Keynes, [9], Chapter 12, speaks of the dependence of "animal spirits" on a "stable business and political atmosphere"), and finds empirical support in a macroeconomic empirical test using the Michigan Survey of Consumer Sentiment. While no empirical tests of the present model applied to the product differentiation problem exist (to the author's knowledge) it would also appear a fertile area for empirical work.

Some remaining problems including the following: The exact form of the h and H functions needs to be further investigated theoretically and ultimately established empirically. For example, Simonton [7] used the sum of the inverses of the probabilities in his study of tastes for classical music (in a parabolic formulation controlling for genre); while Middleton [3] found significant results using the natural-log information-theoretic measure (in a parabolic formulation including both "informational" and "physical" utility). A central challenge to any field work is the identification of the information set available to the subject, and the length of "operational" memory (both of which are handled judgmentally in the works just cited). The relative contributions of "physical" and "informational" elements to total utility would appear to vary across goods and activities (with "fashion" goods being more sensitive to context than "practical" goods, for example). Thus, the functional form of the total utility function (degree of separability of physical and informational components, for example[4]) needs to be explored for differing activities. Moreover, the contributions of "spatial" (contemporaneous) and intertemporal contexts or information sets may vary in differing decisions. All these considerations will affect the exact form of the derived stochastic choice parameters.

Footnotes

See Berlyne [10], Middleton [3,4]. Simonton [7] uses $h(p) = 1/p$, citing computational constraints mitigating against the use of the information-theoretic measure. (Middleton [3,4] also discusses the relationship to Professor Shackle's theory.)

This corresponds to an aggregation of information expectations across characteristics in the information-theoretic specification. See Theil [11], p. 641 ff. and Middleton [3].

Middleton [3] introduces the distinction between "physical" and "informational" utility, which is explored in more detail below in relation to the random utility models.

Middleton [3] uses an estimation form including physical variables, subjective novelty variables (first and second degree), and interaction terms. Simonton[7] includes subjective novelty variables and interaction terms employing dummy variables for musical genre explicitly meant to capture differences in (physical) preferences among genres.

References

[1] Scitovsky, T., The Joyless Economy (Oxford University Press, New York, 1976).

[2] Machina, M., Stochastic Coice Functions Generated From Deterministic Preferences Over Lotteries, Economic Journal (1985), 95.

[3] Middleton, E., Some Testable Implications of a Preference for Subjective Novelty, Kyklos (1986), 39.

[4] __________, A Behavioral Model of 'Animal Spirits', Metroeconomica, (1986), 38.

[5] Smith, T., and Yu, W., A Prominence Theory of Context-Sensitive Choice Behavior, Journal of Mathematical Sociology (1982), 8.

[6] Stigler, G.J., and Becker, G., De Gustibus Non Est Disputandum, American Economic Review (1978), 68.

[7] Simonton, D.K., Thematic Fame, Melodic Originality, and Musical Zeitgeist, Journal of Personality and Social Psychology (1980), 38.

[8] Rink, D.R., and Swan, J.E., Product Life Cycle Research, Journal of Business Research (1979).

[9] Keynes, J.M., The General Theory of Employment, Interest and Prices (Harcourt, New York, 1936).

[10] Berlyne, D.E., Conflict, Arousal and Curiosity (McGraw-Hill, New York, 1960).

Part Three
Managerial Decision-Making in Centralised Economies

MANAGING DIRECTORS' MOTIVATION TO UNDERTAKE RISKY ECONOMIC ACTIONS IN THE CONTEXT OF ECONOMY MANAGEMENT IN POLAND

Joanna SOKOLOWSKA

Department of Psychology
Polish Academy of Sciences,
Pl. Malachowskiego 1,
00-063 Warszawa, Poland

1. THE MOTIVATION TO UNDERTAKE RISKY ACTIONS IN THE CONTEXT OF PERCEIVED REASONS AND FURTHER CONSEQUENCES OF THE OUTCOME.

This study was an attempt to analyze the motivation to undertake risky actions in a natural setting. It was assumed that this problem is connected with two issues that were studied within psychological decision theory - the base rate fallacy and accepted risk level.

Behavioral decision theory provides much evidence of the inconsistency between the calculus of probability and people's evaluation of the possibility of the occurence of a given event. Many mechanisms have been discovered by which people bias their estimates of the possibility of the occurance of certain events, e.g. neglecting base rates or the size of a sample [1,2]. One very important problem here seems to be the often confirmed tendency for people to perceive the world in deterministic categories. In this context it is worthwile to note the results of the well-known experiment by Kahneman and Tversky in which they showed that people ignore statistical information on a frequency of an event (base rate) which, in their opinion, was unrelated to the problem analyzed. On the other hand, it was also found that people use the base rate that they belive to be relevant to the problem considered [3-5]. Regardless of whether this is a bias (as in a chance situation) or not a fallacy (as in a skill situation), it is important to determine the laws governing such a "deterministic" evaluation of the probability of the occurance of a given event.

This problem is the substance of some psychological theories of motivation, the so-called cognitive models of motivation. These models pay much attention to factors influencing evaluation of the probability of success from this point of view. An especially important problem in these models is the attribution of causes to the anticipated or actually obtained outcome. This problem is formulated most broadly in Weiner's attributional model of achievement motivation [6-8]. Weiner believes that the reasons perceived by people as responsible for success or failure in action may be described on the four following dimensions: internality, stability, controlability, and globality.

According to this model the dimensions of stability, controlability, and globality influence the intensity of an individual's expectancies of being successful in action and the change of these expectancies when a certain outcome is obtained. In line with psychological decision theory, one would say that they are modifiers of the relevant objective base rate on the frequency of success and failure in such situations. The problem of the controlability of the outcome was also considered in the psychological theory of decision making, in studies on the perception and acceptance of risk. It was stated that the perceived risk level of action is connected with two factors:

1. Perceived dependency of failure on the possibility of skills' training, supplying proper materials, safeguarding against errors, etc. This dependency is also confirmed by a finding which indicates that people prefer skill to chance situations and prefer to undertake more risky tasks in the former circumstance. They also have greater confidence in the correctness of their judgments when there are specific rules procedures [9-14].
2. Perceived dependency between the reversibility of negative consequences and the possibility of reducing them [15,16].

Generally, the possibility of controlling an undesired event increases the level of accepted risk [12,16-18]. Hence, one can surmise that this is an effect of some overlapping of information on the objective frequency of success and failure and evaluation of one's own possibilities of controlling events.

The next problem concerns assessment of utility. In line with Weiner's model, such dimensions of outcome causes as stability, controlability, and globality increase the strength of the emotional reactions (anticipated or experienced) accompanying a certain event, thereby increasing its utility. Another very important factor concerning evaluation of outcomes is the further consequences for an individual. This problem is perhaps most widely discussed in the Valence-Instrumentality-Expectancy theory, expecially in Vroom's model [21], where the utility of the action outcome is linked with the rewards and punishments that an individual can receive for this outcome. This dependency is given as follows:

$$U_{\mathrm{k}} = \sum_{j=1}^{n} U_{\mathrm{j}} * I_{\mathrm{j}\to\mathrm{k}}$$

where U_{k} is the utility of the outcome k, U_{j} is the utility of the reinforcement (reward or punishment) j, and $I_{\mathrm{j}\to\mathrm{k}}$ is the belief that a given outcome k leads to reinforcement j (instrumentality of a given outcome with respect to a specific reinforcement).

The utility of an outcome increases proportionally to its instrumentality in relation to rewards regarded as valuable or punishment regarded as painful.

2. THE RESEARCH PROBLEM: THE DEGREE OF CENTRALIZATION OF MANAGEMENT OF THE ECONOMY AND THE MOTIVATION TO UNDERTAKE RISKY ECONOMIC ACTIONS.

In line with psychological decision theory and cognitive models of motivation, the choice of direction of action is a function of the outcome utility and the chance of its occurring as an effect of such an action. As stated above, the evaluation of the probability of outcome depends on perceived causes of success and failure in a given action, and the estimation of the outcome utility depends on its perceived further consequences for an agent.

This inquiry concentrated on the motivation to undertake risky actions in the context of perceived reasons for success and failure and their consequences for the agent. The subject of this inquiry were the strategic decisions of managing directors of enterprises. These decisions include selection of the assortment of production, change in technology, and making investments in development. According to previous findings, an individual's chance for success in a given action and evaluation of its riskiness are influenced by such dimensions of source of uncertainty (outcome causes) as stability, controlability, and globality. The studied relation was the connection between perceived controlability of the cause of the outcome of action under risk and evaluation of the riskiness of and preference for this action.[1]

The value of the outcome of risky actions (according to VIE theory) by managing directors of enterprises is linked with the perceived instrumentality of success and failure in these actions with respect to their consequences for the professional career of the agent (e.g. for his promotion or salary). Hence, perceived instrumentality of success and failure for further consequences in risky, careful, and non-task-oriented actions were studied as well as the relation between perceived instrumentality of success and failure in these three kinds of actions and the tendency to chose risky actions.

The perceived instrumentality of the outcome of actions may be linked to the decision maker's perceived independence in the choice of the action and its realization. On the other hand, the perceived instrumentality of the action outcome is connected with the perceived criteria of evaluation used with respect to the enterprise and the managing director. Since the subjects were managing directors of enterprises with no immediate superiors, these problems are related to the system of managing the economy, above all the degree of centralization. This concerns first and foremost the distance from the parametric model of management and the number of commands or personal pressures used (e.g. the suggestion by the government to start up production of a certain kind with the offer of a subsidy or dissatisfaction of the government with the direction of production expressed by withholding allocation of materials for the factory).

3. SELECTION OF SUBJECTS.

Though perception reflects the subjective beliefs of an individual, it also usually reflects the objective features of the situation. Hence, it was decided to study managing directors who are in objectively different situations with respect to the intensity of personal pressures used by the government that cause them to believe that the absolute criterion of profit is barely important. It was assumed that under conditions in Poland two quite different groups of managing directors can be distinguished in the following ways: (1) managing directors of private enterprises based on Polonia or foreign capital, and (2) managing directors of state enterprises that produce so called important products, i.e. important both for satisfying the needs of the domestic market and for earning foreign currency through exports. To verify this assumption 50 pilot interviews were carried out in the spring of 1984 (40 with executives of state enterprises and 10 with executives of private enterprises). The interviews confirmed the above assumptions.

The subjects of the study proper, were managing directors of both state and private enterprises. The information was gathered from the questionnaire between 10 May and 11 September 1985. Questionnaires were given to 80 managing directors of state enterprises and 60 managing directors of private companies. To ensure anonymity the subjects were asked to return the questionnaire by mail. Completed questionnaires were received from 47 subjects - 32 managing directors of state enterprises and 15 managing directors of private companies.

4. REASONS FOR SUCCESS AND FAILURE IN RISKY ACTIONS PERCEIVED BY MANAGING DIRECTORS, EVALUATION OF THEIR RISKINESS AND PREFERENCE FOR THEM.

It was assumed that the importance and controlability of the cause of outcome (i.e. the source of uncertainty) can modify the evaluation of one's chances for success in a given action and the motivation to undertake it. The pilot study revealed 11 reasons mentioned by managing directors as responsible for the outcome in the realization of strategic decisions. These reasons can be collected in the four categories:

- features of the subject: knowledge, ability, and effort put into the task;
- other people: decisions of superiors (administrative authorities or owner) and the quality of the work of subordinates;
- situation determinants: legal and financial regulations, the economic and socio-political situation at home and in the world.
- chance happenings (good or bad luck).

The perceived importance of the above reasons for success and failure were measured in the study proper. Assuming that these 11 factors determine the outcome completely (100%), the subjects were asked to assign to each of them what percentage of influence they believed it had on the outcome. For each of the 11 factors the subjects also separately estimated on a scale of 0-100 perceived control over a given factor.

It was assumed that all subjects would similarly evaluate their own traits and the world economic and political determinants. On the other hand individual differences in the generalized and situational locus of control can appear in evaluation of other people and chance happenings. For these reasons the three following sources of uncertainty were selected for analyzing the link between controlability of these sources and evaluation of the riskiness and preference for them: decisions of superiors, quality of the work of subordinates, chance happenings that could appear during the start-up of a pilot production. The subjects were presented with the description of three risk situations that differed in the sources of uncertainty and were asked to rank these possibilities twice, from most risky to the least risky, and from most preferred to the least preferred. All three possibilities were assumed to have the same "objective" frequency of success and failure. It was assumed that the importance of a given source of uncertainty and control over it perceived by an individual would modify the "objective" information on the frequency of success and failure in this action (objective relevant base rate). Simultaneously, an attempt was made to equalize these possibilities with respect to utility of gains and losses. To reduce individual differences among subjects in evaluation of their utility, a goal of the action was imposed on the subjects - a favorable outcome and a necessary outcome. Presentation of the general assumptions served this purpose. All three possibilities were constructed in such a way as to give at least a favorable outcome in case of success. On the other hand, failure gave an outcome worse than the necessary one.[2]

The results obtained allow the following statements:

1. Subjects ranked lowest the importance of chance happenings for the outcomes they obtained.
2. According to the attributional achievement motivation model, subjects regarded their own traits as most important for success and situation factors as most important for failures.
3. They ranked highest the possibility of controlling their own traits, followed by the quality of the work of their subordinates. The possibility of controlling chance happenings was ranked lowest.
4. The situation regarded by subjects as most risky, in comparison with those regarded as least risky, had a source in uncertainty perceived as more important for achieving success ($t=1.67$, $p=0.05$) or incurring failure ($t=1.66$, $p=0.05$).
5. There was a correlation between the perceived controlability of decisions by superiors and the evaluation of the riskiness of actions in which the superiors were sources of both uncertainty ($r=0.245$, statistically insignificant) and preference for these actions ($r=0.41$, $p=0.05$).
6. No correlation was found between the perceived controlability of the quality of work of subordinates and chance happenings and estimation of riskiness and preferences for those actions in which these factors were a source of uncertainty.

7. It was found that subjects preferred situations which they perceived as less risky (r=0.54, 0.54, 0.53, p=0.05).

The findings can be interpreted in the context of a person's use of information on the objective frequency of success and failure in specific situations (objective base rate). Such information was used in this investigation and it was expected that the subjects would regard it as relevant. In accordance with the empirical findings of the psychological decision theory, it should be used by the subjects. According to cognitive models of motivation, such information, together with subjective opinions on one's possibilities of controlling events, is the basis for making a subjective estimate of the possibility of success and failure in a given situation. The findings of the inquiry suggest that the problem of using objective and subjective information on the frequency of events (objective and subjective base rates) is more complicated.

Besides the two mentioned above factors it seems that there exists a third one - the kind of the source of uncertainty which this information concerns. It seems important to distinguish between chance happenings and events which are caused by non-probabilistic mechanisms. The results of this study suggest that in the situation with a chance source of uncertainty subjects made considerable use of information on the frequency of favorable and unfavorable events. Simultaneously , concerning their own opinions on controlability and on importance of this source of uncertainty, subjects estimated the situation that include this source as the least risky. It appears that if subjects perceived little importance of the uncertainty source then perceived riskiness is not significantly influenced by perceived small controlability of this source. The findings also seem to indicate that in situations in which the source of uncertainty was not chance but rather people, the subjects used still another information besides the objective frequency of success and failure and their own beliefs on controlability and importance of this source. This can be clearly seen in a situation in which the source of uncertainty was the quality of the work of subordinates, regarded by all subjects as generally quite important for the outcome but well controlled by them (x=60%). Subjects were given the objective chance of success equal to 0.60. The very description of the situation contained the possibility of entering into a conflict with the crew. Success could be achieved either by winning this conflict or by alleviating it, but its complete avoidance seemed impossible on the basis of this description. For many subjects this information appeared to be more relevant than the objective frequency of success in such a situation and their own opinions on controlling events of this type. This problem requires further study since it would supply new information on the "deterministic" thinking of people in risky situations.

5. THE DEGREE OF CENTRALIZATION OF MANAGEMENT OF THE ECONOMY, PERCEIVED REASONS FOR SUCCESS AND FAILURE IN RISKY ACTIONS AND THE TENDENCY TO UNDERTAKE THEM.

An indicator of the tendency to undertake risky actions was the number of risky choices in a choice situation between certain and risky actions. The choice was made three times. As before, the subjects were presented the general assumption for a choice situation and given the goal of action - a favorable outcome and a necessary outcome. Choice situations were constructed so that certain actions led to a necessary outcome. On the other hand, risky actions in the case of success gave a better than favorable outcome and in the case of failure a worse than necessary outcome. It was assumed that a certain situation and a risky situation are equivalent. The equalization was made in line with the prospect theory [22].

No differences were found in the frequency of risky choices between managing directors of state and private enterprises with respect to two of the three decision problems. These were choice of co-producers and choice of the level of export production. The probability of success and failure was estimated on the basis of statistical data and the opinions of experts on the world economic situation and the foreign operations of a competitive firm.

Differences were observed between both groups of managing directors in the frequency of risky choices in the third decision problem, where success or failure depended on the decisions of administrative authorities or an owner. Managing directors of private firms chose risky actions more often than managing directors of state companies ($\chi^2 = 7.55$, p=0.01).

It was found that managing directors of state enterprises rated more important the influence of the decisions of the Center on their results than managing directors of private companies rated the importance of the infuence of the company owner. At the same time, managing directors of state enterprises rated lower their own control over the decision than did managing directors of private firms (t=3.13, p=0.01).

These findings confirmed the hypothesis on the dependency between the degree of peremptoriness of the management system and renouncement of the criterion of profit and the importance of controlability of the Center's decisions as perceived by managing directors. The findings also suggest that (1) managing directors of state enterprises avoid situations in which the decisions of administrative authorities are a source of uncertainty for the outcome of their action, and (2) there is a correlation between perceived controlability of this source and the estimation of its riskiness.

6. THE DEGREE OF CENTRALIZATION OF MANAGEMENT OF THE ECONOMY AND THE VALUE OF RISKY ACTION IN THE CONTEXT OF THEIR INSTRUMENTALITY FOR THE PROFESSIONAL CAREERS OF MANAGING DIRECTORS.

Here we measured:

- the utility of 6 rewards and 6 punishments, with measurement limited to ranking them, and
- the instrumentality of certain actions and their outcomes for these reinforcements; the perceived strength of the relation was defined on a scale of 0-100 and expressed

the belief of subjects about the frequency with which a positive or negative outcome of a specific action leads to a given reinforcement.

The rewards and punishments whose utility were measured and the 15 actions about which subjects were asked their opinion were derived from another study on perception of the system of reinforcements by the executives and workmen of both types of enterprises which I carried out in the fall of 1984.

In this study it was found that all subjects similarly evaluated the utility of the presented reinforcements (e.g. promotion and degradation, dismissal, financial rewards and punishments). However, differences were observed between the opinions of the subjects on the effectiveness of certain actions with respect to reinforcements. Table 1 contains information on the average assessment by managing directors of state and private enterprises of the instrumentality of success with respects to rewards in risky actions in comparison with success in careful and non-task-oriented actions. The data in this Table suggest that:

1. Managing directors of private companies perceive success in risky actions as more instrumental in relation to rewards than success in careful and non-task-oriented actions.
2. Managing directors of state enterprises attribute the same instrumentality in relation to rewards to success in risky and non-task-oriented situations actions and only slightly higher instrumentality for success in careful actions.
3. Managing directors of state enterprises evaluated lower the instrumentality of success in every action in relation to rewards than did managing directors of private companies. Hence, managing directors of state enterprises see no effective way of achieving professional rewards.

Table 2 contains information on the average assessment of instrumentality of failure in the three kinds of actions in relation to punishments. The data in this Table suggest that:

1. Managing directors of private companies believe that failure in risky action leads more often to punishments than failure in careful and non-task-oriented actions.
2. Managing directors of state enterprises believe that they are punished more often for failure in careful actions than in non-task-oriented actions, and least often in risky actions.
3. As before, managing directors of state companies believe that they are punished less often than directors of private firms.

These findings suggest that the utility of risky actions is evaluated higher by managing directors of private companies.

7. THE TENDENCY TO UNDERTAKE RISKY ACTIONS IN THE TWO GROUPS STUDIED.

As was described in Section 5, the frequency of choice of a risky action or certain

TABLE 1

Mean values of perceived instrumentality of success for all rewards in risky, careful and non-task-oriented actions.

Actions	Mean values perceived by directors managing state enterprises	Mean values perceived by directors managing private companies	Differences in mean values between both groups
1. Obtaining better outcomes than the others under the same conditions	18.1	28.8	t=2.12 p=0.05
2. Putting great effort into task	13.0	14.8	no difference
3. Observing regulations	9.8	17.8	t=2.36 p=0.05
4. Increase in production quantity level	13.4	15.5	no difference
5. Increase in production quality level	12.9	24.7	t=1.81 p=0.05
6. Completing task on time	10.9	15.1	no difference
7. Increase in profit	15.3	32.3	t=2.65 p=0.01
8. Self-financing of enterprise (lack of deficit)	10.6	8.3	no difference
9. Modernization of production processes	15.7	27.8	t=2.07 p=0.05
10. Decrease in production costs	12.3	16.7	no difference
11. Making good investments in development	15.8	24.9	t=1.95 p=0.05
12. Keeping workmen satisfied	14.6	18.1	no difference
13. Keeping good relations with administrative authorities or with owner	19.2	18.7	no difference
14. Directors own involvment in social and political activity	13.7	6.7	t=2.25 p=0.05
15. Supporting attitute towards social and political organizations (i.e. political parties or trade unions) in the enterprise.	12.8	4.3	t=3.83 p=0.05

TABLE 2

Mean values of perceived instrumentality of failure for all studied punishments in risky, careful and non-task-oriented actions.

	Actions	Mean values perceived by directors managing state enterprises	Mean values perceived by directors managing private companies	Differences in mean values between both groups
1.	Obtaining worse outcomes than the others under the same conditions	12.2	28.9	$t=5.51$ $p=0.01$
2.	Putting too small effort into task	10.1	13.3	no difference
3.	Disobeying regulations	14.4	17.4	no difference
4.	Decrease in production quantity level	12.2	20.7	$t=2.73$ $p=0.01$
5.	Decrease in production quality level	1o.7	25.9	$t=4.54$ $p=0.01$
6.	Deley in completing task on time	13.2	19.9	$t=2.16$ $p=0.05$
7.	Decrease in profit	13.9	31.9	$t=5.11$ $p=0.01$
8.	Financial deficit	19.2	35.2	$t=3.44$ $p=0.01$
9.	Lack of effort towards modernization of production processes	7.5	13.2	$t=1.85$ $p=0.05$
10.	Increase in production costs	9.5	14.8	$t=1.83$ p‘0.05
11.	Losses caused by improper investments	15.6	30.7	$t=2.93$ $p=0.01$
12.	Inducing workmen's dissatisfaction	17.0	13.3	no difference
13.	Bad relations with administrative authorities or with owner	14.7	19.0	no difference
14.	Lack own involvment in social and political activity	9.9	2.6	$t=3.59$ $p=0.01$
15.	Passive attitute towards social and political organizations in the enterprise.	9.4	1.7	$t=3.49$ $p=0.01$

action in the three decision problems was used as an indicator. Differences between the two groups appeared only in one of the three decision problems.

The correlation was checked between the tendency to undertake risky actions and the perceived instrumentality of the results of such actions in relation to reinforcements as well as perceived instrumentality of non-task-oriented actions. As expected, a negative correlation was found between perceived high instrumentality of non-task-oriented actions and the tendency to undertake risky actions. On the other hand, the expected dependency between the perception of high instrumentality of success in risky actions and the tendency to undertake them was not found. This fact seems to require separate interpretation for both groups and for the entire population studied.

This dependency was not found for the entire population studied, most probably because there was a high agreement between the perceived positive and negative instrumentality of certain types of actions, i.e. subjects who believed that success in a given action often leads to reward simultaneously believed that failure in this action very often is punished. This accounts for the fact that the strong motivation to undertake risky actions that yield profit (and as a consequence individual rewards such as promotion, increase in salary , etc.) is accompanied by the strong motivation to avoid such actions from fear of the negative consequences of failure (loss of professional prestige, dismissal, etc.). The psychological theory of decision making states that the negative utility of punishment is always rated higher than the positive utility of rewards. This may account for the stronger tendency to avoid risky actions.

This phenomenon appeared much more distinctly in the group of managing directors of private companies, who rated instrumentality of task-oriented behavior in relation to reinforcements higher than did managing directors of state companies. This conflict between motivation to achievement and the avoidance of failure most probably is "solved" by certain features of the external situation in which managing directors of private firms operate. On the basis of this study, pilot interviews, and information from the board of the enterprises' association of these firms, it was found that their managing directors do not make risky decisions because:

1. There is no business risk; with large gaps in the market every article can be sold. Simultaneously, new regulations make it difficult to form new companies and there is no threat of competition.
2. There is no investment risk resulting from specific features of the legal regulations (e.g. a foreign company can only lease the land on which an investment is made) and their frequent changes (during the time these inquiries were being prepared the legal and financial regulations changed twice).
3. There is no risk in choosing the assortment of production, that would maximize profit. Although there are no regulations limiting profit, owners and managing directors believe that profit above 30% exposes a company to control and the charge of speculation.

4. Export decisions to a large extent are limited by external factors (e.g. the obligation to sell foreign currency to the Polish National Bank, the requirements to have the Ministry of Foreign Trade approve prices in foreign currency, etc.).

The second group of subjects rated the instrumentality of the outcomes of risky actions in relation to reinforcements rather low. At the same time they believe that non-task-oriented behaviors - care to maintain good relations with administrative authorities and satisfaction of the crew as well as their social and political activity - more often lead to some rewards (e.g. promotion, independence in work) than task-oriented behaviors. According to the cognitive models of motivation the tendency to undertake these actions should be stronger, since success is easier and "more certain".

FOOTNOTES

[1] The decisions and actions studied, undertaken by managing directors are typical of their everyday activity, are repetitive, and hence are at the exteme end of the globality dimension. Simultaneously, the possibility of controlling events through person's activity requires perceiving a given cause as unstable. Hence, this two dimensions were only controlled, but not studied in this research.

[2] To construct decision situation similar to actual dacision problems considered by the subjects, these probabilities were based on information gathered from the pilot interviews with executives from both times of enterprises.

REFERENCES

1. Kahneman, D. and Tversky, A., Subjective probability: A judgement of representativeness, *Cognitive Psychol.* **3** (1972) 430-453.
2. Kahneman, D. and Tversky, A., On the psychology of prediction, *Psychol. Rev.* **80** (1973) 237-251.
3. Tversky, A. and Kahneman, D., Causal schemas in judgements under uncertainty, in: Fishbein, M. (ed.), Progress in Social Psychology vol. 1 (Erlbaum, Hillsdale, 1980).
4. Dawes, R. M., Is irrationality systematic?, *The Behavioral and Brain Sciences* **6** (1983) 491-492.
5. Levi, I., Who commits the base rate fallacy?, *The Behavioral and Brain Sciences* **6** (1983) 502-506.
6. Weiner, B., Frieze, I., Kukla, A., Reed., L., Rest, S., and Rosenbaum, R. M., Perceiving the causes of success and failure, in: Jones E. E. et al. (eds.), Attribution: Perceiving the Causes of Behavior, (General Learning Press, New York, 1971/72).
7. Weiner, B., A theory of motivation for some classroom experiences, *J. Educational Psychol.* **71** (1979) 3-25.

8. Weiner, B., An attributional theory of achievement motivation and emotion, *Psychol. Rev.* **92** (1985) 548-573.

9. Cohen, J. and Hansel, C. E., Preference for different combination of chance and skill in gambling, *Nature* **183** (1959) 841-842.

10. Howell, W. C. and Burnett, S. A., Uncertainty measurements: a cognitive taxonomy, *Organizational Behavior and Human Performance* **22** (1978) 45-68.

11. Svenson, O., Risk of road transportation in psychological perspective, *Accident Analysis and Prevention* **10** (1978) 14-29.

12. Svenson, O., Are we all less risky and more skillful than our fellow drivers?, *Acta Psychol.* **47** (1981) 143-148.

13. Fischhoff, B. and Slovic, P., A little learning: Confidence in multicue judgement tasks, in Nickerson, R., (ed.), Attention and Performance (Erlbaum, Hillsdale, 1980).

14. Kahle, L. R., Stimulus conditions self-selection by male in interaction of locus of control and skill - chance situations, *J. Personality and Social Psychol.* **38** (1980) 50-56.

15. McAllister, D. W., Mitchell, T. R., and Beach, L. R., The contingency model for the selection of decision strategies: An empirical test of the effect of significance, accountability and reversibility, *Organizational Behavior and Human Performance* **24** (1979) 228-244.

16. Vlek, Ch., and Stallen, P. J., Rational and personal aspects of risk, *Acta Psychol.* **45** (1980) 273-300.

17. Harvey, J. H. and Smith, W. P., Social Psychology: An Attributional Approach (C. V Mosby, Saint Louis, 1977).

18. Slovic, P. et al., Rating the risk, *Environment* **21** (1979) 14-29.

19. Fischhoff, B. et al., How safe is safe enough? A psychometric study towards technological risk and benefits, *Policy Science* **9** (1978) 127-152.

20. Fischhoff, B. et al., The "public" versus the "experts": Perceived versus actual disagreement about risks, *Risk Analysis* (1983).

21. Vroom, V. H., Work and Motivation (John Wiley, New York, 1964).

22. Kahneman, D. and Tversky, A., Prospect theory: An analysis of decisions under risk, *Econometrica* **47** (1979) 263-191.

JUSTIFICATION OF DECISIONS MADE IN ADVERSE CIRCUMSTANCES

Tadeusz TYSZKA and Piotr GASPARSKI

Department of Psychology
Polish Academy of Sciences,
Pl. Malachowskiego 1,
00-063 Warszawa, Poland

1. INTRODUCTION.

Justification of previously made decisions has so far not attracted attention of researchers. To be sure, there are theories or concepts of post- and pre–decision processes that permit certain predictions concerning justification of choices, but these predictions are rather modest.

First and foremost, the theory of cognitive dissonance, which states that the attractiveness of an alternative chosen increases and the attractiveness of alternatives rejected declines, leads us to expect a tendency toward the predominance of positive evaluations in justifying decisions already made. An identical conclusions follows from the ideas which treat the process of choice as "a search for good arguments" [1]. People, according to this approach, try to structuralize a decision problem in such a way as to arrive at a dominance structure, *i.e.* a set of options such that one of the choice alternatives emerges as definitely better than others [1]; or as Shepard [2] put it, people "try out various frames of mind until they find one (alternative) whose associated subjective weights give one alternative the clearest adventage".

The difference between the theory of cognitive dissonance and the other approaches to the decision process reduces only to the moment in which, after or before the choice, this increase in positive opinions of the alternative chosen occurs.

Not much more can be concluded from both these concepts concerning justification of decisions. Somewhat more specific expectations can be formulated on the basis of ideas associated with the notion of freedom of choice. Namely, one can surmise that one of the consequences of limiting freedom of choice should be weakening of the tendency toward exclusively positive evaluation of decisions made. For eventually the decision maker can attribute negative aspects of his decisions to the limitations in freedom of choice. However, the concept of freedom of choice is understood in various ways [3]. From our point of view we are interested in two interpretations:

A. Freedom of choice can be understood as the attractiveness of available choice alternatives in comparison with the level of aspirations of the decision maker. If available alternatives (at least one of them) exceed his level of aspirations, then the decision maker has the feeling of freedom of choice. However, if the alternatives are below this level, he does not feel that he has freedom of choice (see ref. [4]).

B. Freedom of choice can be understood simply as a function of the number of available choice alternatives and differences in the subjective probability of choosing each of them. The greater the number of available alternatives and the smaller the differentiation of probabilities of choosing each of them, the greater is the feeling of freedom of choice [5].

One can surmise that limiting freedom of choice in each of the above meanings should lead to weakening the tendency toward exclusively positive evaluation of decisions made.

In the present study, carried out in a natural setting, we decided to trace the process of justifying decisions made by managing directors of Polish economic enterprises in a period in which considerable limitations on freedom of choice in both of the above senses could be expected. During the period in which the study was made, the economic situation in Poland was clearly catastrophic. The basic problem for most enterprises was survival rather than development. Simultaneously, in this period the so-called economic reform was introduced, which postulated considerable independence in decisions of state enterprises compared with the traditional central management of the economy in Poland. Despite the implementation of this reform, according to common opinion and various polls, the independence of enterprises deviated considerably in practice from the officially declared principles.

On one hand, we decided to study the perception the managing directors had about the changed decision situation and, on the other hand, to trace the process of justifying decisions that they made. In the latter case we concentrated on the aforementioned decision–making criteria and evaluations of these decisions. Additionally, we also asked the subjects to characterize the riskiness of the decisions and their time horizon. These two characteristics seemed to be especially interesting in justifying decisions made in adverse circumstances.

2. METHOD.

The investigation covered 25 managing directors of state productive enterprises.

The research method was a structuralized interview conducted in the managing director's place of work by a pair of hired, specialized psychologists. As a rule, it was concluded in two hours. The interview in the form of free conversation began with a question about the profile and assortment of production in the enterprise. Then the interviewers asked about specific recent cases of decisions on the changes in the assortment of production. With respect to these cases the interviewer attempted to gain information on:

- origin of the decision made (where the problem came from and who made the decision;

- range of possible choice alternatives and limitations;
- criteria (attributes) considered in a given decision;
- assessments (for and against the decision made);
- risk level (dangers and the probability of their occurring);
- time horizon of the decision made.

After finishing the conversation on the assortment decision, subjects were asked about cases of decisions on supplies, employment , and sales following the same pattern as in the assortment decisions.

Finally, if there was time and the subject had not expressed such opinions earlier, he was asked about his general opinion on the freedom to make decisions and other conditions of the decision situation of the enterprise in the changed system of managing the economy.

In many cases, realization of the above rules for conducting the interview deviated from the initial assumption. It was not always possible to keep the conversation to specific cases, and some information was given in the more general form. Neither was it always possible to complete the plan of the interview (respondents did not have sufficient time). As a result, data on various aspects coming from individual respondents were incomplete. Therefore, the data which we cite in the following section are not systematically based on the responses of all the 25 directors interviewed.

3. RESULTS.

The material obtained was analyzed along two lines: perception of the decision situation of enterprises by their managing directors and justification of the decisions made in this situation.

3.1. Perception of the decision situation.

Data on three matters was obtained here: (1) the situation in supplies, employment, and sales, (2) the felt range of freedom of choice, and (3) the felt certainty and stability of the economic situation.

The situation in supplies, employment, and sales presents a very clear picture. Of the 25 managing directors interviewed, 22 (88%) declared that they have considerable problems with supplies, and the same number had problems with employment. Only four respondents had some troubles with sales; the others stated that they had no such problems.

Supply problems consisted of the lack of possibilities to purchase basic raw materials and means of production, or of shortages and irregular supplies of raw materials, tools, semi-finished products, spare parts, packaging, *etc.* There was also a problem of the lack of foreign currency for indispensable import. The basic problem in employment consisted of the labor shortage in comparison with the needs and of the constant tendency of employees to quit their jobs.

Freedom of decision making was analyzed on two levels: (1) in the context of specific choices presented by respondents, and (2) in the context of spontaneous general opinions on freedom and limitations. As far as the first level is concerned, respondent's statements were analyzed by two judges to determine whether a given decision in the enterprise was made on his own initiative, without apparent outside pressure, or whether, though formally made in the enterprise, it was initiated and forced by the superior authorities or by the external circumstances so that it became the only available course of action.

We introduced two categories of the origin of decisions:

(a) free decisions,

(b) forced decisions.

In the category (b) we included all decisions that had comments attributing the basic role to the external circumstances. For example, "it was the only possibility", "the decision was strictly determined by situation", "it was imposed by the superiors", *etc.* Category (a) included all the remaining cases.

Among 105 decision presented by the respondents, 74 (70%) were classified as free and 31 (30%) as forced decisions. The latter number contains five command decisions, that is such decisions that were directly imposed on the enterprise by its superior authorities.

Opinions of managing directors about the freedom of the decision making in the enterprise are listed in Table 1.

TABLE 1

Frequency of opinions on the freedom of decision making expressed by managing directors of enterprises.

subjects of opinion	declared freedom	declared lack of freedom
general statement	3 (12%)	15 (60%)
assortment decisions	7 (28%)	9 (36%)
supply decisions	1 (4%)	10 (40%)
employment decisions	1 (4%)	11 (44%)

As we can see, 60% of the subjects spontaneously confirmed the existence of serious limitations on the freedom of decision stemming from the functioning of superior institutions. Hence, we find here an interesting discrepancy with the previous findings - at the concrete level respondents rarely mentioned cases of the administrative imposition of decisions.

It is difficult to determine which picture of decision making is "true" - the one resulting from the description of the concrete decisions or the one from general statements. Statements concerning specific cases seem to be more reliable. Nonetheless, we should remember that specific cases were selected by the respondents themselves, who had every reason to talk about the decisions they made themselves rather than about those which were imposed on them.

Besides, this discrepancy can be specious. Speaking generally about administrative limitations respondents as a rule mentioned the special way in which the administration operates, This can be called the method of indirect pressure, *e.g.* through central allocation of raw materials or foreign currency, *etc.* This procedure "hides" the role of the administration in imposing decisions on enterprises and creates a false impression of the minor role of command decisions. However, this does not change the general opinion of managing directors about the command system of directing the enterprise.

Among respondents expressing general opinions about the limitations on the supply and employment decisions, the definite majority confirmed the existence of considerable limitations on the freedom of decisions in both areas. Opinions were more divided on the assortment decisions; the number of persons confirming the lack of freedom was not much higher than the number confirming the existance of freedom or at least more freedom than before the reform.

Finally, more than half of the respondents confirmed that the lack of general stability of the economic system and in particular the non–predictability of legal regulations and decisions made on of the top level controlling the operations of the enterprise. 64% of the respondents who expressed themselves on this matter. were in complete agreement.

3.2 Justification of decisions.

Before we discuss the data on justification on decisions made, we shell briefly describe the kinds of decisions which were mentioned by the subjects. In production, except for one case which consisted clearly of re-profiling the production, these were introductions or changes of new assortments or technologies, or minor organizational changes. Basic decisions of managing directors regarding supplies consisted mainly of putting, often informal, pressure on suppliers, frequently including illegal actions. Finally, the most typical operations in employment were wage increases and other measures to retain or attract employees.

To explain how the managing directors describe their decisions, we present the data on:

- the criteria for selecting a strategy of decision making,
- the evaluation of these decisions,
- their time horizon,
- their riskiness

Asked about the reasons for making individual decisions, managing directors usually mentioned several criteria, ranging in number from one to seven. The frequency with which individual criteria were mentioned in the assortment decisions, which were most thoroughly described by the subjects, is contained in Table 2. The frequencies refer to persons and not to the number of decisions described, *i.e.* they express the number (percent) of respondents who mentioned a given criterion. The classification was made ex post, *i.e.* the categories in the Table are somewhat generalized names of the criteria mentioned by the subjects themselves.

TABLE 2

Frequency of appearance of various assortment decisions criteria.

Decision criterion	Frequency
1. Profit	17 (68%)
2. Adaptation to existing possibilities or limitations is	
Supplies	12 (48%)
Machines and technology	18 (72%)
Sales	15 (60%)
Staff posibilities and skills	6 (24%)
Financial	8 (32%)
Cooperation	3 (12%)
Administrative requirement	4 (16%)
Maintaining production (generally)	5 (20%)
3. Quality of process of production	
High level of technology	3 (12%)
Efficiency of the production process	7 (32%)
Quality of the product	5 (20%)
Production for export	5 (20%)
Anti-import production	3 (12%)
4. Development of the plant	2 (8%)
5. Prestige of the plant	1 (4%)
6. Safety	3 (12%)
7. Customers needs	4 (16%)
8. Benefits for the crew	9 (36%)
9. Organizational changes	6 (24%)

As we can see, profit (economic profitability) is the criterion mentioned by the definite majority. Obviously, we have no grounds to conclude that this is the commonly used criterion for making assortment decisions in enterprises. However, we can infer that this criterion is quite commonly present in the consciousness of the managing directors (if only as a criterion to which they should appeal in justifying a decision).

The next group of seven categories is related to the operating conditions of an enterprise that create specific possibilities or impose limitations on decision making. Mentioning them as a criterion means accomodation of the decision maker to the existing conditions. As we can see, availability of materials, machine and technological possibilities, financial security, staff possibilities and skills, and sales are commonly mentioned criteria of this type.

In light of the findings presented in the previous paragraph all of the criteria but sales create serious problems for the enterprise and thus are important limitations in the assortment decisions. In this sense they concern survival of the plant and the maintaining of production.

In contrast, criteria of quality of process of production, development, *etc.*, except benefits for the crew, are relatively rarely mentioned.

The typical justification of a decision consisted of mentioning some requirement which it should or did meet. The requirements were predominantly of the type postulated by Simon's satisficing model, and occasionally elimination of alternatives, that did not meet some of the criteria, was also mentioned. Thus, although sporadically elements of other decision strategies also appeared, Simon's model seemed to be the dominating form of justifying a decision.

Respondents describing their decisions with respect to the criteria they mentioned, generally expressed themselves in the evaluative way, *i.e.* they attributed positive or negative values to the decisions they made. They were encouraged to do so by the interviewer.

After classifying all the evaluative statements into positive and negative categories, we found the following relationships. The assortment decisions received on the average 1.58 positive evaluations and 0.30 negative evaluations. This dominance of positive evaluations was not so strong in the supply decisions and was totally absent in the employment decisions. The average supply decision received 0.78 positive and 0.30 negative evaluations, and the employment decision had 0.54 positive and 0.54 negative evaluations.

There was an even clearer difference in the proportion of positive and negative evaluations attributed to decisions classified as free and as forced. The former were evaluated mostly positively (on the average 1.20 positive and 0.23 negative evaluations). The latter received more negative then positive evaluations (on the average 0.58 positive and 0.77 negative evaluations).

The relationship between the evaluation of decisions with the perceived freedom of choice and the area of decision concerned is shown by the following regression equation

$$Y = 0.37 + 0.37X_1 + 0.15X_2,$$

where Y is the evaluation of a decision (plus or minus), X_1 is the perceived freedom of choice, and X_2 is the area of decision. F for the regression equation is equal to $20.36(p < 0.001)$, F for $X_2 = 21.85(p < 0.001)$, and F for $X_2 = 4.25(p < 0.05)$.

The typical time horizon attributed to the assortment decisions was 5 to 10 years. The supply and employment decisions were usually presented as improvised, stressing that if they resolve a problem at all, it is at most for a few months. We shell return to this issue in the discussion.

As among criteria of choice relating to economic benefit, here as well financial loss is the most common danger in the minds of managing directors. Other categories of dangers concerning the enterprise as the economic organization are: sales problem, poor quality of production, interruption of production, or bankruptcy. Also mentioned among the dangers were the possibility of being fired or other negative personal consequences, the possibility of negative reactions of the crew, and the danger of employees leaving.

Were these dangers evaluated as realistic? The vast majority of respondents said no. They spoke of them as "theoretical" dangers, "not occurring in practice", "very improbable", *etc.* No one mentioned any such danger that had occurred. However, the respondents often talked about dangers that had not occurred. Only four of the respondents evaluated some of the dangers that they mentioned as possible or real.

4. DISCUSSION.

The findings about the perception of the decision making situation by many directors confirmed in essence the earlier known opinion about the unfavorable position of enterprises in supplies and employment, lack of stability, and limited freedom of decision in practice.

How in such a critical perception of their decision making situation do managing directors justify and evaluate the decisions they make? It turns out that at least as far as unforced decisions are concerned, their evaluations are mostly positive. Shortly, one can say that regardless of adverse circumstances managing directors have the opinion that they make good decisions. Managing directors simply appeal to those criteria of evaluation which are met by their decisions: the production undertaken has the assured raw material base, machines, technology, sales, *etc.*, and so the undertakings can be evaluated positively. Criteria which these undertakings do not meet, *e.g.* quality, development, safety, *etc.* are simply ignored in justifying decisions.

It turns out, however that positive inclination does not hold for decisions that, in the opinion of the decision maker, were forced, with respect to which his choice was very limited in the number of alternatives. Such choices were characterized by the considerable proportion of negative evaluations. One can add that approximately half of the positive opinions attributed to these decisions were relative evaluations - the selected alternative was the best among those possible (which does not mean that it was good).

The difference between evaluation of the assortment decisions and the decisions in supplies and employment may also be explained in terms of freedom of choice. If the situation in supplies and employment is regarded as extremely unfavorable, much more than managing directors would wish, the lack of freedom in the decision making in this sense (see Sect. 1) weakened the tendency to evaluate their decisions favorably.

Thus, our study seems to support the hypothesis about the relationship between the perceived freedom of choice (in the two meanings) and the evaluation of a decision made. However, it says nothing whether it is a pre- or post–decisional phenomenon.

Similarly, on the basis of this study one cannot determine whether the declared long time perspective of the production decisions and the lack of risk are real characteristics of decisions made or are only attributed *ex post* to justify these decisions.

As far as the long time horizon of the decisions is concerned, this can be an authentic reaction of managing directors to the uncertainty of the decision making situation. With the general instability and uncertainty of many other elements, stabilization of the profile of production can ensure some minimal security of operations. On the other hand, attributing a long perspective to the decisions made in adverse circumstances can also be an element of their positive evaluation, which would show that directors are able to cope with an unfavorable situation.

Similarly, as far as the "real" risk is concerned, there can be two sources of such a description of a decision made. Perhaps risk is already reduced in the pre–decisional phase. Kornai [6] notes that a decision maker in a situation of uncertainty does not make risky choices; he tries to acquire information about how to project himself from uncertainty so as to be able to act in conditions of certainty and not uncertainty. As a consequence, in speaking about risk he will consider the safeguards available to him rather than the greatness of the uncertainty itself. These safeguards should, in effect, reduce uncertainty. This interpretation was confirmed in our study in the sense that the subjects did indeed mention numerous safeguards that they took with respect to possible dangers.

However, there is also a possibility that regardless of the perceived level of risk of a decision before it is made, the decision maker has a tendency to raise the security level of his decisions in hindsight. Here we may be dealing with a phenomenon described by Fischhoff [7] as the hindsight bias, consisting of the fact that people exaggerate in the hindsight what they know in the foresight.

Generally, we must stress again that our study does not allow to separate pre- and post–decisional phenomena, so it says nothing about sources of justifications given by decision makers. Furthermore, our findings are based on a rather weak method, and they should be confirmed in better controlled experimental conditions.

REFERENCES

1. Montgomery, H., Decision rules and the search for dominance structure: towards

a process model of decision making, in: Humphreys, Svenson and Vari (eds.), Analysing and Aiding Decision Processes, (Akademiai Kiado, Budapest, 1983).

2. Shepard, R. N., On subjectively optimum selections among multi–attribute alternatives, in Shelley, M. W. and Bryan, G. L. (eds.), Human Judgements and Optimality, (Wiley, New York, 1964).
3. Kofta, M., Wolnosc wybory (freedom of choice), in Gliszczynska, X. (ed.), Czlowiek jako Podmiot Zycia Spolecznego, (Ossolineum, Warszawa, 1983).
4. Steiner, I. D., Three kinds of reported choice, in Perlmuter, L. C. and Monty, R. A. (eds.), Choice and Perceived Control (Hillsdale, New York, 1979).
5. Ajzen, I., Attribution of disposition to an actor: perceived decision freedom and behavioral utilities, *J. Personality and Social Psych.* **18** (1971) 144-156.
6. Kornai, J., Anti-equilibrium. On Economc System Theory and the Task of Research, (North-Holland, Amsterdam, 1971).
7. Fischhoff, B., Hindsight=foresight: the effect of outcome knowledge on judgement under uncertainty, *J. Exptl. Psychol.: HPP* **1(3)** (1975) 288-299.

Part Four
Economic Psychology of the Family

IS ALTRUISM THE DOMINANT MOTIVATION IN THE FAMILY?

Charlotte DeMonte Phelps

Department of Economics, Temple University
Philadelphia, Pennsylvania, 19122, U.S.A.

This paper gives a negative answer to the title question. Altruism is defined as a transfer of money income motivated by affiliation.

1. INTRODUCTION

Economists assume that altruism is the dominant motivation in marriage and decision making in the family. The concept of altruism, as used by economists, usually ties together two attributes: a one-way money transfer and warmth of affection, "love". Becker forges this link in his model of altruism in the family [1,2], as does Boulding in his theory of the grants economy [3].

Becker's argument for the dominance of altruism rests on the interdependence resulting from small numbers and his theory of assortative mating.

> Altruism is common in families not only because families are small and have many interactions, but also because marriage markets tend to 'assign' altruists to their beneficiaries. A selfish beneficiary compares her family income as the mate of her benefactor with the family income of other participants in the marriage market.[1] ...Since the wife's consumption counts twice (it enters both utility functions), they are better off marrying each other than marrying similar persons who are neither benefactors nor beneficiaries. Thus we can readily explain why marriages with caring - or 'love' - are likely to be part of the equilibrium sorting of mates ...([1], pp. 196-197]).

Becker does not consider the possibility that the positive dependence of the husband's utility on his wife's may be attributable to fear rather than love. Boulding posits a spectrum of grant motivation, ranging from love to fear, the latter being a response to a threat. The increase in the husband's utility that accompanies a money transfer may represent a "'negative negative' -- that is, ... the absence of a decrease in utility that would otherwise have taken place ([3], p. 22).

Public opinion may be the source of the threat. Smith analyzes the incentive value of approbation and disapprobation in learning virtuous behavior [4]. If marriage is a sign of virtue (Grossbard-Schectman, [5]), a man may marry to acquire the sign or to avoid the stigma of being unvirtuous. It would be desirable to have a measure of motivation that distinguished between real and faked virtue.

Boulding argues that social systems based on threats are unstable. If the family persists as an organization, it follows that "... the 'integrative' or gift element in grants ultimately dominates ..." ([3], p. 5). The fact that the divorce rate in America has risen over the last thirty years to the highest in the world suggests that the motive for fear has increased relative to the motive for love.

This paper introduces to economic analysis a measure of love, the motive to affiliate (Heyns, Veroff and Atkinson, [6]) and a measure of fear, the motive for power as fear of weakness (Veroff, [7]). Measures of these motives from nationwide surveys of Americans' mental health in 1957 and 1976 show that fear has increased relative to love (Veroff, Depner, Kulka and Douvan [8]).

The measures are based on Thematic Apperception Tests (TATs), a personality test that taps unconscious motives by asking subjects to compose imaginative stories in response to word or picture cues. The tests are said to tap the unconscious because they are based on free association. Veroff found that some people who scored high on his measure of power gave conscious reports of loving relationships (Veroff and Veroff, [9]). An inference is that a person may be an unconscious faker.

This paper analyses the motivation of a sample of 323 white married men with children from the 1957 survey (Gurin, Veroff and Feld, [10]) to test the hypothesis that altruism is the dominant motivation in the family.[2] The sample subjects gave adequate responses to the TAT.[3] The sample is biased towards love and against fear by the restriction that all subjects lived with own parents until they were 16. Approximately 80 percent of people surveyed in 1957 were reared in intact homes. Veroff, Atkinson, Feld, and Gurin found that the effect of broken home background is to lower male affiliation and raise power motivation.

In the survey, all married men were designated head of household. All transferred money income to the members of the household. They were in the industrial labor force or retired.

Becker's theory contrasts altruism and selfishness, while Boulding's theory contrasts love and fear. In Section 2, Erich Fromm's [12] analysis of love and pseudo love is used to support the hypothesis that behavior which is controlling can result from fear motivation. Because Becker's altruist controls family behavior through the use of monetary transfers, his motivation could be fear, not love. My point is that motivation cannot be inferred from behavior. The motive measures make it possible to differentiate transfers motivated by love from transfers motivated by fear.

The motive measures are explained in Section 3. The data are analyzed in Section 4. Conclusions are drawn in Section 5.

2. ALTRUISM, LOVE, AND PSEUDO-LOVE

Becker makes a distinction between being "altruistic," and "effectively altruistic" ([1], p. 173). "Altruistic" means the husband's utility depends on the wife's; "effectively" means that his behavior is changed by his altruism. The behavior cited is the transfer of money income from him to her.

It is my perception that Becker's description of an effective altruist's maximizing behavior is similar to Fromm's description of sadistic love. Sadistic love seeks security in limited control of another person. It requires a submissive (masochistic) partner. Both the dominant and submissive forms of pseudo-love result from anxiety and an inability to be independent.

After weighing the benefits and costs to himself of alternatives, an effective altruist chooses the action which maximizes his own satisfaction and compensates his wife for any initial loss in her satisfaction. The expectation that he will increase (reduce) transfers according to the postive (negative) impact of her behavior on his utility causes her to take account of her impact on his utility. She is said to behave as if she were altruistic. Becker refers to this outcome as economizing the scarce resource "love".

Becker's point of emphasis is that the behavior of a household with an effective altruist is integrated; that is, is consonant with the maximization of the head of household's utility. My point of emphasis is that an effective altruist is exercising limited control over his wife.

The husband may cease to be an effective altruist - i.e., cease contributing to her - if his selfish wife accepts an increase in income which reduces his income by more than he had been contributing to her. Pollak states that the development of such a "corner solution" depends on "implicit assumptions about power or, equivalently, about the structure of the bargaining game" ([13], p. 599). His interpretation, like mine, assumes power motivation.

According to Fromm, in many pseudo-love relationships "the roles change constantly - a continuous struggle for dominance and submission being conceived as love" ([12], p. 518). The hypothesized behavior of the selfish wife and the cornered husband is consistent with that pattern. Note that behavior which Becker terms selfish may be an expression of anxiety.

What then is love? Fromm's answer is that it is "an active striving, the aim of which is the happiness, development and freedom of its 'object'" ([12], p. 519). Love between adults is a relationship between independent equals. In Becker's theory, it is a marriage between two altruists. In Boulding's theory, it is a marriage based on reciprocity.

Love of a parent for a child encourages individuation. Perhaps it is more complex, because the parent must assert authority in socializing the child. In the context of child-rearing, Becker's description of altruism is closer to Fromm's definition of love. Becker observes that parenting requires controlling the behavior of young children who have insufficient information to know what is "good for them" ([1], p. 193). According to Becker, altruists differ from selfish parents by the motive for control. He gives the desire to gain prestige from children's accomplishments as an example of a selfish motive. Another difference is the degree of control. Altruists are less controlling than selfish parents.

In discussing the parent-child relationship, Boulding again draws attention to the role of fear of public opinion as a motivating force.

> Even within the family, parents support the children not only

> because they love them, but also because they are afraid of what the neighbors might say, or fear for their reputation, or even fear the heavy hand of the political authority coming down with legal sanctions for child neglect ([3], p. 4).

Fromm cites a cause of fear other than public opinion. It is the parents' anxiety and inability to be independent.

> The sadistic love is frequently the kind of love that parents have for their children. Whether the domination is overtly authoritarian or subtly 'modern' makes no essential difference. In either case, it tends to undermine the strength of self of the child and leads in later years to the development in him of the very same symbiotic tendencies ([12], p. 518).

In Section 4 the two origins of fear are empirically differentiated.

3. MEASURES OF LOVE AND FEAR

The preceding discussion suggests that the principal motivational distinction in marriage is between love and pseudo-love, the latter being a consequence of anxiety or fear. It is argued that the motive to affiliate is a measure of love and that the motive for power as fear of weakness is a measure of pseudo-love. The manuals for scoring themes of imaginative stories are used to support the argument.

The manual for scoring affiliation (AFF) requires counting references to the desire to establish, maintain or restore a positive affective relation. However, if the characters in the story are lovers, married, or members of the same family, there must be an explicit statement about warmth of affection.

The manual states "...if the mother, father or child is doing something <u>affiliative</u> that might be <u>expected</u> <u>only</u> because she is the mother (father or child), don't score unless further affiliation imagery is given. ...friendly, nurturant acts such as consoling, helping, being concerned about the happiness or well-being of another are regarded as evidence of affiliative feelings provided they are not culturally prescribed by the relationship between the persons" ([6], pp. 206-208).

The restrictive definition of affiliation led me to establish a coding category for culturally prescribed behaviors (CULT). It was assumed that stories about family members not scored for affiliation or power contain themes about culturally prescribed behaviors.

The manual for scoring power as fear of weakness (POW) requires counting references to "thoughts, feelings, and actions of one of the characters in a story which indicate that the character is concerned with the control of the means of influencing a person" ([7], p. 220). The manual states that affective concern can be inferred from statements about "wanting to win a point or show dominance, ..., being ashamed of an incapacity to assert one's self or become dominant, (and) resenting the influence of another and wanting to overcome this" (<u>Ibid.</u>).

The cues that were used to elicit the imaginative stories in the surveys of Americans' mental health were six pictures, representing different life situations. The following is a description of the pictures: ([8], p. 1252)

1. Two men (inventors) in a shop working at a machine.

2. Four men seated at a table with coffee cups.

3. Man (father) and children seated at breakfast table.

4. Man at drafting table.

5. Conference group. Seven men variously grouped around a conference table.

6. Woman in foreground with man standing behind and to the left.

Pictures 3,4, and 6 evoked stories about intra-family social interaction. It is likely that the outcome in Picture 4 is a response to a stimulus not mentioned in the above description; i.e., a picture on the drafting table of the man's family. Almost all the sample respondents viewed the man and woman in Picture 6 as husband and wife.[4]

In deriving motive measures, coders first score for presence or absence of imagery. Only if imagery is present do they code for strength of motive. Research has shown that raw scores for strength of motive vary with the length of the story, and that the length of the story is a function of the respondent's level of education. The motive measures used in this paper are based on presence or absence of imagery and therefore are not subject to educational bias.

Most research on the relationship between motivation and behavior uses measures of strength of motivation averaged over situations. This paper uses situation specific information about presence or absence of motivation.

4. ANALYSIS OF MOTIVATION

Since Becker's argument for the dominance of altruism in the family rests on the assumption that the husband loves his wife, the key picture for testing his theory is Picture 6. Stories about Picture 6 are most often about arguments between husband and wife. In the affiliation stories, the emphasis is on restoring a state of warmth between the couple. In the power stories the emphasis is on one person trying to persuade the other to accept his/her viewpoint.

Sample stories about Picture 6 were coded for reference to money and the control of possessions.[5] 32% of the stories scored for power as fear of weakness contained references to money and the control of possessions. None of the stories scored for affiliation contained such references. My inference is that in marriages based on pseudo-love, money is an instrument for expressing the need for control, rather than warmth of affection.

Table 1 shows the relation between the husband's motivation towards his wife, his children, and the family as a whole. The bottom row shows the absolute frequencies of four kinds of motivation towards wife (Picture

Table 1

Percentage Distribution of Motivation in Picture 6 by Presence of Affiliation and Power in Other Pictures Pertaining to the Family

	AFF	POW	POWAF	CULT
Presence of Affiliation				
Picture 3	26%*	21%	19%	15%
Picture 4	65	57	58	53
Presence of Power				
Picture 3	31	52	46	33
Picture 4	1	0	4	0
N, Column				
Picture 6	74	42	26	181

* 26% of the 74 heads of households who perceive affiliation imagery in Picture 6 also perceive affiliation imagery in Picture 3. 31% perceive power imagery in Picture 3. Some may perceive both affiliation and power imagery in Picture 3.

6). The columns show the husband's perception of his children (Picture 3) and the family as a whole (Picture 4). The AFF column shows the perceptions of a loving husband; the POW column, the perceptions of a husband motivated by fear; the POWAF column, the perceptions of a husband motivated by love and fear; and the CULT column, the perceptions of a husband motivated to perform culturally prescribed acts.

The percentage distribution of the frequencies in the bottom row shows: 23% of Picture 6 stories are affiliative, 13% are about power as fear of weakness, 8% have mixed imagery, and 56% are about culturally prescribed behavior. The salient finding is that a minority of husbands love their wives. Doubt is cast on the validity of Becker's argument for the dominance of altruism in the family. However love is more common than pseudo-love.

To counter the argument that the definition of affiliative is too restrictive to constitute a fair test of Becker's theory, examine the correlation between the husband's motivation towards his wife and his motivation towards his children in Picture 3. The proportion of affiliative husbands who are also affiliative towards their children is 26%, significantly greater than 15%, the proportion of culturally motivated husbands who are affiliative towards their children (p value = .10).[6] The data support Becker's and Fromm's position that loving husbands are also loving fathers.

The table also shows that fear plays a significant role in motivating behavior towards children, confirming Boulding's insight. However 52% of the men who are motivated by fear towards their wives perceive power imagery in the father-children picture, significantly more than the cultural norm of 33% (p value = .05). Given that motivation precedes behavior, this finding supports Fromm's theory that parental anxiety is transmitted to children. The data in the table do not support the hypothesis that men who love their children have lower power motivation towards them.

The strongest evidence for the assumption that love is the dominant motivation in the family comes from stories about Picture 4, the picture of a man at work with a picture of his family on his desk. The cue value for affiliation is higher in this picture than in the other pictures. The fact that the percentage of affiliation imagery perceived in this picture is higher for the men who also scored affiliation in the husband-wife picture supports the inference that the husband-wife picture identifies a segment of the population that is more loving. Because the cue value for arousing a motive varies by picture, an accurate measure of motivation should be based on a large number of pictures.

5. CONCLUSIONS

The motive measures introduced in this paper are used to explain differences in family income in another paper (Phelps, [14]). In that paper, the husband's motivation in work situations is related to his motivation towards his wife. It is necessary to take account of motivation in the work place to explain differences in power motivation towards children and differences in income.

Becker postulates that households headed by altruists maximize family income. The highest family incomes are in households headed by professional and managerial husbands who love their wives. Those households are a minority.

The motive measures introduced in this paper have many other applications. Following Grossbard-Schectman, they can be used to differentiate between real and faked virtue. They can also be used to explain inter-family differences in response to unemployment (Kirchler, [15]). A study showing the relation between Kirchler's measures of love and power and the TAT measures would be welcome.

ACKNOWLEDGEMENTS

My test of Becker's theory of altruism in the family is extended and developed in an article which has been accepted by the Journal of Economic Behavior and Organization [14]. The paper in this volume takes account of comments made by an anonymous referee for that article and comments made by participants at the session on the economic psychlogy of the family at the International Conference on Economics and Psychology, Kibbutz, Shefayim, Israel, 1986.

(FOOT)NOTES AND REFERENCES

1. The gender distinction between altruist and beneficiary is made by Becker for clarity of exposition.

2. The motivation data from the 1976 survey were obtained in early 1986 and are now being analyzed.

3. The definition of adequate response is given in Veroff, Atkinson, Feld, and Gurin ([11], p. 11).

4. I examined sample protocols for Picture 3, 4, and 6. Copies of stories scored for affiliation and power were purchased with funds from a Temple University Grant-in-Aid of Research.

5. The stories were scored for references to money and the control of possessions by my research assistant and checked by me. I did not make a record of scoring reliability.

6. The scoring reliabilities for coding the stories are reported in ([11], p. 9). The percentage of imagery agreement ranged from 73 to 89 for affiliation and from 67 to 84 for power. Given the variability in coding reliability, the choice of a minimum level of significance equal to 10% is rigorous.

[1] Becker, Gary S., 1974, A Theory of Social Interactions, Journal of Political Economy, 82, No. 6, 1063-1093.
[2] Becker, Gary, S., 1981, A Treatise on the Family (Harvard, Cambridge, Mass.).
[3] Boulding, Kenneth E., 1973, The Economy of Love and Fear (Wadsworth, Belmont, California).
[4] Smith, Adam, 1853, The Theory of Moral Sentiments (Henry G. Bohn, London).
[5] Grossbard-Shechtman, Amyra, this volume, Virtue, Work, and Marriage.
[6] Heyns, Roger, W., Joseph Veroff, and John W. Atkinson, 1958, A Scoring Manual for the Affiliation Motive, in: John W. Atkinson, ed., Motives in Fantasy, Action and Society (Van Nostrand, Princeton). pp. 205-218.
[7] Veroff, Joseph, 1958, A Scoring Manual for the Power Motive in: John W. Atkinson, ed., Motives in Fantasy, Action and Society (Van Nostrand, Princeton).
[8] Veroff, Joseph, Charlene Depner, Richard Kulka, and Elizabeth Douvan, 1980, A Comparison of American Motives: 1957 Versus 1976, Journal of Personality and Social Psychology, 39, No. 6, 1249-1262.
[9] Veroff, Joseph and Joanne B. Veroff, 1972, Reconsideration of a

Measure of Power Motivation, Psychological Bulletin, 78, No. 4, 279-291.
[10] Gurin, Gerald, Joseph Veroff, and Sheila Feld, 1975, Americans View Their Mental Health, SSA Study Number 3503, Survey Research Center, Institute for Social Research, Ann Arbor.
[11] Veroff, Joseph, John W. Atkinson, Sheila Feld, and Gerald Gurin, 1960, The Use of Thematic Apperception to Assess Motivation in a Nationwide Interview Study, Psychological Monographs, 94, No. 12 (Whole No. 499).
[12] Fromm, Erich, 1939, Selfishness and Self-Love, Psychiatry, 2, 507-523.
[13] Pollack, Robert A., 1985, A Transaction Cost Approach to Families and Households, Journal of Economic Literature, 23, No. 2, 581-608.
[14] Phelps, Charlotte DeMonte, forthcoming, Caring and Family Income, Journal of Economic Behavior and Organization.
[15] Kirchler, Erich, this volume, Job Loss and Marital Power.

Virtue, Work and Marriage

AMYRA GROSSBARD-SHECHTMAN.
Department of Economics, San Diego State University
San Diego, CA 92182

This paper analyzes the benefits of virtue to employers and derives a demand for virtue and seemingly virtuous behavior. People supply such behavior, in part as the result of incentives employers create. Among the major insights of this market model of virtue are the value of being married, individual investment in virtue, and the value to the state of helping virtue be general rather than specific.

"In the long run, the public interest depends on private virtue" James A. Wilson [1]

I. INTRODUCTION

The public interest depends on private virtue. So do private interests. Firms benefit from virtuous workers to the extent that workers committed to their employer display a smaller tendency to quit and are less likely to destroy their firm's equipment. As was pointed out by Arrow [2] "every commercial transaction has within itself an element of trust". Trust, a component of virtue, facilitates productivity not only within a firm, but also in transactions of all kinds.

People and firms will therefore prefer to associate with virtuous, trustworthy, people. But information on other people's virtue is extremely difficult to obtain. This explains why firms often rely on polygraphs and graphological tests. Firms may also consider their candidates' past behavior in other areas, especially if this behavior has often indicated an underlying tendency for virtue in the past. Such behavior I call "seemingly virtuous behavior." If married men tend to be more virtuous than unmarried men, marital status functions as a signal indicating higher virtue. This is one possible reason why married men tend to earn more than unmarried men. It may also explain a few social aspects of corporate and bureaucratic organizations generally overlooked by economists.

If seemingly virtuous behavior is rewarded, individual may invest in such behavior and in virtue. I apply Becker's [3] distinction between general and specific human capital, and develop a market for seemingly virtuous behavior.

2. THE DEMAND FOR VIRTUE

Virtue, called V, can not be observed. What is observable is behavior v termed "seemingly virtuous behavior." The observer does not know, however, whether v is behavior out of true virtue or faked virtue. I am now analyzing the demand for an individual's seemingly virtuous behavior by another party, such as an employer. Assume $v = v(V)$ has a positive derivative, which means that seemingly virtuous behavior is likely to reflect real virtue. The employer may be basing such generalization on past experience.

V increases a worker's i productivity, as reflected in production function 2
(2) $Q = f(t_i, k, V_i)$, where Q is output, t time worker i spends at work, and K physical capital at work. The cross-derivatives of Q by t and V by V and K are positive, i.e. V reinforces the productivity of labor and capital.

V's positive effect on productivity may be due to V's discouraging effect on the probability to quit, which in turn leads to higher levels of specific training. Workers' virtue also reduces shirking and could save the firm monitoring costs. The worker is less likely to misuse capital. If one also adds time of other workers to the production function, an additional source of shirking lies in the absence of well-defined property rights. Once a worker operates with a team his individual extra work effort is a public good. Therefore, individual workers have an incentive to shirk and be free-riders (Leibenstein [4]) with respect to their team or the firm as a whole. Virtue reduces free-riding tendencies by employees, and therefore increases worker's productivity. Virtue in this context is similar to loyalty or discipline, and the statements above remind of some previous literature. Marxist economists, for instance, wrote about the value employers derive from a well-disciplined work force (Himmelweit and Mohun [5], Bowles [6]). Maital and Maital [7] consider cooperative workers as a benefit to firms. Ouchi [8] finds that loyalty enhances productivity in Japanese firms and Z-organizations in the U.S.

Employers are consequently willing to pay higher wages to more virtuous workers. Given the fact that virtue is not observable and that V and v are positively correlated, employers will be willing to pay higher wages to workers who display seemingly virtuous behavior.

A firm's demand for seemingly virtuous behavior is downward sloping if the marginal utility of V is diminishing. An aggregate demand for v by employers, the sum of individual demands, is depicted in Figure 1. I now discuss factors that could shift that demand.

Employers will demand more seemingly virtuous behavior the larger V's contribution to productivity, and the more v is associated with V. In turn, V is more likley to be valuable to employers (a) in more capital-intensive jobs, (b) when type of contract makes shirking more likely. For instance, if workers are paid by the hour shirking is more likely than if workers are paid by piece-rate, (c) in large corporations or bureaucracies when it is easier for a worker to act as a free rider at the expense of fellow workers, (d) in cases where quites are more costly, in part a matter of industrial structure. In Japan, for example, expected job tenure is higher than in the United States, (e) where a worker is employed in a task more amenable to shirking. For example, it is easier to shirk for a worker employed in marketing than for a worker producing a physical object (see Barzel [9]), and to the extent that emphasis on loyalty hinders creativity, (f) in less creative tasks (see Maital and Maital [7] p. 94 on innovation and corporate culture). The demand for v is also larger the more v is likely to vary positively with V. This is more likely if V is of a more general nature. Before this can be explained, let me give examples of seemingly virtuous behavior. Any human relation can serve as evidence of virtue. Employers may investigate whether a person is known as a good worker, a good son or daughter, a good husband or wife, a good soldier, a good tenant, or a good citizen.

A candidate's observed family behavior often serves as a form of v playing an important role in hiring and promotion. Employers may investigate marital status, duration of marriage, marital fidelity, or number of children. Employers' preference for virtue and married men's higher virtue relatively to unmarried men is one possible explanation for the higher wages married workers have been observed to receive, keeping standard wage determinants constant.[1] Alternative explanations for such marital differentials in men's earnings are (1) that married men acquire more human capital and (2) that the relation between marital status and earnings is spurious. The men with higher incomes are more likely to be married (see Becker's [10] "Economics of Marriage".) The latter and the explanation based on virtue could also account for the fact that married women do not earn more than unmarried women.

The "economics of marriage" explanation is that women earning more are less likely to be married. The "seemingly virtuous" explanation for differential effects of marriage on men and women is that exemplary and stable marital behavior is more likely to indicate true virtue in the case of men than in the case of women. This follows from biologically or culturally given differences which lead women to benefit from marital stability more than men. Men who stay married despite the basic forces driving them in the opposite direction are more likely to be virtuous than women who more often prefer to stay married. This argument is pursued and gender asymetry in individual preferences for commitment in marriage is documented in Grossbard-Shechtman [11].

The value employers place on seemingly virtuous behavior is expected to increase with worker's potential productivity. Therefore, the positive differential between the earnings of married and unmarried men is expected to be larger in the case of corporate executives than among other workers with similar characteristics.

The following are suggestive facts. In 1969, 93.1% of the male managers earning $15,000 or more (nearly all managers) were married. That percentage rose as salaries increased. Senior executives also seem to be much more likely to stay married to the same wife than men in the same age bracket. For instance, according to a recent survey of children (between 14 and 22 years old) of senior executives in U.S. corporations with sales of $70 million or more, only a surprisingly low 8 percent had parents who had ever been separated or divorced (Crossen [12]). In contrast, the father of an average child in that age group who would on the average be 40 years old in 1980 had approximately a 30 percent probability of having been divorced (Schoen et al., [13]). An alternative interpretation seems unconvincing. In principle, causality could run the other way: the high income earned by executive could increase the likelihood of marriage and reduce the likelihood of divorce. But men earning higher incomes have a higher tendency been found to divorce more often than men with average incomes. In particular, Becker, Landes, and Michael [14] have shown that men earning more than would be expected at time of marriage (possibly the case of many successful corporation managers) are more likely to get divorced than men earning what was expected.

Family men (true and faking) also have an incentive to advertise their seemingly virtuous family behavior. Accordingly, Kanter [15] reports that in a large corporation pictures of wives and children adorned men's offices so commonly that they seemed almost mandatory.

The demand for seemingly virtuous behavior is expected to be higher in Japan, where tenure is expected to be larger. Accordingly, rewards to married workers seem more substantial in Japan than in the United States. For instance, although in the United States some doors close to unmarried candidates in the corporate and political world, that is very obviously the case in Japan where firms even act as marriage-brokers (Browning [16]).

Firms also appear to value seemingly virtuous behavior in the form of service to the community. Heroism demonstrated at war often serves as a wage booster in countries with a recent history of war. For instance, when they leave the army Israeli officers with a heroic war record obtain jobs that are better than jobs offered to people with otherwise comparable credentials and experience. It is expected that even at peace time people who volunteer to more dangerous military positions are likely to reap some benefits from it when applying for positions for which a tendency for virtue is particularly appreciated.

A piece of Japanese economic history can also reinforce this viewpoint. An often mentioned partial explanation for 19th century Japan's economic revolution is the availability of a <u>samurai</u> class who had been trained both as warriors and as bureaucrats espousing the Confucion principle of public virtue. These same <u>samurai</u> later became the captains of a modern factory system (see for instance, Clark [17], Morishima [18]). Their Confucian ideology stressing virtue benefited their own advancement as well as that of Japanese industry.

Public employers are expected to value virtuous employees for the same reasons that they are valued by large corporations. The more bureaucratic an organization the more shirking is potentially beneficial and the harder it is to monitor work efforts. It is consequently not surprising that the ultimate employers in a democracy, the taxpayers, seem to pay a lot of attention to seemingly virtuous behavior when voting for politicians. Voters seem to look for leaders capable of transcending self-interested motivations (Hirshleifer [19]). They often value any superficial indication of such motivation as expressed by the apparently virtuous attitudes of politicians towards wife, children, and even grandchildren. Heroism in war (and space) seems to be rewarded in politics too. Finally, politicians can generally improve their public image by ostentatiously attending church services.

In non-democratic regimes aspiring public servants can also reap benefits from displaying seemingly virtuous behavior and from openly espousing benevolent ideologies. Perhaps even more so than in democracies, as the potential losses the public stands to loose from shirking by its "servants" are so large. The traditional Chinese and Japanese tested their bureaucrats for their knowledge of Confucian principles. Candidates for leadership in the Catholic church and Marxist regimes need to appear as staunch defendants of the loftier parts of the official doctrines.

Spouses can also be viewed as each other's employers. Marriage markets of the kind analyzed by Becker [10† and Grossbard-Shechtman [22], [20], [21] establish wages for household labor in ways similar to those observed in more conventional labor markets. It is therefore predicted that people displaying seemingly virtuous behavior outside their marriage receive higher quasi-wages in marriage. Although measurement problems make quantitative applications of this theory to the family harder to come by, the importance of virtue to families may make this theory even more relevant to the family than to the firm or the government (see Maital and Maital [7]).

The generality of virtue is an important element of the demand for seemingly virtuos behavior. If a good husband is also a good worker, his virtue is of a general nature. If what makes a soldier or a worker good is of use to others, his virtue is general and not specific to the context in which he operated. The more virtue is of a general nature, the more seemingly virtuous behavior expressed in one system of behavior is applicable to other spheres, and the higher the demand for v.

3. Supply

3.1 Short Run Supply

At any given time t, an individual can engage in j kinds of seemingly virtuous activities. To the individual some or all v_{tj}'s may be unrelated or negatively related to (the stock of) V. (What made v a positive function of V to the employer was a general trend based on past experience). As an example, a two-period utility function is presented in 3

$$(3)\ U = U_1[v_{11}(V), v_{12}(V), \ldots v_{1N}(V), x_1] + U_2[v_{21}(V), v_{22}(V) .. V_{2N}, x_2] \quad ,$$

where is a discount factor and x_t market goods. Activity v_{t1} is work in period t. Other activities could be various forms of leisure or work performed for a spouse, as in Grossbard-Shechtman [22]. It is assumed that no activities are joint. The individual maximizes 3 subject to time constraint

$$(4)\ T_v = \underset{j=1}{} v_{tj} \quad \text{, and a budget constraint 5}$$

$$(5)\ w_1 v_{11}(V) + w_2(v_{11}, , \ldots, v_{1N}) v_{21}(V)/(1+r) = p_1 x_1 + p_2 x_2/(1+r).$$

The first activity is assumed to be the only one generating income. The individual knows that his wage in period 2, w_2, varies positively with past seemingly virtuous behavior. Consequently, he might invest in some activities v_{tj} with the sole purpose of increasing future wages, or he may engage in more such activity than he would based on its direct utility.

For example, individuals may get married in period one and display exemplary devotion to their family, thereby increasing their wage in period two. Some activities may be consciously chosen in period one in order to advertise one's potential for virtue. Volunteers to the marines or other relatively dangerous assignments may have such investment in mind. (In that sense volunteer activities generate information as a beneficial side effect).

The supply of a seemingly virtuous activity v_j is upward sloping if the marginal disutility of engaging in such activity v_j increases with v_j. By definition virtue implies that an individual gives up some personal utility for the benefit of others. The disutility of v_j can be expressed in terms of the foregone utility of another v_j producing more utility at the margin (follows from the first-order conditions of optimization). The higher the return to v_j in terms of higher wages in the next period, the more a person is willing to engage in v_j and to move along his supply curve. The better the substitutes to v_j available to the individual, the more elastic the supply.

More virtuous people, i.e. people with higher stocks of V, will have a supply that lies to the right of that of people who are less virtuous. It is also expected that for many activities v_{tj} virtuous people will supply a positive number of hours at zero wage. The supply of some activities may be more wage elastic than that of others, depending on various institutional (e.g. religious) and technical constraints.

The individual faking virtue is giving up much less when engaging in a given form of v_j than the individual who really attempts to serve others' needs. Consequently, fakers may supply more of a given type of v_j than genuinely virtuous people.[2]

The aggregate supply of time devoted to a particular seemingly virtuous activity is obtained by aggregating individual supplies.

3.2 Long Run Supply

The model could also be expanded to include investment in V. Virtue may be learned from experience. In that case the stock of V in period 2 would increase when the person engages in seemingly virtuous activities in period 1.3

Individuals could also invest in their stock of V by consciously altering the "internal locus of control" governing their behavior. (If they solely fake virtue they are influenced by an "external locus of control" such as the firm that will reward them[4] or the concerned father analyzed by Becker in the Rotten Kid theorem).

Virtue can be acquired in various ways. Whether the mechanisms for value acquisition involve the intellect, feelings, actions, or a combination of these, is an issue beyond this paper's scope. In any case, deliberate exposure to other virtuous people seems like one possible desirable strategy which involves at least some learning-by-doing.

This type of voluntary reinforcement of one's virtuous tendencies is a case of deliberate character planning, and relates to the idea of pre-commitment which has previously been discussed by economists. Akerloff and Dickens [23], for instance, report that when given freedom in job selection, workers tend to show signs of cognitive dissonance, i.e., they build beliefs whereby they perceive their work as safer than it actually is. Van Raaij [24] mentions that people may take ski or piano lessons in order to learn to appreciate skiing or music, an example more directly related to the learning-by-doing of virtue. Similarly, individuals may seek the company of virtuous people in marriage, friendship, religious groups, or at work.

Precommitment to virtuous groups reminds of Thaler and Shefrin's [25] Christmas clubs and Schelling's [26] discussion of self-management. Exposed to short run benefits obvious to the doer part of their personality (immediate spending) and long run benefits their planner is aware of (Christmas shopping), people may decide to join Christmas clubs where they receive lower interest on their savings but a guarantee that money will be available right before Christmas. Likewise, people may join Alcoholics Anonymous or Weight Watchers [24] or, more relevant here, a group emphasizing virtue.

4. Market and State

A market for seemingly virtuous behavior v_j is generated when the demand for the v_j workers displayed in period 1, by employers in period two is juxtaposed to the supply by workers responding to rewards in period 2. For a given level of faking, in a market with a lot of seemingly virtuous workers, employers end up paying little extra for such workers. Where virtue is scarce, they pay a large bonus for workers who seem to be virtuous. If people become less virtuous over time, this would imply that the bonus to virtuous workers would increase. It is possible for example, as suggested by Charlotte Phelps, that the aggregate supply of seemingly virtuous behavior shifted to the left between 1957 and 1976.

Veroff's measure of power motivation in situations where men and women interact, the measure Phelps [27] used in her own work, increased during those years. This would imply that the premium for marital stability would also have increased during those years.

The demand and the supply are not independent, since one of the factors shifting the demand is the percentage of fakers. The more fakers, the lower the demand and the more the supply shifts to the right, as engaging in v_j is very cheap to fakers.

One can construct separate markets for different kind of workers. In the market for v_j by executives, one expects a high demand for v_j, as virtue is very important to the employer. The more executives are willing to engage in virtuous activities, i.e. the more the supply shifts to the right, the lower the actual reward for engaging in v_j. Employers clearly benefit from a virtuous population.

The state benefits from a virtuous population in its capacity of employer. Moreover, if it relies on volunteering, virtuous citizens with the necessary skills are more likely to volunteer to state institutions such as the army. To the extent that the state embodies the public good, a more virtuous citizenry will also increase the public good (Weisbrod [28], Hirshleifer [19], Maital and Maital [7], Guttman [29]). As a result, it is in the state's interest to promote virtue. The state can do this directly by taking an active role in educating and regulating the public. Alternatively. following this paper's basic argument, the state can encourage individual investments in virtue by emphasizing the generality of individual virtuous tendencies. By promoting the general acceptance of well-established standards of virtue and seemingly virtuous behavior, the state increases the benefits individuals can derive from behaving virtuously.

For instance, let us assume a given "stock" of virtue in the population, where a considerabel part of that virtue is oriented towards in-groups such as specific families, firms, tribes, or religious groups. If such virtue lacks generality the potential benefits individuals can reap from acting virtuously are limited. If the state intervenes and encourages substitution of more universal virtue for the virtue existing within groups, individuals can gain more from being virtuous; consequently more investment in virtue will occur and the total stock of virtue will rise.

States have played a major role in increasing the generality of virtue. One often used strategy towards that goal is for the state to adopt an official religion, such as Anglicanism in England, Confucianism in China, or Lutheranism in Sweden. National standardization of virtuous tendencies can also be achieved through a variety of national symnbols and standards such as royalty, presidency, or a Constitution. Historically, stronger national standards of virtue have often been promoted at the cost of emphasizing differences between the nation and the rest of the world. State religions and more recently fascist nationalistic ideologies such as nazism have frequently strengthened individual incentives to be helpful fellow citizens by instigating extreme forms of hatred towards groups defined as outsiders.

Besides generating repugnant by-products such as mass murder of minorities or wars, institutionalized religions and nationalism have often been detrimental to individual well-being due to beliefs, laws, and policies impeding economic growth. It is therefore difficult to use comparative data to test the hypothesis that states can benefit economically by standardizing the criteria for virtue accepted by their citizens. Nevertheless, I find that some of the most dramatic jumps in economic growth observed in the past can be used as suggestive evidence for the hypothesis advanced here. For instance, Europe's transformation from separate feudal fiefs into national boundaries helped its econmic expansion because it reduced the amount of internal malevolence (violence) inside a country, as is commonly argued by economic historians.

Given the contribution of private virtue to the public interest and the other benefits of virtue mentioned above, one may view the emergence of modern economic growth in Europe as the result not only of the neutralization of inter-tribal and other internal malevolence, but also of the inculcation of national standards of virtue. The same perspective can also be used to integrate the often-noted fact that England and Japan, two of the most noteworthy examples of industrial revolution, are islands in which more of a distinctive national character had developed than in the adjacent mainland. This enabled more investment in virtue, and consequently more economic growth.

As to the United States' economic success, among its characteristics one may count the fact that it is not confined to the fifty states of the union (most multinational corporations originated in the United States) or to a relatively uniform ethnic-national-religious group. These pluralistic aspects of the American economy are related to the open nature of the basic standards for individual virtue promoted in the American Constitution and other institutions central to the United States.

5. Summary

Employers appreciate virtue in workers and are willing to pay a bonus or promote workers who seem to be virtuous. Workers are willing to act as if they were virtuous or to actually be virtuous, in part as a result of the incentives employers give them. Among the insights the market model presented here has generated one can count (1) the value of general virtue versus behavior specifically good for a particular group, (2) a list of the determinants of seemingly virtuous behavior, (3) the idea of investment in virtue, and (4) implications for public policy.

FOOTNOTES

*I am indebted to Joel Guttman for stimulating my interest in this paper, to Jack Hirshleifer, Michael Naughton, Harinder Singh and participants at the Second Annual Conference of the Society for the Advancement of Behavioral Economics and at a Seminar at Bar-Ilan University for helpful comments and to Maureen McDonnell for skillful typing.

1. For more on the relation between marriage and productivity at work, see Grossbard-Shechtman [30].

2. To these hypocrits one can apply the statement by Pope "Hypocrisy is the tribute that vice pays to virtue" (citation contributed by Jack Hirshleifer).

3. This is a major justification rabbis give for the biblical commandments that ment get married and be nice to their wife during the first year of marriage. Note that women are not commanded to get married'

4. These kinds of locus of control have been introduced by Rotter [31]. Becker's [32] concerned father displays what I call seemingly virtuous behavior to his children. It is not clear if he is truly virtuous when he gives goods to his children, see also Phelps [27].

REFERENCES

[1] Wilson, Q., "The Rediscovery of Character, Private Virtue and Public Policy," The Public Interest, p. 16 (Fall 1985).
[2] Arrow, K.J., "Gifts and Exchanges," in Altruism, Morality, and Economic Theory. E. Phelps, Ed., New York: Russell Sage Foundation, 1975.
[3] Becker, G.S., Human Capital, New York: Columbia University Press (1964).
[4] Leibenstein, H., "The Prisoner's Dilemma in the Invisible Hand: An Analysis of Intrafirm Productivity," American Economic Review, Vol. 72, p. 92-97 (1982).
[5] Himmelweit, S. and Mohun, S., "Domestic Labour and Capital," Cambridge Journal of Economics, Vol. 1, p. 15-31 (1977).
[6] Bowles, S., "The Production Process in a Competitive Economy," American Economic Review, Vol. 75, p. 16-36 (1985).
[7] Maital, S. and Maital, S.L., Economic Games People Play. New York: Basic Books (1984).
[8] Ouchi, W.C., Theory Z" How American Business Can Meet the Japanese Challenge, Reading, Mass. (1981).

[9] Barzel, Y., "The Entrepreneur's Reward for Self-Policing," Economic Inquiry, forthcoming (n.d.)
[10] Becker, G.S., "A Theory of Marriage," in Economics of the Family. T.W. Schultz, Ed., Chicago: University of Chicago Press (1974).
[11] Grossbard-Shechtman, A., "A Theory of Marriage Formality: the Case of Guatemala," Economic Development and Cultural Change Vol. 30, pp. 813-830 (1982).
[12] Crossen, C., "Kids of Top Executives Are Crazy About Dad," Wall Street Journal, March 19, 1985.
[13] Schoen, R., Urton, W., Woodrow, K. and J. Baj, "Marriage and Divorce in Twentieth Century American Cohorts," Demography, Vol. 22, pp. 101-114 (1985).
[14] Becker, G.S., E.M. Landes, and R.T. Michael, "An Economic Analysis of Martial Instability." Journal of Political Economy Vol. 85(6), pp. 1141-87 (1977).
[15] Kanter, R.M., Men and Women of the Corporation, New York: Basic Books (1977).
[16] Browning, E.S. "Japan Inc. Becomes a Marriage Broker," Wall Street Journal January 3, 1985.
[17] Clark, R., The Japanese Company, New Haven: Yale University Press (1975).
18] Morishima, M., Why Has Japan 'Succeeded'? Western Technology and the Japanese Ethos. Cambridge: Cambridge University Press (1982).
[19] Hirshleifer, Jack, "On the Emotions as Guarantors of Threats and Promises," in The Latest on the Best" Essays on Evolution and Optimality, J. Dupre, Ed., Cambridge, Mass; M.I.T. Press (1987).
[20] Grossbard, A., "An Economic Analysis of Polygyny," Current Anthropology Vol. 17(4) pp. 701-7 (1976).
[21] Grossbard-Shechtman, A. "The Economics of Polygamy" in Research in Population Economics Vol. 2, J.L. Simon and J. DaVanzo, Eds., Greenwich: JAI Press (1980).
[22] ___________, "A Theory of Allocation of Time in Markets for Labor and Marriage," Economic Journal Vol. 94(4) pp. 863-82 (1984).
[23] Akerlof, G. A. and W. T. Dickens, "The Econmic Consequences of Cognitive Dissonance," American Economic Review Vol. 72, pp. 307-319. (1982).
[24] Van Raaij, F.W., "Attribution of Causality to Economic Actions and Events," Papers on Economic Psychology, Erasmus Universiteit, Amsterdamn, No. 30 (1984).
[25] Thaler, R. H. and H. M. Shefrin, "An Economic Theory of Self-Control," Journal of Political Economy, Vol. 80, pp. 392-406 (1981).
[26] Schelling, T.C., "Egonomics, or the Art of Self-Management," American Economic Review, Papers and Proceedings, Vol. 68, pp. 290-294 (1978).
[27] Phelps, C., "Caring and Family Income: Tradeoffs and Complementarity between Affiliation and Power," this volume.
[28] Weisbrod, B. A., "Comparing Utility Functions in Efficiency Terms, or, What Kind of Utility Functions Do We Want," American Economic Review Vol. 67(4) pp. 991-995 (1977).

[29] Guttman, J. M. "On Welfare Comparisons of Taste-Regimes," Ms. Bar-Ilan University (1985).

[30] Grossbard-Shechtman, A., "Marriage and Productivity--An Interdisciplinary Analysis," in Handbook of Behavioral Economics, B. Gilad and S. Kaisch, Eds., Greenwich: JAI Press forthcoming, (1986).

[31] Rotter, J. B., "Generalized Expectancies for Internal versus External Control of Reinforcement," Psychological Monographs, 80(1) (L966).

[32] Becker, G. S., "Altruism, Egoism, and Genetic Fitness: Economics and Sociobiology," Journal of Economic Literature Vol. 14(3), pp. 817-26 (1976).

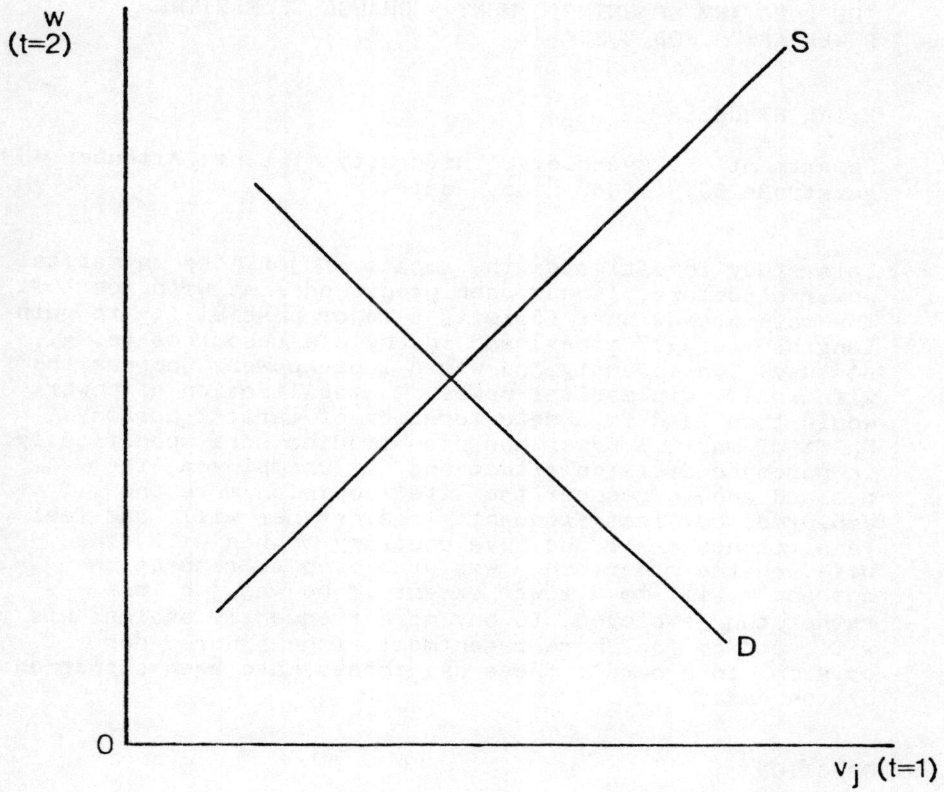

Figure 1. Market for Seemingly Virtuous Activity

THE LONG ARM OF UNEMPLOYMENT - CHANGE OF MARITAL POWER AFTER JOB LOSS*

Erich KIRCHLER

Department of Psychology, University of Linz, Altenbergerstraße 69, A-4040 Linz, Austria

This study investigates the impact of job loss on marital power structure. It has been predicted that with job loss the male breadwinner forfeits a major possibility to gain tangible (e. g., money) and intangible resources (e. g., status). Consequently, he would loose power, whereas the wife would gain marital power. Destabilization of power would then lead to a deterioration of marital harmony. Shift of marital power has been studied more specifically in purchase decision situations. If unemployed, the husband should respect the wife's opinion more than if employed, buy less frequently against her will, and feel less resentment if she buys contrary to his will. The wife, on the other hand, was predicted to respect the husband's will to a lower extent if he was job less rather than employed, to buy more frequently against his will, and to feel more resentment if he ignored her opinion. In general, these hypotheses have been supported by the data.

1. INTRODUCTION

With the economic recession in the industrialized countries of the West, unemployment has again become a major issue in social sciences. Whereas a large body of scientific information about mental and physical health problems of the unemployed individual has been accumulated during the Great Depression and recently (Ferman & Gordus, 1979; Jahoda, 1981; 1982; Kieselbach & Offe, 1979; Wacker, 1983; Warr, 1983a; 1983b; Kelvin & Jarrett, 1985), rather little attention has been paid to the detrimental impact of unemployment upon marital relationships. This study aims to explore some aspects of unemployment and its influence on couples' relationships.

In some cases, unemployment of the husband appeared to have improved the marital relationship. But those were exceptions (cf. Kieselbach & Offe, 1979; Frese & Mohr, 1978; Voydanoff, 1983; Liem & Liem, 1979; Catalano & Dooley, 1979). In general, spouses and families, respectively, lack the necessary strategies to cope with unemployment in a mutual satisfaying way. Families neither seem to be able to protect the unemployed

---

* This study has been supported by the Österreichische Institut für Arbeitsmarktpolitik, Linz, Austria.

member from sever harm nor are they successfully protecting themselves from difficulties caused by unemployment.

With job loss, a family member looses an important source to gain resources for the common use. Not only financial resource contributions diminish with unemployment, (Moen, 1983, Brinkmann, 1976) but also contributions of intangible resources (e. g., status, love; for a taxonomy of resources see Foa, 1971). Job loss of one family member, especially of the male breadwinner, changes the pattern of the member's relative resource contributions.

Resource contributions are an important base of social exchange relationships, such as the family (Nye, 1979; Safilios-Rothschild, 1976; Scanzoni, 1979), and a source of family power (Blood & Wolfe, 1960; Heer, 1965). The more resources a member can give and the more the others are in need of these resources, the higher the member's power. According to resource theory (Blood & Wolfe, 1960), a family member's influence power decreases with diminishing ability to make substantial contributions to the common budget. More generally, according to social exchange theory (Nye, 1979) its attraction or "value" depreciates with devaluation of his/her resource contributions. Thus, loosing his/her job, a family member is expected to forfeit his/her say. This causal relationship has been suggested both by studies during the Great Depression (Komarovsky, 1940) and recently (Schindler, 1979).

Job loss and destabilization of marital power patterns also challenges marital harmony. In a micro-analysis of the processes occuring in everyday life during the first six months of unemployment (Kirchler, 1984; 1985), the unemployed blamed his/her spouse, the own children, and the home in general for his/her bad mood state more frequently than reemployed did. Contrary to the optimism that close relationships become closer during periods of externally caused crises, unemployment undermines marital happiness. As Jahoda, Lazarsfeld & Zeisel (1960, p. 88) put it in their celebrated study of the 1930s, only a few families of Marienthal reported that the spousal relationship had improved after job loss. In general, insignificant dissention between the spouses became a potential issue of sever marital conflict.

In their everyday life married couples must make countless decisions. The responsibility of purchase decisions seems to be a significant area to study marital power and conflict. This study focusses specifically upon employed and unemployed couples' experiences in purchasing situations. If power of the breadwinner decreases after job loss, also his/her say in purchasing situations should decrease.

It can be assumed that marital power is reflected in a spouse's dependency upon the other's opinion in purchasing choices. Dependency is expected to be especially pronounced in situations where only one spouse desires a specific good or service. In such situations, the unemployed is expected to depend more on his/her spouse's agreement than the employed. An unemployed member making an egoistic decision (that is a decision to buy a commodity usefull only to him/her) against the other's will, can be assumed to be more affected by the resulting social costs than the employed member. Assuming that the impact of social costs will be reflected in the individual's feelings of well-being in purchase situations, it can further be expected that the unemployed spouse's mood depends more on the partner's agreement and disagreement, respectively, than the employed partner's mood.

More specifically, if the breadwinner is unemployed he/she is expected to consider the partner's agreement to a greater extent than the employed breadwinner; on the other hand, the unemployed is expected to feel less resentment if the partner decides for a purchase against his/her will than the employed. Moreover, a job less spouse should also realize an egoistic purchase against the other's will less frequently than an employed spouse.

Summarizing, the following hypotheses have been tested:

(a) In marriages with the husband being either employed or unemployed and the wife being a housewife, both spouses perceive the employed husband as outstanding contributor of tangible and intangible resources to the common budget; whereas, the unemployed husband is perceived as contributing a lower part.

(b) The less resources the husband contributes, the lower his marital power. Job loss, devaluation of resource contributions, and decrease of marital power lead consequently to a deterioration of marital harmony.

(c) In egoistic purchasing situations, employed husbands respect the wife's opinion to a lower extent than unemployed husbands, and vice versa, spouses of employed breadwinners respect his opinion to a greater extent than spouses of unemployed husbands.

(d) Employed husbands feel more resentment if the wife buys a commodity against their will than unemployed breadwinners, and vice versa, wives of employed breadwinners feel less resentment if the husband egoistically decides to buy a commodity than wives of unemployed husbands.

(e) Finally, it can be expected that an employed husband realizes more frequently an egoistic purchase against his wife's will than an unemployed husband. On the other hand, the wife of an employed husband buys less frequently against the husband's will than the spouse of a husband without a job.

1.1. Overview

The influence of unemployment upon marital relationships was tested by a questionnaire. Couples with the husband being either employed or unemployed, and the wife being a housewife, were approached and asked to rate their dominance pattern and marital harmony, The couples further had to indicate which spouse contributed the most resources to the common budget, and to describe how they feel in purchasing situations. Both spouses, wife and husband, were asked independently of each other.

2. METHOD

2.1. Subjects

The subjects were 50 couples from Linz, Austria. The husbands were employed in 26 cases; and had no job in 24 cases. They came from the same type of jobs (semiskilled and skilled workers). The wives always were housewives with no paying job.

Student interviewers approached unemployed men at the local Labor Office and asked for permission to visit them at home for presenting the questionnaire to them and their perspective partners. Approximately 5-10 % of the approached unemployed agreed to participate. (The high rejection rate is due to the fact that a high percentage of the unemployed who did not participate were either not married or they did not agree to receive the interviewer at their home). The employed couples were randomly selected from the local telephone book, called and asked for participation, and, if they agreed, visited at their home. Approximately 75 % of the approached employed couples agreed to participate. A more detailed description of the employed and unemployed samples follows in the Results-section.

2.2 Material and Procedure

The subjects were informed that the data were used for a scientific investigation only. No names appeared in the papers to assure complete anonymity.

First, the subjects were asked to rate their well-being in and the frequency of purchasing situations. After an example illustrating the type of situation descriptions and questions, the subjects had to fill out two parts of a questionnaire. While completing the questionnaire, the spouses had no eye contact with each other to ensure privacy. Part one of the questionnaire described two purchasing situations with the subject being the active spouse, that is, with the subject planning to buy a commodity. Part two of the questionnaire described two situations with the partner being the active spouse, and the subject being the passive spouse, in which the subject either agrees or disagrees with the active spouse's purchasing intentions. Figure 1 illustrates the purchasing situations which had to be imagined by both spouses.

The items of the active part read as follows:
"Imagine you want to buy a desirable commodity. The commodity is expensive, and of no use to your spouse. Your spouse thinks

Figure 1: Purchasing Situations

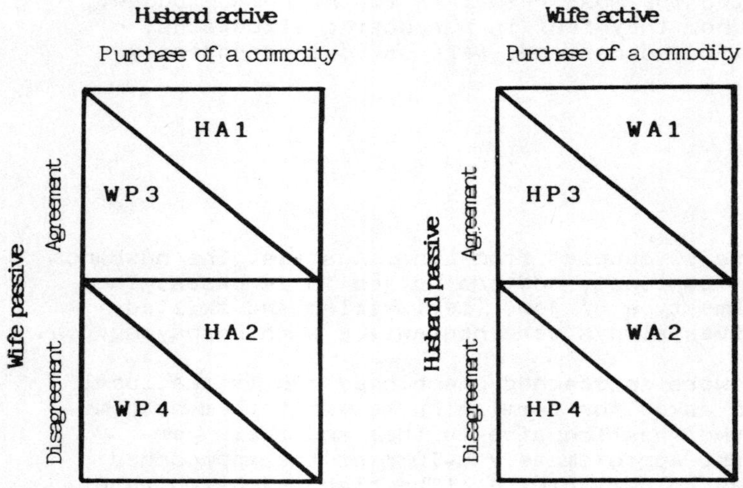

the money for the commodity could be spent otherwise or be saved. Try to imagine the different situations below as vividly as possible and indicate how well you would feel in each situation, and how frequently the specified siutation occurs in your relationship".

The following text specified two different situations: the passive partner either agreed to the purchase or disagreed; the subjects in both cases decided to buy.

1. "Imagine you want to buy the commodity, but your partner disagrees. After a short discussion, however, he/she agrees to the purchase.
Subsequently you visit the shop and buy this commodity. How would you feel ..... How often does this situation occur in your family ....."

The other situations read as follows:

2. "Imagine ..... After a short discussion, however he/she still opposes the purchase. Nevertheless, you visit the shop and buy this commodity. How would you feel ..... How often does this situation occur in your family ....."

The items of the passive part read as follows:

"Imagine your partner wants to buy a desirable commodity. The commodity is expensive, and of no use to you. You think the money for the commodity could be spent otherwise or be saved. Try to imagine ....."

3. "Imagine your spouse wants to buy this commodity, but you disagree. After a short discussion, however, you agree to the purchase.

Subsequently your partner visits the shop and buys the commodity. How would you feel ..... How often does this situation occur in your family"

4. "Imagine ..... After a short discussion, however, you still oppose the purchase. Nevertheless, your partner visits the shop and buys the commodity. How would you feel ..... How often does this situation occur in your family ....."

Each of the descriptions was followed by a scale of well-being and frequency of occurance. The scale measuring well-being ranged from 1 (feeling very bad) to 7 (feeling very good). The scale measuring the frequency of occurence of the specified situation ranged from 1 (almost never) to 5 (almost always). The wording of the questionnaires was gender appropriate for wives and husbands.

Subsequently, the subjects were asked to indicate their marital power structure (two questions asked to indicate how much say the subject and his/her spouse has. The wording of the questions was: "In our relationship my partner has the say"), and marital happiness (four questions asked to indicate how much the spouses loved each other, their happiness, cohesion, and mutual acceptance. The wording of the questions was: "I am happy with my partner", "My partner accepts me as I am", "My partner loves me", and "Our relationship is harmonious"). Each question was followed by a rating scale ranging from 1 (agree) to 5 (disagree).

Next, each respondent indicated how much of each resource out of Foa's (1971) taxonomy; namely status, love, information, money, goods and services; each spouse contributes for the common use. This was assessed by asking each spouse to partition a square, which symbolically indicated 100 % of the common budget of the specific resource, into two parts which correspond to the parts contributed by him/her and his/her spouse. The six resources have been circumscribed according to Foa's (1971, p. 171) definition as follows: "Love" is an "expression of affectionate regard, warmth, or comfort; "Status" is an expression of evaluative judgment which conveys high or low prestige, regard, or esteem; "Information includes advice, opinions, instruction, or enlightment, but excludes those behaviors which could be classed as love or status; "money" is any coin, currency, or token which has some standard unit of exchange value; "goods" are tangible products, objects, or materials; and "services" involve activities on the body or belongings of a person which often constitute labor for another".

Finally, each spouse indicated the following social date: (a) age; (b) education level, (c) years living in the common household; (d) number of children; (e) employment status, and if unemployed, length of unemployment in months; (f) amount of money earned per month; and (g) amount of money at disposal in the household.

After completion of the questionnaire, which took approximately 30 minutes, the couples were debriefed and released.

3. RESULTS

3.1. Comparison of Employed and Unemployed Couples

First, both samples of employed and unemployed couples have been compared in respect of social indexes, in order to assure appropriate hypotheses testing. As Table 1 shows, no differences in demographic characteristics have been found between employed and unemployed couples except for the husband's average monthly income. It is not surprising that unemployment insurance is significantly lower than the average income of employed men.

Table 1: Demographic Characteristics of Employed and Unemployed Couples

	Employed Couples (n = 26)	Unemployed Couples (n = 24)	t-test F	df	p
Age					
Husband	31.88 (8.632)	29.54 (10.048)	.89	48	.38
Wife	30.15 (9.160)	27.48 (8.687)	1.02	48	.31
Education					
Elementary School					
Husband	3	2			
Wife	3	4			
Middle School					
Husband	11	11			
Wife	16	11			
High School					
Husband	12	11			
Wife	7	9			
Months Living in a Common Household	94.27 (92.929)	76.92 (96.016)	.65	48	.52
N of Children					
0	12	9			
1	6	12			
2	3	3			
3	5	0			
4	1	0			

Husband's Monthly Net Income (Austrian Shillings)	15,326	10,104	2.47	45	.02
Duration of Unemployment (months) 1	-	3			
2	-	5			
3	-	3			
4 to 6	-	6			
6 to 12	-	5			
more than 12	-	2			

Note: Numbers indicate means of frequencies, standard deviations (in parentheses), and F-values, degrees of freedom, and probabilities.

3.2. Husband's Employment Status and Perception of Resource Contributions

Hypothesis (a) predicted that the husband would be perceived as contributing the major part of resources to the common budget if he had a paid job, and a considerable lower part if he had no job. Resource contributions of husband and wife were measured by assessing the percentage of both spouses' contributions of the six resources (Foa, 1971). A 2 (employment status) by 2 (sex, within factor) Manova on spouses' perception of husband's contributions of the six resources as dependent variables, yielded a significant main effect for unemployment status ($F(7,33) = 3.42$; $p = .01$). No interaction effect and no main effect for sex have been obtained. Univariate analyses yielded significant effects for husband's contributions of money ($F(1,39) = 20.07$; $p = .00$) and status ($F(1,38) = 5.20$; $p = .03$). As shown in Table 2, both spouses perceived the employed husband as contributing more money to the common budget and providing more status related resources than the unemployed husband.

Table 2: Unemployed Husbands' and Wives' Perception of Resource Contributions

	Employed Couples (n = 26)		Unemployed Couples (n = 24)		Analyses of Variance		
					Main Effect "Employment Status"		
Type of Resource	Husband	Wife	Husband	Wife	F	df	p
Love	47.62	49.87	51.95	46.54	< 1	1,39	.81
Money	67.04	75.43	42.64	46.43	20.07	1,39	.00
Services	43.12	41.73	44.05	40.58	< 1	1,39	.98
Goods	52.88	51.34	49.92	50.11	< 1	1,39	.50

Status	56.75	64.42	48.92	50.54	5.20	1,38	.03
Information	47.87	52.01	46.10	41.34	2.38	1,39	.13
Average Resource Contributions	52.55	55.80	47.26	45.92	3.42	6,33	.01

Note: Numbers indicate the percentage of perceived husband resource contributions. The wife's contributions can easily be computed by substracting the husband's part from 100 %.

As Table 2 shows, employed husbands rated their contributions of money higher (67 %) than the wives' contributions of money (33 %), and so did the wives (75 % versus 25 %). Unemployed husbands, on the other hand, indicated to contribute less money (43 %) than the wives (57 %). Similar results have been reported by the wives (46 % versus 54 %). Also the husbands' contributions to the marital status were higher when they were employed (husbands' and wives' estimations were 57 % and 64 %, respectively) rather than unemployed (49 % and 51 %, respectively).

3.3. Marital Power and Harmony by Husband's Employment Status

With decrease of resource contributions, power of the husband was predicted to decrease too. Power has been assessed by asking each spouse separately who had the most say in the partnership. Answers on the two power questions were averaged and analyzed by a two way analysis of variance (employment status, sex). Both spouses reported significant decrease of husband's power after job loss ($M = 3.47$ and 2.99 for hubands with and without jobs, respectively; $F(1,48) = 9.85$; $p = .003$). No main effect for sex and no interaction effect were found.

Similarly as for marital power, ratings on marital happiness have been averaged and analyzed by a two-way Anova. No significant main and interaction effects have been obtained ($F(1,48) < 1$).

It has been predicted that with job loss the breadwinners also loose a substantial source to gain resources for the common use. Decrease of resource contributions would then be followed by a decrease of marital power, and consequently, destabilization of established power patterns would challenge marital harmony. These linear causal relationships have been investigated by a path analysis, including the following variables: (a) length of unemployment (length of unemployed husbands was indicated in months out of job; employed husbands scored zero), (b) average spouses' perception of husband's resource contributions, (c) spouses' ratings of marital power, and (d) average spouses' ratings of marital harmony. The resulting path diagram is presented in Figure 2.

Figure 2: Path Analysis of Length of Unemployment, Husband's Average Resource Contributions, Husband's Marital Power, and Marital Harmony

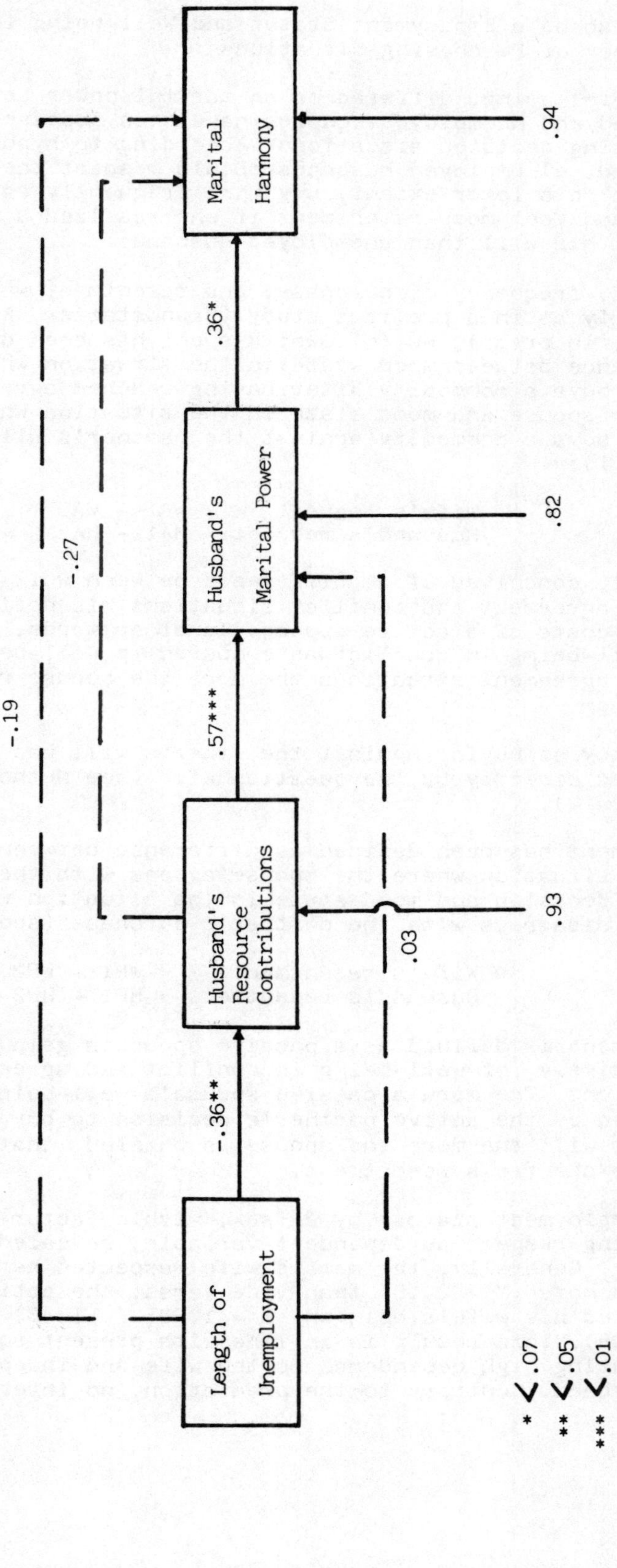

3.4. Husband's Employment Status and Well-being in and Frequency of Purchasing Situations

In the following, differences on marital power between employed and unemployed couples have been assessed in purchasing decision situations. According to hypotheses (c), (d), and (e) employed husbands should respect their wife's opinion to a lower extent, buy more frequently against her will, and feel more resentment if she realized a purchase against his will than unemployed husbands.

Respect, frequency of purchase, and resentment were assessed, similarly as in a previous study (Brandstätter, Kirchler & Wagner, in press), as follows: Respect has been defined as difference between mood state in the situation where the spouse buys a commodity after having reached agreement with his/her spouse and mood state in the situation where the spouse buys a commodity against the partner's will (see Figure 1):

Wife's respect = WA1 - WA2
Husband's respect = HA1 - HA2

Respect, conceived of as difference between well-being in mutual agreement and conflict situations, is defined by the social costs of a active spouse. In other words, the lower the well-being in conflict as compared to well-being in mutual agreement situations the more the spouse respects the other.

Frequency of buying against the other's will has been assessed directly by the questionnaire (see Method section, question 2).

Resentment has been defined as difference between mood state in the situation where the spouse agrees with the partner's buying decision and mood state in the situation where the spouse disagrees with the partner's purchase (see Figure 1):

Wife's resentment = WP1 - WP2
Husband's resentment = HP1 - HP2

Resentment is defined as a passive spouse's gain and loss, respectively, of well-being in conflict and agreement situations. The more a passive spouse's well-being is affected by the active partner's decision to buy against his/her will the more the spouse is puzzled, that is, the more he/she feels resentment.

A 2 (employment status) by 2 (sex, within factor) Anova including respect as dependent variable, revealed a main effect for sex. Generally, the active wife respected her husband's opinion more ($M = 2.18$) than vice versa, the active husband respected his wife's opinion ($M = 1.52$; $F(1,48) = 7.34$; $p = .009$). This result is in line with present societal roles, attributing high dependence to the wife and independence to the husband. Contrary to the prediction, no interaction effect and no main effect of employment status have been found. However, the longer the husband was out of a job, the more he started respecting his wife's opinion. The correlation between husband's length of unemployment and respect amounted to $r(24) = 0.36$; $p = .04$; the correlation between length of unemployment and the wife's respect amounted to $r(24) = -.19$; $p = .19$).

The second 2 by 2 Anova with frequency of buying against the other's will revealed, was expected, a significant interaction effect ($F(1,48) = 9.27$; $p = .004$). No significant main effects were found. As shown in Figure 3, employed husbands realized an egoistic purchase against their wife's will more frequently than unemployed husbands; whereas, the wives bought less frequently against their husband's will if he was employed rather than unemployed.

Figure 3: Frequencies of Employed and Unemployed Husbands' and Wives' Purchases against the Partner's Will

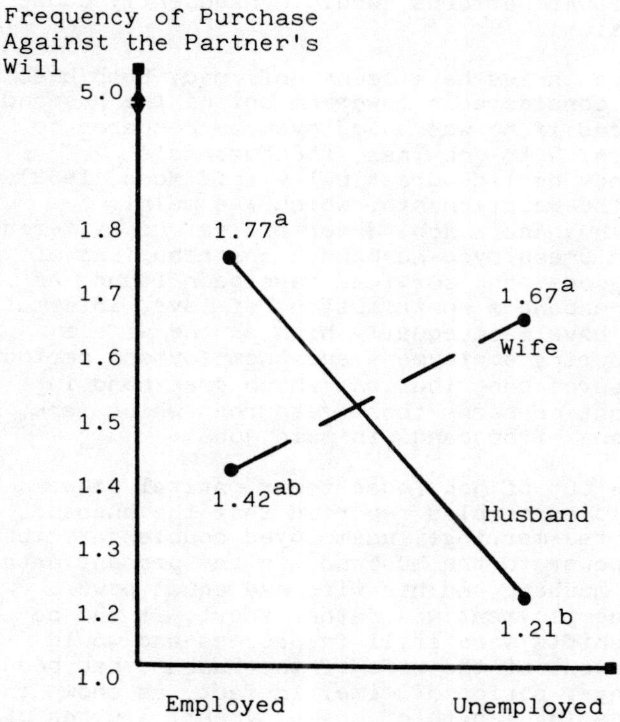

Note: Different superscripts indicate significant differences

In the last Anova, with resentment as dependent variable, the interaction effect sex by employment status slightly missed significance ($F(1,48) = 3.24$; $p = .078$). Both main effects were not significant. Unemployed husbands felt less resentment if their wife bought against the husband's will ($M = 1.88$) than employed husbands ($M = 2.19$). The wives, on the other hand, were most puzzled if their jobless husband realized a purchase against their will ($M = 2.42$ and 1.88, respectively, for wives with unemployed and employed husbands). Again, the correlation between length of unemployment and puzzledness indicated that the longer the husband was jobless, the less puzzled he was if his wife bought contrary to his opinion ($r(24) = -.45$; $p = .01$; the correlation with the wife's resentment was $r(24) = -.14$; $p = .26$).

4. DISCUSSION

It has been argued that with job loss, the male breadwinners also loose a substantial source to gain resources for the common use. Decrease of resource contribution was hypothesized to lead to a crucial loss of marital power. Moreover, destabilization of power patterns, would consequently cause marital dissatisfaction.

In general, these hypotheses have been confirmed. Both husband and wife reported a considerable lower amount of the husband's resource contributions if he was unemployed as compared to employed breadwinners. With job loss, the husband's contributions of money decline drastically (cf. Moen, 1983). But also status of the relationship, which was mainly associated with the husband's job, deteriorates. No differences between employed and unemployed husbands' contributions of love, information, goods, and services have been found. As Table 2 shows, the husband's contributions of love, information, goods, and services have been equally high as the wife's contributions both during employment and unemployment periods. The decrease of resource contributions which goes hand in hand with unemployment concerns those resources which are specific contributions of husbands in paid jobs.

Breadwinners who are out of job loose their marital power position. While employed couples reported that the husbands had the most say in the marriage, unemployed couples attributed significantly less power to the husband. In the present data, both the unemployed husband and his wife had equal power. Since duration of unemployment was rather short, it can be assumed that power shifts were still in process and would have been more in favour of the wife if the husband had been out of job for a longer period of time. In fact, as shown in Figure 2, with increasing length of unemployment, sources of resources to contribute to the common budget decreased and consequently, marital power structure changed which then is followed by a deterioration of marital harmony. This causal relationship is in line with those reported by Komarovsky (1940) and Schindler (1979). It also corresponds to the assumptions made by resource theory (e.g., Blood & Wolfe, 1960), and more generally by social exchange theory (e.g., Homans, 1961; Nye, 1979).

The specific area of family life which has been chosen in this study for the investigation of unemployment and marital power, was couple purchase decision making. It has been predicted that the employed breadwinner was less dependent on his wife than the unemployed breadwinner. Husbands in paid jobs should buy a desired commodity against the wife's will more frequently than husbands without paid jobs. Wives, on the other hand, should consider the employed partner's will more than the unemployed partner's will. If the wife was buying a commodity against her husband's will, he should feel more resentment if he was employed rather than unemployed.

The first hypothesis has not been confirmed. This may be due to the short duration of unemployment (husbands were out of job 5 months on the average; see Table 1). However, the correlation between husband's respect of the wife's opinion and length of unemployment and the wife's respect of the husband's opinion and length of unemployment indicate that a comparison between long term unemployed and employed couples might reveal results confirming the hypothesis.

Another indicator of power changes is the frequency of purchases in conflict situations. As predicted, husbands out of work realized their egoistic purchases less frequently than employed husbands. The wives, on the other hand, became less dependent on the husband when he was out of job, and bought more frequently against his will.

While short time unemployment did not significantly affect the active spouse's readiness to respect the other's will, the passive spouse has been affected. The employed husband felt more resentment if the wife bought a commodity against his will than the unemployed husband, and vice versa, the wife felt most resentment if the unemployed husband realized a purchase against her will. Again, these results were the stronger the longer unemployment endured (see correlations between resentment of husband and wife, respectively, and duration of unemployment).

Summarizing, unemployment affected intrafamily resource contributions, marital power structure, and marital happiness. The unemployed bradwinner forfeited possibilities to gain both tangible and intangible resources, and consequently, his power in the relationship decreased. The longer unemployment endured, the more the husband became dependent on his wife, and the more the wife became independent of her husband in purchasing decision situations. Further investigations focusing on the impact of short and long term unemployment could provide insight into the dynamics of change and restabilization of marital power, and relate power shifts and restabilization to the couple's emotional experiences.

REFERENCES

Blood, R.D. & Wolfe, D.W. 1960. Husbands and Wives. The Dynamics of Married Living. Glencoe, Il.: Free Press.

Brandstätter, H., Kirchler, E. & Wagner, W. In press. Rücksichtnahme und Betroffenheit von Ehepartnern in Konfliktsituationen. In: H. Todt (ed.). Sozialwissenschaftliche Probleme der Familie. Berlin: Duncker & Humblot.

Brinkmann, C. 1976. Finanzielle und psychosoziale Belastungen während der Arbeitslosigkeit. Mitteilungen aus der Arbeitsmarkt- und Berufsforschung, 9, 397-413.

Catalano, R. & Dooley, D. 1979. Does economic change provoke or uncover behavioral disorder? A preliminary test. In: L.A. Ferman & J.P. Gordus (eds.). Mental Health and the Economy. Kalamazoo, Mi.: W.E. Ubjohn Institute.

Ferman, L.A. & Gordus, J.P. 1979. Mental Health and the Economy. Kalamazoo, Mi.: W.E. Upjohn Institute.

Frese, M. & Mohr, G. 1978. Die psychopathologischen Folgen des Entzugs von Arbeit: Der Fall Arbeitslosigkeit. In: M. Frese, S. Greif & N. Semmer (eds.). Industrielle Psychopathologie. Bern: Huber.

Foa, U.G. 1971. Interpersonal and economic resources. Science, 171, 345-351.

Heer, D.H. 1965. The measurement and bases of family power: an overview. Marriage and Family Living, 25, 133-140.

Homans, G. 1961. Social Behavior: Its Elementary Forms. New York: Wiley.

Jahoda, M. 1981. Work, employment, and unemployment. American Psychologist, 36, 184-191.

Jahoda, M. 1982. Employment and Unemployment. Cambridge: Cambridge University Press.

Jahoda, M., Lazarsfeld, P.F. & Zeisel, H. 1960. Die Arbeitslosen von Marienthal. Allensbach: Verlag für Demoskopie.

Kelvon, P. & Jarrett, J.E. 1985. Unemployment. Its Social Psychological Effects. Cambridge: Cambridge University Press.

Kieselbach, T. & Offe, H. 1979. Psychologische, gesundheitliche, soziale und politische Probleme als Folge von Arbeitslosigkeit - Ein kritischer Überblick. In: T. Kieselbach & H. Offe (eds.). Arbeitslosigkeit. Individuelle Verarbeitung, gesellschaftlicher Hintergrund. Darmstadt: Steinkopff.

Kirchler, E. 1984. Arbeitslosigkeit und Alltagsbefinden. Linz: Trauner.

Kirchler, E. 1985. Job loss and mood. Journal of Economic Psychology, 6, 9-25.

Komarovsky, M. 1940. The Unemployed Man and his Familiy. New York: Dryden Press.

Liem, G.R. & Liem, J.H. 1979. Social support and stress: Some general issues and their application to the problem of unemployment. In: L.A. Ferman & J.P. Gordus (eds.). Mental Health and the Economy. Kalamazoo, Mi.: W.E. Upjohn Insitute.

Moen, P. 1983. Unemployment, public policy, and families: Forecasts for the 1980s. Journal of Marriage and the Family, 45, 751-760.

Nye, F.I. 1979. Choice, exchange, and the family. In: W.R. Burr, R. Hill, F.I. Nye & I.L. Reiss (eds.). Contemporary Theories about the Family. Vol. 2. New York: Free Press.

Safilios-Rothschild, C. 1976. The dimensions of power distribution in the family. In: H. Greenbaum & J. Christ (eds.). Contemporary Marriage. Structure, Dynamics, and Therapy. Boston: Little, Brown.

Scanzoni, J. 1979. Social processes and power in the families. In: I. Burr, R. Wesley, R. Hill, F.I. Nye & I.L. Reiss (eds.). Contemporary Theories about the Family. Research Based Theories Vol. 1. New York: Free Press.

Schindler, H. 1979. Familie und Arbeitslosigkeit. In: T. Kieselbach & H. Offe (eds.). Arbeitslosigkeit. Individuelle Verarbeitung, gesellschaftlicher Hintergrund. Darmstadt: Steinkopff.

Voydanoff, P. 1983. Unemployment and family stress. In: H.Z. Lopata & J.H. Pleck (eds.). Research in the Interweave of Social Roles: Families and Jobs. Vol. 3. Greenwich, Co.: JAI Press.

Wacker, A. 1983. Arbeitslosigkeit. Frankfurt am Main: Europäische Verlagsgesellschaft.

Warr, P. 1983a. Work and unemployment. In: P.J.W. Drenth, H. Thierry, P.J. Willems & C.J. de Wolff (eds.). Handbook of Work and Organizational Psychology. London: Wiley.

Warr, P. 1983b. Job loss, unemployment, and psychological well-being. In: E. van de Vliert & V. Allen (eds.). Role Transitions. New York: Plenum Press.

GENDER DIFFERENCES IN FAMILY EFFECTS ON HUMAN CAPITAL AND EARNINGS: AN EMPIRICAL STUDY OF SIBLINGS

David Neumark*

1. INTRODUCTION

Families affect the earnings of their children. From the perspective of empirical research on earnings, these effects can be of two types. First, families can influence the accumulated amount of human capital of their children, measured by ability, schooling, experience, etc., creating intra-family correlations in these characteristics that, in turn, lead indirectly to intra-family correlations in earnings.[1] Second, families can have direct effects on earnings, manifested in intra-family correlations in residuals of standard earnings equations.[2]

This paper uses data on siblings to estimate and compare the magnitudes of both types of family effects for men and women. It extends the research of Shackett (1981) and Bound, Griliches and Hall (1986, hereafter BGH), which applied methods for studying male sibling pairs (Behrman, Taubman and Wales, 1977; Behrman, et al, 1980; Chamberlain and Griliches, 1975) to data incorporating sibling pairs in which one or both members are female. More generally, it responds to Griliches' (1979) call to study the role of the family in determining the labor market outcomes of its offspring.

Two previous empirical findings provide the direct motivation for this research. Shackett (1981) found that in wage regressions that included IQ as well as the standard independent variables, there was a significant correlation in the residuals for brother-brother (.18) and sister-sister (.22) sibling pairs, but for the mixed-gender pairs, the correlation was essentially zero.[3] This suggests that the second type of family effect--the direct effect on earnings--acts differently for men and women. BGH, on the other hand, in studying family effects on IQ, schooling and earnings, conclude that with respect to the first two, "Families and schools treat brothers and sisters symmetrically" (p. 98). Together, these findings suggest that gender differences in family effects are important only with respect to direct effects on earnings unrelated to the measures of human capital that typically enter a wage equation.

This paper extends the previous research in three ways. Most importantly, labor force experience is added to the model of BGH.[4] As is often the case with latent variable models of the type used in this paper, the results obtained depend partly on the parameterization of how experience enters into the model. In this case more than one reasonable parameterization exists, and the choice among these cannot be determined empirically, due to a lack of identification. Under either of the two

---

*Department of Economics, Harvard University. This material is based upon the second essay of my dissertation (Neumark, 1987b), for which the support of a National Science Foundation Graduate Fellowship is gratefully acknowledged. Any opinions, findings, conclusions or recommendations expressed within are my sole responsibility and do not necessarily reflect the views of the Foundation, or of others who contributed to the development of this paper.

that seem most plausible a priori, significant family effects on experience for both men and women are found. Findings with respect to the "symmetry" with which families treat brothers and sisters in affecting labor force experience depend, however, on the parameterization.

The second way in which the previous research is extended is to focus explicitly on the impact of these family effects on intra-family wage correlations. The empirical results show that family effects on the amount and accumulation of ability, schooling and experience explain more of the intra-family wage correlation of sisters than of brothers. Whether this is due to differences in the family effects on these variables for men and women, as opposed to differences in returns in the labor market to these variables, is important in assessing the role of the family in determining the human capital and earnings of men and women. The paper provides evidence that, to some extent, this finding is due to differences in returns.

Lastly, the role of observable family background variables in explaining family effects on human capital and earnings is explored, although only cursorily.

Lurking beneath the surface of this exploration of family effects on human capital and earnings is the broader issue of the role of the family in determining the marked differences between men and women in pay-related labor market characteristics and earnings. (See, e.g., Lloyd and Niemi, 1979.) As will become clear, this paper does not focus on inter-gender differences in means of the dependent variables, but rather on intra-gender variation. What information can this possibly provide on family effects on differences in means?

To make the issue more concrete, consider a question that would appear to be directly applicable, namely whether families systematically train, teach or socialize their female offspring to pursue the types of labor market careers reflected in these differences. The problem that arises is that unless one is willing to assume that, with respect to career choices, brothers and sisters are identical from the outset, the family effects on the differences between a brother and a sister are fundamentally unidentifiable, since gender differences in tastes or aptitudes cannot be distinguished from differences in environment (in this case within the family).[5] Only if these family effects also vary across families, within gender, and only from this variation, can their effects be identified. Thus, for example, the impression that for women labor force experience is much more of a choice variable than for men could lead to the hypothesis that socialization within the family plays a significant role in determining how much a woman works, and that some of this effect may explain the overall lower experience of women. At the same time, the considerable heterogeneity among women in patterns of accumulation of labor force experience (Heckman and Willis, 1977) suggests that this effect might be partially identified via intra-gender variation. Partial confirmation of the hypothesis would be provided by finding a larger role for family effects in explaining the variation in the experience of women, relative to men.

Thus to the extent that there is intra-gender variation in family effects, research along these lines can be used to explore indirectly the role of the family in generating male-female differences in the labor market. More importantly, this argument implies that, in general, in the search for explanations of these differences between men and women, only hypotheses concerning those influences on labor market behavior that vary within genders can be fruitfully studied empirically.

Overall, the empirical findings are ambiguous. On one hand, the similarity of the magnitude of the family effects on ability, schooling and experience of men and women--i.e., the similarity in the amount of the variation in these variables explained by family effects--suggests that at least those parts of the family effects that vary within gender have little to do with broader differences in the human capital of men and women. On the other hand, "asymmetry" in the family effect on experience for men and women, under one parameterization, suggests that the source of this effect differs for men and women, leaving open the possibility that socialization lies behind the effect for the latter.

Section 2 reviews past research on family effects on human capital and earnings, and discusses its relation to this paper. Section 3 describes the data set used. Section 4 discusses the basic recursive model of human capital and earnings, and the empirical findings that motivate the research topic and the strategy used. Section 5 presents a more complete econometric model of human capital and earnings that models family effects with a latent variable structure. Section 6 presents and discusses empirical results for this model. Section 7 summarizes the results and discusses potential extensions and applications of this research.

2. PAST RESEARCH ON FAMILY EFFECTS

Previous research has studied the role of family effects in the determination of earnings and earnings-related characteristics, and the ability of observable variables to capture these family effects. In discussing this work, it is essential to distinguish between studies using observed and unobserved family variables or effects.

With respect to earnings, the general findings are accurately summarized by Griliches (1979). "Measured parental characteristics... appear to affect earnings primarily via their effect on the level of achieved schooling. The market does not appear to pay for them directly. Unmeasured "family" characteristics have a substantial though not large effect on the variance of earnings (10-15 percent), but their interpretation is obscure," (p. S59). The only evidence that is in disagreement with this summary is that in two studies (Sewell and Hauser, 1975; Conlisk, 1971) parents' income enters the earnings equation significantly. Aside from this, direct family effects on earnings remain unexplained by the available variables. A variety of conjectures as to the source of these effects has been offered. Corcoran, Jencks and Olneck (1976) offer two explanations. "One possibility is that certain families socialize their children and develop non-cognitive skills which are largely independent of test scores and educational attainment but still valuable to employers...Another possibility is that some families encourage their children to maximize earnings, while others encourage their children to maximize other forms of psychic income," (pp. 433-435). Evidence of the importance of non-cognitive skills that are uncorrelated with the usual variables in earnings equations is given in Filer (1981).

More concrete results are available for the role of family background in determining ability and schooling. Sewell and Hauser (1975) find that father's education, occupational status and income, and mother's education and income affect offsprings' earnings through their positive effects on ability and schooling. Olneck (1977) demonstrates that father's education and occupation, and the number of siblings, partly determine ability and schooling.

This paper utilizes models with unobservable family effects, extending them to sister-sister and mixed-gender pairs in addition to brother-brother pairs. This permits the comparison of the roles of family effects for men and women. By incorporating labor force experience into

children in response to both the characteristics of the children, and the parents' preferences concerning inequality among their offspring. This work, however, should not be viewed as standing in opposition to the more standard approach to studying family effects. Rather, it contributes to the first of the two questions that Sewell and Hauser (1977) claimed could be addressed with sibling data. "(1) How and why are siblings different from one another?, and (2) How and why are siblings more like one another than unrelated persons?" (p. 255). With respect to same-gender sibling pairs, the approach followed in this paper attempts to answer only the second question. But the analysis of mixed-gender pairs to study gender differences in family effects can potentially help to explain how and why brothers and sisters differ.

3. THE DATA

The data used come from the National Longitudinal Survey of Young Men and Young Women (Center for Human Resources Research, 1984). Data are used from 1966 through 1980 for the men, and from 1968 through 1982 for the women. Since the original surveys were done for the same age group (14-24) for each gender, apart from the two year difference the data set used constitutes a panel on a cohort of men and women followed over the same fourteen years of their lives.

The variable names and definitions, as well as sample descriptive statistics, are given in Table 1. One variable that requires comment is EXP, which measures accumulated years of post-schooling work experience, as well as work experience of persons who were attending school part-time, but did not report going to school as their primary activity, and did not later return to school. The variable was constructed from job history and individual year survey questions, using algorithms created and described in Shackett (1981), and updated for the present research. The measure of work experience is based on weeks worked, not hours; analysis of the sensitivity of results to other definitions and dimensions of labor force experience is beyond the scope of this paper.

The data file used was derived from the nearly 5,000 siblings in the original sample of just over 10,000. For individuals in this sibling sample the latest available observation was chosen subject to the criteria that i) the respondent was 21 years of age or older, ii) the respondent held a job at the time of the survey, and iii) all of the variables in Table 1 were available. This led to a cross-sectional data file, with observations scattered over the fourteen years of the survey (although heavily concentrated at the end). The last step was to match up the sibling pairs left in this data file, first matching up same-gender pairs, and then mixed-gender pairs, never letting the same individual appear in more than one pair. This led to a final sample of 161 brother-brother pairs, 184 sister-sister pairs and 178 brother-sister pairs.

Some of the numbers in Table 1 are indicative of the sample inclusion criteria that have been imposed, suggesting that there are potentially important interrelations between the selection criteria and the values of the observed variables. If the imposition of these criteria has resulted in missing data that are missing non-randomly conditional on the available data (Rubin, 1976), then estimates based on the restricted sample will be inconsistent estimates of the population parameters. This paper follows BGH in assuming that the missing data are missing randomly conditional on the available data. In the case in which observations with missing data are dropped, as in this paper, this is equivalent to assuming that no sample selection bias is thereby induced. (In BGH, this assumption is further exploited to pool over varying patterns of missing data.) In

4. THE MODEL AND PRELIMINARY RESULTS

In keeping with the traditional structure utilized in research in this area, the basic model considered is three recursive equations in schooling, experience and earnings.

$$\text{(1)} \qquad SCH = \gamma_1 X_1 + \epsilon_1$$

$$\text{(2)} \qquad EXP = \beta_1 SCH + \gamma_2 X_2 + \epsilon_2$$

$$\text{(3)} \qquad LNW = \beta_2 SCH + \beta_3 EXP + \gamma_3 X_3 + \epsilon_3$$

The view of the process determining these variables that best accords with the recursive structure is that parents are largely responsible for choosing the level of schooling, individuals' accumulated labor supply decisions determine experience at any point in time, and current wages are determined in the labor market given these and other characteristics. Cross-equation errors can have non-zero correlations due to simultaneity in the determination of these variables, or errors in measurement.

The simplest view of family effects on human capital and earnings variables is given by the correlations that remain after removing the influence of exogenous variables that make siblings similar, but that have nothing to do with family effects per se. Given the recursive structure (1)-(3), the appropriate way to remove this influence is to estimate the reduced form of the model. The OLS estimates of the reduced form are given in Table 2. The individual covariances and cross-sibling correlations of the reduced form residuals are given in Table 3. The latter indicate substantial intra-family correlations.

The correlations in Table 3 constitute the main empirical motivation for this research. For wages, the pattern of positive correlations for same-gender pairs, but no correlation for mixed-gender pairs, was already discussed. The schooling correlations were also studied by BGH, although in this sample the brother-sister correlation is somewhat smaller. The experience correlations are strongly suggestive of the utility of extending the family effects framework to incorporate labor force experience as well.[6]

Most directly, the goal of this paper is to uncover and estimate the structure of family effects that underlies the correlations in Table 3. These are reduced form residual correlations, so they provide no information on the channels through which family effects act. The same question with respect to direct and indirect effects on wages can actually be asked with respect to experience and schooling. For example, for experience the question is whether the correlations in Table 3 arise from effects on schooling, which in turn affect experience, or whether instead there are direct effects on experience. The other major focus will be on determining whether, and if so how, the underlying structure differs for men and women.

The inadequacy of the available family background variables in capturing these family correlations dictates the choice of methodology for answering these questions, which is discussed in the next section. This is demonstrated in Table 4, which presents intra-family correlations of residuals following "second stage" regressions of the reduced form residuals on a set of family background variables[7] including parents' educational goal, father's education, mother's education, number of siblings aged 14-24 in the initial survey, and a dummy variable for whether one of these siblings was of the opposite gender.[8] The schooling and experience correlations fall somewhat, but still remain substantial.

Table 1. Descriptive Statistics and Variable Definitions

	Mean (Std. Dev.) Men (N=500)	Women (N=546)	Variable Definition
IQ	103.700 (15.379)	103.588 (15.765)	IQ score
SCH	14.220 (2.288)	13.357 (2.235)	Highest grade completed
EXP	7.136 (4.243)	5.583 (3.605)	Post-schooling work experience
LNW	6.492 (0.566)	6.059 (0.579)	Logarithm of hourly rate of pay at current job
MIN	0.148 (0.355)	0.187 (0.390)	Dummy variable=1 for non-white
URBAN	0.796 (0.403)	0.784 (0.412)	Dummy variable=1 for SMSA
SOUTH	0.288 (0.453)	0.289 (0.454)	Dummy variable=1 for South
SOUTH66(68)	0.256 (0.437)	0.295 (0.456)	Dummy variable=1 for South in initial interview
AGE	29.290 (3.862)	28.311 (4.460)	Age
AGE66(68)	17.808 (2.516)	18.995 (2.412)	Age in initial interview
MST	0.668 (0.471)	0.614 (0.487)	Dummy variable=1 if respondent is married, spouse present
DEPS	1.210 (1.232)	0.789 (1.066)	Number of dependents, excluding spouse
YRSM	5.704 (4.798)	5.855 (5.341)	Years since first marriage

support of this assumption, they argue that wage equation parameters have been shown to be relatively insensitive to corrections for selectivity. More generally, in models such as the one explored in this paper, explicit account is taken of many of the unobservables that might give rise to selectivity bias.

the model, it provides an analysis of family effects on an additional important determinant of earnings. Potentially, this analysis opens up a perspective on family effects that differs substantially from the view of some researchers, who model family effects on ability (Leibowitz, 1974) and schooling (Behrman, Pollak and Taubman, 1986; Sheshinski and Weiss, 1982) as human capital investment of parents in their children. Decisions with respect to labor force experience, however, are principally made outside of the parents' home. It therefore seems more appropriate to view family effects on experience as effects on the tastes or preferences of children that affect their later decision-making.

The second issue considered in previous research, and one that is crucial in determining and evaluating the empirical methodology used, is the ability of observable variables to capture the family effects of interest. If they can do so, then data on individuals, with relatively simple models, can be used to study the questions considered above. However, much evidence from samples of siblings, in which the size of intra-family correlations explained by observable variables can be compared with the actual correlations, seriously calls into question the adequacy of these variables. Such findings with respect to direct family effects on earnings were already discussed. For similar evidence with respect to family effects on human capital variables, see Olneck (1977) and Sewell and Hauser (1977). This necessitates the use of models with unobservable family effects. Such models have more complicated structures, typically positing the presence of latent variables in a number of equations, which may be either for various indicators for one individual (e.g., Griliches and Mason, 1972), or for members of the same family (i.e., sibling models).

In the present context, sibling models are advantageous since the effects of the latent family-related variables are identified from cross-sibling correlations, so that the interpretation of these variables as family effects is less tenuous. Nonetheless, the estimated effects of these variables must be interpreted with caution, since they capture "all the influences on which brothers are "closer" to each other than a randomly drawn pair from the same population," (Griliches, 1979, p. S59). As much as is possible, explicit account is taken of this potential problem of interpretation by modelling family effects as latent variables uncorrelated with a set of exogenous variables for which siblings are similar, but that are not family-specific.

Two related criticisms of sibling models and their results--one empirical and the other conceptual--must be mentioned. While empirical results show that family effects are statistically significant determinants of earnings and measures of human capital, a great deal of variation remains unexplained, in particular with respect to earnings and schooling. Corcoran, Jencks and Olneck (1976) conclude that despite the incorporation of unobserved family effects, "most of the variance in eventual earnings is still within families," (p. 433). In reviewing a large number of studies of family effects, Leibowitz (1977) notes that "none of the studies reviewed...was able to account for much more than 50% of the variance in earnings or schooling," (p. 30).

On a conceptual level, Michael (1977) criticizes the restriction of the focus of attention of sibling studies to common factors. "If parents respond to differences in children's attributes by promoting the comparative advantages of each child...then similarity among brothers is not evidence of the importance of family characteristics nor is dissimilarity evidence of its lack of importance," (p. 166). Sheshinski and Weiss (1982) and Behrman, Pollak and Taubman (1986) respond positively to this criticism by studying the allocation of parental resources to

Table 2. Reduced Form Regression Results[a]

Dependent Variable:	Men (N=500) SCH	EXP	LNW[b]	Women (N=546) SCH	EXP	LNW[b]
Independent Variable:						
CONST	13.308 (0.730)	-5.738 (1.592)	4.379 (0.309)	12.719 (0.753)	-8.172 (1.176)	4.870 (0.219)
AGE66(68)	0.056 (0.041)	-0.071 (0.078)	-	0.047 (0.040)	-0.052 (0.054)	-
MIN	-0.684 (0.294)	0.783 (0.502)	-0.120 (0.059)	-0.506 (0.259)	-0.049 (0.351)	-0.036 (0.052)
SOUTH66(68)	0.076 (0.239)	0.415 (0.675)	-0.035 (0.078)	-0.546 (0.223)	-0.140 (0.401)	0.057 (0.058)
AGE	-	0.484 (0.058)	0.047 (0.008)	-	0.543 (0.037)	0.013 (0.008)
SOUTH	-	-0.768 (0.640)	-0.042 (0.074)	-	-0.322 (0.388)	-0.099 (0.056)
URBAN	-	-0.695 (0.434)	0.200 (0.051)	-	-0.263 (0.304)	0.214 (0.044)
MST	-	-0.036 (0.450)	0.102 (0.052)	-	0.140 (0.281)	-0.005 (0.042)
DEPS	-	0.018 (0.179)	-0.018 (0.021)	-	-0.336 (0.137)	-0.073 (0.020)
YRSM	-	0.096 (0.053)	0.001 (0.006)	-	-0.021 (0.035)	0.004 (0.005)
R^2	.014	.232	.443	.027	.398	.531

[a] Standard errors are given in parentheses.
[b] Interview year dummy variables were also included. Since these also pick up the cohort effect captured by AGE66(68) in the other equations, AGE66(68) was dropped from this equation to avoid perfect multicollinearity.

The brother-brother wage correlation is essentially unchanged, while the sister-sister wage correlation falls to insignificance. The next section outlines a strategy for studying the family effects underlying the intra-family correlations in the endogenous variables using a latent or unobservable variable structure that takes full account of these correlations.

Table 3. Covariances and Correlations of Reduced Form Residuals[a]

Individual Males

	SCH	EXP	LNW
SCH	5.159		
EXP	-4.825	13.83	
LNW	0.229	-0.080	0.179

Individual Females

	SCH	EXP	LNW
SCH	4.860		
EXP	-1.602	7.822	
LNW	0.177	0.094	0.158

Brother-Brother

	SCH	EXP	LNW
SCH	.562		
EXP	-.259	.260	
LNW	.089	-.018	.168

Sister-Sister

	SCH	EXP	LNW
SCH	.397		
EXP	-.241	.229	
LNW	.173	-.045	.155

Brother

		SCH	EXP	LNW
	SCH	.247	-.139	.133
Sister	EXP	-.243	.151	-.083
	LNW	.033	.055	-.025

[a] Covariances are given for the individual males and females. Correlations are given for the sibling pairs.

5. AN UNOBSERVABLES APPROACH TO FAMILY EFFECTS

The strategy in this approach is to parameterize the intra-family correlations in a way that allows direct and indirect effects on the endogenous variables, but at the same time uses some prior restrictions on how these effects operate to keep the parameterization parsimonious, interpretable, and of course identified. While not the only criterion, a statistical test of the validity of the parameterization is given by examining how well the model fits the data.

The complete model is given by

$$IQ = \beta_1 A + \gamma_1 X_1 + \epsilon_1 \tag{4}$$

$$SCH = \beta_2 A + \beta_3 W + \gamma_2 X_2 + \epsilon_2 \tag{5}$$

$$EXP = \beta_4 A + \beta_5 SCH + \beta_6 S + \gamma_3 X_3 + \epsilon_3 \tag{6}$$

$$LNW = \beta_7 A + \beta_8 SCH + \beta_9 EXP + \beta_{10} D + \gamma_4 X_4 + \epsilon_4 \tag{7}$$

Table 4. Cross-Sibling Correlations of Reduced Form Residuals from Second Stage Regressions on Family Background Variables

	Brother-Brother			Sister-Sister		
	SCH	EXP	LNW	SCH	EXP	LNW
SCH	.278			.229		
EXP	-.068	.166		-.156	.166	
LNW	.078	-.009	.165	.082	.015	.096

		Brother		
		SCH	EXP	LNW
	SCH	.198	-.078	.066
Sister	EXP	-.141	.069	-.030
	LNW	.002	.076	-.049

This model contains four unobservable family variables or "factors," A, W, S and D, all of which are assumed to be uncorrelated with the exogenous variables X_i, i=1,...,4. A is unobservable ability, which has both a family and an individual component, for which IQ is an error-ridden measure. W is a family factor, uncorrelated with A, which captures the component of family wealth or tastes for schooling that is independent of ability. Ability should enter the schooling equation if its "productivity" differs in the labor market and in the production of further human capital via schooling (Leibowitz, 1974). Empirical evidence that a second factor is needed in the schooling equation was first provided by Olneck (1977), who found that "families who have sons with higher test scores also tend to have sons whose educational attainments exceed the attainments expected on the basis of test scores alone," (p. 142).

S, in the equation for EXP, is another family factor, also assumed to be uncorrelated with A. Leibowitz (1977) asserted, without empirical support, that one of the channels of family effects on earnings must operate through experience. Among the reasons she suggested were the transmission of "aggressiveness," a "taste for money income" or the "Protestant ethic" from parents to children (p. 29). The inclusion of this third factor allows for the estimation and interpretation of this effect. In one of the parameterizations considered, S is possibly correlated with W. This is equivalent to allowing W and a factor orthogonal to it to enter the EXP equation. The interpretation of this parameterization is that the same unobservables that underlie family effects on schooling have an independent effect on experience. For example, family wealth, which probably affects schooling, may also affect the work experience of people at relatively young ages. An alternative parameterization, which affects the estimated parameters of the experience equation, but not the other parameters of the model, or the overall goodness-of-fit, is also considered. First, a non-zero covariance is allowed between ϵ_2 and ϵ_3, to capture either simultaneity in choices of schooling and experience, or measurement error in schooling. Without some other restriction, though, this covariance and the correlation between W and S cannot be identified. A restriction that allows identification of these two parameters is to restrict β_5 to equal -1, so that the only effect of schooling on experience is a "timing effect," whereby controlling for age, one more year of schooling implies one less year of experience. This is less restrictive than it may at first seem, since the experience measure is post-schooling experience. But it does rule out effects of schooling on the labor supply decisions that are cumulatively captured in EXP. Since it seems inappropriate in an initial empirical study to rule out a correlation of W with S, a third parameterization that sets this correlation to zero is ruled out. The other two, however, with $\sigma_{23} = 0$, and $\beta_5 = -1$, alternatively, are considered.

D captures direct family effects on wages. It is uncorrelated with the other unobservables that should only affect the measures of human capital. Evidence of direct effects on wages was already discussed.

As the discussion concerning the EXP equation emphasizes, while having a structural interpretation, the assumptions concerning the correlations among the unobservables partly reflect restrictions needed to identify the model. The restrictions chosen are thought to best capture the nature of the family effects. Furthermore, the specifications used most closely follow BGH in studying family effects on ability, schooling and earnings, adding to their model in the least restrictive manner equations that allows experience to be influenced by family effects.

Even if the ϵ's are assumed to be uncorrelated across equations, for an individual this model is underidentified. To see this, note that there are ten moments (the ten unique elements of the variance-covariance matrix of IQ, SCH, EXP and LNW) with which to identify fifteen parameters--the coefficients of the endogenous variables (β_5, β_8 and β_9) and the latent variables (β_1, β_2, β_3, β_4, β_6, β_7, β_{10}), σ_i^2, i=1,...,4, the residual variances, and ρ_{WS}, the correlation of W and S.[9]

But use of sibling data allows the identification of the parameters of the model, including some covariances among the ϵ's, given assumptions on the intra-family correlations of the variables A, W, S and D, and the residuals. For same-gender pairs, denoting pair members by i=a,b, and the expectations operator by E, these assumptions are

(8) $$A_i = f_i + g_i \qquad f_a = f_b \qquad Ef_i^2 = 1 \qquad Eg_a g_b = 0 \qquad Eg_i^2 = \tau$$

(9) $$W_a = W_b \qquad EW_i^2 = 1$$

(10) $$S_a = S_b \qquad ES_i^2 = 1 \qquad EW_i S_i = \rho_{WS}$$

(11) $$D_a = D_b \qquad ED_i^2 = 1$$

(12) $$EAW = EAS = EAD = EWD = ESD = 0$$

(13) $$E\epsilon_{ka}\epsilon_{k'b} = 0 \qquad k,k'=1,\ldots,4,\ k \neq k' \qquad E\epsilon_{1i}\epsilon_{ki} = 0 \qquad k=1,2,3$$

$$E\epsilon_{2i}\epsilon_{3i} = \sigma_{23} \text{ if } \beta_5 = -1, \qquad E\epsilon_{2i}\epsilon_{3i} = 0 \text{ if } \beta_5 \text{ unrestricted}$$

(14) $$E\epsilon_{ki}A = E\epsilon_{ki}W = E\epsilon_{ki}S = E\epsilon_{ki}D = 0 \qquad k=1,\ldots,4$$

These restrictions imply that part of A (f), and W, S and D are pure family factors that are the same across same-gender siblings. A also has an individual component; the ratio of the variances of the individual to the family components is τ. The family factors are uncorrelated with the residuals, and all of the residuals are uncorrelated across siblings. (Covariances between the ϵ's of the SCH, EXP and LNW equations, not considered in this discussion for the sake of clarity, can arise from measurement error in SCH and EXP, or simultaneity.)

Ten moments or covariances have now been added, but only one additional parameter (τ). Thus the necessary condition for identification, that the number of moments is at least as great as the number of parameters, is satisfied. It is straightforward to show that every parameter is indeed identified. This is most easily done by writing out the twenty unique elements of the covariance matrix of (IQ_a, SCH_a, EXP_a, LNW_a, IQ_b, SCH_b, EXP_b, LNW_b) implied by the reduced form of the model.[10] The twenty resulting equations can then be solved for the sixteen parameters, some of which are overidentified. Writing out the model this way for the mixed-gender sib pairs, for whom family factors can differ, allows the introduction of four additional parameters--ρ_A, ρ_W, ρ_S and ρ_D--that measure the correlations across genders in these factors.

Two important assumptions are implicit in this approach. First, it is assumed that the parameters of the model are the same for each member of same-gender pairs. There is conflicting evidence as to the importance of birth order effects on IQ and schooling (Leibowitz, 1974; Sewell and Hauser, 1979). In reviewing evidence on the effects of sibling position, Griliches (1979) concludes that "The data examined seem to support these theories, but the observed effects are rather small (relative to other sources of variance in educational and economic achievement)," (p. S61). Furthermore, birth order effects need not imply that parameters must differ across siblings due to these effects. For example, controlling for age of siblings might adequately capture the phenomenon (as well as controlling for spacing effects).

Second, it is assumed that the set of parameters that are relevant for members of same-gender and mixed-gender pairs are identical, for each gender. This means that potential family composition effects are ignored. This second assumption may be of particular relevance, given evidence that family effects on daughters may depend on whether the family has any sons, a phenomenon that could conceivably be reflected in the parameters of the model. Relaxation of these assumptions remains for future consideration.

The model is estimated using LISREL (Joreskog and Sorbom, 1984), which estimates the structural parameters of the model by minimizing a function of the difference between the actual variance-covariance matrix of the variables in the model and the variance-covariance matrix implied by the structural parameters. This is a method-of-moments estimator, but if it is assumed that the data are distributed multivariate normally, it is equivalent to maximum likelihood estimation.

As in BGH, to reduce the computational burden the model is estimated by first regressing the dependent variables on the exogenous variables of the reduced form equations. Then these "pre-processed" variables are used to estimate what is in essence the model in (4)-(7) in the endogenous variables and the unobservables. This limited information procedure leads to consistent, efficient and asymptotically normally distributed estimates of the structural parameters of this "sub-model," which are the parameters of interest in this application. For this result to hold in a simultaneous equations setting, the parameters must be identified solely from covariance restrictions--which they are in this case due to the unique structuring of the residuals that sibling data are assumed to provide. Further explanation of this approach is given in BGH and in Neumark (1987b).

To implement this methodology, the reduced form regression coefficients are estimated with OLS. Then the pre-processed values of the endogenous variables are input into LISREL, using the multi-sample feature to accomodate the brother-brother, sister-sister and brother-sister pairs. This amounts to estimating three systems of equations (one for each type of sib pair) in eight variables (the four endogenous variables for each sibling), with restrictions across equations and across systems of equations.

6. EMPIRICAL RESULTS

The sufficient statistics from which the model is estimated are the variances and covariances of the residuals from the reduced form regressions for the endogenous variables. Some of these, and the correlations implied by the rest of them, were given in Table 3, and are suggestive of the estimates that will result from the maximum likelihood estimation, in particular the magnitudes of the family effects. The brother-brother and sister-sister matrices are quite similar. Other than the relatively higher SCH correlation for brothers (.562 vs. .397), the elements of the matrices are quite close. The brother-sister matrix, however, does reveal some differences, which suggests that the family effects work differently for men and women. The cross-sib intra-family wage correlation is much lower (-.025) than either the brother-brother or sister-sister correlations (.168 and .155, respectively). The schooling and experience intra-family correlations are also lower than for the same-gender pairs. However, the cross-sib matrix is not that different, suggesting that there may not be large differences in the workings of the family effects. Of course, these covariance matrices obfuscate more complex interractions among these variables that the full system estimates will reveal.

The maximum likelihood estimates of the unconstrained model, using the parameterization that $\sigma_{23} = 0$, and constraining σ_{24} and σ_{34} to zero, are given in Table 5. Estimates of the model using the parameterization that $\beta_5 = -1$ are given in Table 6. Considering first the estimates that are the same under either parameterization, one question is whether the overall goodness of fit achieved by the model is sufficient to explain the underlying data. The χ^2 statistic given is the statistic for the likelihood ratio test for the unconstrained model that freely fits the 56 unique covariances implicit in Table 3 (considering IQ as well), compared to the restricted model implied by the equations (4)-(7) and the associated assumptions. The χ^2 statistic with 18 degrees of freedom is an insignificant 17.97, at the 5% level.

The equations for IQ are similar for men and women, although the ratio of the individual to the family variance is higher for males (.403) than for females (.144). The schooling equations, however, indicate that in the IQ-schooling relationship this outcome is attenuated, since ability has a smaller effect on the schooling of women (.856) than of men (1.270). The magnitude of the coefficient of the second family factor, W, is nearly the same for men (1.108) and women (1.059). It should be noted, though, that the unexplained variance in schooling is higher for women than for men (2.895 vs. 1.647 out of an overall variance of about 5).

Turning to the log wage equation, the schooling coefficient is higher

Table 5. Maximum Likelihood Estimates, σ_{23} = 0 Parameterization[a]

χ_{18}^2 = 17.97

	Men				Women			
Dep. Var.:	IQ	SCH	EXP	LNW	IQ	SCH	EXP	LNW
Ind. Var.:								
SCH	-	-	-1.267 (.183)	.045 (.015)	-	-	-.020 (.103)	.024 (.009)
EXP	-	-	-	.014 (.006)	-	-	-	.025 (.006)
A	9.749 (.780)	1.270 (.140)	.598 (.301)	.035 (.029)	10.39 (.649)	.856 (.125)	-.554 (.171)	.100 (.022)
W	-	1.108 (.136)	-	-	-	1.059 (.150)	-	-
S	-	-	1.504 (.262)	-	-	-	1.202 (.247)	-
D	-	-	-	.163 (.040)	-	-	-	.104 (.050)
σ^2	74.83 (13.05)	1.647 (.245)	7.102 (.764)	.139 (.015)	67.24 (13.11)	2.895 (.301)	5.967 (.592)	.128 (.013)

τ_m = .403 (.141) τ_f = .144 (.110)

ρ_{WS}^m = .373 (.269) ρ_{WS}^f = -.757 (.262)

ρ_A = .838 (.107) ρ_W^b = .476 (.250) ρ_S = -.009 (.354) ρ_D = -.620 (.750)

[a] Asymptotic standard errors are given in parentheses.
[b] Correlations between W for males and S for females, and vice versa, were also estimated under this specification, but are not reported.

for men (.045 vs. .024) while the experience coefficient is higher for women (.025 vs. .014), as is the ability coefficient (.100 vs. .035) although none of these differences are significant. The low schooling coefficient for women is troubling. It is not solely the result of controlling for unobserved ability, since in results unreported here, the schooling coefficient in the same log wage equation estimated with OLS was .048 for women, and .068 for men. Thus this is to some extent simply a characteristic of the sample. The estimates of the ability and schooling coefficients are rather imprecise, however, reflecting multicollinearity between A and SCH, which was also found in BGH.

The estimated coefficients of D capture direct family effects on wages. The original covariances are .030, .024 and -.004, for

Table 6. Maximum Likelihood Estimates, β_5 = -1 Parameterization[a]

χ^2_{18} = 17.97

	Men				Women			
Dep. Var.:	IQ	SCH	EXP	LNW	IQ	SCH	EXP	LNW
Ind. Var.:								
SCH	-	-	-1.000	.045 (.015)	-	-	-1.000	.024 (.009)
EXP	-	-	-	.014 (.006)	-	-	-	.025 (.006)
A	9.749 (.780)	1.270 (.140)	.260 (.148)	.035 (.029)	10.39 (.649)	.856 (.125)	.285 (.149)	.100 (.022)
W	-	1.108 (.136)	-	-	-	1.059 (.150)	-	-
S	-	-	1.421 (.255)	-	-	-	.796 (.436)	-
D	-	-	-	.163 (.040)	-	-	-	.104 (.050)
σ^2	74.83 (13.05)	1.647 (.245)	7.219 (.764)	.139 (.015)	67.24 (13.11)	2.895 (.301)	8.748 (.849)	.128 (.013)

τ_m = .403 (.141) $\qquad \tau_f$ = .144 (.110)

ρ_{WS}^m = .187 (.205) $\qquad \rho_{WS}^f$ = .162 (.368)

σ_{23}^m = -.439 (.300) $\qquad \sigma_{23}^f$ = 2.838 (.407)

ρ_A = .838 (.107) $\qquad \rho_W$[b] = .476 (.250) $\qquad \rho_S$ = .131 (.625) $\qquad \rho_D$ = -.620 (.750)

[a] Asymptotic standard errors are given in parentheses.

[b] Correlations between W for males and S for females, and vice versa, were also estimated under this specification, but are not reported.

brother-brother, sister-sister, and brother-sister pairs, respectively. The cross-sibling covariance that remains after controlling for the human capital variables is simply the square of the coefficient on D, which is .027 and .011 for brother-brother and sister-sister pairs, respectively, implying that in the complete model indirect effects capture about half of the wage correlation or covariance for sister-sister pairs, but almost none for the brother-brother pairs. These differences, however, are not statistically significant. The model was estimated constraining the coefficients of D to be equal for men and women, and ρ_D to equal 1. The χ^2 value, with two degrees of freedom, was an insignificant 4.74, at the 5% level.

In general, point estimates of these wage covariance parameters are not robust. Unpublished results associated with BGH give, for early wages, original (reduced form) covariances of .022 and .013 for men and women, respectively, while the corresponding residual covariances, after controlling for human capital variables, are .023 and .005. For late wages the original covariances are .018 and .043, for men and women, while the residual covariances are .015 and .026. Furthermore, results unreported here indicate that the incorporation of EXP into the model, in contrast to the model of BGH, is not responsible for these differences. Lastly, the cross-sibling wage correlations in Shackett (1981), cited in the Introduction, are higher than any of the correlations implied by the above estimates. The variability of the point estimates suggests that these estimates are sensitive to the precise sample definition. Nevertheless, the principal result that family effects capture approximately one-half of the sister-sister wage covariance, while for brothers they capture essentially none of it, is robust over both sets of estimates in Bound, Griliches and Hall, as well as those of this paper.

The choice of parameterization becomes important in estimating the parameters of the experience equation. In Table 5 the schooling and ability coefficients differ sharply for men and women. Net of other effects, and given that age is controlled for, there is essentially an identity between schooling and experience, unless schooling changes the labor supply behavior whose cumulative effect is captured in experience. In the absence of this effect, schooling would enter the experience equation with a coefficient of -1, since time spent in school would simply be deducted from time that would otherwise be spent working. However, schooling does affect labor supply and participation decisions. The large negative coefficient for men (-1.267) suggests that schooling leads to the accumulation of slightly less experience (although the coefficient is not significantly different from 1). The extremely small schooling coefficient for women (-.020) suggests that for them, the opposite is true. Schooling has such a large, positive effect on accumulated experience that the "loss of time" effect is essentially wiped out. With respect to ability, however, the reverse holds; its direct effect, net of its effect on experience via schooling, is to increase the experience of men, and to decrease that of women. The family effect on experience, measured by the coefficient on S, is statistically similar for men (1.504) and women (1.202). The higher point estimate for men is offset by the higher initial variance in their experience (13.83, vs. 7.822 for women).

In Table 6, in which the parameterization β_5 = -1 is used, with σ_{23} unconstrained, the parameter estimates of the experience equation for women change drastically, while for men they are relatively unaffected. For women, the estimate of σ_{23} is positive (2.838) and statistically significant, so that under this parameterization there appears to be considerable simultaneity in the schooling and experience outcomes of women. Allowing for this simultaneity, in turn, leads to sharply different coefficient estimates. In the estimates in Table 5, the loading of this simultaneity onto the SCH coefficient, and the high positive correlation between SCH and W, and SCH and A, caused the coefficient on A, and the estimate of ρ_{WS}, to be negative. Now, however, the parameters are closer to those for the men. Because of these differences, in what follows results that hinge on this parameterization are given for both cases. Unfortunately, the three parameters ρ_{WS}, σ_{23} and β_5 cannot be separately identified, without the addition of some other outcome variable that also depends, say, on W and S, and on no additional latent variable.

The sensitivity of wage equation estimates to errors in measurement or simultaneity, and the use of sibling data as natural instrumental variables for studying these effects, have been explored thoroughly by Griliches (1979). In the estimates presented, σ_{24} and σ_{34} have been constrained to zero. Measurement error will lead to negative covariances and hence downward biases in the SCH and EXP coefficients, while simultaneity will have the opposite effects. In these data, allowing these covariances to be free leads to almost no improvement in the fit of the model, increased variance of the coefficient estimates, and imprecisely estimated covariances. In brief, the data are not sufficiently informative to distinguish between parameterizations with and without these covariances constrained to zero. Detailed results are given in Neumark (1987b).

In addition to the constraint on the wage residual covariances tested above, there are a variety of other constraints on the model that can be tested. An important set of constraints can be used to answer the type of questions considered in BGH, as to whether the family effects differ for men and women. From the high correlation between A for men and A for women (.838), it is apparent that setting ρ_A equal to one will not worsen the fit of the model considerably. Instead, the model was constrained to have ρ_A and ρ_W equal to one, a constraint that BGH could not reject. Although the estimate of ρ_W (.476) is considerably lower than their estimate of .90, the constraint still could not be rejected. The χ^2 statistic with four degrees of freedom was an insignificant 7.58 at the 5% level.[11] Unlike in that paper, however, the constraint that the coefficients of A and W are equal for men and women in the IQ, SCH and LNW equations, conditional on the factor covariances being equal, was rejected, at the 5% level, with a χ^2 value with four degrees of freedom of 13.58. Thus in these data it appears that unobserved ability and the second unobservable that affects schooling are the same for men and women, in that they act in the same "direction," but their impacts on the endogenous variables differ by gender.

The same type of question concerning the correlation between the latent family variables for men and women can be asked with respect to S. While the results just discussed are independent of the choice of parameterization, now this choice affects the results. The estimate of ρ_S, conditional on the restriction that the factor correlations for A and W are equal for men and women, was -.016 with a standard error of .369. While this standard error is large, when the restriction that ρ_S equals one was tested, the χ^2 statistic with two degrees of freedom was significant, at the 5% level, with a value of 6.87. In this case, then, the finding of "symmetric" treatment of brothers and sisters does not carry over to family effects on labor force experience. But with the other parameterization, the estimate of ρ_S was .308, with a standard error of .599. Thus $\hat{\rho}_S$ was not significantly different from one, although it was estimated very imprecisely. This was borne out by estimating the model with this restriction imposed, yielding an insignificant χ^2 statistic for testing this restriction of 1.06, with two degrees of freedom.

Having considered this evidence on the structure of the unobservables, it is of some interest to return to the role of observable family background variables, as discussed at the end of Section 4. The implication of the specification of the recursive model with family effects, in (4)-(7), is that OLS estimation of the equations would lead to inconsistent coefficient estimates, since the residuals are correlated. Given that the family effects are interpreted as orthogonal to the exogenous variables, though, if consistent parameter estimates of the coefficients of the endogenous variables, as estimated in this section, are imposed, the remaining coefficients can be consistently estimated with OLS. (These estimates will still be inefficient, however, since both cross-sibling and individual cross-equation residual correlations are ignored.) To maintain consistency with the interpretation given to family effects in this section, the effects of observable family background variables can then be studied by regressing the residuals from these regressions on the family background variables. These estimates are given in Table 7, and are suggestive of some of the determinants of the unobservable family effects just estimated. The overriding factor, however, is the extremely low explanatory power of the family background variables, except for schooling for males, which cautions against over-interpretation of the findings.

In Table 7, father's education has a relatively larger influence on the education of males, while mother's education has the dominant effect for females. This is in accordance with past research (Leibowitz, 1974; Sewell and Shah, 1968). The other notable finding is that the OPPGEN variable enters all of the equations for males with positive coefficients, and all of the equations for females with negative coefficients. Only in the wage equation does it enter significantly, with an order of magnitude that is quite meaningful in a log wage specification. Looking at the signs in all of the equations, however, suggests that in all respects women do worse if they come from a household in which there was at least one brother, whereas brothers do better if they come from a household with at least one sister. This is reflected in schooling, which may be thought of as due to conscious investment decisions on the part of parents (as in Behrman, Pollak and Taubman, 1986), in experience, which may be due to socialization effects, and in wages. This seems to imply that all of the family effects with respect to these three variables are "allocated" towards males, and away from females. The finding for wages may also lie behind the lack of correlation in wage residuals for mixed-gender sibling pairs, as discussed earlier.

The final issue considered returns to the intra-family cross-sibling wage correlations. The estimates presented in this section indicate that the family effects generating these correlations are almost exclusively direct effects on wages for men, independent of the human capital variables A, SCH and EXP, while for women about half of the correlation derives from indirect family effects on wages through effects on the measures of human capital. An interesting question, though, is whether this result stems from differences in family effects on the human capital of men and women. An alternative explanation is that differences in the coefficients of the wage equations for men and women are such as to amplify the effect on wages of family effects on A, SCH and EXP for women, and to dampen these effects for men.[12] The latter explanation does not diminish the importance of the result, but it does imply that the explanation of the finding is to be found more in differences in how labor markets reward the human capital of men and women, than in how families treat them.

Table 7. Second Stage Regressions on Family Background Variables, Using Consistent Estimates in Recursive Model[a]

Dep. Var.:	SCH	EXP[b]	EXP[c]	LNW
		Men (N=500)		
Ind. Var.:				
CONST	-10.285	-1.435	1.044	-0.014
	(0.817)	(1.346)	(1.337)	(0.183)
PEDGL	0.558	0.078	-0.059	0.006
	(0.051)	(0.083)	(0.083)	(0.011)
FED	0.143	0.100	0.068	0.004
	(0.034)	(0.056)	(0.056)	(0.008)
MED	0.108	-0.033	-0.059	-0.002
	(0.038)	(0.063)	(0.063)	(0.009)
NSIBS	-0.389	-0.183	-0.073	-0.063
	(0.122)	(0.200)	(0.199)	(0.027)
OPPGEN	0.335	0.304	0.193	0.096
	(0.174)	(0.286)	(0.284)	(0.039)
R^2	.375	.027	.017	.022
		Women (N=546)		
CONST	-4.250	2.910	-0.930	-0.276
	(0.598)	(0.792)	(0.877)	(0.111)
PEDGL	0.131	-0.072	0.050	0.011
	(0.027)	(0.036)	(0.040)	(0.015)
FED	0.041	-0.015	0.015	-0.001
	(0.032)	(0.043)	(0.047)	(0.006)
MED	0.193	-0.177	-0.005	0.018
	(0.042)	(0.055)	(0.061)	(0.008)
NSIBS	-0.005	0.155	0.166	-0.011
	(0.118)	(0.156)	(0.173)	(0.022)
OPPGEN	-0.101	-0.204	-0.346	-0.073
	(0.186)	(0.246)	(0.273)	(0.035)
R^2	.144	.059	.016	.043

[a] Standard errors are given in parentheses. MFED, MMED and MPEDGL were also included.

[b] $\sigma_{23}=0$ parameterization.

[c] $\beta_5=-1$ parameterization.

One way to obtain some evidence regarding this question is to consider the intra-family wage covariances "explained" or implied by the structural parameter estimates, compared to the fitted covariances,[13] and to calculate what these explained covariances would be if, for example, men were subjected to the family effects on human capital by which women were influenced.

The explained covariance for same-gender pairs was calculated for the following cases: i) all own-gender parameters, ii) own-gender parameters, but substituting opposite-gender parameters for family effects on the human capital variables (β_3, β_6, ρ_{WS}), and iii) own-gender parameters, but substituting opposite-gender wage equation parameters (β_7, β_8, β_9). These calculations show that it is the different wage coefficients for men and women that drive the higher estimate of the indirect family effects, or the lower estimate of the residual wage correlation, for women. For example, using the estimates in Table 5, for the own-gender parameters the family unobservables explain 24 percent of the brother-brother fitted wage correlation, and 52 percent of the sister-sister fitted wage correlation. When opposite-gender family effect parameters are substituted, these numbers are more or less unchanged. In fact the explained sister-sister correlation rises, and the explained brother-brother correlation falls. But when opposite-gender wage equation parameters are substituted, the situation is reversed. 35 percent of the brother-brother wage correlation is explained, in contrast to 26 percent of the sister-sister correlation.[14] The results are nearly identical using the estimates from the alternative parameterization of the model in Table 6. This last set of results should only be taken as indicative, but in that light it implies that to some extent the higher indirect effects of families on the wages of women are due to differences in the returns to human capital variables of men and women, rather than to stronger family effects on the human capital of women.

7. CONCLUSION

Four principal results emerge from this research. First, families do affect the earnings of their children. For women a large part of the effect is due to family effects on human capital variables, while for men a large part of the effect remains unexplained, something that shows up only in the residual of the wage equation even in a complete model of the determination of earnings. However, the research indicates that the greater role of indirect effects via human capital variables in explaining the intra-family wage correlation of women is partly due to different returns to the human capital of men and women, and not only to differences in family effects.

Second, the "symmetry" of family effects on the human capital of men and women is called into question once experience is added to the model. The issue, however, cannot be determined decisively due to a lack of identification of all of the relevant parameters. While the magnitude of the family effect on experience is similar for men and women, its statistical structure under one parameterization is quite different. Therefore evidence that men and women are subject to different influences within the family, which would tend to support the notion that differences in family effects lie behind the male-female experience differential, is inconclusive.

Third, results concerning the role of observable family background variables are supportive of the view that family effects differ by gender. There is some evidence of what might be interpreted as gender-role modelling effects on schooling, as well as general, although weak evidence that direct family effects on human capital and earnings favor male offspring. This question, however, bears further exploration.

Fourth, Shackett's (1981) original finding of correlated wage equation residuals, at least for male sibling pairs, still remains an unexplained empirical puzzle.

This research has implications for other, related work on gender differentials in the labor force. A standard technique for the measurement of discrimination decomposes the average wage differential between men and women into a part due to discrimination (different regression coefficients) and a part due to differences in characteristics (Neumark, 1987a; Oaxaca, 1973). Reference is typically made to the possibility that discriminatory processes cause differences in characteristics which are ignored in the estimates of wage discrimination. While not addressing this technique directly, this paper begins to look at how differences in labor market characteristics may be generated, in this case within the family.

Along similar lines, this work is suggestive of the importance of looking at "sex-role" socialization and its effect on gender differentials in the labor force, as part of the research program proposed by Corcoran and Courant (1985). With respect to the accumulation of labor force experience, this paper suggests that within one potentially important component of the socialization process--the family--men and women may be subjected to different influences. Whether, and to what extent, this constitutes "sex-role" or other socialization, as well as alternative empirical approaches to this issue, remain subjects for further research.

Lastly, the models of the accumulation of schooling and experience that have been used are overly simple. Given the findings of significant, and in some cases different family effects on these variables for men and women, it seems worthwhile to develop richer models of the accumulation of these variables, which incorporate family effects, and that exploit to a greater extent the longitudinal nature of the available data. In doing so, consideration will also have to be given to the endogeneity of marital and childbearing behavior. In addition to explicitly increasing knowledge concerning how families affect the human capital of their children, such models should also contribute to the understanding and scope of related models of individual behavior.

ACKNOWLEDGEMENTS

I am grateful to John Bound and Zvi Griliches for many helpful discussions, and to Yoram Ben-Porath, Reuven Gronau, Lawrence Summers, and participants in seminars at Ben-Gurion University, Haifa University, Harvard University, The Hebrew University, the Technion and Tel Aviv University for valuable comments.

NOTES

[1]See Leibowitz (1977) for a summary of related research findings.

[2]For evidence of this type of effect, see Shackett (1981), and more extensive work in Bound, Griliches and Hall (1986).

[3]These findings were partly corroborated by BGH, whose results are discussed further below.

[4]They discuss the inclusion of this variable, but omit it because the models with unobservables that are used in this research do not permit the appearance of endogenous variables in more than one functional form. Thus, for example, one cannot have an equation for experience (EXP), and a log wage equation in which EXP and its square appear. In this paper this standard non-linearity in the log wage equation is omitted, and a linear approximation is used.

[5]Behrman, Pollak and Taubman (1986) estimate a model with parameters that measure parental "preferences" for boys or girls in schooling investments. But this effort requires two assumptions. The first, made explicitly, is that "education decisions are made entirely by the parents" (p. 49). The second allows for the first to be mitigated somewhat, as long as children make some of their own education decisions "on the basis of investment calculations" (p. 49). In either case, different tastes of males and females are ruled out.

[6]A comparison of the samples used in this paper and the larger one in BGH suggests that the sister-sister correlation in experience is larger in the population (Neumark, 1987b).

[7]In general, stepwise regression procedures such as these are not desirable, since their effect is to load onto the variables included in the first regression all of the effect of the variables in the second regression that is correlated with the former. In the present case, however, family effects are viewed precisely as the intra-family correlations that arise net of, or orthogonal to, exogenous variables that are not family-specific.

[8]The mnemonics for these variables, used in Table 7, are PEDGL, FED, MED, NSIBS and OPPGEN, respectively. Dummy variables were used for cases missing data for these variables.

[9]The γ's are not counted because, as explained below, the model is estimated for the endogenous variables after regressing them on the exogenous variables. At any rate, their identification is trivial.

[10]Strictly speaking, the covariance matrix of eight variables has 36 unique elements. But it is assumed that sib-ordering is irrelevant, which is imposed by replicating the data with the original order of siblings reversed so that, e.g., $\text{Cov}(IQ_a, IQ_b) = \text{Cov}(IQ_b, IQ_a)$. This leaves 20 unique elements in the covariance matrix.

[11]There are four, and not two, degrees of freedom because of the cross-sib, cross-gender correlations in different unobservables. The tested restriction implies, for example, that the correlation between W for men and S for women must be equal to the correlation between W and S for women.

[12]This does not explain the high residual covariance for men, which arises from factors uncorrelated with these human capital variables, but it does potentially account for the higher explained covariance for women.

[13]The fitted covariance differs from the actual covariance since the model is overidentified. It is used since it is the sum of the explained and the unexplained fitted covariances. The actual covariances are .030 for

brothers and .024 for sisters, while the fitted covariances are .035 and .023, respectively.

[14]The contrast is exaggerated because the residual covariances will not necessarily fall as the explained covariances rise, since the residuals are already uncorrelated with the right-hand side variables. Nonetheless, even if the residual covariances are kept constant, the qualitative result that differences in wage equation parameters explain part of the greater indirect effect for women remains the same.

REFERENCES

Behrman, Jere R., Zdenek Hrubec, Paul Taubman and Terence E. Wales. 1980. *Socioeconomic Success: A Study of the Effects of Genetic Endowments, Family Environment and Schooling* (Amsterdam: North-Holland Publishing Company).

Behrman, Jere R., Robert A. Pollak and Paul Taubman. 1986. "Do Parents Favor Boys?" *International Economic Review*, 27(1): 33-54.

Behrman, Jere R., Paul Taubman and Terence E. Wales. 1977. "Controlling for and Measuring the Effects of Genetics and Family Environment in Equations for Schooling and Labor Market Success," Taubman, ed. (1977).

Bound, John, Zvi Griliches and Bronwyn H. Hall. 1986. "Wages, Schooling and IQ of Brothers and Sisters: Do the Family Factors Differ?" *International Economic Review*, 27(1): 77-105.

Center for Human Resources Research. 1984. *The National Longitudinal Survey Handbook* (Columbus: Ohio State University).

Chamberlain, Gary and Zvi Griliches. 1975. "Unobservables with a Variance-Components Structure: Ability, Schooling and the Economic Success of Brothers." *International Economic Review*, 16(2): 422-449.

Conlisk, John. 1971. "A Bit of Evidence on the Income-Education-Ability Interrelation." *Journal of Human Resources*, VI(3): 358-362.

Corcoran, Mary E. and Paul N. Courant. 1985. "Sex Role Socialization and Labor Market Outcomes." *American Economic Review*, 75(2): 275-278.

Corcoran, Mary, Christopher Jencks and Michael Olneck. 1976. "The Effects of Family Background on Earnings." *American Economic Review*, 66(2): 430-435.

Filer, Randall K. 1981. "The Influence of Affective Human Capital on the Wage Equation." In Ronald G. Ehrenberg, ed. *Research in Labor Economics*, 4: 367-416.

Griliches, Zvi. 1979. "Sibling Models and Data in Economics: Beginnings of a Survey." *Journal of Political Economy*, 87(5, Pt. II): S37-S64.

Griliches, Zvi and William Mason. 1972. "Education, Income and Ability." *Journal of Political Economy*, 80(3, Pt. II): S74-S103.

Heckman, James J. and Robert Willis. 1977. "A Beta-Logistic Model for the

Analysis of Sequential Labor Force Participation by Married Women." *Journal of Political Economy*, 85(1): 27-58.

Joreskog, Karl G. and Dag Sorbom. 1984. *LISREL VI: Analysis of Linear Structural Relationships by the Method of Maximum Likelihood* (Chicago: National Resources).

Leibowitz, Arleen. 1974. "Home Investments in Children." *Journal of Political Economy*, 80(3, Part II): S108-S138.

________________. 1977. "Family Background and Economic Success: A Review of the Evidence," in Taubman, ed. (1977).

Lloyd, Cynthia B. and Beth T. Niemi. 1979. *The Economics of Sex Differentials* (New York: Columbia University Press).

Michael, Robert T. 1977. "Family Background and Achievement: A Comment," in Taubman, ed. (1977).

Neumark, David. 1987a. "Employers' Discriminatory Behavior and the Estimation of Wage Discrimination." Mimeo.

_______________. 1987b. "Gender Differentials in the Labor Force: Measurement, Causes and Probes." (unpublished Ph.D. dissertation, Harvard University).

Oaxaca, Ronald. 1973. "Male-Female Wage Differentials in Urban Labor Markets." *International Economic Review*, 14(3): 693-709.

Olneck, Michael R. 1977. "On the Use of Sibling Data to Estimate the Effects of Family Background, Cognitive Skills, and Schooling: Results from the Kalamazoo Brothers Study," in Taubman, ed. (1977).

Rubin, Donald B. 1976. "Inference and Missing Data." *Biometrika*, 63(3): 581-592.

Sewell, William H. and Robert M. Hauser. 1975. *Education, Occupation and Earnings: Achievement in the Early Career* (New York: Academic Press).

____. 1977. "On the Effects of Families and Family Structure on Achievement," in Taubman, ed. (1977).

Sewell, William H. and Vimal Shah. 1968. "Parents' Education and Children's Educational Aspirations and Achievements," *American Sociological Review*, 33(2): 191-209.

Shackett, Joyce. 1981. "Experience and Earnings of Young Women." (unpublished Ph.D. dissertation, Harvard University).

Sheshinski, Eytan and Yoram Weiss. 1982. "Inequality Within and Between Families," *Journal of Political Economy*, 90(1): 105-127.

Taubman, Paul, ed. 1977. *Kinometrics: Determinants of Socioeconomic Success Within and Between Families* (Amsterdam: North-Holland Publishing Company).

Part Five
Behavioural Aspects of Fertility and Migration

The Changing Motivation for Having Children

Paul J. Albanese, Assistant Professor of Economics

Department of Economics, Middlebury College,
Middlebury, Vermont 05753, U.S.A.

1. INTRODUCTION

The predominant motivation for having children changes in a systematic way over the course of economic development, and each of these motivations is reflected in a characteristic pattern of fertility. A change in the predominant pattern of fertility which characterizes a population, therefore, is the result of a change in the motivation for having children. The purpose of this paper is to provide a theoretical examination of the systematic changes in the motivation for having children which occur in the course of economic development. It will be argued that the predominant motivation for having children changes from an economic motivation in traditional societies, to a social motivation in transitional societies, and ultimately to a psychological motivation in modern societies.

The theoretical concept of the demographic transition has long been the grand historical generalization which demographers have used to express the relationship between economic development and population change. Since the introduction of this concept by Frank W. Notestein [1] in 1945, demographic transition theory has fascinated demographers from many disciplines and has been explored from many theoretical points of view. Perhaps the most important understanding that has come out of this investigation is the realization that the demographic transition cannot be attributed to any single factor.

The present investigation will focus primarily on the theoretical aspects of the fertility decline of the demographic transition. This has been the primary preoccupation of economists, and the present approach will use the contributions that economic theory has made to an analysis of the fertility decline as a theoretical foundation. However, no single theoretical approach can encompass all of the factors which have contributed to the fertility decline. In an effort to broaden the behavioral foundations of the economic analysis, the relationship between economics and psychology will be explored.

To illustrate the theoretical analysis of the systematic changes in the motivation for having children, a case study of the generational change in the size of the Italian family in the United States will be presented. Table 1 makes a generational comparison of the number of children ever born to two cohorts of immigrant Italian women with two cohorts of American born Italian women.

Among immigrant Italian women in the United States that were captured by the 1940 census of population, the number of children ever born averaged around five children. However, among the American born Italian women captured by the 1970 census--the children of the Italian immigrants--the number of children ever born averaged just over two children.

The interpretation of the abrupt generational change in the size of the Italian family in the United States will be used to evaluate the various theories of fertility determination.

However, the wider implications of the generational change in the size of the Italian family can be seen when it is considered as a concentrated case study of the demographic transition. While the Italian immigrants were largely from rural and agricultural areas, they emigrated predominantly to the large industrial cities in the United States. Thus, the children of the Italian immigrants were born into a fundamentally different economic, social, and cultural system than that of their parents, and one aspect of their adaptation to living in the United States

TABLE I: GENERATIONAL CHANGE IN THE SIZE OF THE ITALIAN FAMILY IN THE UNITED STATES

Immigrant Italian Women: 1940*			American Italian Women: 1970**		
Age	Born	Number of Children Ever Born to Married Women		Born	Age
55-64	1876-1885	5.245	2.151	1906-1915	55-64
45-54	1886-1895	4.710	2.323	1916-1925	45-54

SOURCES: *U. S. Bureau of the Census, Census of Population: 1940, <u>Differential Fertility, 1940 and 1910: Women by Number of Children Ever Born</u> (Washington, D. C.: Government Printing Office, 1945): 128.

** U. S. Bureau of the Census, Census of Population: 1970, <u>Women by Number of Children Ever Born</u> (Washington, D. C.: Government Printing Office, 1973): 41-44.

is the remarkable change in the size of their families. The interpretation of this change will provide valuable insights into the factors that have contributed to the historical decline in fertility.

The paper will be divided into four sections: Section II will provide a brief overview of critical contributions to demographic transition theory. Section III will lay the theoretical foundation for an economic analysis of fertility determination, and provide a critique of the limits of applicability of these approaches. Section IV will explore the relationship between economics and psychology as a way of expanding the economic analysis of fertility to include social and cultural factors, as well as psychological factors. Section V will contain brief concluding remarks.

2. A BRIEF OVERVIEW OF DEMOGRAPHIC TRANSITION THEORY

The consideration of the generational change in Italian family size as a concentrated case study of the demographic transition provides an opportunity to investigate the implications of a number of theoretical approaches. In "Population--The Long View" (1945), Notestein placed special emphasis on the "growth of huge and mobile city populations", and the "growing individualism and rising levels of popular aspiration developed in urban industrial living" ([1], p. 40).

It will be shown subsequently that these are critical factors contributing to the fertility decline. However, in Notestein's original conception of the demographic transition, the population was viewed on an aggregate basis, and this gave the appearance of a gradual transition of birth and death rates for a country.

Since Notestein's earlier work there have been four theoretical developments which have made important contributions to the analysis of the demographic transition. In a study published in 1965, the United Nations [2] reached the conclusion that "fertility levels might ... be due ... at least partly to culturally determined circumstances affecting the interactions between fertility and economic and social changes" ([2], p. 143).

The position taken by the United Nations placed special emphasis on culture, and on the relationship between cultural, economic, and social factors affecting fertility behavior, especially <u>changes</u> in fertility patterns. In essence, the United Nations' point of view is that culture is the envelope of social and economic factors, and therefore influences the way in which social and economic factors affect fertility behavior.

In a general sense, this point of view argues against any one factor as the determinant of fertility behavior, whether it be economic, social, or cultural. However, in a more specific sense, it provides direct support for the strategy employed here of selecting a culturally distinct group within a population as a case study. Successive waves of immigration have made substantial contributions to the growth of the population in the United States. The result has been the creation of significant cultural variations within the population that must be accounted for in the study of American historical demography. The abrupt generational change in the size of the Italian family in the United States raises a fundamental question with regard to the general significance of ethnic factors in American fertility patterns.

A further contribution in this direction was made to demographic transition theory by the Princeton Office of Population Research, as a result of the European Fertility Project. It was demonstrated that a decline in fertility can spread rapidly through a region inhabited by a distinct linguistic or religious group, only to be halted at the boundary [3]. There are two important implications that can be drawn from the contributions of the European Fertility Project: In general, it further supports the necessity of disaggregating a population into significant groups, whether they are distinct linguistic or religious groups, or culturally distinct groups. In addition, the approach goes one important step further by arguing that within a distinct linguistic or religious group, the fertility decline can be very rapid. Thus, by aggregating the population the actual pattern of the fertility decline may be disguised, and appear to be gradual, when in fact the transition is actually abrupt.

What is clearly called for is the disaggregation of a population into significant groups which are characterized by common patterns of behavior, and therefore, will have a common pattern of fertility. In the Princeton study, this meant disaggregating European populations into regions containing distinct religious or linguistic groups. For the present case study, what is called for is the disaggregation of the population of the United States into culturally distinct ethnic groups.

Another contribution to demographic transition theory that warrants attention in this selective survey, especially for its substantive contribution to economic approaches to the fertility decline, is Deborah S. Freedman's "The Relation of Economic Status and Fertility" (1963). Freedman [4] argued for the need to distinguish between the general concept of the relative economic and social status of a group, and a more limited concept of the relative income of a family within an economic and social status group ([4], p. 415). It will be shown subsequently that the simple recognition of the stratification of society into significant economic and social status groups is critical to an understanding of the fertility decline. For the present investigation the primary implication is that the case study must be further disaggregated by generations within an ethnic group, because there was a significant change in the relative economic and social status of the American born generation of the children of the Italian immigrants.

A final contribution that must be noted has been made by John C. Caldwell in "A Restatement of Demographic Transition Theory." Caldwell [5] strongly emphasized the need to study how the individual demographic innovator differs from their parents, and has argued that the failure to investigate in detail the way of life of the individual constitutes a research failure in understanding the demograhic transition ([5], p. 335).

The insights from these various approaches have been combined in the designation of the case study of the generational change in the size of the Italian family in the United States as an opportunity to investigate the fertility decline of the demographic transition. Disaggregation of the population into culturally distinct ethnic groups is dictated by the impact of immigration on the demographic history of the United States. Further disaggregation of a single ethnic group into separate generations is determined by the differential opportunity for economic mobility of the Italian immigrants and their American born children in this country. A detailed case study of a single socioeconomic group is essential, and for this reason the present investigation will ultimately focus primarily on the American born generation of the children of the Italian immigrants. Finally, the need to focus on the individual coincides with the individual orientation of the economic theory of the consumer, and further, facilitates expandsion of the behavioral foundations of economic theory through the establishment of the relationship between economics and psychology. This is accomplished by relating the economic theory of the consumer to psychological theories of the personality, and more precisely by using theories of personality development to study the process of preference formation [6] [7].

3. ECONOMIC THEORIES OF FERTILITY DETERMINATION

A highly selective survey will be presented of the theoretical contributions that have been made by economists to unraveling the demographic transition. Economists have concentrated on the theory of the fertility decline, and the work of three economists will be emphasized and examined in a critical way: Gary S. Becker [8] [9], Richard A. Easterlin [10] [11], and Harvey Leibenstein [12]. Each of these approaches represents an application of some variant of the economic theory of the consumer, and it is this theoretical foundation which will be related to psychology in an endeavor to expand the limits of applicability of economic theory.

The application of the economic theory of the consumer to fertility behavior essentially began with Gary S. Becker [8] in "An Economic Analysis of Fertility" (1960). While many ideas were introduced in this article, it was Becker's quantity-quality argument that was subsequently brought to fruition in A Treatise on the Family (1981). In the intervening period, Becker [13] introduced the concept of time into the economic analysis of consumption behavior in "A Theory of the Allocation of Time" (1965), which was subsequently elaborated with Robert T. Michael [14] in "On the New Theory of Consumer Behavior" (1973).

The result became known as the "household production function" approach, in which tastes and technology determined the allocation of income and time in the production of "commodities" by the household. This is a critical innovation, because "the observation that all activity takes scarce time is crucial to the claim that all human pursuits come within the purview of neoclassical economic analysis", and it "is the foundation stone for his [Becker's] enterprise of apprehending the most varied aspects of human behavior 'from the economic point of view'" ([15], p. 20).

Becker states his interpretation of the fertility decline in the following way: "I am convinced that the most promising explanation is found in the interaction between the quantity and quality of children, for it implies that the demand for children is highly responsive to price and perhaps to income, even when children have no close substitutes" ([9], p. 107). In essence, his approach argues that parents choose not only the number of children that they will have, but also the quality of each child, and, in the course of economic development, parents simply choose higher quality children, and therefore, must decide to have fewer children.

The quantity-quality argument is subject to two criticisms, one obvious and one not so obvious, which severely undermine the theory. An obvious criticism is that parents simply do not have separate choices to make between the quantity of children and their quality. The quantity-quality distinction is an artificial separation of what is essentially one choice into two choices. Parents simply do not have a choice about the so-called "quality" of each child, but are compelled by social considerations to raise each child at the same status. Furthermore, that status is determined by the relative economic and social status of the parents [4] [12]. This is the critical insight behind the quip made by James S. Duesenberry [16] in commenting on Becker's original 1960 article: "Economics is all about how people make choices. Sociology is all about why they don't have any choices to make."

The failure to recognize the significance of social considerations is a fundamental weakness of the basic theoretical framework of the economic theory of the consumer, without regard to whether it is the conventional version of the theory or the household production function approach. The inadequate social foundation of the theory stems from the assumption of given tastes or preferences upon which the theory is based. As a result of this assumption, the social basis of the theory is indistinguishable, that is to say, the theory cannot distinguish between an individual, a family, friends, peer groups, the local community, or economic and social classes [17]. The theory simply assumes that tastes or preferences are given, and it is irrelevant whether they represent any one of these social organizations. It is no wonder that economists that accept the validity of the assumption of given tastes or preferences have been slow, if not loathe, to recognize the significance of social considerations for economic analysis.

A not so obvious, but far more fundamental criticism of Becker's argument comes from the observation that a change in the pattern of fertility reflects a change in fertility preferences. The quantity-quality argument reduces to nothing more than a sophisticated disguise for what must be recognized as an undeniable change in preferences. This observation is central to the explanation of changes in the motivation for having children, and will be elaborated using the case study of the generational change in the size of the Italian family in the United States.

However, at this point a digression is in order to document the antagonistic attitude displayed by Becker and his colleagues in the Chicago School toward the appropriate role of tastes and preferences in economic analysis, and to demonstrate that this aggressive display betrays a basic sensitivity and vulnerability on this issue ([15], p. 9).

In the defensive "De Gustibus Non Est Disputandum" (1977), Becker and George J. Stigler simply dismiss tastes or preferences as an explanatory variable by merely asserting that "tastes neither change capriciously nor differ importantly between people" ([18], p. 76). The attribution of changes in tastes to capriciousness must be regarded as pure rhetoric, however, the assertion that tastes are "similar among people", and "that no significant behavior has been illuminated by assumptions of differences in tastes" must be taken somewhat more seriously ([18], pp. 76, 89). By not acknowledging the critical role of tastes or preferences in consumer theory, according to Becker and Stigler, "all changes in behavior are explained by changes in prices and income, precisely the variables that organize and give power to economic analysis" ([18], p. 89).

The critical implication of this statement is that not only are Becker and Stigler willing to accept the assumption of given tastes or preferences, but having done so, they are prepared to ignore any of the theoretical limitations imposed by that assumption. As a consequence, a controversy surrounding the appropriate role of tastes or preferences has grown out of the application of the economic theory of the consumer to an analysis of fertility behavior. One side is represented primarily by the views of Becker, and has become known as the Chicago-Columbia School. The other side, representing virtually every other economist has become known as the Pennsylvania School, primarily after the work of Richard A. Easterlin.

In "Toward a Socioeconomic Theory of Fertility: A Survey of Recent Research on Economic Factors in American Fertility", Easterlin [10] called for the elevation of taste considerations bearing on choice to a position equal to that of income and prices in economic theory. With regard to expanding the limitations of economic analysis, he argued that "perhaps the greatest obstacle so far to development of a unified socioeconomic theory of fertility, and correspondingly, the most promising opportunity for advance, lies in the subject of tastes" ([10], p. 133).

What is so important about Easterlin's challenge is that it addresses the two limitations thus far enumerated: it calls for specific attention to tastes, rather than simply ignoring their role entirely, and it advocates the investigation of taste factors as a way of overcoming the inadequate social foundations of economic analysis. Easterlin [10] concluded that "an adequate framework for fertility analysis calls for explicit attention to preference phenomena and the factors entering into their formation" ([10]. p. 135).

The call for an investigation of preference formation is the most promising opportunity for advance in expanding the behavioral foundations of economic analysis. However, even this issue evinces an antagonistic attitude from the Chicago-Columbia School, and again, it stems directly from a sense of vulnerability. In "On the New Theory of Consumer Behavior", the argument is put forth that, "if behavioral responses are attributed to differences in tastes, not much more can be said since there is no useful theory of the formation of tastes" ([14], p. 39). Instead, the household production function approach substitutes technology for taste considerations, with the easy argument that economists do profess to know something about technology [14].

The problem with ignoring taste considerations is tied to the fundamental limitations of the assumption of given tastes or preferences, and clearly reveals why the Chicago-Columbia school shows so much sensitivity on this issue. Whenever the question of why a consumer has a certain set of preferences is asked, the theory becomes circular, and simply resolves into nothing more than saying the consumer behaves as they behave [19]. This results from the fact that with ordinal utility theory, "the consumer's market behavior is explained in terms of preferences, which are in turn defined only by behavior" ([20], p. 91).

To avoid this circularity, the formation of preferences must be systematically investigated, rather than simply being ignored. This facile approach was countered by Easterlin, along with Robert A. Pollak and Michael L. Wachter, in "Toward a More General Economic Model of Fertility Determination: Endogenous Preferences and Natural Fertility": "The notion that economists have an acceptable theory of systematic differences in household technology, but do not have a definitive theory of taste formation, is hardly justification for excluding or neglecting hypotheses related to tastes" ([11], p. 116).

In this article, Easterlin and his colleagues provide a general analytic framework which attempts to systematically incorporate as many relevant factors bearing on fertilty behavior as possible. This theoretical framework must be regarded as the best effort of economists to combine the contributions of numerous disciplines, and to communicate across disciplinary boundaries in an effective way. Accordingly, they argue that, "A framework that incorporates research on taste formation along with other social and economic variables will extend the range of empirical problems potentially amenable to treatment" ([11], p. 117).

While this general framework is the most fertile yet produced by any discipline, it is not as analytically satisfying as the specific contributions made by Harvey Leibenstein [12] in "The Economic Theory of Fertility Decline" (1975). Leibenstein's theory explicitly takes into account the stratification of the population into social and economic status groups, as the following methodological statement attests: "The alternative that suggests itself, ... , is that populations are divided into social status groups that have different tastes, who may to some degree have different desires for children (but not simply because of an income difference), and who especially see the whole cost structure of their expenditures, including expenditures for children, from the viewpoint of vastly different preference structures" ([12], p. 3).

The recognition of the stratification of the population into economic and social status groups is integral to Leibenstein's interpretation of the fertility decline. Leibenstein's crucial contribution to fertility analysis is the recognition that it is a change in relative economic and social status that brings about a change in family size. The change in fertility patterns which conventionally characterizes the fertility decline, that is, the change from a pattern of natural fertility to a pattern of replacement fertility, is primarily the result of a change in relative economic status, followed by an adjustment to the appropriate social status. This is the fundamental contribution which Leibenstein has made to the theory of the fertility decline.

What Leibenstein has succeeded in doing is formulating a model of the process of rising to a higher relative economic status which incorporates a concomitant change in social status. Leibenstein's critical contribution lies in the way in which the change in relative economic status and the fertility decline are related in his theory. The expresss purpose of Leibenstein's theory is "to explain the decline in fertility that accompanies sustained economic development" ([12], p. 1). In the course of sustained economic development, according to Leibenstein [12], job formalization and professionalization increases, and this results in the income stream becoming "steady" and "stable". Thus, the rise in relative economic status provides a steady and stable source of income, which allows the pattern of consumption to change to reflect the appropriate social considerations of the new status.

While Leibenstein must be given credit for applying this concept of the labor market to explain the fertility decline, the fundamental idea did not originate with him. In fact, it is the the concept of the dual labor market which has been extensively investigated by Michael J. Piore [21]. The dual labor market consists of a secondary and a primary labor market, and Piore provides the following striking description of the secondary labor market: "the jobs tend to be unskilled, generally, but not always low paying, and to carry or connote inferior social status; they often involve hard or unpleasant working conditions and considerable insecurity; they seldom offer chances of advancement toward better-paying, more attractive job opportunities; they are usually performed in an unstructured work environment and involve an informal, highly personalistic relationship between supervisor and subordinate" ([21], p. 17).

The primary labor market is characterized by a hierarchical organization of labor which provides the possibility of upward mobility. It is Piore's contention that "such a hierarchy is critical to the motivation of the labor force, that is, that it is basically the accumulation and maintainance of social status, not income, that induces people to work" ([21], p. 33). In addition, Piore argues that the movement from the secondary to the primary labor market brings an inevitable shift in job aspirations toward a steady, stable, and preferably rising source of income which characterizes the primary labor market ([21], p. 78).

The concept of the dual labor market is implicit in Leibenstein's theory, and it is essential for his explanation of the fertility decline. Making the structure of the labor market explicit gives precise meaning to a change in relative economic status, viz., it is represented by the movement from the secondary to the primary labor market, making possible a steady, stable, and rising source of income. The change in relative economic status results in a change in social status, and the entire pattern of consumption changes to reflect the new economic and social status.

In Leibenstein's theory the fertility decline results from the way in which the pattern of consumption changes to reflect the new economic and social status. As a family rises to a higher status, an increasing proportion of income is spent on commodities which reflect the new status [12].

In essence, what this means is that alternative consumption bundles become available through the market which are substituted for children [12]. Leibenstein concludes that, "to some degree, higher status groups rely more on the market" ([12], p. 24).

One further clarification can be made using Leibenstein's theory of the fertility decline, a clarification which was first made by Deborah Freedman [4]. A clear distinction can be drawn between the concept of relative economic and social status and relative income. The stratification of society into economic and social status groups is based on a range of factors, including income, occupation, education, and so on. Relative income is a more limited concept which refers to income relative to the average income within an economic and social status group [4]. This distinction is crucial for fertility theory because fertility is positively related to relative income, but negatively related to relative economic and social status [4].

Leibenstein's main theoretical contribution is the understanding that it is a fundamental change in relative economic and social status which is essential to the fertility decline [12]. Despite the scant attention which his theory has received since its publication in 1975, it must regarded as the most viable theory of the fertility decline yet produced.

The limits of applicability of Leibenstein's approach stem from the ranges of family size which he correctly chose to address. Leibenstein [12] divided the desire for children into three categories--low-, medium-, and high-parity children, where low parity meant zero to three children, medium parity represents four to six children, and high parity represents seven or more children. While these ranges can be regarded as arbitrary, the important point is Leibenstein [12] restricted his theory of the fertility decline to a change from high to medium parity fertility patterns, and did not concern himself with the motivation for having children in the low parity range. Thus, what he was concerned with is what is conventionally defined as the fertility decline, the change from a pattern of natural fertility to a pattern of replacement fertility, which is described here as a change from a predominance of an economic motivation to a social motivation for having children. In other words, when children no longer contribute time and income to the support of the family, the economic motivation for having children is lost, and the social motivation becomes dominant.

An additional criticism of the limits of applicability of Leibenstein's theory can be made with regard to the role of preference change. Leibenstein [12] explicitly recognizes the significance of differences in preferences, which is clear from the methodological statement that each social status group has different tastes, and views the cost structure of their expenditures from vastly different preference structures. It is also clear from the recognition that the structure of preferences is different for each economic and social status group, that a change in the relative economic and social status will involve a change in the structure of preferences. However, the role of changes in preferences is only implicitly recognized and requires more extensive elaboration.

4. PREFERENCE CHANGE AND THE FERTILITY DECLINE

The affirmation of the importance of the role of tastes or preferences as an explanatory variable in economic theory is a central objective of this paper. Because the economic theory of the consumer is based on the assumption of given preferences, the theory cannot be called upon to investigate the origin of those preferences without becoming circular. Therefore, it is clear that we must go beyond economic theory to investigate the nature of preferences. What this means is that to avoid this circularity, it is essential to systematically incorporate useful contributions from other disciplines into the basic framework of the economic theory of the consumer. The objective of such an endeavor is not to replace the economic theory of the consumer with an alternative theory, but to broaden the behavioral foundations of the theory.

A promising opportunity for advance lies in relating the disciplines of economics and psychology as a way of investigating the nature of preferences. Notable among the many contributions on the relationship between economics and psychology are Tibor Scitovsky's The Joyless Economy: An Inquiry into Human Satisfaction and Consumer Dissatisfaction (1976), and Shlomo Maital's Minds, Markets, and Money: The Psychological Foundations of Economic Behavior (1982). Scitovsky [22] argued that what economists think of as differences in tastes are in fact different types of personalities, and that different personality types can be ranked along a continuum. Maital's main contribution, I believe, lies in advocating that economists should study the development of personality as a way of integrating economics and psychology [23].

A major objective of each of these approaches is to draw insights from existing psychological theories to illuminate economic theory. A specific objective here is to relate psychological theories of the personality to an investigation of the nature of the consumer's preferences, and ultimately to apply the insights gained to fertility theory. However, this is not the time or place to delve deeply into the substantive issues involved in forging a theoretical relationship between economics and psychology [6] [7]. An effort will be made here to deal with the conceptual issues which are relevant for an application to fertility behavior.

To begin with, an understanding of the development of personality can contribute to an understanding of the formation of preferences. This is the way out of the circularity imposed by the assumption of given preferences, and this approach also provides a way of overcoming the criticism that the social basis of the theory of the consumer is inadequate. Economists must perforce begin with an investigation of the individual, before we can proceed to larger social aggregates such as the couple, the family, the household, and so on. The advantage of starting with the study of the personality development of the individual is that modern theories of personality development are based on the significance of interpersonal relations, which means that the theories start from a social basis [24] [25] [26].

A further advantage of the investigation of the personality is that the level of personality development can be arrayed along a continuum of personality development. The concept of a continuum of personality development has been elaborated by Otto F. Kernberg, particularly in his influencial articles on determinants of interpersonal intimacy [27] [28] [29] Intimacy in an interpersonal relationship is considered an achievement, and the degree of success or failure in achieving intimacy has been used as an overall organizing concept to rank the level of personality development along the continuum.

Two profound implications for fertility theory can be drawn from this analysis. The first implication concerns the predominant motivation for having children after the economic and social motivation are no longer predominant. The motivation for the need for intimacy is loneliness, and the emergence of intimacy as an analytic concept in psychology can be related directly to the fertility decline. The historical decline in fertility has increased the incidence of isolation and, therefore, the incidence of the experience of loneliness, and this increasing incidence of loneliness is the motivation behind the increasing interest in intimacy.

The historical argument that the decline in fertility has increased the motivation for intimacy can be used to illuminate the motivation for having children when there is no significant economic or social motivation. In questionaire surveys which asked urban middle class couples with small families why they had children, the foremost response was for happiness, love, and companionship, and the most important specific reason in this category was the avoidance of loneliness, followed by the love and affection afforded by the parent-child relation [30]. In terms of the classification of the motivation for having children, the predominant motivation becomes psychological; i.e., the need for intimacy.

This contribution alone is a powerful justification for the use of the insights of psychology to illuminate economic analysis. However, a further, and perhaps more fundamental insight is available pertaining to changes in preferences. An understanding of the systematic way in which preferences change has proven to be a rather intractable area of research for economists. The major reason for this strikes at the very foundations of the economic theory of the consumer, and dates from its inception.

Cardinal utility theory had its origin in Jeremy Bentham's hedonic calculus, which was based on the concept that there were quantifiable "simple pleasures" and "simple pains" [31]. When economists borrowed Bentham's theoretical framework, they only extracted the pleasureable side of the equation, and ignored completely the negative aspects of consumption. Thus, "utility" became associated only with the satisfaction of wants ([32], p. 1055).

This omission has direct relevance for understanding the intractability of preference change: What motivation could a consumer possibly have to change their preferences if only pleasure is experienced from consumption? If the consumer only maximizes utility, why change? Not being able to recognize the unpleasureable aspects of consumption leaves the economic theory of the consumer one-sided, and, therefore, unable to anticipate preference change because it is disappointment with one's choices that leads to change [15].

The way out of this dilemma stems directly from the determinants of intimacy: The first precondition for intimacy in an interpersonal relationship is that another significant person must be perceived as both good and bad, that is, as a whole person. Failure to integrate the good and bad aspects of one person means that every other person is treated as either all-good or all-bad ([26], p. 30). Thus, by using the development of personality as a way of understanding preference formation, the most fundamental flaw in the foundation of the economic theory of the consumer can be overcome.

A further illumination of the insights of psychoanalytic theory can be drawn on to complete the analysis of preference change and the changing motivation for having children. The second precondition for an intimate relationship is the integration of satisfying sexual relations into an interpersonal relationship ([29], p. 81). This opens the way for the internalization of a value system in an intimate interpersonal relationship. In an intimate relationship, sexual intercourse and orgasm leads to the experience of transcendence, in which boundaries of the self are abandoned, and a new common social boundary forms around the couple ([29], p. 106) [33]. It is this new social boundary which forms around the couple that protects them from parental prohibitions and demands, which in this case represents the culture of the immigrant Italians. This permits the American born children of the Italian immigrants to change in ways that are more appropriate to the dominant culture which they are born into and live. For the generation of American born Italian men and women, this explains how family size could change so abruptly: It was part of the broader process of adaptation and cultural change in the United States [6]. This confirms the position taken by the United Nations, that fertility levels are at least partly the result of culturally determined circumstances affecting the interactions between fertility and economic and social changes ([2], p. 143).

5. CONCLUSION

The changing motivation for having children over the course of economic development can be characterized in the following way: At lower levels of development the predominant motivation for having children is primarily economic; i.e., children contribute time and income to the support of the family. The choice is one of having as many children as possible, and a natural pattern of fertility is the outcome. At higher levels of development, when the structural change in the economic system warrants the designation as a developed country, the predominant motivation for having children is primarily social; i.e., children become a reflection of the relative economic and social status of their parents. The choice is one of how many children to have, and a pattern of replacement fertility is the outcome. At the highest levels of development, the predominant motivation for having children is primarily psychological; i.e., children satisfy a basic human need for intimacy, and to avoid the devastating experience of loneliness. The choice then becomes one of whether to have children or not, and the decision has been moving in the direction of having one child or none in the more advanced developed countries.

ACKNOWLEDGEMENTS

This paper was originally prepared while I was a Research Fellow at the Center for Population Studies at Harvard University. I would like to acknowledge the helpful comments made on various stages of this paper by Harvey Leibenstein, Oded Stark, and Hank Gemery.

REFERENCES

[1] Notestein, Frank W., Population--The Long View, in: Schultz, Theodore W., (ed.), Food for the World (Chicago: University of Chicago Press, 1945) pp. 36-57.

[2] United Nations, Department of Economic and Social Affairs, Population Bulletin of the United Nations, Number 7-1963, with Special Reference to Conditions and Trends of Fertility in the World (New York: United Nations, 1965).

[3] Coale, Ansley J., The Demographic Transition Reconsidered, International Population Conference, Leige, 1973 Vol. I (Leige: IUSSP, 1973) pp. 62-63.

[4] Freedman, Deborah S., The Relation of Economic Status and Fertility, American Economic Review 53, 3(June 1963) pp. 414-426.

[5] Caldwell, John C., A Restatement of Demographic Transition Theory, Population and Development Review 2, 3&4(September/December 1976) pp. 321-366.

[6] Albanese, Paul J., Toward a Methodology for Investigating the Formation of Preferences, Ph. D. Dissertation, Harvard University, November 1982.

[7] Albanese, Paul J., The Nature of Preferences: An Exploration of the Relationship Between Economics and Psychology, Journal of Economic Psychology, forthcoming, 1986.

[8] Becker, Gary S., An Economic Analysis of Fertility, in: Demographic and Economic Change in Developed Countries (New York: Columbia University Press, 1960) pp. 209-230.

[9] Becker, Gary S., A Treatise on the Family (Cambridge: Harvard University Press, 1981).

[10] Easterlin, Richard A., Toward a Socioeconomic Theory of Fertility: Survey of Recent Research on Economic Factors in American Fertility, in: Behrman, S.J., Corsa, Leslie Jr., and Freeman, Ronald, (eds.) Fertility and Family Planning: A World View (Ann Arbor: University of Michigan, 1969) pp. 127-156.

[11] Easterlin, Richard A., Robert A. Pollak, and Michael L. Wachter, Toward a More General Economic Model of Fertility Determination: Endogenous Preferences and Natural Fertility, in: Easterlin, Richard A., (ed.), Population and Economic Change in Developing Countries (Chicago: University of Chicago Press, 1980) pp. 81-150.

[12] Leibenstein, Harvey, The Economic Theory of Fertility Decline, Quarterly Journal of Economics 89:1 (February, 1975) pp. 1-31.

[13] Becker, Gary S., A Theory of the Allocation of Time, Economic Journal 75, 299(September 1965) pp. 493-517.

[14] Becker, Gary S., and Michael, Robert T., On the New Theory Of Consumer Behavior, Swedish Journal of Economics 75, 4(December, 1973) pp. 378-396.

[15] Hirschman, Albert O., Shifting Involvements: Private Interests and Public Action (Princeton: Princeton University Press, 1982).

[16] Duesenberry, James S., Comment, in: Demographic and Economic Change in Developed Countries (New York: Columbia University Press, 1960) pp. 231-240.

[17] Sen, Amartya K., Rational Fools: A Critique of the Behavioral Foundations of Economic Theory, Philosophy and Public Affairs 6, 4(Summer, 1977) pp. 317-344.

[18] Becker, Gary S., and Stigler, George J., De Gustibus Non Est Disputandum, American Economic Review 67, 2(March, 1977) pp. 76-90.

[19] Sweezy, Alan R., The Interpretation of Subjective Value Theory in the Writings of the Austrian Economists, Review of Economic Studies 1, 3(1934) pp. 176-185.

[20] Samuelson, Paul A., Foundations of Economic Analysis (Cambridge: Harvard University Press, 1947).

[21] Piore, Michael J., Birds of Passage: Migrant Labor and Industrial Societies (New York: Cambridge University Press, 1979).

[22] Scitovsky, Tibor, The Joyless Economy: An Inquiry into Human Satisfaction and Consumer Dissatisfaction (New York: Oxford University Press, 1976).

[23] Maital, Shlomo, Minds, Markets, and Money: Psychological Foundations of Economic Behavior (New York: Basic Books, 1982).

[24] Fairbairn, W.R.D., Psychoanalytic Studies of the Personality (London: Rutledge & Kegan Paul, 1952).

[25] Sullivan, Harry Stack, The Interpersonal Theory of Psychiatry (New York: W. W. Norton, 1953).

[26] Kernberg, Otto F., Object Relations Theory and Clinical Psychoanalysis (New York: Jason Aronson, Inc., 1976).

[27] Kernberg, Otto F, "Barriers to Falling and Remaining in Love", Journal of the American Psychoanalytic Association 22 (1974) pp. 486-511.

[28] Kernberg, Otto F, "Mature Love: Prerequisites and Characteristics", Journal of the American Psychoanalytic Association 22 (1974) pp. 743-768.

[29] Kernberg, Otto F., "Boundaries and Structure in Love Relations", Journal of the American Psychoanalytic Association 25, (1977) pp. 81-114.

[30] Espenshade, Thomas J., "The Value and Cost of Children", Population Bulletin 32, 1(April 1977).

[31] Bentham, Jeremy, The Principles of Morals and Legislation (New York: Hafner Press, 1948).

[32] Schumpeter, Joseph A., History of Economic Analysis (New York: Oxford University Press, 1954).

[33] Albanese, Paul J., "Intimacy and Sexuality in the Italian Family in the United States", in: Juliani, Richard N., (ed.), The Family and Community Life of Italian Americans (New York: Italian American Historical Association, 1983) pp. 173-176.

Relative Deprivation and Migration

by

Oded Stark and Shlomo Yitzhaki*

Mailing Address:

Oded Stark
Department of Economics
Harvard University
Littauer Center
Cambridge, Massachusetts 02138

March 1987

* Harvard University and Bar-Ilan University; The Hebrew University of Jerusalem and The World Bank, respectively. This is a revised version of Harvard University, Migration and Development Program, Discussion Paper No. 20. The paper was presented at the International Conference on Economics and Psychology, Shefayim, Israel, July 1986.

ABSTRACT

In this paper we define the relative deprivation of a person with income y as an increasing function of the percentage of individuals in the person's reference group whose income is larger than y. We obtain his satisfaction by adding up the marginal utilities of income over the range of income a person possesses. We model migration from one reference group to another as a response to relative deprivation and satisfaction: We say that a strong incentive to migrate exists if relative deprivation decreases while satisfaction rises with migration and that a weak incentive exists if the individual increases or decreases his satisfaction and deprivation at the same time by migrating. We derive conditions under which different incentives, weak or strong, hold for different individuals. We obtain the result that in general the richest individual in a society will not have a strong incentive to migrate but may have a weak incentive to migrate, whereas the poorest individual may have a strong incentive to migrate and also a weak incentive to migrate. Our analysis enables us to explain several perplexing migratory phenomena, identify income inequality as a distinct explanatory variable of migration and establish an incentive to migrate in situations where the utility-social welfare approach does not.

I. Relative Deprivation: The Basic Approach

The theory of relative deprivation is a theory about the feelings raised by social inequalities. The original conceptualization of the theory appears in the famous three-volume research monograph *The American Soldier: Adjustment During Army Life*, (1949). The theory has been applied to several fields in order to model social behavior. (See Crosby (1979) for an excellent review.) However, as pointed out by Merton and Kitt (1950), the concept of relative deprivation is not formally defined in *The American Soldier*. Therefore it is not surprising that Crosby (1979) counts four versions of the theory and that in general there is no agreement on what is the exact meaning of the term relative deprivation. In this paper we follow the approach developed in Yitzhaki (1979, 1982) and Stark (1984a, 1984b) which may be viewed as the economist's interpretation and quantification of the work of Runciman (1966). Runciman defines four conditions for an individual to feel relatively deprived: "We can roughly say that [a person] is relatively deprived of X when (i) he does not have X, (ii) he sees some other person or persons (possibly including himself at some previous or future time) as having X (whether or not that is or will be in fact the case), (iii) he wants X, and (iv) he sees it as feasible that he should have X." (Runciman (1966), p. 10).

The relativity of the concept is due to (ii) and (iv). The feeling of deprivation is defined by (i) and (iii). Replacing (i) with (i') "the person has X", where X represents a bundle of commodities x, enables us to interpret (i') as representing the utility or disutility derived from x, while (iii) eliminates disutility and thereby ensures utility. An individual's utility is a function of the commodities he has, whereas deprivation is the loss in forgone utility, due to not having commodities. Obviously, having x also means not having more than x or being deprived of having more than x. Formally, if u(x) is an index of the satisfaction from having x then -u(x) can serve as an index of the deprivation of having no more than x. Maximizing u(x) subject to an income constraint yields the same result as minimizing deprivation, -u(x), subject to the same constraint. Hence we can argue that the deprivation concept and the utility concept are two sides of the same coin; whereas utility is defined on "having," deprivation is defined on "not having."

However, there are two major differences between a relative deprivation approach and the utility, or the welfare function, approach. One, related to the relativity of the concept, emerges from the existence of reference groups in the society. How reference groups are formed and dissolved is a complicated issue that we hope to explore in the future. For the moment, we assume that the entire society constitutes the reference group and later on, when modeling migratory behavior, that society consists of two such groups. This assumption simplifies the presentation at the cost of ignoring an important dimension of the relative deprivation approach.

The other major difference between the relative deprivation approach and the welfare function approach relates to the marginal utility of income. Under the utility approach, the marginal utility of income is a function of income alone and hence does not depend on the income of others. Under the relative deprivation approach, each unit of income can be viewed as Runciman's x, and the feeling of deprivation which arises from not having the unit is an increasing function of the number of individuals in the reference group who have it.[1] Note, however, that envy or altruism are not postulated; what counts is how individuals evaluate what they have (satisfaction) and what they do not have (deprivation).

Assume a continuous income distribution. Then, each income unit (Runciman's x) is represented by an income range $[y, y+\Delta y]$ where $\Delta y \to 0$. Let $F(y)$ be the cumulative distribution of income. Then $1-F(y)$ is the percentage of individuals whose income is higher than y. Hence $1-F(y)$ represents the percentage of individuals who have the commodities represented by the income range $[y, y+\Delta y]$ and the feeling of deprivation is an increasing function of the percentage of individuals who have income larger than y, i.e., $1-F(y)$.

Let $h(1-F(y))$ be the deprivation from not having $[y,y+\Delta y]$, where $h(0) = 0$ and $h' > 0$. Then an individual whose income is y is deprived of all units of income above y. Thus we can write:[2]

$$D(y) = \int_y^{\infty} h[1-F(z)]dz \tag{1}$$

In order to simplify the discussion, we shall assume for now a simple form of $h[1-F(y)] = 1-F(y)$. In Section III we return to the more general form $h(\cdot)$.[3]

The deprivation function is defined on "not having." But it might be more convenient to work with a concept defined on "having." It is fairly easy to obtain such a concept by adding up the marginal utilities of income on the range of income that the individual possesses. We call this function the satisfaction function (the gratification function). Formally,

$$S(y) = \int_0^{y} h[1-F(z)]dz \tag{2}$$

which, given our assumption on the form of h, becomes:

$$S(y) = \int_0^{y} [1-F(z)]dz \tag{3}$$

The satisfaction and the deprivation functions complement each other in the following manner:

$$D(y) + S(y) = \mu \tag{4}$$

where μ is mean income.[4] Hence in evaluating a change in the well-being of an individual in a given reference group, it does not matter which function is used. However, once we bring in migration, since the individual moves from one reference group to another, it may well happen that satisfaction and deprivation increase or decrease in tandem.

We now briefly note the main properties of the functions.

a. $\frac{\partial S}{\partial y} = [1-F(y)] \geq 0; \quad \frac{\partial^2 S}{\partial y^2} = -f(y) \leq 0$, that is, the marginal satisfaction is non-negative and non-increasing. Intuitively, the individual will be more satisfied the more valued are the commodities he possesses. This value is an increasing function of $1-F(y)$, the fraction of individuals in the reference group who possess these commodities. In a society in which possessing a car is uniformly desirable, having a car is more valuable to an individual when many individuals possess cars than when only few do.

b. An increase in the income of a person who is poorer than the individual, such that the individual's rank remains intact, increases satisfaction but does not affect deprivation.

c. An increase in the income of someone richer than the individual does not affect the individual's satisfaction, but it increases his deprivation.

d. The deprivation of an individual can be written as the percentage of persons who are richer than the individual times their mean excess income, that is:

$D(y) = [1-F(y)]\ E(z-y|z>y)$ where z is the income of the richer persons.[5] Hence, for a given mean excess income of persons richer than the individual, the individual's deprivation is an increasing function of the percentage of such persons; and for a given percentage of persons richer than the individual, the individual's deprivation is higher the larger is their mean excess income.

e. The satisfaction of an individual can be written as:[6]

$$S(y) = \mu\left[\frac{\partial \phi(F)}{\partial F(y)}\,(1-F(y)) + \phi(F)\right] \tag{5}$$

and his deprivation as:

$$D(y) = \mu[1-\phi(F) - \frac{\partial\phi}{\partial F}[1-F(y)]] \quad (6)$$

where, as before, F is the cumulative distribution function, that is, the rank of the individual in the society, $\phi(F)$ is the Lorenz curve, that is, the percentage of total income received by individuals with incomes lower than that of the individual and $\frac{\partial\phi}{\partial F}$ is the slope of the Lorenz curve. It is worth noting that $\frac{\partial\phi}{\partial F} = \frac{y}{\mu}$, that is, the income divided by the mean.

Using the absolute Lorenz curve,[7] that is, the Lorenz curve where incomes are _not_ divided by mean income, enables us to portray S(y) and D(y) graphically as in Figure 1.

OAB is the absolute Lorenz curve. The curve passes through (0,0) and $(1,\mu)$; it is convex and its slope is equal to y. The line AC is tangent to the Lorenz curve at $F(y^*)$. Hence, BC is the deprivation of an individual with income y^* whereas CD is his satisfaction. To obtain this note that $CE = y^*[1-F(y^*)]$ and thus $CD = y^*[1-F(y^*)] + \mu\phi[F(y^*)]$ which upon rearrangement gives (5). Equation (6) can be derived geometrically in a symmetrical manner.

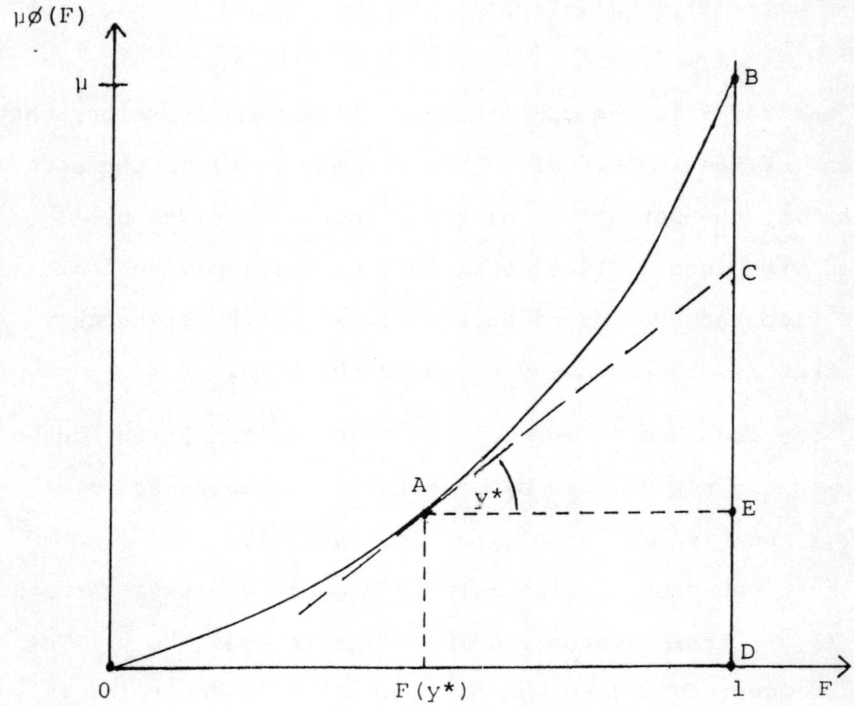

FIGURE 1

A Diagrammatic Presentation of Deprivation and Satisfaction

II. Deprivation and Migration

An individual who feels deprived in his own community has an incentive to migrate. This incentive is inversely correlated with the possibilities for deprivation reduction through intra-community mobility. Of course, actual migration is a function of other considerations such as incurred costs, whether pecuniary or psychic, opportunities for migration and attitudes toward risk (risk aversion). Our objective in this section is to examine the migration predictions of the pure relative deprivation theory. Since other variables are ignored, the discussion is restricted to whether a relative deprivation incentive to migrate exists and if so whether it is strong or weak. (We define these magnitudes below.) The predictions of the relative deprivation theory may be compared to the predictions of the utility theory, which are closely linked with those of the human capital approach. The prediction of the latter theory is fairly simple; an incentive to migrate exists if thereby expected lifetime income, appropriately discounted and netted, increases. Since the time dimension is fully and smoothly captured through the discounting procedure, there is no need to distinguish between short-run and long-run considerations.

However, in the case of a deprivation theory it is crucial to differentiate between the short run and the long run. In the short run the migrating individual probably continues to associate himself with his origin reference group. In this case, an individual will have an incentive to migrate only if his income increases, a conclusion which replicates the prediction of the utility theory/human capital approach.

In the long run, though, the migrating individual presumably associates with his new society, and refers to *it* as his new reference group.

In real life there is presumably a medium-run in between, wherein the individual may associate himself simultaneously with two reference groups, although not necessarily attaching the same weight to each. The passage from the short-run to the long-run may indeed be characterized by a gradual reduction in the weight attached to the origin reference group and a corresponding increase in the weight attached to the reference group at destination. The current paper deals only with a situation in which migration is accompanied by a complete (perfect) substitution of the reference groups, i.e., the long-run. This is a departure from our focus in earlier work on relative deprivation and migration (Stark 1984a, 1984b).

Since the society a migrant leaves and the the society he joins are different, it may happen that a migrating individual feels less deprived but also less satisfied in his new society or more satisfied yet more deprived. He feels more deprived if in the new society others have more goods than he does and more satisfied if he has more goods than before. Unless we explicitly model tastes, in such a case it is not clear which consideration dominates. We shall say that in situations of this type there is a weak incentive to migrate. That is, a weak incentive to migrate exists if by migrating the individual increases or decreases his satisfaction <u>and</u> deprivation at the same time. The implication of this condition is that it may then happen that some individuals will be motivated to migrate. We shall say that a strong incentive to migrate prevails if by migrating satisfaction increases <u>and</u> deprivation decreases. Then, migration is more likely, i.e., likelier than when the incentive to migrate is weak.

Thus, an individual who considers migrating from society A to society B has a strong incentive to migrate if $D_B < D_A$ and $S_B > S_A$ where D,S are deprivation and satisfaction respectively. It is assumed that both societies are large, so that the effect of migration by an individual on the distribution of income by size in both societies can be ignored.

Formally, a satisfaction incentive exists if

$$y_B[1-F_B] + \mu_B\phi_B > y_A[1-F_A] + \mu_A\phi_A \quad (7)$$

and a deprivation incentive exists if

$$\mu_B[1-\phi_B] - y_B[1-F_B] < \mu_A[1-\phi_A] - y_A[1-F_A] \qquad (8)$$

Rearranging terms, the satisfaction condition for an incentive to migrate (the S condition, hereafter) can be written as

$$y_B - y_A > \mu_B F_B[\frac{y_B}{\mu_B} - \frac{\phi_B}{F_B}] - \mu_A F_A[\frac{y_A}{\mu_A} - \frac{\phi_A}{F_A}] \qquad (7a)$$

and the deprivation condition (the D condition hereafter) as

$$y_B - y_A > (\mu_B - \mu_A) + \mu_B F_B[\frac{y_B}{\mu_B} - \frac{\phi_B}{F_B}] - \mu_A F_A[\frac{y_A}{\mu_A} - \frac{\phi_A}{F_A}] \qquad (8a)$$

Note that the terms in square brackets are non-negative. To see this, recall that $\frac{y}{\mu}$ is the slope of the Lorenz curve whereas $\frac{\phi}{F}$ is the slope of the line connecting the Lorenz curve to the origin. Since the Lorenz curve is convex, the non-negativity is ensured. Consequently, it can be easily seen from (7a) and (8a) that if the social parameters are identical, that is, if $\mu_A = \mu_B$, $\phi_A = \phi_B$ and $F_A = F_B$, then the prediction of the deprivation theory will be identical to the prediction of the utility theory; in both cases $y_B > y_A$ is a sufficient condition for an incentive to migrate.

However, if the social parameters differ across societies then a deprivation theory based prediction will be dependent on six parameters; of course not all of them are independent. To render the analysis tractable we shall thus initially restrict our attention to specific cases, where some of the parameters are given. As an aside we point out that if $\mu_A = \mu_B$, that is if the two societies have the same mean income then the S and the D conditions are identical. However, if $\mu_B > \mu_A$, then fulfillment of the S condition is a necessary condition for the D condition to hold whereas if $\mu_B < \mu_A$ then the D condition is a necessary condition for the S condition to hold.

a. Migration of the Richest Person

For the richest person in society A, $\phi_A = F_A = 1$. Then the S condition (Eq. 7) is:

$$y_B[1 - F_B] + \mu_B\phi_B > \mu_A \tag{9}$$

while the D condition (Eq. 8) is

$$\mu_B[1 - \phi_B] - y_B[1 - F_B] < 0 \tag{10}$$

By using Figure 1, it is easy to see that the D condition cannot be satisfied. On the other hand, the S condition is fulfilled if:

$$y_B > \frac{\mu_A - \mu_B \phi_B}{1 - F_B} \qquad (11)$$

However, if $\mu_A = \mu_B$, even the S condition cannot be fulfilled. To see this, replace y^* by y_B in Figure 1. BE is $\mu - \mu\phi[F(y_B)]$ and AE is $1-F(y_B)$. Since the absolute Lorenz curve is convex, its slope at A--which is y_B--is smaller than BE/AE. Therefore (11) is invalidated. Hence in this case the richest person in the society has no incentive to migrate. Intuitively, since relative deprivation is bounded from below by zero, the richest individual whose deprivation in A is zero cannot possibly lower it through migration. Note though that if the society at destination is richer than the society at origin, that is, if $\mu_B > \mu_A$ and the individual is expected to be the richest individual in B then, since (7) collapses to $\mu_B > \mu_A$, he can be said to have a strong incentive to migrate. (We say "can" since deprivation decreases only in the weak sense, i.e., it remains unchanged.)

Thus we conclude that in general the richest individual will not have a strong incentive to migrate but may have a weak incentive to migrate.

b. <u>Migration of the Poorest Person</u>

For the poorest individual in A, $F_A = \phi_A = 0$. Hence the S condition is

$$y_B - y_A > \mu_B F_B [\frac{y_B}{\mu_B} - \frac{\phi_B}{F_B}] \tag{12}$$

and the D condition is

$$y_B - y_A > (\mu_B - \mu_A) + \mu_B F_B [\frac{y_B}{\mu_B} - \frac{\phi_B}{F_B}] \tag{13}$$

The right-hand side of (12) is non-negative, hence the satisfaction condition is met if $y_B - y_A$ is sufficiently large. From the D condition we can conclude the following: If $\mu_B > \mu_A$ then the poorest individual has an incentive to migrate if y_B is greater than y_A by a large magnitude. Moreover, the richer (in terms of μ_B) society B is, the greater the income increase would have to be to cause migration. On the other hand, if $\mu_B < \mu_A$ then the poorest individual in A may still have a weak incentive to migrate even if his income declines! A poor person may very well endure less deprivation if he were to leave a rich society and join a society where only few persons possess goods which he does not possess. That we do not typically observe migratory moves of this kind must then have to do with the nonfulfillment of the S condition. And indeed, since the S condition cannot be fulfilled in this case, the overall condition for a strong migration incentive does not hold.

Consider now a situation wherein the income of the poorest individual in B is larger than it is in A, i.e., $y_B > y_A$. Assume that conditions (12) and (13) hold. We now wish to check whether under a specific shock to the parameters, conditions (12) and (13) hold a fortiori. We increase the individual's rank in B, i.e., we assume that F_B is larger. However, we keep μ_B and ϕ_B intact. Intuition might have led us to anticipate that the increase in rank will make (12) and (13) hold a fortiori: A higher rank is associated with a more appealing prospect. Apparently this is not the case. By inspecting (12) and (13) we note that in each case, the right-hand side where F_B enters multiplicatively is larger. This is portrayed with the help of Figure 2. The absolute Lorenz curve in society B is OAC and the individual considered is at A. Since $\mu_B\phi_B$ is kept constant, then increasing F_B means that the new absolute Lorenz curve must pass in the region $\overline{AE}$. Since y_B is the same, its slope when it intersects with $\overline{AE}$ is equal to the slope at A. Since μ_B is kept constant, the new curve must pass through C.

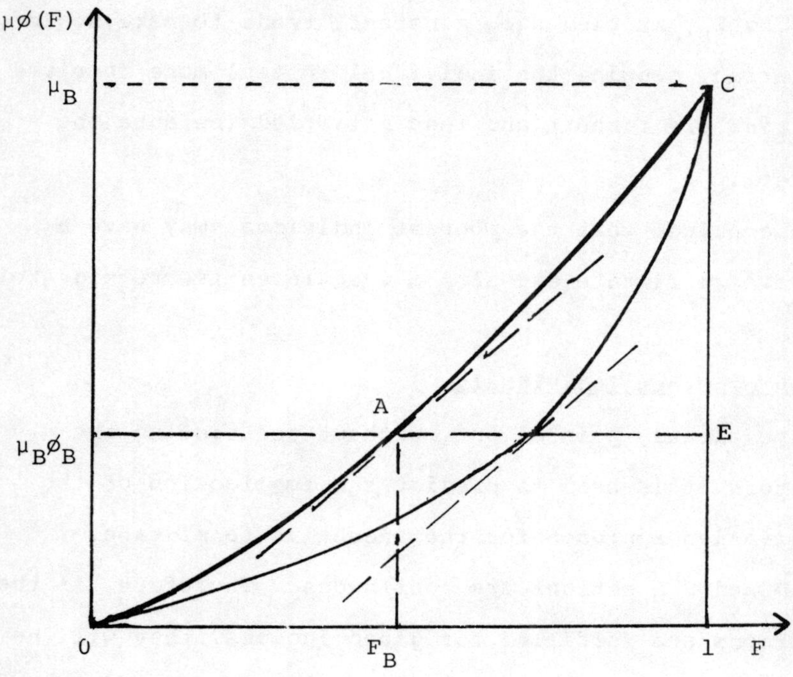

FIGURE 2

Hence increasing F_B, keeping $\mu_B \phi_B$ constant, tends to make society B less egalitarian, causing the individual to feel more deprived (because the rich are richer) and less satisfied (because the poor are poorer).

Thus, we conclude that the poorest individual may have a strong incentive to migrate and also a weak incentive to migrate.

c. <u>Migration of Other Individuals</u>

As we have already pointed out, without restricting the social parameters it is hard to predict the implication of the relative deprivation approach for the incentive to migrate. However, the D and S functions are continuous. Therefore, if the S and D conditions are fulfilled for given incomes, they will be fulfilled in their neighborhood of these incomes. Since we have found that the incentive to migrate for the poorest individual in the society is greater than for the richest, we may conclude that the relative deprivation approach predicts that for a given income differential, the poor have a higher incentive to migrate.

If we restrict $F = F_A = F_B$, that is, assume that the rank of the individual does not change, and assume also that $\phi_B = \phi_A = \phi$, then from (7a) the S condition becomes

$$y_B - y_A > \frac{(\mu_A - \mu_B)}{1 - F}\phi \qquad (14)$$

while from (8a) the D condition is

$$y_B - y_A > \frac{[\mu_B - \mu_A][1 - \phi]}{1-F} \tag{15}$$

and as can be seen from equation (14), the richer society B is, the larger the incentive to migrate for a given difference in incomes. On the other hand, from equation (15), we note that the richer society B is, the larger the income difference $y_B - y_A$ would have to be, in order to have a D incentive to migrate.

An interesting case arises when the individual will be the richest in B. In this case $\phi_B = F_B = 1$. The S condition is

$$\mu_B > y_A[1-F_A] + \mu_A\phi_A \tag{16}$$

whereas the D condition is

$$0 < \mu_A[1-\phi_A] - y_A[1-F_A] \tag{17}$$

The D condition is always fulfilled. Moreover, even the S condition may be fulfilled. This may hold even if $y_B < y_A$. Thus we may conclude that there is always a weak incentive for the second in line to move into a society in which he may be the top man and sometimes--and despite a decline in income--even a strong incentive exists. (See also Frank (1984, 1985)).

III. Deprivation and Migration: A Generalization

Hitherto we have employed a specific formulation of the theory of relative deprivation. Our main motivation in choosing the formulation has been to simplify the presentation. In this Section we adopt a general formulation of the theory. In the preceding Sections we have assumed that the intensity of deprivation of an individual is an increasing linear function of the number of individuals in the reference group who possess commodities the individual does not have. Yet it is possible to argue that the intensity of deprivation is also determined by the utility function as this function weighs the importance of the commodities and that rather than being linear in the number of individuals with higher income, deprivation is a monotonic increasing function of this number. We now incorporate these considerations, intimating as we do so that the implications of our approach for the incentive to migrate do not change in any qualitative way. However, the satisfaction and the deprivation incentives do change quantitatively, i.e., they may become weaker or stronger, depending upon the utility function.

Assume that an individual who does not have the commodities represented by the income range $[y, y + \Delta y]$ feels deprived of $u'(y)$, the marginal utility, and that the intensity of this feeling is, as before, an increasing function of the proportion of the individuals who are not deprived of this income range, that is $1 - F(y)$.

The deprivation of an individual whose income is y will be

$$D_u(y) = \int_y^{\infty} u'(z)[1 - F(z)]dz \tag{18}$$

while the satisfaction will be given by

$$S_u(y) = \int_0^y u'(z)[1 - F(z)]dz \tag{19}$$

For simplicity it is assumed that $u(0) = 0$. Then, the sum of $D_u(y)$ and $S_u(y)$ is equal to μ_u, the expected value of the utility function,[8] and the derivatives of $S(y)$ with respect to income have the same signs as before. The only property that requires modification concerns the relationship between $S_u(y)$ and $D_u(y)$ and the Lorenz curve. It can be shown that

$$S_u(y) = \mu_u[\frac{\partial \phi_u(F)}{\partial F} [1 - F(y)] + \phi_u(F)] \tag{20}$$

and

$$D_u(y) = \mu_u[1 - \phi_u(F) - \frac{\partial \phi_u(F)}{\partial F} [1 - F(Y)]] \tag{21}$$

where $\phi_u(F)$ is the cumulative percentage of μ_u that is derived from incomes lower than y, while $\frac{\partial \phi}{\partial F}$ is the slope of the curve.[9] Using the property $\frac{\partial \phi_u}{\partial F} = \frac{u(y)}{\mu_u}$ we can write the D and the S conditions as in (7a) and (7b) except that each y is translated into u(y), and ϕ and μ now carry the subscript u. Having defined the equivalent equations to (7a) and (7b), we can easily redo the preceding analysis with respect to migration. The qualitative conclusions do not change. For example, the richest person in the society may have only a weak incentive to migrate while the poor individual may have a weak incentive as well as a strong incentive. But of course, both incentives now depend on the properties of the u function as it affects the magnitudes of the parameters.

Assume, alternatively, that h[1-F(y)] is not linear. For example, let $h[1-F(y)] = [1-F(y)]^v$ where v>1 is a given constant. Then the satisfaction function is given by

$$S(v,y) = \int_0^y [1-F(z)]^v dz \tag{22}$$

In this case rather than portraying S(y) and D(y) using the absolute Lorenz curve (recall Sections I and II) we would need to utilize a weighted integration of the area below the Lorenz curve (as in Yitzhaki (1983)). Taking the analysis one step further in the generalization ladder we may express the satisfaction function as

$$S_u(y) = \int_0^y u'(z)h[1-F(z)]d(z) \tag{23}$$

where $h'>0$. Clearly if $h(\cdot)$ converges to a constant, the satisfaction function collapses into the conventional utility function.

IV. Concluding Comments

Students of migration have often failed to take note of the fact that the migration process is blurred by quite a lot of noise--as if it were that the main "regular" phenomenon is accompanied by some "irregular" satellite phenomena. The latter have usually been accounted for by ad hoc explanations and described as anomalies: Migration in the "wrong" direction, in our terminology from A to B while $y_B < y_A$, cannot possibly be explained by those same variables accounting for migration in the "right" direction, that is, from A to B while $y_B > y_A$. Our approach has the valuable characteristic that not only does it add a layer of explanation to the main phenomenon but also that it explains the accompanying phenomena and does so in a novel way.

For example, migration by retired persons, especially to communities characterized by a high ratio of retirees, might be construed as a strategic move aimed at preempting the likelihood of an increase in relative deprivation due to an anticipated, continued growth in the income of the non-retirees (but not of the retirees) in the retirees' origin reference group. The relative deprivation approach may thus give rise to life cycle based migratory predictions.

Return migration by successful migrants which is, by definition, a form of migration, is very often associated with a departure from a rich society (economy) to a less rich one. It appears as though maximal overall gains associated with migration accrue if at appropriate points in time, _two_ substitutions of reference groups take place: One, associated with the first move; the other, accruing as a successful migrant decides to return when _rank-wise_ his progress in the receiving community appears to grind to a halt.

Our analysis also has a bearing upon phenomena other than migration narrowly defined. For example, the third most senior executive in one corporation departs to become the chief executive officer in another corporation in a move which cannot possibly be sustained by considerations of income or income growth prospects.

We have seen that inequality _per se_ has a bearing on migration propensities. The fad in empirical migration research of characterizing--hence ranking--sending and receiving societies (sectors) by their mean income alone may thus omit an important explanatory variable. Our theory gives rise to the belief that migration depends on the inequality in the distribution of income by size in the sending and receiving societies, that it is positively correlated with inequality in the society of origin, and that it is negatively correlated with inequality in the society of destination.

On the basis of our discussion in Section II we may also note that the incentive to migrate is not a function of income levels but rather, and exclusively so, of income differentials. In order to verify this we may return to equation (3). Note that if we add a constant amount to the income of each and every individual, then satisfaction changes exactly by this constant whereas deprivation does not change at all. Hence if we add the same constant amount to all incomes in A as well as in B, conditions (7) to (17) will remain exactly the same; absolute levels of income play no role at all. This cannot be said to hold under the utility-welfare function approach where, due to declining marginal utility, addition of a constant amount reduces the incentive to migrate throughout. Notice though that the conclusion pertaining to the robustness of conditions (7) to (17) may not hold once a u function is introduced (as in Section III).

FOOTNOTES

[1]Runciman uses the example of promotions and writes: "The more people a man sees promoted when he is not promoted himself, the more people he may compare himself with in a situation where the comparison will make him feel relatively deprived," (1966, p. 19).

[2]For a detailed and explicit derivation of this equation from Runciman's axioms see Yitzhaki (1982).

[3]The reader might question our definition of D(y), pointing out that intuitively 1-F(y) might do just as well. Unfortunately, such is not the case. If, for example, the income of an individual who is richer than our reference individual increases, F(y) remains unchanged and so does 1-F(y). Yet a proper measure of relative deprivation should be sensitive to there now being more income units the reference individual is deprived of. D(y) as defined in (1) exhibits such sensitivity.

[4]Proof: $S(y) + D(y) = \int_0^\infty [1-F(z)]dz$

and by using integration by parts where $u = z$ and $v = 1-F(z)$ we obtain

$$\int_0^\infty [1-F(z)]dz = [1-F(z)]\, z\Big|_0^\infty + \int_0^\infty zf(z)dz = \mu.$$

[5]Proof:

Using integration by parts where

$v(z) = 1-F(z)$, $v'(z) = -f(z)$; $u(z) = z$ and $u'(z) = 1$ and the property $\lim_{y\to\infty} [1-F(y)] = 0$ we obtain

$$D(y) = \int_0^\infty [1-F(z)]dz = -[1-F(y)]y + \int_0^\infty zf(z)dz.$$

Using the conditional density function

$$f^*(z|z>y) = (1/[1-F(y)]f(z)$$

we insert f(z) into the last integral to obtain the expression as in d.

[6]Proof:

$$S(y) = \int_0^y [1-F(z)]dz$$

and by using integration by parts

$$S(y) = y[1-F(y)] - \int_0^y zf(z)dz = \mu[\frac{y}{\mu} [1-F(y) - \phi(F(y))]]$$

where ϕ is the Lorenz curve. Noting that $\frac{y}{\mu} = \frac{\partial\phi}{\partial F}$ completes the proof.

[7]Shorrocks (1983) refers to the absolute Lorenz curve as the "generalized Lorenz curve."

[8]Proof:

$$S_u(y) + D_u(y) = \int_0^\infty u'(z)[1-F(z)]dz$$

using integration by parts, we get

$$u(y)[1-F(y)]\Big|_0^\infty + \int_0^\infty u(z)f(z)dz = \mu_u + u(0)$$

assuming u(0) = 0 completes the proof.

[9]Proof:

$$S_u(y) = \int_0^y u'(z)[1-F(z)]dz =$$

which by using integration by parts decomposes to

$$= u(y)[1-F(y)]\Big|_0^y + \int_0^y u(z)f(z)dz$$

$$= \mu_u[\frac{u(y)}{\mu_u}[1-F(y)] + \frac{1}{\mu_u}\int_0^y u(z)f(z)dz]$$

$$= \mu_u[\frac{\partial\phi_u(F)}{\partial F}[1-F(y)] + \phi_u(F)]$$

where $\phi_u(F) = \frac{1}{\mu_u} \int_0^{\infty} u(z)f(z)dz$ is the percentage of u derived from income lower than y.

The derivative of $\phi_u(F)$ with respect to F (the cumulative distribution of income) is derived indirectly by

$$\frac{\partial \phi_u(F)}{\partial F} = \frac{\partial \phi_u / \partial y}{\partial F / \partial y} = \frac{u(y)f(y)}{\mu_u \; f(y)} = \frac{u(y)}{\mu_u} .$$

REFERENCES

Crosby, F. (1979). "Relative Deprivation Revisited: A Response to Miller, Bolce, and Halligan," The American Political Science Review 73, No. 1, 103-112.

Davis, A.J. (1959). "A Formal Interpretation of the Theory of Relative Deprivation," Sociometry 22, 280-296.

Frank, R.H. (1984). "Are Workers Paid Their Marginal Products?" The American Economic Review 74, No. 4, 549-571.

Frank, R.H. (1985). "The Demand for Unobservable and Other Nonpositional Goods," The American Economic Review 75, No. 1, 101-115.

Merton, R.K., and A.S. Kitt (1950). "Contributions to the Theory of Reference Group Behavior" in K.K. Merton and P.F. Lazarsfeld (eds.), Contributions in Social Research, Studies in the Scope and Method of "The American Soldier." Glencoe, IL: The Free Press, 40-105.

Runciman, W.E. (1966). Relative Deprivation and Social Justice: A Study of Attitudes to Social Inequality in Twentieth-Century England. Berkeley: University of California Press.

Shorrocks, A.F. (1983). "Ranking Income Distributions," Economia 50, No. 197, 3-17.

Stark, O. (1984). "Rural-to-Urban Migration in LDCs: A Relative Deprivation Approach," Economic Development and Cultural Change 32, 475-486. (a)

Stark, O. (1984). "Discontinuity and the Theory of International Migration," Kyklos 37, 206-222. (b)

Stouffer, S.A., E.A. Suchman, L.C. DeVinney, S.A. Star, and R.M. Williams, Jr. (1949). The American Soldier: Adjustment During Army Life. Princeton, NJ: Princeton University Press.

Yitzhaki, S. (1979). "Relative Deprivation and the Gini Coefficient," The Quarterly Journal of Economics 93, 321-324.

Yitzhaki, S. (1982). "Relative Deprivation and Economic Welfare," European Economic Review 17, 99-113.

Yitzhaki, S. (1983). "On an Extension of the Gini Inequality Index," International Economic Review 24, 617-628.

Behavioural Variability in Migration

Eliezer B. Ayal

Department of Economics
University of Illinois at Chicago
Box 4348, Chicago, IL 60680
U.S.A.

ABSTRACT

Migration, especially rural to urban migration, has been historically associated with economic development. There is, however, substantial variability in the nature, degree and speed of migration among different societies, and within societies.

There is an almost universal agreement by now that the ultimate determinant of migration is the wish to improve the material standard of living of the individual and his/her family. Yet there is ample evidence that there are substantial differences in the migration response to such economic incentives among individuals, families, and communities, reflecting the above mentioned variability.

This paper reports on empirical studies conducted in Southeast Asian countries which investigate the various factors which promote or inhabit migration. The factors studied include a wide range from religious affiliation to family land ownership.

Besides presenting such evidence, this paper attempts to find explanations for the differences in migration response. It is doubtful that a general theory would apply to all circumstances. But there are elements that empirical works reveal to be present across cultures. For example: level of education, previous move from original location, family or "network" relationship to migrants, and marital status affect the decision to migrate in most countries. Institutional factors such as the presence of active recruiting agencies affect migration both as suppliers of information and as providers of actual work and pay contracts.

The paper ends with an examination of various theoretical and empirical implications including the role of non-economic factors and of micro and macro modeling.

BEHAVIORAL VARIABILITY IN MIGRATION

Eliezer B. Ayal

1. INTRODUCTION

In the past, as well as at present, the process of economic transformation from a country with low per capita income to an industrialized country has been accompanied, and partly caused, by rising urbanization. A large share of such increased urbanization comes from rural-to-urban migration. There are, of course, various types of migration besides the permanent rural-to-urban migration, as will be seen below. Nonetheless, with the obvious exemption of urban-to-urban migration, the majority of the migrants originate from rural areas. Because lifestyles in the rural areas in most LDC is guided by traditional culture, ascriptive relationships, and constraining social units (such as extended families), standard economic models of migration might not provide a sufficient explanation or prediction. Moreover, migration often is a culmination of changing attitudes reflecting social and psychological evolution in isolated traditional societies. Such changes can be subtle and are not always obvious until some symptoms appear, such as migration. But there are differences in migration responses to economic incentives between adjacent villages which otherwise appear to be indistinguishable in occupational structures and ways of life. There are differences also within the same village, and even within the same family. Therefore, one cannot escape the suspicion that psychological factors also play a role.

Some regions seem to continuously be a source of outmigration. Such regions often exhibit characteristics which make them obvious candidates for outmigration even to the casual observer, such as persistent poverty and backwardness. Nonetheless, it is legitimate to ask why economic alternatives to migration do not develop in those regions. The apparent absence of opportunities within such regions might be a powerful push for emigration, once the psychosocial evolution made people ready for seeking improvement in their lives.

These are some of the reasons why it is important to understand the relationship between migration and the so-called "non economic factors." Such factors play a role in all stages of migration, from the emergence of an inclination towards migration, through actual migration and the continued interaction between migrants and their places of origin, to the kinds of living conditions of, and regrouping formed by, migrants at the destinations.

There follow a number of implications for the analysis of migration. For example: to what extent the decision to migrate is motivated by ambitions of individuals as distinguished from a collective decision by the family? Similarly, it is important to study the venues through which information leading to migration is communicated and interpreted. Another important area of interest is how the intention to migrate results in actual migration. Since actual migration requires the expenditure of resources to finance the move, it seldom occurs on the spur of the momment. Besides out-of-pocket costs there are also the opportunity costs of the rural job foregone, as well as other condiments such as a rent-free lodging place in the village. Here, again, family support is often required, with all the implied reciprocal commitments.

Once at the destination, there are a number of possibilities, including the question as to whether the migrant will stay there; if so, how long and in what type of urban sub-community will he/she live? If he/she intends to move further, the same questions will arise regarding the new place. Another, related, question is the continuing interaction or lack of it with the family and community of origin. A major type of continued relationship is the flow of remittances which was likely an important consideration leading to the emigration in the first place.

2. THE ECONOMIC THEORY OF MIGRATION

By now there is wide agreement about the economic theory of migration, especially of permanent place-to-place migration. Moreover, other social scientists also tend to agree that current and potential standard of living differences between the origin and destination are the ultimate determinants of migration.

A short-hand portrayal of the prevailing economics approach is as follows: Migration is a form of investment in human capital. Migration takes place when the discounted long term expected gains (the benefits) more than compensate for the costs. The latter include foregone earnings and amenities, moving costs and incurred obligations to the "folks back home." The following empirical findings are consistent with the basic economic model: it is increasingly found that, contrary to what had been previously assumed, migrants tend to be more skilled and more educated than those left behind. Similarly there is the related evidence that potential and actual migrants tend to be well informed about the prospects at the destination. In fact, recent studies record that unemployment among migrants is often smaller than among the natives at the destination areas, which suggests that migration is a systematic and informed behavior.

But there are a number of important issues which economic theory has not been able to answer. Among them: the continued rural urban income differentials in spite of very large rural/urban migration. (Empirical works, mostly testing and/or revising the Harris-Todaro model, have not yet resolved the issue.) The same can be said about the lack of a satisfactory economic explanation for the diverse migration responses to the intersectoral income differentials.

Economic models tend to ignore the "push" factor in migration. The most important one, of course, is the rural population growth which in most LDC outspaces the urban population growth in absolute numbers. Although one could argue that since such population growth results in lower average rural income and that therefore the economic model would pick it up anyway, it is not quite so. Migration has its own dynamics, and the average rural income is too aggregative to serve as a causal variable capable of explaining the variability of migration response. It could be, and was, argued, for example, that since the educated and skilled were found to have a higher than average propensity to migrate, we have to use a model that clearly differentiates between different skill groups. The increase in the rural ratio of labor over capital and land, due to population growth, keeps down rural wages and the incentive for labor-substituting capital investment in that sector which could have raised the average income there. This generally low rural wage keeps the income of the rural skilled disproportionately lower than their urban counterparts. Such a gap could explain both the persistance of the rural/urban wage differential, and the higher incentive to migrate found among the rural skilled.

Because the attraction of the cities (and some foreign countries) goes beyond higher wages, a purely economic model cannot fully account for migration, although the incorporation of the externalities within such a model will go a long way to meet this challenge.

3. EVIDENCE FROM SOUTHEAST ASIA

The empirical results presented here are based on recent research done in and on Southeast Asian countries. Among the reasons for that: (1) these are very good works; (2) the area has been rarely mentioned in the well known works on migration; (3) it is one of the areas in the developing world where rural to urban migration is still the major factor in urbanization; (4) among them, the Southeast Asian countries encompass practically all kinds of migration; and (5) the area is composed of populations following vastly different religions.

Because religious differences are believed to affect the status of women; family structure and obligations; mobility, and other relevant attributes, a short survey of the religious affiliations in the different countries might be useful here, especially for those who are not familiar with Southeast Asia. It should be pointed out, though, that empirical research has not yet categorically established precise relationships betwen specific religions and migration patterns.

The predominant religion in Thailand is Theravada Buddhism. In the Philippines it is Catholicism. In Indonesia it is Islam. In peninsular Malaysia the Malays are Muslim, the Chinese have the amalgam of the Chinese religions and traditions, and the Indians of Malaysia and Singapore are mostly Hindu.

We begin with Thailand. A combination of Theravada Buddhism; a family system based on bilateral inheritance and kinship; a substantial equality between the sexes; and a history of poverty-driven migration in the Northeast helps explain the rich variety of migration types in Thailand.

The Chinese tradition is different, but we must remember that the Chinese in Southeast Asia, especially in Thailand and the Philippines, have been influenced by the surrounding cultures. Their families are patrilineal, with strong family control over spouse selection, dowry payment, marriage arrangements and inheritance. There is marked preference for male over female children. These factors limit the freedom of movement of individuals, especially single women. Thus migration decisions are substantially family decisions. In southeast

Asia this is primarily relevant for penisular Malaysia. In the other countries there are no Chinese villages. There, almost all the Chinese live in cities except for individual or small clusters of trading families in villages. Since the brunt of the migration is out of villages, most of the migrants in these countries are indigenous non-Chinese.

Most Filipinos are Catholic, with a relatively small sprinkling of Protestants. They retain, however, a significant amount of extended family features. Moreover, like in many other Southeast Asian countries, the status of women is closer to that of men than in most Latin American Catholic countries. Nonetheless, the long Spanish-Catholic rule has left lasting marks on Philippine society. In the extreme south there are areas populated by Muslims, but they have not yet fully integrated into Filipino society, nor have they migrated to other parts of the country, except as university students.

Of all the religions in Southeast Asia, Islam is the most male oriented. The attitude toward women's role in society and family is such as to place severe restrictions on their freedom of movement. The obvious effect on migration is that it makes the migration of single women rather complicated. However, the spread of education and outside influences, such as exposure to foreign values through various media, have been loosening the traditional constraints. This is more evident in Indonesia than in Malaysia and among the Muslims in South Thailand, and the Philippines.

Similar to many countries in the Third World, migration, especially rural to urban migration, has been substantial in Southeast Asia and has accelerated in recent years. Data are easily attainable from various publications, including series of periodical reports by international organizations such as the United Nations and the World Bank. Space limitation will preclude a sufficiently comprehensive documentation here. A more useful and challenging use of space would be to present some important recent research, unlikely to be well enough known beyond a very small group of specialists.

3.1 Thailand

One of the great advantages of studying Thailand is that it often contradicts generalizations made on the basis of experience elsewhere. In the context of this paper we can mention the near absence of unemployment in the capital, Bangkok, and the extreme primacy of Bangkok when Thailand is compared to countries with similar per-capital income. In other contexts Thailand has provided valuable perspectives for assessing claims about the alleged impact of colonialism (Thailand was never a colony) or of a response to Western cultural impact.

Migration in Thailand is of long standing. In fact, much of the southern part of central Thailand, including Bangkok, was settled mostly during the last two centuries. In this century, especially since World War II, the migration has acquired more and more the rural/metropolitan characteristic (as opposed to inter and intra regional migration which was previously predominant, and which still continues to some extent).

In recent years Thailand has joined the countries which export contract labor abroad, especially to the Middle East. The incentives for the migrating workers are the usual ones which could be covered by the envelope statement: the wish to improve the material standard of living of the individual and his/ her family. However, a decision to go abroad on contract surely differs from a decision to migrate to a town in the next province. Moreover, we have found that sometimes two villages that previously were barely distinguishable from each other differ significantly in the percentage of their working population which responded to such incentives from abroad. In other words, the same material incentives seem to bring about different levels of actual response in terms of migration. Such differences were observed not only between villages as mentioned above but also between households in the same villages, similar to what was observed in internal migration.

The statistical services in Thailand have continuously improved in recent years. Numerous censuses and surveys were conducted, including the collection of data on migration. Also increasing in recent years have been in-depth studies, some innovative both in methodology and results. The rest of this section relies heavily on the Fuller et al. (1983) book [3] which will be specifically cited when referring to features unique to that study. It is selected because it incorporates various strands and approaches in an interdisciplinary analysis. Another unique feature of the book is the policy-relevant experimental study of three villages compared with three control villages.

That experiment was involved with the provision of information about employment prospects in towns. This is related to an already previously noticed phenomenon: that the flow of migrants is not correlated to the census type of information the government has been distributing about job openings. Migrants tended, instead, to follow the information provided by friends and relatives who have had experience in other destinations.

Before proceeding to comment on the experiment, the results of the analysis of the pre-experiment decision-making model have to be reported. The method used to investigate the relationships between the variables was through a set of regression equations using path analysis. The good reasons for selecting the method cannot be discussed here. It is sufficient to say that the nature of the variables and the assumed relationships among them called for this method of multivariate analysis.

THE VARIABLES

(1) MOVES 1. This variable is based on previous moves to either Bangkok or a Northeastern town during the latest three years.

(2) CONTACTS 1. Friends, relatives, or other personal contacts in Thai towns whom the interviewees know well enough as ones able to provide detailed information.

(3) INFO 1. Information about urban areas. The variable was an index based on responses to questions showing knowledge about: jobs, trade schools, wages for three occupations, and rental costs.

(4) EVAL 1. These were evaluations by the interviewees of the quality of life and expectations of possibilities in the village versus Bangkok and Northeastern towns. The questions included even such items as whether it is a pleasant place, or what do they think is the respect locals have towards villagers. The interesting thing is that in almost all categories, including "the opportunity to be rich," many ranked their own village higher than the urban areas.

(5) PLAN 1. These were subjective estimates by the villagers of the probability that they would move to Bangkok or a Northeast town. These were divided between whether they will "definitely" or "probably" move or not move, or "not sure." A distinction was made between those mentioning one year and those having a longer time horizon called "five years."

(6) MOVES 2. Actual moves during the year between the two interviews. These moves include not-yet-permanent moves, such as an exploratory visit or temporary employment.

The results of the analysis can be seen in Figure 1 and Figure 2 which include only statistically significant relationships ($p < .05$). All are positive as hypothesized.

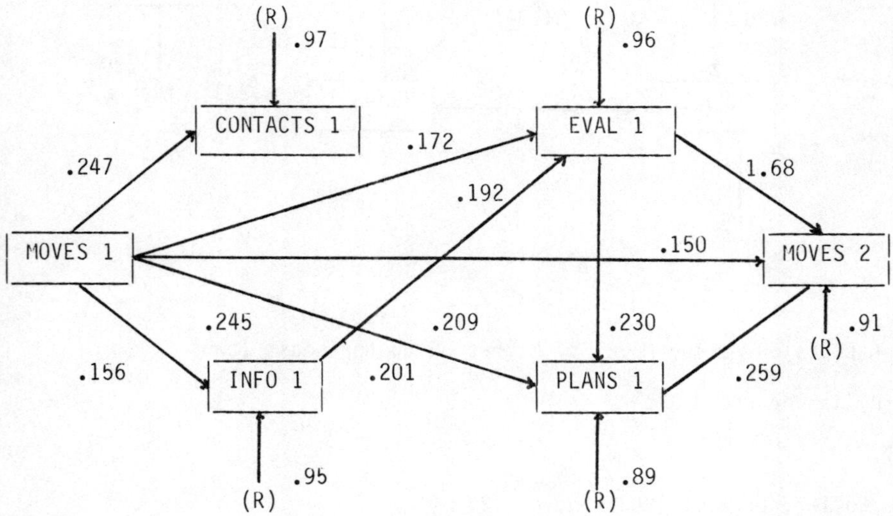

FIGURE 1

A Decision-Making Model of Migration to Bangkok

Note: (R) is the residual.

Source: Fuller, et al., 1983 [3], p. 122.

As can be seen from these figures, there are relatively strong links among these variables and the directions of causality are the ones expected. The differences between the migration to Bangkok vs. Northeast Towns might be of some interest, especially since it was also the concern of the experiment. In terms of the summary pictures presented in Figures 1 and 2 we see no significant relationship between CONTACTS 1 and neither PLANS 1 nor EVAL 1 in the case of migration to Bangkok. In the case of migration to Northeast towns, notice the absence of significant relations between MOVES 1 and INFO 1 and between EVAL 1 and MOVES 2. This does not necessarily mean they are entirely absent, but they do not pass the strict statistical significance test for direct influence.

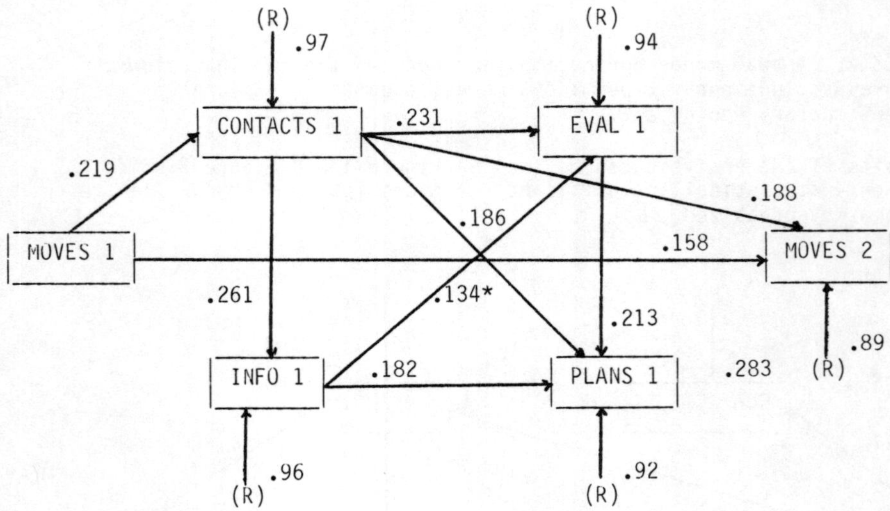

FIGURE 2

A Decision-Making Model of Migration to Northeast Towns

Note: (R) is the residual.

*P < .07

Source: Fuller, et al., 1983 [3], p. 123.

Information is an important element in the process, even beyond its influence on EVAL 1 and PLANS 1 as seen in Figures 1 and 2. For the purposes of Fuller et al., it had additional importance by virtue of its being amenable to modification by external sources, unlike some of the other variables.

Their main purpose in the experiment was to provide information to the experimental villagers that will influence them to move to towns in the Northeast (the region where these villages were located) rather than to Bangkok. They selected three "experimental" villages and three "control" villages. The latter were not provided with information about job availability and opportunities in the Northeast towns. For a number of technical reasons the experiment cannot yet be declared a success. Since one of these reasons is that the checking of the results was done only seven months after the initiation of the information program, we should wait for the follow-up reports.

3.2. The Philippines

The Lee study [6] is selected for a number of reasons besides the high quality of the research. An important feature is that it studies the *intention* to migrate irrespective of the possible destination, or even whether or not it ends up in actual migration. In other words, the investigation separates between the decision to move, which does not require knowledge about the conditions at the possible destination, and the actual move. A related, and equally important feature of Lee's study is the investigation of the characteristics of the place of origin and how these characteristics affect the decision to migrate by some people and the decision not to by others.

The area she studied is the Ilocos Norte provice of the Philippines, which has been a migrant-exporting area for many years. Although relatively poor, the province has shown economic progress, including urbanization. Although some of the past migrants moved within the province, or went abroad (such as those recruited by the Hawaii Sugar Planters' Association), the focus of the research is on those whose conception of migration was a move to elsewhere in the Philippines. This is the right focus since most migration studies have been done on migration within the same country, which will allow comparison.

Her main groups of "independent" variables are: (1) commitment to family, job and place (a negative incentive). (2) "Resources for moving" which are a combination of human capital such as education and migration experience together with household material resources. (3) "Community Resources" which is a basket of the various conditions and amenities in the community. The more attractive these are, the less likely the intention to move elsewhere.

In her study these three broad categories are subdivided into more detailed sub-categories, both well studied ones such as age, sex and marital status; as well as kinship, occupation, accessibility to community amenities, electrification, etc.

Space does not allow getting into the various details and the intricacies of the study. The following should suffice for now. The intention to migrate was determined by a "yes" answer to the following two questions: (a) "Do you intend to move away from this *barangay* (one of the units which make up a municipality) within two years?" And (b) "Do you intend to move away from this *barangay* sometimes in the future?"

Hers is a contextual analysis, the individual behavior within the social context. She uses a binary qualitative choice model (either "yes" or "no") using the maximum likelihood logit function.

Table 1 summarizes the result of the analysis of the complete model,

TABLE 1

Comparison of Predicted and Obtained Signs of Coefficients for Each Variable

Variable	Measurement level	Sign: Expected	Sign: Obtained	Sign: Group for which significant effect found
COMMITMENT TO FAMILY, JOB, AND PLACE				
Age	individual	-	ns	(-) single group and no migration experience group
Sex (male = 1)	individual	?	ns	(+) married group
Being single	individual	+	+	
Farm occupation	individual	-	ns	(-) older female group
Land ownership	household	-	ns	(+) nonfarmers and younger male group
Competition for land within a family	household	+	ns	
Internal linkages	individual	-	ns	(-) younger male group
REOURCES FOR MOVING				
Education	individual	+	+	
Migration experience	individual	+	+	
Perceived adequacy of economic conditions	household	+	ns	
External linkages	household	+	+	(+) nonfarmers and younger male group
COMMUNITY RESOURCE				
Urban residence	individual	+	+	
Density	community	+	+	
Tenancy rates	community	+	ns	(+) farmers and old male group
Irrigation	community	-	-	
Employment opportunities	community	-	-	
Electrification	community	-	-	
Community services	community	-	-	
Intermunicipal transport	community	-	ns	
Education facilities	community	-	-	

ns = not significant

Source: Lee (1985)[6], Table 5.9, pp. 114 and 115.

which includes all the items making up the three groups of variables: commitment, resources for moving, and community resources. But further comments are required for a broader prospective. The commitment variables, when analyzed alone, were all significant. But when the resources for moving were added, that significance disappeared except for a positive effect on migration of being single.

Land ownership turns out to be a major determinant in favor of migration among the young and non-farmers. Land, it might be recalled, is an important asset the sale of which can provide resources for moving. At the same time, when the explanatory variables were evaluated at their mean values, the competition for land (as measured by agricultural density) emerged as the most decisive factor encouraging migration. In general, local employment opportunities and community services decrease migration plans among the married, but not the single.

3.3. Malaysia

There are very few studies of Malaysia which explicitely examine the non-economic factors in the migration decisions in that multi-racial country.

There are, of course, some sensitive issues there relating to race and religion. There is a precarious balance among the communities, especially between the Chinese and Malays with preferential political and economic treatment given to the latter. This finds expression also in the kind of projects which the government supports and which have an impact on the opportunities provided to prospective migrants.

The impact of Islam is still felt in Malaysia. A number of studies on Indonesia indicate that overall, there is near equality between the numbers of men and women migrants to Jakarta, which is one indication of the relatively lax attitude toward Islam in that country. In Malaysia, on the other hand, the majority of the rural-to-urban Malay migrants in the 1960s were males. In the 1970's the share of Malay women migrants increased somewhat (Ariffin 1984) [2]. These were usually pre-organized and supervised young females directed toward light assembly industries which were female-labor-intensive. It is interesting to note that in this respect Muslim Malaysia is similar to non-Muslim Taiwan, which also has had the tradition of keeping young daughters at home until marriage (Huang 1982) [5].

The migration patterns differ among the communities, but it is not easy to isolate the effect of religion since the communities differ also in occupational structures, living arrangements, including the rural-urban distribution, and in the relative concentration of communities in the individual states. Another complicating factor was the forced resettlement during the "Emergency" of the 1950's.

The best source, albeit somewhat dated, for the kind of analysis and information we seek here is Pryor (1977) [7].

Pryor presents his own research and summarizes works by others. Here are some of the findings:

Migrants in Malysaya tend to be young (15-34, and especially 20-24 years of age). Among the Malays, they tend to be male, especially when young and moving long distances. Female migrants come primarily from among the non-Malay, and they move short distances. Those who move to the capital district are most likely to be Malays or Indians, rather than Chinese.

Being single or, if married, having or desiring small families, favors migration. While employment-related reasons for migration tend to be emphasized, the presence of relatives or friends at the destination area is often crucial to the migration process.

Service workers, clerical and professional occupations, are prominent among migrants. And, as was often found in studies on other countries, achieved level of education or the search for education are among the major causes for choosing migration.

The latest, more conventional, study to be cited here is Wah and Ee (1985) [8]. Among its findings are: more than half of the states have a net out-migration while the clearly top "beneficiary" is the state of Selangor where the capital city is located. On the other hand, the most important component of internal migration was rural/rural migration (62% of all migration), and the second was urban/urban. The conventional reason given for the former is the government's rural development policy. Lastly, as one might expect, distance has had a deterrent effect on labor mobility.

4. CONCLUSIONS AND GENERALIZATIONS

Although some of the findings cited here tend to confirm findings in other studies, they also provide elements which are new both in the analytical process employed and in the results. There are many theories about what causes migration, its consequences and implications. The reference here, of course, is to voluntary migration. There were huge migrations in history caused by conquests, natural calamities, and other non-voluntary population movements which are beyond the scope of our subject.

Because we deal with a voluntary phenomenon, a central question is what is the decision unit, and how it arrives at a decision. Then there is the question as to what forms a relevant basis for making such decisions. There is also the determination of what is the proper process of modeling for both the theoretical and the empirical study of migration. The area of the policy implications lies beyond the scope of this paper. I would just make an aside: it is amazing how many policy recommendations, especially those devised to combat the alleged ill effects of migration, have been put forward. This in the face of the stark reality that we know very little about the good or bad consequences of migration.

In fact, we do not have a full-fledged theory about the causes of migration either, beyond the rather trite statement that people move in order to improve their and their families current or future well-being. It is clear that no one model would apply equally to different communities and situations. Certain attributes do appear fairly regularly as contributing to migration. Such are, for example, education and scarcity of employment opportunities in the place of origin. But even these raise some questions. For example, maybe the investment in education is undertaken in preparation for a future move. Nor is it clear, as the Thailand study shows, that the average income at the destination is a determining factor, as opposed to the finding of specific job opportunities.

Different kinds of migration involve different risks, prospects, and cultural and social adjustments, as well as different decision processes. Permanent rural-to-urban migration differs from circular or commuting. These, in turn, differ from international migration. The extent of the information flows, the required resources, and the extent of continued interaction with the place of origin, are examples of such variability.

A legitimate question could be raised as to whether the micro-level research of the kind reported here, including the psycho-social considerations, is worth the trouble. In other words, it could be argued that the macro consequences would not be much affected by these details. Although the documented variability among the different situations indicates that these are significantly more than mere details, the question deserves to be addressed. For an example of an examination of these issues as related to the more general subject of economic development see Ayal (1973) [2].

Some of the results cited here help highlight the insights gained from micro studies. The Thailand study showed the differences between the determinants of migration to Bangkok versus Northeast towns. The Philippines study shows that land ownership encourages the decision to migrate. Another interesting insight gained from the latter is how the importance of the individual characteristics wash out when the "resources" variables are brought in. This tends to increase the importance of the family as the migration decision unit. The Malaysian example shows that who moves where and why depends, inter alia, on ethnic and religious factors and has important political, economic, as well as spatial and income distribution implications. On the other side of the coin, actions by government encourage certain types of transport and travel possibilities, which, when accompanied by the reduction in the relative cost of travel, have changed some migration patterns. Circular migration is partly replacing permanent migration. The terminal-time on-contract Asian migration to the Middle-East oil exporting countries is another example of development assisted by improved travel conditions.

There remains the problem of proper modeling. There have always been difficulties for economists trained in neoclassical theorizing as to how to incorporate in their models the obvious fact that actual behavior is more complex than profit maximizing. Some of the noneconomic factors come through the back door, so to speak, such as when dealing with the role of innovation, adjustment costs, etc. There have been attempts at building explicitly behavioral models of the firm and even of governmental organizations which have allowed for modifications of the simple maximization assumption. And, of course, in some branches of labor economics they could not escape from dealing with psychological and organizational variables.

A big problem with detailed behavioral modeling on the micro level is how to handle the diversity among the units, such as we have with the variety of migration decisions and decision units. It might miss the point unless complemented by analysis on a more macro level. For example, does it matter that Mr. X and his family decided to migrate? Would others have done so instead of him if he didn't? Are the overall conditions favoring certain kinds of migration? How does migration itself change the overall conditions? There have been efforts done in this direction but a lot more has to be done, especially to get a comprehensive analytical perspective.

REFERENCES

[1] Ayal, Eliezer B. (ed.), *Micro Aspects of Development* (New York: Praeger Publications, 1973).

[2] Ariffin, Y., "Migration of Women Workers in Penisular Malaysia: Impact and Implications," in Fawcett, Y. C., S. Khoo and P. C. Smith (eds.) *Women in the Cities of Asia* (Boulder: Westview Press, 1984).

[3] Fuller, Theodore D., Prerasit Kamnuansilpa, Paul Lightfoot, and Sawaeng Rathanamongkolmas, *Migration and Development in Modern Thailand* (Bangkok: Social Science Association of Thailand, 1983).

[4] Houser, Philip M., Daniel B. Suits, and Naohiro Ogawa (eds.), *Urbanization and Migration in ASEAN Development* (Tokyo: National Institute for Research Advancement, 1985).

[5] Huang, N. L. C., "Spatial and Behavioral Aspects of Rural-Urban Migration: The Case of Female Movement in Taiwan" (Taiwan: Taiwan Population Study Center, National Taiwan University Research Report, 1982).

[6] Lee, Sun-Hee, *Why People Intend to Move, Individual and Community-Level Factors of Out-Migration in the Philippines* (Boulder: Westview Press, 1985).

[7] Pryor, Robin Y. (ed.), *Migration and Development in South East Asia* (Kuala Lumpur: Oxford University Press 1979).

[8] Wah, Lai Yew and Tan Siew Ee, "Internal Migration and Economic Development in Malaysia," in Houser et al. (eds.) [4], *Urbanization and Migration in ASEAN Development* (Tokyo: NIRA, 1985).

Part Six
Expectations

Testing for Rational Expectations in Experimental Predictions

Friedel Bolle

Universität Hamburg
Von-Melle-Park 5
2000 Hamburg 13

Introduction

There is general agreement among economists that the expectations of market participants - about future prices, technical progress, the availability of resources, etc. - have a strong influence on individual decisions as well as on aggregate demand and supply. Unfotunately, up to now there has been no convincing method for the modelling of these expectations. The most elegant way of getting round this deficit is to utilize "Rational Expectations" (RE). This hypothesis which was first used by Muth (1961) assumes that the economic agents know the future values of the variables or at least the correct distribution of these values (for an overview see Ramser, 1978; Kantor, 1979).

In this paper I will report about experiments where subjects have to predict in sequence the next value x_{t+1} of a given time series $(x_\tau)_{\tau=1,...,t}$. I want to test the hypothesis that - after a sufficiently long learning time - the subjects choose a prediction

$$(1) \qquad \tilde{x}_{t+1} = Ex_{t+1} + u_{t+1}$$

where Ex_{t+1} is the expected value of x_{t+1} under the correct ditribution of x_{t+1} and where u_{t+1} is a random variable with $Eu_{t+1}=0$, which is uncorrelated with other residuals and has further properties as reported below. Thus the following investigation will concentrate on the residuals u_t for which several tests will be carried out.

The tests used are partly those described in the literature about testing for RE (see Aiginger, 1981, Zimmermann, 1984, and the literature cited there). The advantage of an experiment is that the stochastic process is known exactly, while for field data the investigator, too, has to make assumptions about the form of this stochastic process. In addition, the investigator has to make assumptions about the available information - usually the minimal assumption that only the past values of the predicted variables are known. This is a severe oversimplification for the analysis of field data whereas it is completely appropriate for experiments. Experiments also have the additional advantage that the same situation can be presented twice, giving rise to stronger tests of hypotheses.

My experiments are closely connected with those of Becker (1967) and Becker and Leopold (1985). These investigations are focussed on interpersonal comparisons and on the isolation of a number of attibutes of the decision process, but they do not test a complete theory about individual prediction behaviour.

For comparisons sake I have used the same stochastic process

$$x'_{t+1} = x'_t - [0.5x'_{t-1}] + w_{t+1} \tag{2}$$

where $[a]$ is the largest integer which is smaller or equal to a, and where w_{t+1} is a random variable with

(3) $$\text{Prob}(w_{t+1}=z) = \begin{cases} 1/6 & \text{for } z=1,2,3,4,5,6 \\ 0 & \text{otherwise} \end{cases}$$

The actual series presented was[1)]

(4) $$x_t = x'_t + 10.$$

Comparisons with the results of Becker and Becker/Leopold as well as the investigation of learning behaviour will be the theme of my subsequent work. This paper concentrates on testing the RE hypothesis.

In the next section the experiments are described, and in the following sections, tests and results are presented. For two of eight subjects the RE hypothesis is not rejected by any of eight tests on the 5% level of significance. For five subjects there are hints that the learning process was ongoing in all periods and/or that there were systematic deviations from RE. For these five the RE hypothesis is rejected by at least two tests. The results of one subject are not so clear-cut and will be discussed below in more detail.

The experiments

The experiments were undertaken with eight students from an undergraduate course in economics. All of them had just finished

---

1) Becker (1967) proposed such a transformation to exclude possible "format effects" of the series (x'_t).

an elementary course in statistics.

The task of the subjects was to predict the next value of a time series. They were given this time series (x_τ) in a graphical/numerical form as shown in Figure 1 for t=25; they were asked to predict x_{t+1}. Then they got - on a new sheet of paper - a representation of the time series up to t+1; etc.

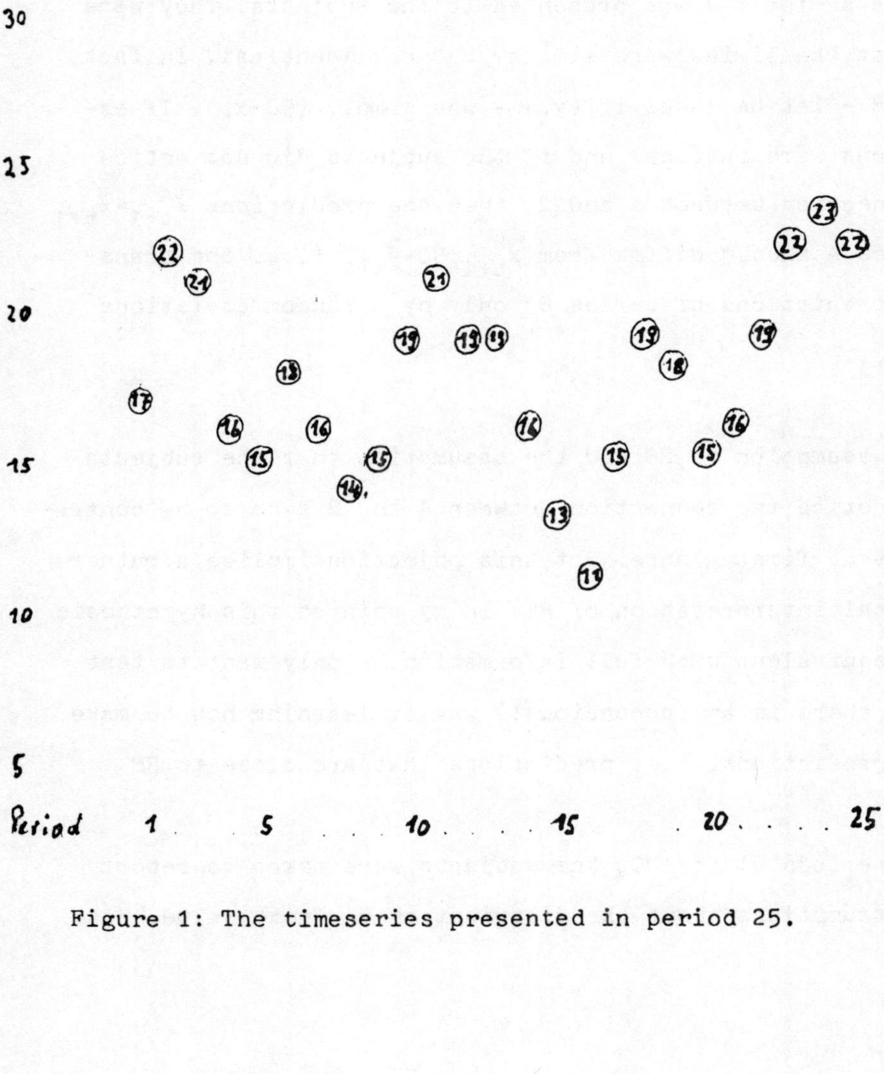

Figure 1: The timeseries presented in period 25.

The first prediction required was that of x_{11}, the last one that of x_{100}. The subjects were told that there were systematic as well as stochastic elements in the development of the series, that nobody could predict the next value exactly but that one could do more or less good in predicting.

After the first series (called series A) a second series (called series B) was presented to the subjects. They were told that the siries were similar but not identical. In fact, series B - let us label it (y_t) - was simply $(50-x_t)$. If expectations were rational and if the subjects did not notice the connection between A and B, then the predictions $\tilde{x}^A_{t+1}=\tilde{x}_{t+1}$ of series A should differ from $\tilde{x}^B_{t+1}=50-\tilde{y}_{t+1}$ (i.e. the transformed predictions of series B) only by random deviations $u^A_{t+1}-u^B_{t+1}$.

The assumption of RE and the assumption that the subjects do not notice the connection between A and B seem to be contradictions at first glance. But this objection implies a rather mechanical interpretation of RE. In my opinion this hypothesis is not equivalent with full information. I only want to test whether there is an (unconcious!) way of learning how to make "good" predictions, i.e. predictions that are close to RE.

For periods 91 to 100, the subjects were asked to report their assumptions about the distribution the next value. Most answers were rather peculiar (two times probability 1 was given to one value). The most one could derive from these answers is that prediction is oriented to the value with the maximal subjective probability, or perhaps to the median value, but not to the expected value under under the reported distribution. It seems to me, however, that predictions were not made on the basis of estimated distributions but vice versa. So I will ignore these answers in the rest of the paper.

To guarantee sufficient motivation and a clear goal function, the subjects were promised that the one having the least squared errors would earn DM 12o.-. The subjective estimation of the experimenter was that all the subjects tried to do their very best.

In the following I will assume that the subjects needed some time to learn how to make good predictions but that finally - after period 50 - they used a constant prediction rule. The tests will show, however, that for some subjects we have reason to suspect that learning lasted more than 40 periods. An overview of the results is given in table 1 on page 13.

A test of unbiasedness, symmetry, and identity

All subjects chose only integer for prediction so that u_t^A and u_t^B have values ± 0.5, ± 1.5,.... In the first test, called USI, we will investegate whether u_t^A and u_t^B are distributed symmetrically and identically with median values ± 0.5.

Let us assume, for example, that the maximal deviation from RE is 2.5. Then, for this subject, a χ^2-test is performed for the following structure of classes[1] (NoC=Number of cases).

NoC $u_t^A = 2.5$ is $50a_2$	NoC $u_t^A = 1.5$ is $50a_1$	NoC $u_t^A = 0.5$ is $50a_0$	NoC $u_t^A = -0.5$ is $50a_0$	NoC $u_t^A = -1.5$ is $50a_1$	NoC $u_t^A = -2.5$ is $50a_2$
NoC $u_t^B = 2.5$ is $50a_2$	NoC $u_t^B = 1.5$ is $50a_1$	NoC $u_t^B = 0.5$ is $50a_0$	NoC $u_t^B = -0.5$ is $50a_0$	NoC $u_t^B = -1.5$ is $50a_1$	NoC $u_t^B = -2.5$ is $50a_2$

This is a stronger test than the usual test of $Ex_t=0$. It turned out that this class structure was rejected at the 5% level for subjects 4 and 7. For subject 7 a slightly different hypothesis was testet as well, namely that predictions are centered around the larger of the two median values $Ex_t+0.5$. Let us call this hypothesis RE+. With RE+, subject 7 also passes the first test.

1) Note that u_t^B is the deviation of transformed predictions $\tilde{x}_t^B$ from the transformed RE. The transformation changes the sign of u_t.

Two tests of minimal variance

In the first of these tests I investigated whether the distribution P_u of u_t (estimated in the last section) can be used to predict P_d, the distribution of differences $d_t = \tilde{x}_t^A - \tilde{x}_t^B$. If RE is not a "best theory" in the sense that u_t shows "minimal deviations", then this fact will be revealed by the test of the hypothesis $P_d = P_u \oplus P_{-u}$[1][2]. If there are systematic deviations from RE, P_d will show a higher concentration on small differences than $P_u \oplus P_{-u}$. Again we use a χ^2-test.

Taking the example from the last section we compute $P_u \oplus P_{-u}$ by:

$$\begin{aligned} &\text{Prob } (\tilde{x}_t^A - \tilde{x}_t^B = 0) = 2(a_o^2 + a_1^2 + a_2^2) \\ &\text{Prob } (\tilde{x}_t^A - \tilde{x}_t^B = 1) = \text{Prob } (\tilde{x}_t^A - \tilde{x}_t^B = -1) = 2(a_o a_1 + a_1 a_2) + a_o^2 \\ &\quad \vdots \\ &\text{Prob } (\tilde{x}_t^A - \tilde{x}_t^B = 5) = \text{Prob } (\tilde{x}_t^A - \tilde{x}_t^B = -5) = a_2^2 . \end{aligned} \tag{6}$$

a_i are the probabilities which were estimated in the USI test. Let us take subject 5 as an example. The estimated frequency of the class with $x_t^A - x_t^B = 0$ is 8.3. The empirical frequency is 21. This shows that decisions were more constant than predicted by the u_t which arise from the RE hypothesis. This class contributes to the χ^2-value with 19.4 which is significant alone.

This test is called BT (test of best theory) and rejects the RE hypothesis for five of the eight subjects. RE+ for subject 7

---

1) Note that the requirement of minimal variance is not restricted to any class of estimators as in the regression test below.

2) A similar test has been proposed by the author (Bolle, 1981) for theories about yes-no-decisions.

is not rejected.

In the next test, called Korr AB, the coefficient of correlation r_{AB} of residuals u_τ^A and u_τ^B is computed. BT and Korr AB supplement each other. Korr AB may be more powerful in detecting small but uniform deviations from RE; but if, in addition, there is a change of behaviour from A to B in some situations then these effects may add up to a correlation coefficient near 0. The structure of the empirical distribution P_d, however, may remain significantly different from $P_u \oplus P_{-u}$. In the case of subject 1, Korr AB shows a significant magnitude while test BT is passed. In the cases of subjects 3 and 6 the situation is vice versa.

A test of unbiassedness and miminal variance

As a next test we compute the regression line

$$(7) \quad \tilde{x} = a + b \cdot Ex ,$$

and test the hypotheses a = o and b = 1. These two subtests are, of course, rather similar to the tests described above; but we cannot exclude the possibilty that there is supplementary information. Let the situation be as shown in Fig. 2. The deviations from RE may have a mean value of 0 but they may be too large. The regression line may show significantly smaller deviations. This is a test of whether RE is the best of all linear hypotheses, whereas BT tests whether RE is generally a best theory. At least in our cases BT turns out to be stronger than the regression test (see table 1).

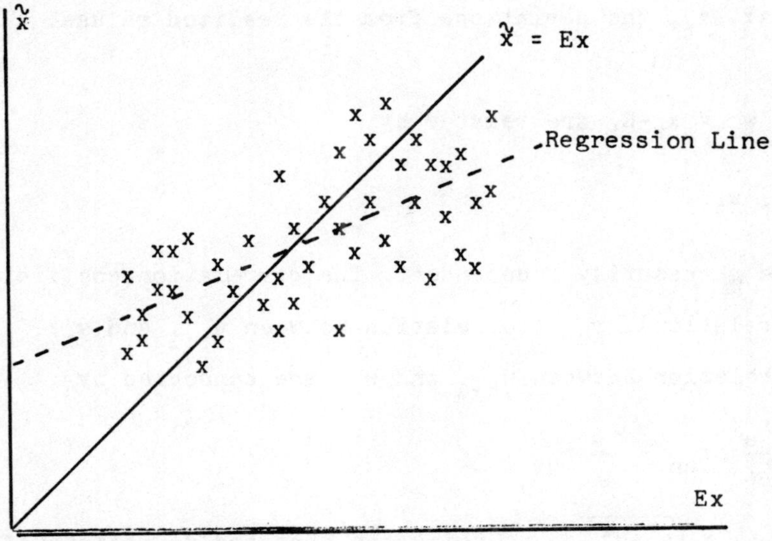

Fig. 2: An example of the regression (7).

Two tests of learning behaviour

The first test investigates autocorrelation of the residuals. This test is often called a test of sufficiency (see Aiginger, 1981) In our study this correlation is statistically important and shows, if significant, autocorrelation is tend that there are regularities beyond RE; but it is not so easy to explain without further information.

In field studies the observed value x_{t+1} serves as a proxy for Ex_{t+1}, and one can interpret the test of autocorrelation as being a test of the plausible hypothesis that the prediction error in t+1 is influenced by the observed error in t. The experimental situation allows us to compute the true residuals, but these true deviations cannot be observed by the subjects. So we also correlate

u_{t+1} with $v_t = \tilde{x}_t - \tilde{x}_t$, the deviations from the realized values.

u_t, v_t and $w_t = x_t - E_t$ are related by

(8) $v_t = u_t - w_t$.

u_t and w_t are necessarily independent. The correlation coefficients r_{uu} (autocorrelation), r_{uv} (correlation between u_{t+1} and v_t), and r_{uw} (correlation between u_{t+1} and w_t) are connected by

(9) $v_{uw} = \frac{\sigma_u}{\sigma_w} r_{uu} - \frac{\sigma_v}{\sigma_w} r_{uv}$

with σ_u, σ_w, $\sigma_v = \sqrt{\sigma_w^2 + \sigma_w^2}$ being the standard deviations of u,w and v.

In Table 1 the r_{uu} and r_{uv} values are given. r_{uw} turns out to be insignificantly low for all subjects and is therefore left out of the table. This result shows that the random deviations have only little influence on behaviour. So only large v_t values or perhaps aggregate v_t values from earlier periods have influence on the predictions. It is also plausible that the r_{uu} are larger than the r_{uv}. If we set $r_{uw}=0$ we get

(10) $r_{uv} = \frac{\sigma_u}{\sigma_v} r_{uu} < r_{uu}$.

The results

The level of significance of a single test is identical with the type I error. If our criterion for the rejection of RE is "one of the tests shows significant values on the 5%-level" then the type I error which arises from this criterion is considerably larger than 5%. At least the tests USI, Korr AB, and the tests based on r_{uu} and r_{uw} (the results of the latter are not included in Table 1) are mutually independent so that the type I error can be expected to be 20% or 25% or even more. Under such a point of view perhaps we should not reject RE+ for subject 7.[1)]

For subjects 1 and 3 we must conclude that their behaviour deviates from RE and that this deviation consists of or is accompanied by a "slow" learning process. For subjects 5 and 6 the learning process seems to have nearly vanished in the last 50 periods, but there are constant deviations from RE. The regression coefficients for both are significantly larger than 1 which means that their predictions are more extreme than RE in both directions.

For subject 4 there are several sources of deviation from RE. Firstly, behaviour in A and B is - with regard to means -significantly different. While predictions in A are centered around Ex, those in B are centered around Ex+1 (in transformed values). Secondly, however, the large coefficient of correlation r_{AB} points out that there are important repetitions of behaviour (which are not described by RE). Thirdly, the large values of r_{uu} and r_{uv} make it probable that a "fast" learning process is still going on.

---

1) In addition, his correlation coefficient $r_{AB}=0.29$ just surpasses the critical value 0.28.

Subjects 2 and 8 have passed all the tests. Interestingly, these are the subjects with the smallest and the largest size of error, respectively. According to McNees (1978), a large error term should be an indicator for the usefulness of searching further for better hypotheses. On the other hand, one has to take into consideration that if systematic deviations are responsible for the greater part of the error, it should be relatively easy to detect them. Thus we do not want to regard the size of error as a sort of additional test. Its only function is to give us information about the proximity of RE to individual predictions.

Test \ Subject	1	2	3	4	5	6	7	8	7,RE+
USI	-	-	-	5%	-	-	5%	-	-
BT	-	-	5%	1%	1%	5%	1%	-	-
r_{AB}	0.45	-	-	0.59	5%	-	5%	-	5%
Regr. b=1	-	-	-	-	1.30	5%	5%	-	-
Regr. a=0	-	-	-	5%	-5.8	5%	5%	-	-
r_{uu}	0.31	-	0.37	0.61	-	-	-	-	-
r_{uv}	-	-	-	0.37	-	-	-	-	-
$1-R^2$	0.41	0.26	0.30	0.38	0.29	0.41	0.38	0.53	0.31

Table 1: Results of tests for Rational Expectations. Nonsignificance on the 5% level is labelled "-". Correlation coefficients (regression coefficients) which are different from 0 (from 1) on the 1% level are given.

Of special interest, I think, is the close approach to RE by subject 2. The size of error does not even give the full truth because predictions were limited to integer values. Subject 2's predictions consisted 57 times of one of the median values and had therefore, the "inevitable" distance ± 0.5 from RE; 37 times his deviations were ± 1.5; 5 times ± 2.5; once 3.5. This shows that it is possible to learn to make good predictions - but there seem to be large individual differences with respect to the velocity of learning as well as to the quality of the result.

References

Aiginger,K. "Empirical Evidence on the Rational Expectations Hypothesis Using Reported Expectations", Empirica, 1, 1981, 25-72.

Becker,O. "Eperimentelle Untersuchung der Erwartungsbildung für eine Zeitreihe", in: H. Sauermann (Ed), Beiträge zur experimentellen Wirtschaftsforschung, Tübingen, 1967, 226-254.

Becker,O., Leopold,U. "A univariable Pridiction Expiriment", in: H. Brandstätter, E. Kirchler (Eds), Economic Psychology, Proceedings of the 10th IAREP Annual Colloquium, Linz, 1985, 159-167.

Bolle,F. "Ein Test für Theorien über Ja-Nein-Entscheidungen", Zeitschrift für exp. und ang. Psych., 28, 1981, 15-22.

Kantor,B. "Rational Expectations and Economic Thought", J. Ec. Lit. XVII, 1979, 1422-1441.

McNees,St.K., "The Rationality of Economic Forecasts", AER, Pap. and Proc., 1978, 301-305.

Muth,J.F., "Rational Expectations and the Theory of Price Movements", Econometrica, 29, 1961, 315-335.

Ramser,H.J. "Rationale Erwartungen und Wirtschaftspolitik", Zeitschrift für die ges. Staatswiss., 134, 1978, 57-72.

Zimmermann,K.F. "On Rationality of Business Expectations: A Micro Analysis of Qualitative Responses", Beiträge zur angewandten Wirtschaftsforschung, Universität Mannheim, Jan. 1984.

EXPERT AND AMATEUR INFLATION EXPECTATIONS

Abraham Friedman   Zur Shapira

School of Business
The Hebrew University
Jerusalem, Israel

Recent analyses of inflation by economists suggest that it cannot be stopped by monetary or fiscal policies alone. It is argued that a major element determining inflation is consumer expectations of inflation and therefore dealing with consumer expectations may lead to a better way of handling inflation.

The subject of expectations is of major importance in economics. One of the more developed theories of expectations is the theory of "rational expectations" (cf. Muth, 1961) which argues that the expectations of firms and individuals tend to be distributed for the same information set similarly to the objective probability distribution of outcomes. This theory has far-reaching implications (Begg, 1982). Yet studies conducted by economists raise doubts as to whether people's expectations can be described by the theory. Turnovsky (1970) and Leonard (1982) examined price and wage expectations and found that they differ from what a rational expectations model would predict. Brown and Maital (1981) examined the expectations of expert economists who participated in the annual Livingstone survey and found that while there were no biases in the experts' expectations there was only a partial use of the available information. These researchers suggest that one should pursue a concept of partial or limited rationality for developing models of expectations.

Expectation formation is basically a psychological subject. The relevance of psychological studies to the development of economic models of consumer behavior is a subject long advocated by behavioral scientists such as Katona (1974) and Simon (1979). The limited correspondence between economic assumptions about the rational consumer and individual choice behavior has been demonstrated in a series of studies conducted by Kahneman and Tversky (1979, 1981). Their findings and results of other studies (cf. Lichtenstein *et al*., 1977; Shapira & Venezia, 1981) suggest, among other things, that:

a. Judgmental procedures are governed by heuristics which lead to systematic biases.

b. Dynamic judgmental and decision processes are characterized by partial calibration, partial learning and departures from normative rules of optimal stopping.

These findings seem relevant for inflation expectation formation in situations where information is partial and the situation changes continuously.

Would experts fare better than amateurs in forming inflation expectations? Studies in behavioral decision making within a variety of professions came out with inconclusive evidence. Some argue for the superiority of experts and others argue for no difference between experts and non-experts (cf. Kahneman, Slovic & Tversky, 1982). Studies of the formation of inflation expectations are rather scarce. Blomqvist (1983) compared the accuracy of inflation expectations of "informed" and "uninformed" subjects. The former were members of the Economic Society in Helsinki while the latter were sampled from the personnel of the Swedish School of Economics at Helsinki. He found that "informed" subjects made better predictions that "uninformed" subjects. The present paper reports preliminary findings about the accuracy of the factors affecting inflation expectations of experts and amateurs.

Method and Data

Background

The early 1980's in Israel were characterized by a high rate of inflation. From around a 50% annual rate in the late 1970's the CPI rose to 133% in 1980, 101% in 1981, 131% in 1982, 190% in 1983, 445% in 1984, and 185% in 1985. The first part of 1981 was characterized by pre-election economic measures that increased consumer spending, later labeled by the then Minister of the Treasury as the "correct economics". In October 1983, inflation that remained on the same high level it had reached in the previous three years became a clear cost to the economy. The balance of trade had worsened, the external debt was growing rapidly, and the rate of savings was decreasing. Yet the G.N.P. and employment were increasing. At this time the "bank stocks" crisis occurred. The government introduced a new economic policy: the shekel was develued by 23%, government subsidies were slashed, and budget cuts were proposed. This policy brought about a higher level of inflation (16% per month), improvement in the balance of trade, reduction in the local economic activity, and erosion of real wages. The same Minister of the Treasury proposed a dollarization program which eventually led to his forced resignation. Since then there have been joint attempts by the government, the Labor Federation (Histadruth), and the Manufacturers Association to arrive at three package deals where prices and wages are frozen for a certain period of time.

In July 1985 an emergency program for the stabilization of the Israeli economy was adopted. This program had two goals: a large and fast reduction in the level of prices, and improvement of the balance of trade. One of the main vehicles for achieving these goals was a major and quick change in inflation expectations. The program involved budget cuts including a drastic cut in government subsidies for basic consumer products, a substantial reduction in available credit, and wage erosion. The emergency economic plan succeeded in reducing the rate of inflation. The expected rate of increase in the CPI for 1986 was 25%. Nevertheless, the plan did not lead to improvement in the balance of trade.

The Amateurs Sample

The Israel Institute for Applied Social Research runs a monthly "Current Survey" of attitudes of the Israeli Jewish urban adult population. On three occasions (March 1981, May 1983 and November 1983) questions were asked about sources of information regarding inflation, as well as items pertaining to the estimation of the lagged rate of inflation for a variety of consumer goods and the CPI. Sample sizes for these three studies ranged from 485 to 563. In practice the data was collected in interviews where a closed format questionnaire on inflation expectations and other social and economic items was administered to the respondents. The sampled population included the Jewish inhabitants of the four largest cities and some smaller townships.

The Experts Sample

The data on expert expectations is drawn from a longitudinal survey of presidents of industrial firms conducted by the Israeli Manufacturers Association. There are about 400 corporate members in this Association which represents most of the private sector industry in Israel.

Every three months a survey questionnaire is sent to the presidents of the corporations and an average of 140 (35% response rate) are returned. The questionnaire consists mainly of ten items regarding: (a) Firm's performance -- volume of production, level of financial expenditures, cost of production factors (inputs) and number of employees; (b) Local market sales -- volume of sales, number of orders, price of products; (c) Export -- volume of sales, number of orders and prices. For each of these items the presidents of the firms are asked to assess the level for the previous three months and to state their expectations for the relevant levels over the next three months. Almost all the items are on a five category scale. The data presented here are from five surveys: April 1983, July 1983, July 1984, October 1984, and January 1985. Thus, the data presented in this paper allow three comparisons of predicted vs. actual changes, as only consecutive surveys can be compared. For example, actual values obtained in July 1983 are compared to predictions made in April 1983.

Results and Discussion

Amateurs Data

The predicted and observed increases in prices of different goods at three points in time are presented in Table 1. One should note that the actual increases are indicated in percentages of increase from six months prior to the specified date. On the other hand the predicted changes, for the previous six months also, are mean responses on a five point rating scale. Thus, a direct comparison is not immediately available. Nevertheless, one can compare the order of the magnitude of increases of each of the product categories in the two time intervals. While the correspondence between the predicted and actual increases seem to be rather good, the analysis of the mispredictions shows that they are spread over categories and time points. However, the general trend suggests that the more information the consumer has about the particular product category, the more accurate the prediction is. Thus, the prediction of change of prices of fruits and vegetables is good for all three periods. Data presented in Table 2 suggest that a person's labor market status affects the accuracy of his/her predictions.

Table 1. Average Increases in the Prices of Product Categories, Actual and Predicted (amateur sample)

Product Category	March 1981[a]		May 1983[b]		November 1983[c]	
	Actual	Predicted	Actual	Predicted	Actual	Predicted
Fruits & Vegetables	188.3	3.15	220.3	3.54	117.2	2.77
Clothing	157.2	3.17	133.2	3.45	119.2	3.54
Durable Goods	152.0	2.79	149.1	3.20	174.1	3.47
CPI - Lagged	152.7	3.36	153.3	3.53	179.2	3.60
CPI - Expected	147.7	-.01	179.2	.52	219.1	.51

Note: Both actual and predicted increases are based on a six month period. Predicted increases are means of responses given on 5 point rating scales, except predicted CPI ahead was a 3 point scale - larger = +1; same = 0; smaller = -1.

[a]N = 485 to 521
[b]N = 530 to 546
[c]N = 533 to 563

<u>Experts Data</u>

The predicted and observed changes in different production variables are presented in Table 3. These data are actually the mean differences between matched pairs; that is, a firm's data was entered only if its president responded at both points in time. Due to missing data on various categories the sample size changes between categories. There is a remarkable difference between the three periods. The accuracy of prediction at the first period (April 1983 - July 1983) was mixed. In almost all the items, the observed values were higher than the predicted ones. These differences were significant for financial expenditures, number of employees, and sales and orders on the local market. The accuracy of prediction at the second period (July 1984 - October 1984) is remarkable: there were no mispredictions. On the other hand, there are many mispredictions in the third period (October 1984 - January 1985) regarding the firm's production variables as well as the local market parameters. It is interesting to note that the results are counter to our naive hypothesis. In the third quarter of 1983 the state of the economy was rather unstable. The rate of inflation was 5% per month, yet there were problems with the balance of trade. Furthermore, since the exchange rate of the U.S. dollar did not match the rate of inflation, people sold stocks and bonds and bought dollars, which were

Table 2. Average Increases in the Prices of Product Categories Predicted by Labor Market Status.

Product Category	March 1981					May 1983					November 1983				
	Total Population	Wage-Earner	Self-Employed	Retired	Housewife	Total Population	Wage-Earner	Self-Employed	Retired	Housewife	Total Population	Wage-Earner	Self-Employed	Retired	Housewife
Fruits & Vegetables	3.15	3.07	2.88	3.48	3.39	3.54	3.51	3.68	3.68	3.63	2.77	2.71	2.64	3.06	2.76
Clothing	3.17	3.10	3.11	3.35	3.35	3.48	3.51	3.56	3.56	3.50	3.54	3.49	3.65	3.59	3.65
Durable Goods	2.79	2.78	2.76	2.91	2.78	3.20	3.14	2.97	3.28	3.36	3.47	3.43	3.49	3.58	3.52
C.P.I. - Lagged	3.36	3.30	3.29	3.56	3.35	3.53	3.56	3.52	3.53	3.49	3.60	3.62	3.62	3.48	3.69
C.P.I. - Expected	-.01	-.06	.03	0	.10	.52	.46	.41	.58	.67	.51	.46	.53	.47	.60
N (minimal)	485	247	47	53	96	530	281	44	59	113	533	290	33	84	94

Table 3. Mean Differences Between Predicted and Observed Changes On Production Variables (Expert Sample)

Category	July 1983[a] vs. April 1983	October 1984[b] vs. July 1984	January 1985[c] vs. October 1984
Firm's Production			
Production volume	-.210	-.217	-.493**
Cost of production input	-.103	.014	.522**
Financial expenditures	-.410**	-.129	1.642**
Number of employees	-.308**	-.121	-.176
Local Market			
Sales	-.419*	-.043	-.357**
Orders	-.465**	-.014	-.371**
Price of products	-.023	-.044	.662**
Export			
Sales	-.261	.064	-.116
Orders	.000	.255	.195
Price of products	-.160	.149	.049

* $\underline{P} < .01$
** $\underline{P} < .005$

[a]N = 23 to 43
[b]N = 41 to 59
[c]N = 42 to 70

relatively "cheap", instead. This led to the "bank stocks" crisis in October 1983 and to another government stabilization program. This program succeeded in reducing the trade deficit yet inflation went out of control, climbing to 17% per month. In the first part of 1984, there was considerable volatility regarding measures of economic performance, and a great deal of turbulence in the economy. By contrast, the fourth quarter of 1984 was marked by a relative decline in inflation (5.2% in January 1985 vs. 13.5% in May 1984) due to the package deal structured by the government, the Labor Federation and the Manufacturers

Association. The package deal agreement was supposed to stabilize the system, and it actually decreased inflation although at a rather high cost.

What is the explanation for the mispredictions? Two possible reasons come to mind. First, the October 1984 survey showed a remarkable decline in the optimism index of the respondents. Regardless of the forthcoming package deal which began November 2, 1984, most executives were pessimistic about their business and the local market. This may have led to the underestimation of production volume, sales, and orders on the local market. The other three financial indices show an overestimation that may be due to a disbelief in the power of the package deal agreement to freeze wages and prices. A second explanation may be a psychological one: during periods of change for the better (October 1984) or change for the worse (October 1983) businessmen had difficulty in predicting the expected economic developments. However, in "stable" periods, even though economic conditions were highly volatile, they had little problem in predicting economic developments. Perhaps, as far-reaching as it may sound, those executives got used to the dynamic-turbulent situation and were able to predict short term (three months) changes well enough. But when an artificial, exogenous mechanism was to bring equilibrium to the system, those manufacturers who were able to predict a turbulent free market, were wrong (perhaps from disbelief) in predicting changes in a very controlled economic environment. According to this explanation, the most important variable affecting prediction is the change in economic parameters and not their actual size.

It is interesting to note that the problem of misprediction in periods of expected change (i.e., October 1983) occurred in the case of the amateurs as well as the experts. Yet, the predictions of the amateurs for almost all the variables (clothing, CPI lagged, and CPI expected) were too high while the predictions of the experts (regarding financial expenditures, number of employees, local sales, and local orders) were too low.

Conclusion

The data presented in this paper are only preliminary in nature. In general, it gives credit to both consumers and manufacturers in predicting changes in prices and other economic variables. The results seem to indicate that apart from using differing information, experts and amateurs do not differ with regard to their interpretation of economic information. For both groups the most important variable that affected the accuracy of their predictions was the regularity or change of the economic conditions and not their actual level.

REFERENCES

Begg, D. K. (1982) The Rational Expectations Revolution in Macro-economics. Oxford: P. Allan Publishers.

Blomqvist, H. C. (1983) "On the formation of inflationary expectations: Some empirical evidence from Finland, 1979-1980", Journal of Economic Psychology 4, 319-334.

Brown, B. and Maital, S. (1981) "What do economists know? An empirical study of expectations", Econometrica 49, 491-504.

Kahneman, D., Slovic, P., and Tversky, A. (eds.) (1982) Judgment Under Uncertainty: Heuristics and Biases. New York: Cambridge University Press.

Kahneman, D. and Tversky, A. (1979) "Prospect theory: An analysis of choice under risk", Econometrica 47, 263-291.

Katona, G. (1974) "Psychology and consumer economics", Journal of Consumer Research 1, 1-8.

Leonard, J. (1982) "Wage expectations in the labor markets: Survey of evidence on rationality", Review of Economics and Statistics 64, 157-161.

Lichtenstein, S., Fischhoff, B., and Phillips, D. (1977) "Calibration of probabilities: The State of the art", in H. Jungerman and G. de Zeeuw (eds.), Decision Making and Change in Human Affairs. Holland: Reidel.

Muth, J. (1961) "Rational expectations and the theory of price movements", Econometrica 29, 315-353.

Shapira, Z. and Venezia, I. (1981) "Optional stopping on nonstationary series", Organizational Behavior and Human Performance 27, 32-49.

Simon, H. (1979) "Rational decision making in business organizations", American Economic Review 69, 493-513.

Turnovsky, S. (1970) "Empirical evidence on the formation of price expectations", Journal of the American Statistical Association 65, 1441-1454.

Tversky, A. and Kahneman, D. (1981) "The framing of decisions of the psychology of choice", Science 211, 438-458.

Part Seven
The Kibbutz

Professional Managers in the Kibbutz

AMIR HELMAN
RUPPIN INSTITUTE
MAY 1986

ABSTRACT

The founders of the Kibbutz strove to build a unique, democratic society, without managers and leaders.

In the last two decades a process of "Institutionalization" and "Professionalism" took place.

The Kibbutz tried to avoid "stratification" by its special effort to keep rotation among its office-holders.

Researchers found that the average time in the most important managerial jobs is only 2-3 years.

In our research we follow the careers of the principal office-holders after they had finished their "chosen task".

We found a group of "professional managers", mainly men, graduated in economics and management, aged 40-50, with experience as economic coordinators or treasurers. They exchange managerial-jobs and thus kept a special sort of "horizontal rotation".

1. THE KIBBUTZ - GENERAL DESCRIPTION

The specific contribution of the kibbutz to the human experience is its attempt to translate socialist principles into every day practice within a community based on voluntary membership.

In Israel there are about 250 Kibbutzim, with a total population of 120,000 people, which is less than three percent of the Israeli population. The kibbutz is a communal village with a total population ranging approximately from 50 to 2000 persons, with an average of 4 or 5 hundred.

Usually all the permanent adult residents know each other personally. This enables the kibbutz to rely heavily on informal social control, a feature of great importance to the running of the community.

The kibbutz is a voluntary society in its nature: persons who are currently members may leave whenever they wish, and non-members may join at any time (provided their candidacy is approved by a stated proportion of the existing membership). The means of production are owned communally and production is carried out collectively. No wages are paid: the kibbutz supplies the basic needs (Education, health, food, clothing, social services and so on), and in addition a personal allowance to all members on an agreed, equitable basis.

The inherently democratic nature of the kibbutz is enshrined in the composition of the general assembly which consists of all adult members and meets 30 to 40 times a year; it is the central organ and the ultimate source of authority. The machinery of kibbutz decision making and control is however based on an elaborate network of committees, offices, and functions.

The secretariat which meets weekly is the main decision making organ. It is composed of the principal office holders, who were elected by the general assembly for two years, and include the general secretary, the economic coordinator, the labour coordinator, the treasurer, and the coordinator of education etc.

The economic committee is probably the most important committee, which deals with the current problems of the production sector, discusses annual and long term plans, general investment planning, and the allocation of labour. The kibbutz' main ideal, derived from Marx's Communistic ideas "from each according to his ability, to each according to his needs". This ideal intentionally disconnects the usual relationship between a person's income and his consumption.

2. THE DILEMMA: VALUES AGAINST EFFICIENCY

The kibbutz has a special problem, because of its main values intentionally appear as opposed to economic efficiency. We can present a few typical examples:

1. The kibbutz can use hired labor from outside, increasing its income, but is forced to give up part of its ideal not to exploit others, and to rely only on its self-labor.

2. The introduction and incentives and rewards for effort. Although the kibbutz can expect higher income, it weakens the main ideal of breaking the connection between one's production and consumption.

3. Abolishing rotation of efficient managers in industry is another step which endangers the idea of a classless society, without "elites" or a managerial group.

An extremely idealistic society, such as a religious puritan sect, may have more lofty goals, which they try to fulfil, with economics only a necessary means to achieve these primary targets. They would choose a point which would enable them to accomplish the highest standard of their values.

On the other hand, the real materialist, for example, the homo-econimicus, who is motivated only by his natural instincts, and as a consumer would tend to prefer material possessions over spiritual ones, and thus would prefer to give up his values when they prevent or reduce his economic achievements.

The founders of the kibbutz had a very strong tendency to be as close as possible to the highest rate of accomplishing their values. They were in fact almost like religious people who strove to build a new society, based on freedom, equality, mutual aid, tolerance and brotherhood; a society without exploitation, discrimination, or despotism.

The image portrayed by the kibbutz is one of a highly self-conscious microcosm, whose members are intent upon preserving the values around which their society was created: a devotion to social justice and equalitarianism, along with a high sense of national identity and national dedication.

But the kibbutz, like all social movements, passed from a "charismatic" into a "routine" phase in the course of its development. Second and third generations in the kibbutz admire their parents' revolution, but for them it is the life they were born to, and got used to.

In the last two decades, we can find a gradual, but very clear tendency to prefer economic efficiency over kibbutz values. This process is taking place without any decision, and even unconsciously, without definition and recognition of this simple "possibility frontier curve". The appearance of "professional managers" in the Kibbutz is in contradiction to some of its main ideals.

3. THE PROCESS OF INSTITUTIONALIZATION AND "PROFESSIONALISM"

Until the Second World War the Kibbutz existed as a homogeneous, intimate group of friends, with pure and complete democracy, which included spontaneous relationships without formality and without crystallized establishment. The organization structure was weak and undefined and the general assembly meetings were informal, and discussed each problem and matters of the Kibbutz.

R. Cohen (1946) explains the socio-economic organization from his point of view: "self management of the society in the Kibbutz, reached its full utterance when each member fully participated in all Kibbutz matters. The establishment of the Kibbutz does not enforce its own desires on the members, and it only acts according to the society's needs and to serve the members... the managers are equal to all other members, in their satisfaction and their duties... In order to keep this equality we need the rotation among the leaders... When we use our democratic methods, we increase the direct influence of each member on all society matters, and we increase the value and initiative and awareness of each member." (P. 267).

A. Daniel (1972) points out the stabilization and crystallization of the organization during 1940-1948. The feeling of lack of a democratic stabilized frame brought to the establishment of a very complicated organization, with a lot of committees.

After the establishment of the Israeli State, the process of establishment of the democratic organization is taking place, when demographic, social, economic and ideological changes transfer the decision making emphasis from the general assembly toward the smaller committees.

Gradually the secretariat of the Kibbutz became stronger, when the economic Coordinator stands out as the dominant factor in charge of the economic sphere.

The process of "Professionalism is especially felt when the main economic staff begins to do their job during the work-day (and not only in the evenings after their usual work).

The professionalism, the complication of the problems, increasing of the population and its trend to heterogeneous and multiple ages society, with a lot of "secondary groups", begin to decrease and weaken the importance of the general assembly.

E. Cohen (1963) wrote that "The General Assembly stopped dealing with the real important topics, which are now transferred to the Kibbutz establishment; its main task now is the approval of some of the economic Plan prepared by the center, and dealing with many peculiar and insignificant matters." This development is clearly in contrast to the original idea of direct democracy, participating, abolishing of alienation and equality of members' value, which were some of the basic values of the Kibbutz formation.

The decrease of Kibbutz democracy, and the professionalization brought a concentration of power into the hands of the economic coordinator and the treasurer, who were two delegates of the economic sector in the Kibbutz secretariat. Some experts warned that this could lead to the appearance of a new, very strong "Elite", which keep in their hands all the important and essential decisions. It could bring about a bureaucratic hierarchic organization, which means complete destruction of the Kibbutz' special structure.

Much research done in the Kibbutz did not succeed in finding real classes or research groups. But in the economic sphere they found the beginning of Professionalism. Y. Talmon found signs of development toward more stratification, by profession differentiation. E. Cohen found in each Kibbutz a group of members who, most of the time, take the most important roles (and at the same time, many members remain passive permanently and were never in office). Cohen and Leshem found that in spite of the fact that Kibbutz members prefer the democratic way as the good method for solving problems in the Kibbutz, they prefer another attitude, when dealing with economic problems.

Very special organization crystallized in the Kibbutz: there is central planning, as we find in the preparation of the economic plan. On the other hand it is very decentralized and the general assembly is the supreme authority for approval of all the Plans. It seems that every member has the ability and right to reject, to change, to improve and add to the economic plan made by the economic establishment.

But in reality a real contradiction is created between the efficient personal decision of the "experts", who are involved in every detail of the Kibbutz' problems, and who are able to reach a high level of decisions, and between the collective decision of the general assembly.

Formally the Kibbutz has the last decision, as to the aim and strategy of the economic activities in the hands of the members, and the decision is not with the experts and managers, but the general assembly is relegated to deal mainly with marginal matters, the number of participants is lessening, and even its standard of discussion is not very high. It is especially clear that not many economic problems are dealt with in the assembly.

A sociological study, conducted in one of the kibbutzim (in 1975), points out that only four general meetings in a year dealt with economic topics. Its conclusion is that public interest in economic matters is trifling. Decisions in this sphere are reached by a handful of economists and administrators.

Another research done by Reuven Cohen in (1975) concentrated on the alienation which is growing between the leaders and the led.

> "Two separate and more or less polarized groups were created in each Kibbutz - the leading and the led... The leading group identifies itself fully with the aims and existence of the system... but it does not determine the general character of the kibbutz-society. The different behavior of the led constantly undermines the position and behavior of the leading group. They are generally aware of every I deserve.. They take anything they can get from the system and hardly ever interfere with this operation. They regard all values of the system as outdated."

The discrepancy between R. Cohen of (1946) and R. Cohen of 1975 (not the same person) is astonishing: complete democracy in 1946, and hierarchy and almost classes in 1975.

In a research done lately in Ruppin Institute (Helman 1985) we found that there are clear signs of crystallizing a group of "permanent managers". The Kibbutz keeps its idea of rotation, and a manager should finish his job after a few years. But instead of returning to "regular jobs", he is usually moved to manage in a parallel environment. The Kibbutz needs the manager's skills and experience, and the manager prefers to express himself in several managerial jobs, and we find a special sort of "Horizontal rotation" in the Kibbutz.

4. STRATIFICATION AND ROTATION

The rigid rule of oligarchy presumes that in each society one can expect the gradual appearance of hierachy and stratification. Any attempt to create an organization with direct democracy and equality, would contradict the functional requirements and the efficiency of society.

Many experts were eager to examine the Kibbutz in order to see whether it is really possible to function in a classless society, without managers and leaders. In 1951 Eva

Rosenfeld examined one Kibbutz and discovered the first signs of stratification: The veteran members were chosen for the most important management-jobs. But only during the Sixties and Seventies, after the "industrial revolution" took place in the Kibbutzim, the questions of stratification, alienation and classes really appeared.

A researcher from one Kibbutz (Kresl G) wrote a book in which he described many details about the behavior of a few managers in his own Kibbutz.

"They gain decisive influence, power, prestige, authority and even material advantages. They also make sure that they keep their important jobs, by creating the impression that all the other members depend on their special skills."

Many researchers oppose Kresl and claim that stratification in the Kibbutz is completely impossible, because of the highly important ideal and implementation by rotation: Each manager is chosen for a short period (2 - 3 years) and then is replaced by another chosen member.

Shefer Y. (1977) checked 5 main management-jobs (secretary, economic coordinator, treasurer, industrial-manager and work coordinator in 14 Kibbutzim. He discovered that managers on the average rotate every 2.4 years. "We avoid monopolization of power, and prevent the appearance of permanent and professional managers."

Talmon's (1970) research focused on 6 kibbutzim, and she claimed that it is impossible to find any significant "Elite".

Rosner and Cohen examined 13 Kibbutzim (with 4000 members), during the years 1966-1976; their findings show that 200 members served in the 4 main management-jobs. The average time in office was 2.5 years, and only 50 of them served in these jobs for 5 years. Their conclusion was that "the data proves that there is no trend towards monopolization of the central management-jobs, and that the mechanizm of rotation is still working exactly according to the normative values". Rosner and Cohen also claim that the success in preventing obligarchy due to the manager's special disadvantages and "negative compensation".

But all these researches ingnore a very important question: To where does the manager return after his rotation? Does he return to his regular or previous job? Or does he, once a manager, become a managed-worker? Or does he prefer to stay in some other managerial job?

5. THE "PROFESSIONAL-MANAGERS" - FINDINGS

In order to examine the appearance of "Professional Managers", we focused on the groups of Kibbutz' principal office holders: secretaries, economic-coordinators and treasurers. We tried to follow their careers, after they had finished their "chosen task", until the end of 1984.

The research was done in the "Ruppin College for Managers" in 1985, and the basic information was gathered by students of economics who intend to be the economic-coordinators of their Kibbutzim in the future. We examined all the secretaries, economic coordinators and treasurers who were in office during the years 1970 - 1984, in 30 Kibbutzim. During these 15 years, there were 636 management-tasks. In an average Kibbutz 21 members serve in these three main jobs: 10 secretaries, 6 economic coordinators and 5 treasurers.

We tried to find some characteristics of these office-holders:

(a) Sex: The Kibbutz was founded as a society managed by men. Only two women (out of 180) served during the last fifteen years as economic-coordinators. There were only 4.8% women among the treasurers, and even as secretaries we found only 51 women (out of 291), which is 17.5% of the total number of secretaries. In 10 of the Kibbutzim, there was not even one woman who served as a secretary during the last 15 years.

(b) Age: The average age, at the beginning of the task was 40. Economic coordinators are slightly younger (37), while the secretary of the Kibbutz was 43, and the treasurer is 40 years old. Only 16% of these office-holders began their managerial jobs when older than 50.

(c) Education: 80% of the economic coordinators were graduates in economics, management or agriculture. Less than 8% were only high-school graduates. In 21 (out of 30) Kibbutzim, all the economic coordinators were academic studies graduates. The same goes for the treasurers. On the other hand only half of the secretaries were University graduates.

Our aim was to follow these office-holders' careers and work in the Kibbutz, after they had finished their chosen tasks, until December 1984.

In order to do this, we examined 364 office-holders during 1970 - 1980. We tried to find out how many years they had worked in "management", and for how many years they have devoted to "non-management" work (agriculture, industry, services and other regular jobs).

As "management" we define not only the main "classical" three (secretary, economic coordinator and treasurer) but also the top managers of Kibbutz' industries, management jobs outside the Kibbutz (mainly in regional-industries, movement's-centres, etc.)

Here we had an astonishing surprise: not only that the original idea of "returning to work" does not exist, but many of the "task holders" work most of their time in managerial jobs. We can prove this with the example of the 97 members, who served in these 30 Kibbutzim during 1970 - 1980 as economic coordinators: 20% of them did not proceed with any managerial-jobs, but 80% of them entered other managerial jobs. These 78 economic coordinators, who entered the "management world", devoted 77% of their years of work to management jobs. An average economic coordinator in the last 11.5 years worked 9 years in "management", and only 2.5 years in "non-management" jobs. He managed in his Kibbutz industry, in the Movement, regional industries, again in the secretariat of his Kibbutz, as delegate abroad etc. In these jobs he spent almost 80% of his work time. Even in the 23% of his "non-management" jobs, he was not exactly a "labourer", as we include with the "non-management" jobs also advanced study, costing, or second degree management in the Kibbutz.

It is interesting to find what happened to the 19 economic coordinators (out of 97), who had left management altogether. Did they return to agriculture? Have 20% really to be "labourers", according to the original idea of rotation? It seems that the answer is: "no". Eight of them were simply unable to proceed with their careers: one had died and seven decided to leave the Kibbutz. The other 3 were sent for a long time to study, 3 other members entered work as cost-accountants which is very close to the Kibbutz' establishment. One member, who was 60 years old, entered the service sector, and only 4 (out of 97) returned to agriculture, and stayed completely out of the "management sector".

Quite similar results were found with the 93 treasurers: 80% of those who returned to management devoted 75% of their work-years to managerial jobs. Among their 25% "non-managerial" time, at least 10% was spent in studies and as accountants.

Again, from the 19 members who removed themselves from "management", only one returned to his previous work in agriculture.

Among the 174 secretaries of the Kibbutzim during that period (1970 - 1980), 80 members (and mainly the women) returned to their former jobs, and left the "management sector". 94 secretaries (54%) who continued as managers, devoted almost 2/3 of their time to managerial jobs, mainly in the Center of the Kibbutz' movement.

We found a group of 246 Kibbutz members, who had worked in

the last 11 years, about 8 years (72% of their work time) in "management". 60 members worked 100% of their time in "management".

We found a group of managers, mainly men, graduates in economics and management, aged 40 - 50, with experience as economic coordinators or treasurers who are definitely "Professional Managers". Their main tasks, most of the time, are managerial jobs. Although they did not manage permanently in one place, and we found a very clear rotation in each office and task, these certain members did not travel "up and down". Instead they always exchanged places, and thus kept a special sort of "horizontal rotation".

6. REASONS FOR THE "HORIZONTAL ROTATION"

There are many important reasons for the appearance and development of this special sort of rotation in the Kibbutz:

(1) Lack of professional managers among Kibbutz' members, and effort to use the experience and the skill of the most suitable people for the job.

(2) Tremendous increase in the demand for managers. Development of new industries and additional outside organizations, require many managers.

(3) Prolonged and profound preparation for management, increases the educational gap between the manager and the "regular member".

(4) Increase in complexities of the subjects.

(5) The evasion of other "specific professionals" (engineers, architects, teachers, academics etc.) from entering managerial jobs.

(6) Lack of appropriate jobs for members of the age 40 - 50, (who became too old for agriculture, and in any case need a "transferance" to another job).

(7) The need of "self-actualization", for people with a high level of initiative.

(8) The passive and indifferent attitude of a large part of the public.

(9) The change in the Kibbutz' attitude towards "management", and a growing recognition of management as a profession.

BIBLIOGRAPHY (H = Hebrew)

Barkai H. (1977) GROWTH PATTERNS OF THE KIBBUTZ ECONOMY North-Holland Publishing Company. Contribution to Economic Analysis 108.

Cohen E. (1963) H. Changes in the Social Structure of the Work in the Kibbutz". THE ECONOMIC QUARTERLEY. No. 40. (P. 378-388).

Cohen R. (1946) H. THE BASIS OF KIBBUTZ ECONOMY Hakibbutz Hameuchad Publication.

Cohen R. (1975) H. "What happened to us?" SHDEMOT Forum for Kibbutz Movement No. 52.

Daniel A (1972) H. THE COOPERATION-VISION AND REALIZATION University Library. Am-Oved - Culture and Education.

Helman A. (1980) "Income Consumption relationship within the Kibbutz system". INTERGRATED COOPERATIVES IN INDUSTRIAL SOCIETY (Ed: Bartolke et al). Van Gorcum. Assen. The Netherlands.

Helman A. (1985) H. "Horizontal-Rotation and signs of appearance of new managerial class". YAHAD, Forum of Kibbutz United Movement.

Kresl G. (1983) H. "TO EACH ACCORDING TO HIS NEEDS" "Guma" books of Science and Research.

Michels R.(1959) POLITICAL PARTIES. Dover Publications. New York.

Rosenfeld Eva (1951) "Social stratification in a classless Society" AMERICAN SOCIOLOGICAL REVIEW. No. 6.

Shefer Y. (1977) H. INTRODUCTION TO KIBBUTZ SOCIOLOGY. Ruppin Institute.

Talmon-Garber Y. (1972) FAMILY AND COMMUNITY IN THE KIBBUTZ. Harvard University

THE TRANSITION FROM A "SIMPLE" INDUSTRY TO A "SOPHISTICATED" ONE IN THE FUTURE KIBBUTZ *

Dan Bar-On, PhD **
Department of Behavioral Sciences
Ben Gurion University
Beer Sheva, Israel

Amittai Niv, D.B.A.
Director of the Academic Program
The Ruppin Institute, Israel

* This article is based on a research project initiated and generously supported by Yad Tabenkin, the United Kibbutz Federation research institute.

** Authors' names appear here in alphabetic order. They equally share the authorship of this article.

The Kibbutz is a quasi autonomous, social and economic entity that differs from its surrounding society by its values (egalitarianism, broad social mission), principles ("from everybody according to his or her ability, to everybody according his or her needs) and its operating system (self ruling democracy). As a total system (one performs all his or her roles and satisfies all his or her needs within his Kibbutz) that has an active approach and mission towards the rest of the world, the Kibbutz is engaged in an intensive exchange with its external environment. To survive as a unique entity, it has to strike a delicate balance between organizational efficiency and preserving its unique social features. Failing to meet the first challenge will lead to stagnation, giving up part of its main social features will end with assimilation into the rest of the world. (Niv, 1976). One important aspect of this dilemma is the issue of size.

Inherent in the structure of the Kibbutz, as in any other type of commune, is the conflict between community values (small size, intimacy and a great emphasis on the quality of communal life) and the needs of the organization to produce at maximum efficiency. This contradiction is especially apparent in Kibbutzim where, due to their very nature, they try to attain both these objectives. They aim to maintain an egalitarian lifestyle with an emphasis on values and ideology while, at the same time, aspiring to the goals of material success as presented by the wider society. It is from this contradiction that the uniqueness of the dilemma of scale derives: in order to be a community the Kibbutz must be small and intimate. On the other hand, in order to be an efficient organization it must develop, rapidly as possible, the advantages of scale.

Much of the successful survival of the Kibbutz during its first eighty years can be attributed to its agricultural nature. During these years most of its resources, activities and income were in this domain. A typical Kibbutz has between five and ten different agricultural branches (i.e. cotton, cowshed, poultry, apple orchards, etc.). The branch itself constitutes of the production unit (i.e. raising cotton). almost all `auxilary activities' such as research and development of new crops and cultivating methods. Initial preparation of raw materials, final processing of the crops, and marketing are performed by large scale cooperative organizations, as described by Bar-on and Niv (Bar-on and Niv, 1985). By creating these large umbrella organizations, Kibbutzim are able to enjoy both worlds: To maintain their small and intimate operating units within their physical and organizational borders while, at the same time, enjoy the advantages of scale where they are needed. The rapid industrialization process experienced by the Kibbutz at present constitutes a serious deviation from this ideal pattern. Kibbutz ability to cope with the challenges imposed by its industry will determine, to a large extent, its continuing survival as a unique system.

THREE GENERATIONS OF KIBBUTZ INDUSTRY

The beginning of Kibbutz industrialization date back to the second world war. The agricultural export branches (mainly citrus), were paralyzed through lack of transportation and a reduction in foreign markets. On the other hand the British army became a sizable customer in the local market. Especially of food preserves and metal products. Several of the enterprises established at that time were later dissolved. Others formed the infrastructure for continued industrial development. Industrial enterprises of that time had several characteristics in common: they were large in relation to the Kibbutzim which had established them. They were labor intensive and employed several dozen workers each. Technology was simple and physical conditions were hard.

The second wave of Kibbutz industrialization reached its climax between the mid-sixties and mid-seventies. Several factors were involved. An increasingly large number of Kibbutzim fully utilized the land, water and especially, the production quotas allotted to them. Any further income would have to come from non-agriculture sources. The accepted standard of living in the movement and the desire to make the Kibbutz more attractive in this respect to potential candidates created great pressures for increased income. During that period most of the Kibbutzim experienced an increase in population due to internal growth and the joining of new members from outside. The Kibbutz "labor market" not only grew during these years but became also more diversified. New and young members nurtured expectations for jobs that are more `sophisticated' than the ones offered by the industry of the first wave. During this period more than two hundred Kibbutz industrial enterprises were formed. At the end of the process in the early eighties less than a handful of Kibbutzim were left without at least one industrial enterprise.

An important advantage of these enterprises is their small size and simple nature. The number of workers required and their level of professional expertise allowed most of these operations to remain within the boundaries (both physical and organizational) of the Kibbutzim to which they belonged. This appears to explain the optimal correlation between the character of industry in the second generation and the size of the average Kibbutz.

By and large, this industry operated within a comfortable environment within which products, technology and market stay stable most of the time. Auxiliary activities such as R & D, marketing and professional management were unnecessary. To overcome other problems of scale, most Kibbutzim joined loosely organized umbrella associations. For instance, `clubs' to exchange information, committees to coordinate purchasing of raw materials and sales of finished goods and a central institution to coordinate R & D efforts. Interkibbutz cooperation reached its extreme form in more than thirty industrial partnerships between two (and sometime three or more) Kibbutzim.

In 1985 total output (sales) of all Kibbutzim was 1.9 billion dollars. More than 60% of which were of industrial products. Kibbutz industry outperforms Israel's industry by all relevant indicators. In a way, these data support the fundamental ideology of the Kibbutz which assumes a strong relationship between the nature of the social system and its economic performance.

But two developments over the last two years have cast a shadow over the positive picture painted here. The first concerns the large number of Kibbutzim searching, with only partial success, for an industrial enterprise. Either as a replacement to the existing one or as an addition to it. The second concerns the performance of Kibbutz industry over the last ten years.

THE PRESENT SITUATION: IS IT AN AGING INDUSTRY?

During the late seventies and early eighties Kibbutz industry suffered a clear slowdown in all important indices. Part of it was in absolute terms and another, relatively to the average growth rates of Israel's industry. Table 1 summarizes key data as published by Kibbutz Industrial Association.

TABLE 1: RELATIVE GROWTH OF KIBBUTZ AND ISRAELI INDUSTRY 1980 - 1981 (BASE INDEX - 100)

YEAR	SALES		INDUSTRIAL EXPORTS		INVESTMENTS	
	KIBBUTZ	AVERAGE	KIBBUTZ	AVERAGE	KIBBUTZ	AVERAGE
1980	100	100	100	100	100	100
1981	104	109	108	109	99	106
1982	107	110	104	103	67	132
1983	119	112	105	100	120	163
1984	137	122	137	119	105	137

Source: Kibbutz Industries Association Report, 1985.

One of the more important conclusions of a study based on these data (Borochov Et Al), defines the problem in the following way:

"The most striking expression of the declining growth rate (of Kibbutz Industry in recent years) is actually to be found in investment figures which point to a real decline of approx. 36% in absolute terms between 1972 and 1982. Which means an annual decline in investments of approx. 4.3%. At the same time investments in industry throughout Israel as a whole grew approx. by 88%. Which is a positive annual average growth rate of approx. 6.5%. The cause for concern arising from this data lies in that the main explanation for the decline in investments on the part of the Kibbutz industries is not due to financing or liquidity problems but to a dearth of new investment projects."

There are at present over 350 Kibbutz owned industrial enterprises. It is, therefore, impossible to talk about Kibbutz industry in general or in average terms. Yet, it is clear that as a whole, the industrial sector of the Kibbutz is going nowadays through fundamental changes. The more apparent are its maturation and aging. Which means that already in the near future this generation of Kibbutz industry will fail in meeting the above mentioned expectations as a modern employer of the young labor force and as the main source for maintaining or raising the existing standard of living of the Kibbutz.

Various factors are involved in this situation. The more obvious are technological advancements, changes in the general economy of Israel, changes in the level and direction of occupational education within the Kibbutz and the tendency of single Kibbutzim to cooperate in developing large scale industrial operations. The interplay between these factors, and many other not mentioned here, adds to a complex problem, a problem that cannot be treated by `manipulating' one single factor. Furthermore, most of the factors involved in the situation change not only at a rapid pace but, also, in unpredictable and unfamiliar directions. The Kibbutz faces, therefore, not only a complex reality but also a situation of an accumulating second-order change. It is reasonable to assume that the problems presented here will not be solved by another dose of "more of the same". It is a situation that calls for reconstruction of existing "maps" and change in basic assumptions. In other words, we enter the third generation of Kibbutz industry.

THE THIRD GENERATION

In July 1984 ten senior decision and policy makers of the Kibbutz Movement and several academics met to explore possible direction for future development of Kibbutz industry. Each participant in that meeting was asked to prepare and present a scenario of future Kibbutz industry. Surprising or not, all these scenarios had two common denominators: first, all defined new spheres of activity (i.e. bio-technology, water processing, recycling and utilization, introduction of robotics into new areas in agriculture). Second, all, without exception, `left' the confines of the single Kibbutz and drew comprehensive organizational configurations of one kind or another. If these scenarios reflect the state of mind and terms of reference of key decision makers within the Kibbutz Movement, one may conclude that expected development of Kibbutz industry in the near future will give rise to a further confrontation with the old dilemma of scale. Besides the general consent about the transition to a larger scale of the Kibbutz industrial enterprise, the specific proposals that were suggested varied extremely. Each one represented differing aspects of the dilemma of scale. The main ones are described in detail below:

1. A broadening and deepening of the activities of the Kibbutz movements' umbrella organizations (to include R & D, import and export). Thus, those enterprises, new and established alike, which come under the authority of the various Kibbutzim, will be relieved from the heavy burden entailed by these support functions. A further advantage of scale may be enjoyed by the single enterprise by enlarging the scope of activities of those organizations working to regulate competition among and between Kibbutzim and their representation to the outside world.

2. Encouragement of existing initiatives for developing industrial activity within regional organizations. Althougћ the latter were set to deal with the agricultural produce of their members, it would be relatively easy to direct them towards `pure' industry.

3. An industrial enterprise under the ownership of two or more Kibbutzim. This involves the broadening and development of the existing approach regarding the autonomy and self containment of the single Kibbutz. Within the Kibbutz Movement today there are more than thirty such partnerships.

4. A corporation, the seeds of this idea are already appearing in several of the inter-Kibbutz partnerships existing today. The intention here is to group together some of the activities carried out separately at present into an integrated product line bearing a common brand name. For instance, a group of several Kibbutzim that get together in order to develop, manufacture and sell medical equipment. Each Kibbutz will specialize in producing one item of a wide line of products. The partnership would concentrate on improving existing products, developing new items for the existing line and forming and developing an effective marketing network.

5. Large scale industry in a big Kibbutz. The settlement concept of the Kibbutz Movement stated, as it does today, that a new Kibbutz must grow at a gradual pace. It is commonly accepted that eight to ten years are needed for a new Kibbutz to stand on its feet as an economic entity. This concept of a growing Kibbutz has several important advantages. Among them are Movement's increasing capacity to act as a settling factor in the country. This is done by starting as many as possible small nucleas in different parts of the country; the distribution of economic risks by the Movement over a large number of projects; the opportunity to suit the size of the Kibbutz at any time to the production capacity at its disposal and finally, a gradual development of capabilities of the single Kibbutz in the spheres of technology and management.

   One of the scenarios presented at that meeting took an opposite approach: the economic infrastructure of the Kibbutz in the future, it is assumed, will be industrial. Since industry of the future will require in part of its components advantages of scale, the future Kibbutz has to be big right from its establishment. Which requires a radical change in the settlement strategy of the Movement as well as in the "practical theory of the development of the single Kibbutz".

6. The employment of hired labor in the more problematic areas, especially in areas that require technical or managerial training and skills. Since Kibbutzim do not have, at present, members who have the right background, they can employ professionals from the outside. The problem with this solution is that it makes the Kibbutz dependent on external resources, which is in clear conflict with the need to be autonomous and independent.

7. The aquisition of external know-how. Just as acquiring the physical means of production in the second generation was accompanied by the aquisition of the necessary know-how, so entry into the third generation requires a similar process. The difference between past experience and present situation, it was mentioned, is in the rapid development and obsoleteness of such know-how. Which makes the aquisition of it an ongoing process and not a single effort.

8. Sub-contracting. One of the tested means of entering the second industrial generation was through association with a leading manufacturer in that particular market or technology. Kibbutzim who entered such a partnership saved the costs and risks associated with the more problematic phases of the construction of a new enterprise (i.e. the development of new products and production processes, penetration into new markets, and the formulation of a business strategy for the long range future.) This last scenario suggested a similar set for nowadays' start ups to facilitate entry into the more demanding third industrial generation.

IS SMALL BEAUTIFUL?

An awareness of the dilemmas of scale characterizes all the scenarios described in the preceding section. On the one hand these "new views of the world" are intended to add to the third generation of Kibbutz industry the dimension of scale. Indeed, the logic behind each of these views reflects an awareness of this dimension of size. On the other hand, the reservations that go together with this concept express a deep concern for the fate of the Kibbutz community under the new conditions. The circumstances urging the Kibbutz to adopt a new generation of industry require renewed efforts to come, again, to terms with the old dilemmas of scale. This new reformulation of the old dilemma is charaterized by the fact that whatever changes are made, whether efficient organization is sacrificed for the quality of community life or vice versa, Kibbutz industry remains within the same rigorous constraints as drawn by the dilemma.

The scenarios presented here may be placed on an organizational efficiency - community intimate scale as follows:
umbrella organization (1) - large Kibbutz (5) - external know-how and skills (7) - employment of salaried workers (6) - sub-contracting (8) - joint enterprise (3) - corporation (4) regional organi ation (2).

The umbrella organizations leave a maximum measure of management autonomy and freedom in the hands of the Kibbutz. Within the given framework their ability to exert a positive influence on the business performance of a particular industry is the smallest of all the above scenarios. An industry situated within a regional organization - the possibility located at the other extreme of the continuum - is the most likely to reap the maximum benefits of scale. It, also poses the greatest threat to the integrity of the Kibbutz community.

All our scenarios describe the main feature of the transition from the second to the third generation as a shift from small to large enterprises. We defined the issues associated with this process as a dilemma because we see them as bearing impossible choices: each of the possibilities here described carries unintended consequences' that make the choice of that option almost impossible. The solutions that go toward the 'organization efficiency' pole have a negative impact on the 'community' pole, and vice versa. Why, then, is a small enterprise discouraged by Kibbutz policy makers? So far the need to move on to the third generation has been justified by two types of empiracal proof; the fact that in recent years the number of Kibbutzim looking for new industrial enterprises has been growing while at the same time there has been a significant decline in existing industrial performance. These two tendencies, so it is claimed, testify to the structural change which has recently taken place within the Kibbutz as well as within its broader relevant environment. This empirical finding, per se, does not justify a change in concept. Especially in a complex situation where circumstantial variables have so far not been taken into account. It would, therefore, also seem justifiable to base the need for a change in attitiude towards the scale factor on rational - analytical considerations. In this case such considerations may be presented by means of a model comprising of three components: Firstly, what are the aims of the industry as far as the Kibbutz itself is concerned? Secondly, to what extent may industry help the Kibbutz accomplish its objectives in relation to the relevant environment? Finally, what means, chiefly in the realm of skills and capabilities, does the Kibbutz have at its disposal to achieve these two objectives? In its simple form the model appears as follows:

EXHIBIT 1: A MODEL FOR RECONSTRUCTION OF THE SIZE PROBLEM IN KIBBUTZ INDUSTRY.

RESOURCES AND CAPABILITIES	OBJECTIVES
Material resources. Capital. Know - how. Goodwill. Technological skills. Business capabilities (finance, marketing, planning, etc). General management skills.	Re. The Kibbutz: To provide employment and income in line with the standards and quality of life accepted by the Kibbutz Movement and/or among the Israeli upper middle class.

Re. The relevant environment (Israeli society): preservation of its function as a pioneer and leader in critical facets of life. specifically, ideological, operational, commercial and technical leadership in the more advanced or vital branches of the economy.

MEDIATING FACTORS
Techno - industrial developments in Israel and throughout the world.

OBJECTIVES: AS DEPENDENT AND INDEPENDENT VARIABLE. Over the past ten years changes in the formulation of these objectives have indeed taken place with regard to both the inner workings of the Kibbutz and the external environment. These changes are, however, mainly quantitative in nature (i.e., more of the same: there is a greater range of jobs available, professional and management development takes place at a faster rate and there is a steady rise in income so that the Kibbutz continues to appear attractive from the point of view of the standard of living it can offer its members. The decisive factor, as far as external objectives are concerned, is the position of the Kibbutz as a leader in the Israeli economy. This is not only a central component of Kibbutz ideology but it also plays a vital role in its continued survival.

THE MEDIATING FACTORS: QUALITY AND INTENSITY OF CHANGE

This is not the case as regards the resources currently commanded by the Kibbutz. Although some are available they must be suited to changing conditions (e.g. improvements in general financial management must take place so that the Kibbutzim can raise the funds required for continued industrial development). However, the greatest change finds expression in new factors which did not exist in the past and which are likely to play a decisive role in the near future. These comprise the "mediating factors" appearing in the model. They may be defined as follows: firstly, a long list of new products likely to bring about a fundamental change in the style of life of the West. The most outstanding change to have taken place in the most recent past is the computerized communications revolution - where computers are being integrated into sophisticated communications systems. Secondly, the development of new materials is opening up far reaching possibilities for the development of new products and the improvement of existing ones. Light and heavy metals, crystals and semi-conductors are among the more well known examples. Thirdly, the development of techniques and systems which not only make mass production possible but make the production process flexible is a characteristic which did not exist in the past. Such techniques include, for example, the use of robots on production lines, the construction of sophisticated conveyor-belt systems and full computerization of warehouse management. Fourthly, the sophisticated marketing systems will, on the one hand, make it possible to "sell large quantities within a short time at a reasonable price" and, on the other, will include efficient information systems so that the organization (to which these systems belong) can react in `real time'. All four processes described here have already rapidly begun to make their mark. The life cycle of most products is becoming shorter and a `generation' which in the past lasted many decades, now lasts less than one year in the more sophisticated industries. It is clear that an accelerated rate of change not only affects the products themselves but all the components mentioned above.

RESOURCES AND CAPABILITIES: KNOW-HOW AS A DECISIVE FACTOR.

It is obvious that the more a Kibbutz moves into the third generation of industry, the importance of know-how increases. We apply the term know-how, both basic and applied, to a wide range of aspects of the industrial world: as part of the product itself, as a key factor in the design and development of new materials, as a component in the improvement of production processes and the development of effective marketing strategies. As mentioned before, almost all the experience and know-how accumulated by Kibbutzim throughout the second generation of industry is production related. Both, staying updated in this area and adding other dimensions of business operations seems to be, under present circumstances, an enormous challenge for the average Kibbutz.

A SHORT INTERMETSO: THE ENORMOUS DANGER OF SUCCESS.

Most attention in the Kibbutz situation, as is the case in other contexts, is paid to the danger of failure in new business start ups. This is the place to mention one unique danger only an organization - community like the kibbutz face. This is the danger of success. We have already some evidence of Kibbutzim which very successfully coped with the difficulties and challenges associated with the formation of a new enterprise of the third generation. To find out that very soon they reach a point in which the new enterprise `spills over' its natural boundaries. The size of the community put very clear limits to further growth. On, the other hand, not responding to such opportunities, immediately calls in undesired competitors that may, and sometime do, challenge the initial achievements.

THE SECOND GENERATION CURRENT STATE OF AFFAIRS

The second generation of Kibbutz industry is entirely different from that described above. Most of its products are conventional, raw materials are standard, production methods are in line with the capabilities and experience required in agriculture and sales, mainly to the local markets, are made in accordance with traditional methods. Above all, the second generation enterprises have not undergone any fundamental changes since they were set up about twenty years ago. The structural change taking place today inside and outside the Kibbutz calls for a transition from the stable conditions of the second generation to the far reaching changes which must be made within short time spans. Of the seven factors mentioned as being the main resources available to the Kibbutz, four clearly suit the requirements of the second generation industry. However, they do not suit those of the third.

Technical know-how and, up to a point, business skills, were normally, acquired in conjunction with the elementry equipment of the second generation. Technological improvements over the years did not force radical changes in the basic understanding and operation of the enterprise, But this is no longer the case. At a time when one is moving towards increasingly innovative industry, the necessary know-how is complex; it continuously calls for numerous and rapid changes and a substantial part of this cannot be acquired or passed on.

The ability to absorb, digest and develop the needed know-how depends, in large part, on the technological skills available to the enterprise. In enterprises of the second generation these factors are more or less balanced. this is not so as regards third generation industry. Table 2 summarizes the "inventory of industrial knowledge" in the Kibbutz Movement.

These data raise a question not only on Kibbutz industry's ability to develop its own know-how. They also indicate the difficulties associated with the successful application of external knowledge.

It seems that the Kibbutz, which has always been in the forefront precisely as regards the ability to absorb and develop technical know-how, mainly in agriculture, now lags behind the more advanced Israeli industry.

TABLE 2: TECHNICAL AND BUSINESS EDUCATION IN THE KIBBUTZ, APRIL, 1986

FIELD	GRADUATES NON DEGREE	BACHELOR DEGREE	MASTER DEGREE	DOCTOR DEGREE	PRESENT STUDENTS
MECHANICAL ENGINEERING	220	140	6	0	180
PRODUCTION MANAGEMENT	80	30	6	0	45
ELECTRONIC & ELECTRONICS	95	25	7	0	85
CHEMICAL ENGINEERING	20	19	1	0	10
OTHER TECH. ENGINEERING	300	100	4	0	20
COMPUTER ENGINEERING	10	10	0	0	10
COMPUTER SCIENCES	60	30	6	0	110
CHEMISTRY	60	35	10	0	27
PHYSICS	40	20	7	2	14
MATHEMATICS & STATISTICS	105	60	7	1	35
ECONOMICS & MANAGEMENT	500	190	35	7	190
TOTAL	1490	659	99	10	726

SOURCE: Statistics Department, United Kibbutz Movement

The seriousness of the problem increases the more one moves from the basic skills of operations and maintenance to the improvement of existing products and the development of new ones. The growing scarcity of skilled manpower in the technological sphere is attributed to a decline in the effectiveness of Kibbutz schools with regard to passing on knowledge and developing an ability to learn - both vital factors in modern industry. The tendency among the majority of elementary and high school students is away from science subjects. Only a handful of graduates at a high level in math, chemistry or physics. A great deal of time and energy is required to bring about a change in this situation. Also change is needed in the outlook of parents, teachers and the `Kibbutz street'. It is clear beyond doubt that the dearth of technological skills is preventing the Kibbutzim from entering, as an independent entity, the new industrial era.

Less obviously lacking but no less important are the commercial capabilities required by modern industry. This is especially so as far as effective marketing systems are concerned. The transition to the third generation requires a strategy which will clearly define the unique skills of the system, the type of business it is specializing in, the section of the market within which it wishes to operate and the mechanisms to be developed so that the real situation may be correctly read. Such a strategy should also examine risks and identity opportunities. One is concerned here with a business operation of an entirely different nature from that characterizing the second generation of Kibbutz industry. The difficulties entailed in building modern marketing units are not only qualitative (e.g. training talented academics) but also quantitative in some respects. To effectively `cover' the various aspects of business and to attain a wide geographical reach, large units are essential and a single Kibbutz enterprise is unable to take on such tasks.

Finally, there is the question of general management skills. In addition to specific management skills (e.g. production management, purchasing, finance, marketing) the need for general management skills will grow at a steady pace Skills are necessary beyond those possessed by the `classical' entrepreneur who could, during the second generation, manage the whole business either from `out of his head' or with the aid of a small notebook. The ability to manage a particular branch of agriculture or to fulfil a specific management task constitutes only a part of what is required of the general manager of the future. Training programs and personal career development must be adjusted to suit these needs.

A heavy investment in, both, materials and time is necessary to develop the skills and abilities required by the four areas detailed above. For instance, the outlook of Kibbutz students must be changed to create a better match between their personal orientation and needs and opportunities created in Kibbutz `job market' by further industrialization. It will, however, take almost a decade until the first engineers and researchers complete their training. The same applies to training general managers or experts in specific fields. It is widely accepted in the Kibbutz Movement that the Kibbutzim do not have the time required to carry out such a training program. The gap between existing skills and capabilities and the challanges of the third generation of Kibbutz industry may be reduced by creating enterprises on a different scale from that which is currently accepted. Although small is beautiful from the point of view of community requirements, small scale enterprises are an obstacle where creating efficient organizations is concerned. It has been stated that this obstacle may be overcome through cooperation between two or more Kibbutzim.

LARGE IS OBLIGATORY, IS IT POSSIBLE?

Kibbutz agriculture developed firstly as a result of the ongoing cooperation among the farmers themselves within the quasi-autonomous agricultural sector and, secondly, as a result of cooperation between the farmers and external bodies such as research institutes, government agencies, marketing organizations and committees within the movement. Cooperation in the agricultural sector covers nearly all fields of activity (research, joint production of raw materials, joint processing and organized marketing). Furthermore, cooperation takes place at all levels: between two or more Kibbutzim and at regional and national levels. This is not the case in industry. It may be said that the single Kibbutz producer builds and maintains a high wall between himself and his Kibbutz colleagues. Before generalizing about the difference between agriculture and industry one should point out the lessons to be learned from the few instances of inter-Kibbutz industrial cooperation.

In 1985 there were more than thirty business enterprises run by two or more Kibbutzim. There were also six partnerships between Kibbutzim and external, non-Kibbutz bodies. The commonly held view within the Kibbutz movement is that such partnerships are difficult to manage. Indeed, the majority are not over successful and, on the whole, it is more worthwhile to give them a wide berth. On the other hand, the scale required to enter the third industrial generation is such that inter-Kibbutz cooperation is one of the only existing means of achieving this end. What do we know about inter-kibbutz cooperation?

Very little. To date no comprehensive research on this subject has been carried out. The information presented here is based on an initial survey recently carried out by students of the first author of this paper as part of their field work at the Ruppin Institute. An analysis of approximately twenty cases of inter-Kibbutz cooperation in industry brought to light a list of factors which consistently appear in each case and which are likely to have a decisive influence on the setting up and functioning on inter-Kibbutz industry. The following important factors should be pointed out:

1. THE SPECIFIC BRANCH OF INDUSTRY. The greatest number of partnerships is in plastics and the smallest in bio-technology. This reflects, to a great extent, the general structure of Kibbutz industry. But it also shows the more

specific connections between the nature of the specific industrial branch in the Kibbutz context and other related factors, for instance, it is quite probable that the basic technology of plastics makes it possible to distribute the various departments and operations over a wide geographical area. The term `industrial sector' includes various components: A line of products, typical markets, a given structure of competition and accepted technology. Each one of these, and especially combinations of two or more of them, create a unit which has some influence on the behavior of the various factors within what is defined as the branch.

2. NUMBER OF PARTNERS. The majority of partnerships are made up of two Kibbutzim, but there are some of three or more. The biggest number to date is six. The number of partners has an obvious efffect on the scale of the enterprise and it may also testify to the relative weight of each partner and the relative share of the burden borne by each. The more partners involved, the more difficult it is to manage the enterprise and the more complex are the relations among the partners.

3. CHARACTERISTICS OF PARTNERS. In the majority of partnerships there is a `senior' partner (from the point of view of scale, experience and economic backing) and one or more `minor' ones. A small minority of partnerships are comprised of similar and equal in size partners. What type of combination of scales is preferable? And in what situation?

4. PHYSICAL LOCATION OF THE ENTERPRISE. Is the location of any significance as regards the enterprise's ability to attract personnel and generate an identification with the workplace? Does location have any effect on the tendency to split the production process into autonomous operation units scattered among the partners?

5. FORMAL CONTRACTS. The formal contract is supposed to formalize relations between the partners in a comprehensible and systematic fashion. The contract usually deals with decision making processes in a joint set-up, the accepted method of distributing income and profits, the norms for assigning central tasks, the method of determining investment policy and, finally, the joint work, training and promotion programs for the permanent employees. Over and above the existence of a legal document laying down inter-partnership relationships there is, of course, the question of the possible connection between the articles of the contract and the chances of success of a given partnership.

6. THE SUCCESS OF THE PARTNERSHIP. This is of course the main dependent variable in this analysis related to scale. Furthermore, the term `success' is a problem in itself. Is one conecerned here with the classical economic criteria of

profit, return on investment or growth? Or is one concerned with more community oriented aspects such as the satisfaction of the employees or with the correct management of the enterprise by the partners? Or is one talking about a combination of the two groups of factors - a combination which may contribute to the integration of the whole system? It is clear that the choice of any of these criteria will not only define the relevant questions but will also determine, to a large extent, the possible answers.

As was mentioned above, research on inter-Kibbutz cooperation is still in its initial stages. Thus, other than providing a typology of cooperation, no definite conclusions are available except for one highly important finding: When one analyses the distribution of the dependent variable i.e. the success of the partnership from the point of view of the two most important aspects - the economy and the community - there is no escaping the conclusion that the number of maximal successes throughout the Kibbutz Movement is no more than five. However, we do know much about the subjective perceptions of many of the key persons in Kibbutz industry. They all point in the same direction: They define the `natural' situation in agriculture as being cooperative. Industry, on the other hand, is perceived, almost by definition as a competitive one.

The economic and community facets of the Kibbutz organization constitute two poles of the same axis. Simple movements along this axis (i.e. more economic efficiency at the expenses of the community aspect) are not a good solution for a Kibbutz aspiring to maintain its unique character. The solutions to the problem require the enterprise to break away from this axis or from the original definition of the dilemma. The two examples presented below are different in nature but they both show what possibilities exist for breaking out of the dilemma in a creative manner.

EXHIBIT 2. LEARNING SPACE FOR KIBBUTZ INDUSTRY: AN ILLUSTRATION FROM FOOTWARE INDUSTRY

PRODUCTS/TECHNOLOGIES

	OLD	NEW
OLD	TRADITIONAL SHOE INDUSTRY	OLD SHOE BY CAD/CAM TECHNOLOGY
NEW	HIGH FASHION SHOES	NEW AND YET UNKNOWN FOOTWARE BY YET UNKNOWN TECHNOLOGIES

HOW HIGH SHOULD ONE JUMP?

One way to cope with the dilemma is by reformulating the problem of moving from the second industrial generation to the, third one. Instead of abandoning existing obsolete enterprises and making an enormous and impossible jump into high-technology, one can instead make a gradual transition. Exhibit 2 shows the range of possibilities available.

The great majority of Kibbutz industrial enterprises are to be found in the section referring to `obsolete technology and products'. Transition to the more advanced section requires both learning and the accumulation of experience which will provide the system, the enterprise or the Kibbutz with skills for carrying out the `new operations' (e.g. utilizing the newest technology to produce a conservative product such as shoes or the use of existing technology to produce a new product such as fashionable shoes). In both cases one is talking of a gradual progress along the learning curve to a point close to the position where the system is located at present. On the other hand, the transition to a new product developed and produced by sophisticated technologies is difficult and complex. Thus, the enterprise climbs too high up the ladder with regard to the present capability of the system. This impression is confirmed by various studies carried out in rapidly growing industries in the United States. A common conclusion to most of these studies is that organizations are highly successful in those areas allied to the ones they succeeded in in the past. Those who tried to `take a shortcut' and jumpt too high did not get very far.

THE KIBBUTZ MOVEMENT AS AN INVESTMENT FIRM

Three hundred and fifty industrial enterprises constitute a substantial sector of the Israeli economy. the splitting of Kibbutz industry into small units makes each one sensitive to the disadvantages of a small scale. Theoretically speaking, bringing all of them under a single roof will not only create an extremely important leverage for scale but will also strengthen the movement itself and contribute by that to the fulfilment of some aspects of its basic ideology. The problem here is, and this is another facet of the initial dilemma of size, that by giving up part of the control over its industrial enterpise, the single Kibbtz loses a central component of its communal nature that combines `life' and `business' into one intergrated sphere.

CAN THE KIBBUTZ LEARN?

The main theme of this paper is that the Kibbutz, by its nature, contains a dilemma of size. It aspires to be, at the same time, an intimate community and a successful business enterprise. To survive in the long run, it has to meet the challange of modern industry. The challange is, in our case, serious because the single Kibbutz seems to lack needed resources (especially know-how) while most Kibbutzim failed, until now to create scale by cooperation. Future progress of the Kibbutz along this front can be by learning to cooperate or by developing creative solutions to the dilemma. A systematic discussion of this last question regarding Kibbutz potential for further learning, is beyond the scope of this paper. It has to include a precise definition of the factors associated with accumulating experience, encouragement of experimentation, risk taking and sharing, mechanisms for sensing changes in the environment and, above all, a creative balance between preserving the fundamental values that makes the Kibbutz a unique social experiment and the ongoing need to adapt and develop. In other words, the key to the size dilemma is, to a large extent, within the Kibbutz itself.

REFERENCES

Bar - on D. and Niv, A. **AN OUTLOOK ON THE REGIONAL ENTERPRISES**, Tabenkin Institute, 1985. (In Hebrew)

Borochov, D. (Ed.) **THE PERFORMANCE OF KIBBUTZ INDUSTRY DURING THE YEARS 1973 - 1983**, National Consultants, 1984

Niv, A. **A SEARCH FOR A THEORY ABOUT THE SURVIVAL OF COMMUNES** A doctoral dissertation, Harvard Business School, 1976

SEX DIFFERENCES IN MATE SELECTION ON THE KIBBUTZ

---oOo---

Ada Lampert

Ruppin Institute, 60960

I S R A E L

ABSTRACT

Sex differences in three aspects of mate selection are tested and interpreted as a function of differential parental strategies that evolution might have selected for each sex. For females, whose parental investment is high, it was predicted that they would emphasize, while choosing a mate, his status and his nurturant behavior. For males, whose parental investment is relatively low, it was predicted that they would emphasize the relatively quick, first impression choice, of high quality genes. 300 youngsters females and males, 15-24 years of age, took part in an "imaginative mate selection", scoring 36 items, indicating the three groups of selection criteria, with four grades, from "very essential for me" down to "not essential". Results give strong support to all three hypotheses. Sex differences in personal development were tested by dividing the sample into three age stages. It was found that females show a steady pattern of choice, from puberty on, while males reduce their emphasis on genes selection, and increase emphasis on mate's nurturant behavior, as they approach marriage age.

1. INTRODUCTION

The social sciences tend to investigate human mate selection from the perspective of cultural, social and economic differences and as an expression of personal preference (see for example Murstein, 1980). Such "environmental" variables afford no insight into the innate "biological" determinants of human behavior. Recent developments in sociobiological theory provide a framework which implies biological evolutionary thought, to human personality structures such as needs, emotions and ideas and to social and cultural structures (e.g. Lumsden & Wilson 1981; 1982). This study will attempt to test some aspects of mate-selelction in humans from a socio-biological point of view.

Insofar as reproduction is the ultimate criterion of natural selection, the closer a human behavior is to the actual act of propagation, the more logical it is to seek its evolutionary origins. In this sense, the selection of a partner for procreation is critical enough to warrant some assumptions of underlying genetic foundations. Sexual reproduction requires a partnership between the two parents. As in most species (Dawkins, 1976), in humans too, this is between unequal parties (Barash, 1981; Mellen, 1981; Rossi, 1984), because the "parental investment" (Trivers, 1972) of females is greater than that of males. On the Kibbutz as well, in spite of the egalitarian norms, women were found to invest more in the care of their children than men (Lampert, 1981). This difference between the sexes affects the process of mate selection of each gender. Women who will invest much in every child are at high risk in every sexual encounter and were, therefore, selected for a strategy of careful and meticulour selection. Men, who will invest less, can afford to be less careful and more adventurous when they select a partner.

Barash (1981) lists three main criteria for mate selection:

1. Good genes.
2. High Status.
3. Care-Giving Dispositions.

It is our aim to look for sex differences in the emphasis on each criterion, as a result of differential parental investment.

The significance of the first criterion is exhausted at the instant of fertilization when the genetic complement of offspring is irreversibly fixed. The importance of the other two criteria is exerted during the prolonged process of child growth when it needs care and nurturance to bring its genetic repertoire to optimal expression. The parental investment of a woman is greater than that of a man, both during fertilization (ovum vs. sperm) as well as during the stages of child growth (pregnancy, lactation, and care). Even if the human species is characterized by a continuous extension of the share of fathers in care of their offspring (see for example Mead, 1967), there is still a tendency on the part of men to desert pregnant women or women with small children (Van den Berghe, 1980), and thus to contribute only to fertilization. While the commitment of mothers to their children is great and irrevocable, fathers are typified by a considerable variance in their childcare dispositions (Bradwick, 1979; Rossi, 1977; 1984). If we were to depict the evolution of the human family as a development on a time continuum which begins at "time zero" at which fathers donate to the partnership only sperm, and which continues with a growing contribution of fathers to the provision and care of their children; it would be possible to identify a process of increase in the importance of fatherhood, a process which is still ongoing and which produces a great variance in the childcare dispositions of men. Some men already care for their children with much devotion, while some are still content to limit themselves only to fertilization. Motherhood, on the other hand, almost does not vary. It is already high and final at "time zero" and, therefore, has small variance. In other words, women were selected according to their ability to identify men with childcaring dispositions and thus they enhance these tendencies in the human species. A father with a greater care giving disposition and a high status ensures an improved probability of success for his offspring. (On feminine hormonal adaptations which enhance the selection of caring men, such as concealment of ovulation and syncronization of menstruation, see for example Turke, 1984).

spring. (On feminine hormonal adaptations which enhance the selection of caring men, such as concealment of ovulation and syncronization of menstruation, see for example Turke, 1984). Men, on the other hand, were selected at "time zero" by their ability to identify women with good genes, insofar as their risk to encounter a woman with weak caregiving dispositions is small; both because motherhood is self evident, as well as because they invest only sperm. During evolution, on the time sequence we presented, the risk men take in selecting partners, gets greater as they become more fatherly and invest more. Therefore men are selected also according to their ability to choose with care a motherly-caring partner.

The selection of good genes, especially such that affect physical traits, is made visually, and men at present are, indeed, aroused more and faster than women by the sight of a potential partner (Symons, 1979). The determination of status and caring dispositions demands a more thorough investigation and may require additional sources of information. This, therefore, is a transition from a quick visual choice to a more careful selection.

Under the assumption that the rise of fatherhood is still an ongoing process, that maternal investment is still greater than paternal investment and that women, therefore still select with more care than men, and that there must be a priority in the criteria of selection, the following hypotheses about intersexual selective differences can be formulated:

1. Men put greater stress than women on "good genes".
2. Women put greater stress than men on "high status".
3. Women put greater stress than men on "caregiving dispositions."

2. METHOD

2.1. Subjects

The sample comprises 300 young Kibbutz residents (who were born on the Kibbutz), 150 women and 150 men. An age range of 15-24 was chosen to represent the period in life at which mate selection activity is at its highest, from sexual maturation to the age of marriage.

Subjects were chosen at random in 30 different Kibbutz settlements. As part of modern western society the Kibbutz can serve as a sample for the study of a greater society. However, the Kibbutz is typified by a social structure in which women and children have no economic dependence on men, and a high social status has no economic remunerations. Such structure ensures an untainted examination of mate selection on the criterion of social status. On the Kibbutz such selection is evidence of inate behavior rather than of economic consideration.

2.2. Instrument

In constructing the questionaire no effort was made to validly incorporate the entire meaning of the concepts "good genes" "high status" or "caregiving dispositions". The intention was merely to examine intersexual differences in the reaction to some items that could serve as indicatiors of these concepts. 12 items were formulated for each concept as follows:

A. Good Genes - 1. Facial beauty 2. Physical beauty 3. Physical health 4. Musical talent 5. Physical strength 6. Verbal ability 7. Mental health 8. Beautiful hair 9. Intelligence 10. Technical aptitude 11. Sportsmanship 12. Beautiful skin

B. High Status -1. Scholastic achievements 2. Social popularity 3. Ethnic origin 4. Leadership 5. Personal philosophy 6. Occupational achievements 7. Persuasive ability 8. Financial resources 9. Social recognition 10. Familial status 11. Military achievements 12. Property

C. Caregiving Disposition - 1. Willingness to care for others 2. Sensitivity 3. Ability to manage 4. Industriousness 5. Fidelity 6. Warmth 7. Devotion 8. Love of children 9. Feeling of others 10. Compassion 11. Consideration for others 12. Ability to give

The 36 items were given to every subject arranged in a column and intermixed. The assignment was defined as "an imaginary exercise in selecting a partner". Subjects were asked to give each item one of four possible grades:

1. Most important to me.
2. Very important to me.
3. Fairly important to me.
4. Not very important to me.

A forced sequence of priorities was dictated to subjects by limiting their use of every grade to 9 times only, so as to compel them to prioritize.

2.3. Procedure

30 interviewers from 30 Kibbutz settlements, selected at

Annonimity was guaranteed. The task was completed in 10 - 15 minutes and many of the subjects reported enjoying the imaginary exercise.

3. RESULTS

All three hypotheses are supported by the study:

1. Men stress "good genes" in mate selection more than women do.
   The mean score for men (N=150) was 29.0;
   The mean score for women (N=150) was 26.4;
   The difference between the sexes is significant
   ($F(1) = 48.9$, $p < .001$)

2. Women stress "High Status" in mate selection more than men do.
   The mean score for women (N=150) was 23.8
   The mean score for men (N=150) was 22.6
   The difference between the sexes is significant
   ($F(1) = 13.1$, $p < .001$)

3. Women stress "Caregiving Disposition" in mate selection more than men do.
   The mean score for women (N=150) was 39.8
   The mean score for men (N=150) was 38.4
   The difference between the sexes is significant
   ($F(1) = 14.6$, $p < .001$)

Even though the differences between men and women in percentages are small (3.5% - 8.5%) I believe they point at different behavioral tendencies (in the process of mate selection). The differences found fit the stated hypotheses and are evidence of the Parental strategies that characterize the sexes, with men tending more than women to make a quick selection while women stressing, more than men the continued care of children after birth.

There is much similarity between the sexes in the overall importance they accord each criterion. Both sexes gave the highest importance to "caregiving dispositions" and the lowest to "status", but as the questionaire was not structured to represent these concepts validly, we shall not compare among the criteria and concentrate on the intersexual differences within each.

4. DEVELOPMENTAL PERSPECTIVE

The 300 subjects are in the 15 - 24 age range. This period between physical maturation to mean age of marriage is, naturally, the most relevant for mate selection. We shall not address here the question why 10 years elapse from sexual maturation to marriage, but we shall look at the changes in selective behavior during ontogenic development. To do so, we divide the sample into three age groups: 1. 15-18; 2. 18-21; 3. 21-24. Every group is further divided into subgroups of 50 women and 5 men. The developmental sequence is presented in FIGURE 1 :

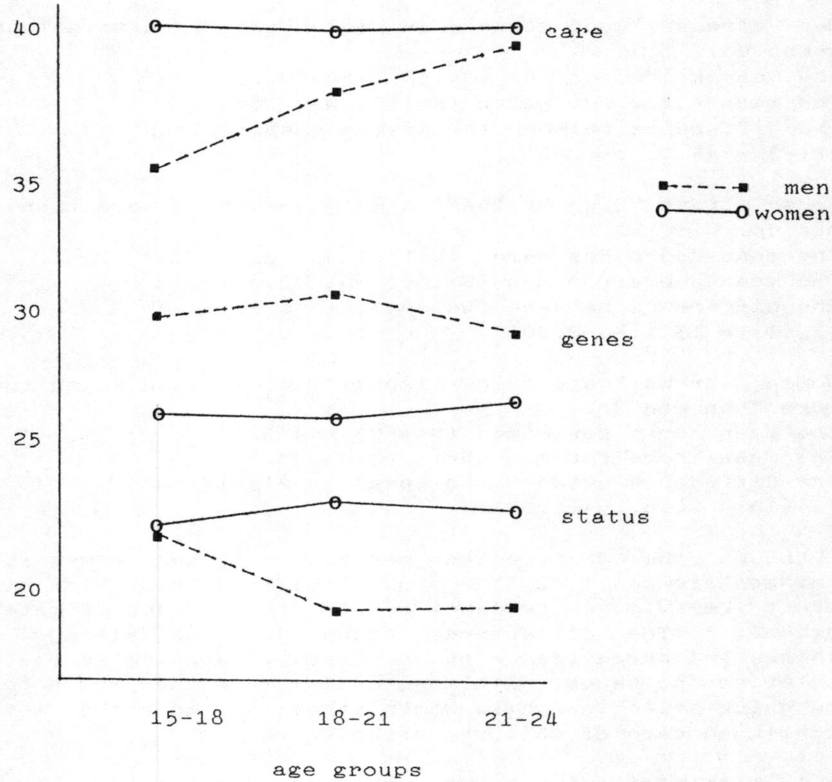

FIGURE 1
Developmental perspective on sex differences in mate selection.

The most striking intersexual difference is that the selective behavior of women does not change significantly between the ages of 15 and 24; while men undergo a development which affects the importance they attach to the criteria at different ages. The importance of caregiving disposition increases as they get closer to the age of marriage, while the importance of status and genes decreases. The ontogenic changes in men are significant for all three criteria: "Good Genes" ($F(2) = 4.2$; $p = .018$), "High Status" ($F(2) = 6.3$; $p = .002$), and "Caregiving Disposition" ($F(2) = 6.8$; $p = .002$).

5. DISCUSSION

Derived from the assumption that fathers' parental investment is smaller than that of mothers, and therefore sex is less hazardous for them, we formulated an hypothesis that the selelctive strategy of men is characterized by the relatively quick selection made on the basis of good genes reflected in the partner's appearance, more than that of women. Indeed the findings of this study point at the greater stress put on the "good genes" of their mate. This finding fits the assuption that men "fall in love" more quickly than women (Murstein, 1980), and also that men are more sexually aroused by external appearance than women (Symons, 1979). Since men invest less than women after fertilization, they put more attention than woman on selection that is relevant to the moment of fertilization. Men can largely depend on women to undertake the care and nurturance of the child. Our results suggest that criteria that are relevant to the continued growth of the child - "high status " with implications to vital resources, and "caregiving dispositions" that ensure that child's wellbeing - are stressed more significantly by women than by men. Women, even if they are secure in their own commitment to care for their child were further selected to prefer men who would assist them in parenting.

The tendency of women to value status of partners more than men has been demonstrated in many previous studies and is generally accepted by social science. It fits general political conditions which accord men a higher social status and thus make this preference of women a logical choice (Murstein, 1980). Rosenblatt (1974), adopting a non-biological social-cultural point of view, maintains that the interest of women in the status of men would disappear when society abolishes intersexual status disparities. The Kibbutz presents a special case in this regard. Unlike any other human society, the Kibbutz has eradicated any connections between personal status and economic remunerations. Though personal prestige differences among individuals on the kibbutz persist, and though men wield greater power than women (Tiger & Shepher, 1975), neither prestige nor power have any economic expression. The Kibbutz has thus split the "status" concept and abolished the usual interdependence between value and resources. Furthermore, physical survival on the kibbutz is guaranteed to all irrespective of any other person (spouse, parent). Under such conditions there is no "logic" in the excessive attraction of women to the status of men and a theoretical framework based on environmental explanatory variables should have predicted the same attention to status for both sexes. However, the young women who participated in this study, who were born and raised on the kibbutz under conditions of economic equality for every one, where wife is not dependant on her husband nor child on his parents, still exhibits this tendency of all other women. The special case of Kibbutz women, therefore, indirectly points at the underlying genetic-evolutionary foundation of selection strategy that has not disappeared after three generations of an egalitarian society. The evolution of human kind is a web of interconnected genetic and cultural changes. Cultural change is quicker and more elastic than genetic change (Stebbins, 1982; Wallace, 1983). The presistance of traditional selection patterns among Kibbutz women living under new conditions is evidence, I believe, of the slowness of the genetic change. More than that, the fact that the sex difference emerges only after males' puberty suggests an hormonal, that is genetic basis for it, on their part. They become less interested in womens' status as they grow up. In the Kibbutz as in any other place.

As expected on the basis of intersexual differences in parental investment and the assumption that human evolution is characterized by a growing tendency for parenting among men (selected for by women), the study demonstrates a greater stress women put on the caregiving dispositions of their partners. If all men would limit themselves to fertilization only, there would have been no sense in trying to select for caregiving dispositions. If, on the other hand, all men were equal to women in caregiving dispositions, both sexes would have exhibited the same attention to this criterion in the selection process. The difference, thus suggests a greater parental interest of women as well as a growing tendency for fathering in men - an evolutionary process which is determined by feminine selective strategies.

A discussion of fatherhood as a variation along the continuum of human family development draws special attention to the developmental perspectives of this study. In the introduction we presented an imaginary time sequence of human family evolution in which at "point zero" males bestow their offspring only with sperm, while at present they augment sperm with a prolonged and intensive parental care. Motherhood does not change along this sequence. It is equally strong and total at point zero and the present. The evolution of the family, from this point of view, is the evolution of man changing from male into father.

When the findings of this study are looked at from a developmental orientation (Fig. 1), an analogy is found between the evolution of the human family in the last few million years and the ontogeny of young people from age 15 to age 24. As the evolution of the family is characterized by a greater change in the strategy of fathers than of mothers, so the ontogney of women is stable while the ontogeny of men changes. In the same manner by which evolution shifts the strategies of men from a stress on the moment of fertilization to a stress on the care and nurturance of children, the 10 years of development of a contemporary young man shifts the relative weight of the criteria he employs for mate selection. The relative importance of the "good genes" criterion is reduced while the relative importance of "caregiving disposition" goes up. The relative weight of the "status" criterion goes down. This may seem to refute the premise that men are increasingly interested in the resources that are necessary for child raising. However, the intersexual division of labour which attends the evolution of the human family, has made status a predominantly masculine intra-sexual affair. This has led mature men to pay only little interest in the status of their prospective mates.

It is beyond the scope of this study to claim that "Ontogeny recapitulates Phylogeny" but it does point to an interesting similarity between the two.

REFERENCES

Barash, D. **Sociobiology: The Whisperings Within** Glasgow, William Collins Sons & Co. 1981

Bardwick, J.M. **In Transition** N.Y. Holt, Rinehart & Wilson, 1979

Dawkins, R. **The Selfish Gene** Oxford University Press, 1976.

Lampert, A. **Parental Investment, Relative Vulnerability and Maladjustment** Ph. D. dissertation, University of Tel Aviv.

Lumsden, C.J. & Wilson, E.Q. **Genes, Mind and Culture** Harvard University Press, 1981

Lumsden, C.J. & Wilson, E.O. **Promethean Fire: Reflections on the Origin of Mind** Harvard University Press, 1982

Mead, M. **Males and Females: A Study of the Sexes in a Changing World** N.Y. William Morrow & Company, 1967

Mellen, S.L.W. **The Evolution of Love** San Francisco, Freeman & Company, 1981.

Murstein, B.I. "Mate Selection in the 1970's" **Jour. of Marriage & the Family**, 42, 777-792, 1980

Rosenblatt, P.C. "Cross-cultural perspective on attraction" in T.L. Huston (ed.) **Foundations of Interpersonal Attraction** N.Y. Academic Press, 1974

Rossi, A.S. "A Biosocial Perspective of Parenting" **Deadalus** vo. 106, 2, 1977

Rossi, A.S. "Gender and Parenthood" **American Soc. Review**, vol. 49, 1984

Stebbins, G.L. **Darwin to DNA, Molecules to Humanity** W.H. Freeman & Company, 1982

Symons, D. **The Evolution of Human Sexuality** Oxford University Press, 1979

Tiger, L & Shepher, J. **Women in the Kibbutz** N.Y. Harcourt, Brace & Jounvich, 1975

Trivers, R.L. "Parental investment and sexual selection" in Campbell, B. (ed.) **Sexual Selection and the Descent of Man, 1871-1971** Chicago, Aldine, 1972

Turke, W.P. "Effects of Ovulatory Concealment and Synchrony on Protohominid Mating Systems and Parental Roles" **Ethology and Sociobiology**, 5, 33-44, 1984.

van Den Berghe, P.L. "The Human Family: A Sociobiological Look" in Lockard, J.S. (ed.) **The Evolution of Human Social Behavior**. N.Y. Elsevier, 1980

Wallace, B. (ed.) **Human Culture: Theodosius Dobzhansky and Ernest Boesiger** Columbia University Press, 1982

Part Eight
Values and Attitudes

THE STRUCTURE OF SOCIAL VALUES IN ISRAEL

Shlomit Levy

Israel Institute of Applied Social Research
19 Washington Street, P.O.Box 7150
Jerusalem, Israel

Facet theory suggests looking at the concept "social value" as a multivariate one. A faceted definition is presented of the varieties of social values, considering the different aspects of the concept discussed in the literature. Values as ends-in-themselves are called here "guiding principles" and are studied according to a specially detailed mapping sentence. Results are given for Israel data, gathered in October 1983 on a national sample of 1162 adult Jewish respondents (excluding kibbutzim). The theoretical interest here lies in the correspondence between the relative sizes of the observed correlation coefficients (among the value responses) and the facet design of the content of the values. This was pursued by making a geometric representation of the correlation matrix by means of SSA (Similarity Structure Analysis) and seeing how the facets correspond to partitions of the geometric space. Lawful partitioning roles were found for the major facets, generating a cylinder. As in previous studies on other topics, the facet of area of life (family, religion, economy, work, social, etc.) plays a polarizing role in the cylinder. In this study, some of the areas had an orientation of being either egotistic or altruistic. Also, some of the areas were studied either as permissive or authoritarian. These orientations correspond to the circular order of the areas of life. The facet distinguishing internal from external behavior plays a modulating role in the cylinder, the internal being central and the external (including the economic ones) being peripheral. An axial role is played by the facet distinguishing situational from behavioral social percepts.

1. "VALUE" AS A SPECIAL CASE OF "ATTITUDE"

Facet theory suggests looking at the concept "social value" as a multivariate one. An outcome of literature survey, and of our cooperative research with the Working Group on Values and Social Problem Indicators for Contemporary Europe, is a faceted definition of the varieties of social values to be presented below. This definition has proved to yield viable and cumulative empirical hypotheses.

Any review of the research literature on "values" immediately reveals that the concept has been rather vague. In dealing with it, various researchers have related to different things. Their definitions are complex and unclear, and almost invariably include external aspects that are but empirically related to the concept "value" (are but correlates) One example out of many is that of Scott's (1965) definition: "Value is an individual's concept of an ideal relationship (or state of affairs), which he uses to assess the 'goodness' or 'badness', the 'rightness' or 'wrongness', of actual relationships that he observes or contemplates." And he adds: "A value is a hypothetical construct assigned to that class of hypothetical constructs known as the individual's phenomenology--the way one views the world and himself in relation to it." The definition is unclear--as is the concept "attitude" from which the author attempts to distinguish it. In this connection, the author says later in his discussion, "value"--as opposed to "attitude"--can serve as public justification for the act. The definition continues to sprawl toward the end of the discussion in the same chapter, bringing in additional external correlates.

Scott's definition is to a certain extent close to those of Kluckhohn (1951) and Parsons (1954, 1964). The point of departure of these researchers for their attempt to classify value systems is the assessment of people's relatedness to their actions. Such assessments can be numerous and varied, as Robin Williams writes in his entry on "values" in the International Encyclopedia for the Social Sciences (Vol.16, p.283): "The term 'values' may refer to interests, pleasures, likes, preferences, duties, moral obligations, desires, wants, needs, aversions and attractions, and many other modalities of selective orientations".

According to the above definition, almost any relatedness could be defined as a value. In her discussion of the concept "system of values", Ethel M. Albert says: "A value system, then, represents what is expected or hoped for, required or forbidden. It is not a report of actual conduct but is the system of criteria by which conduct is judged and sanctions applied." In concluding, she adds: "For the forseeable future, it is doubtful whether a definition of values can be produced that embraces all the meanings assigned the term and its cognates, or that would be acceptable to all investigators" (International Encyclopedia of the Social Sciences, 1968, vol.16, p.288).

A number of years later (1976), the concept remained rather vague in the literature. For example, Rokeach, who has been much involved with the topic, says in his attempt to define "value":

> "To say that a person 'has a value' is to say that he has an enduring belief that a specific mode of conduct or end-state of existence is personally and socially preferable to alternative modes of conduct or end-states of existence" (Rokeach, M. 1976, 157-160)."

Study of change in values over time is an empirical problem. Therefore, as Guttman (1982) claims, inclusion of "stability over time" as part of the <u>definition</u> of the concept "value" renders longitudinal research meaningless. However, Rokeach himself continues to claim that his definition is compatible with those suggested by Kluckhohn and Williams, who like Scott, are aware of the dynamics over time. This vagueness points to the fact that a systematic classification of values must relate to the problem of type of assessment, of which dynamics is but one example.

The facet approach enables viewing each of the previous attempts at a definition as emphasizing a specific aspect of the multi-faceted concept. But, there must be something that unifies them all, namely, the common range.

Examining the items used for research on values shows that the range of these items is usually ordered from positive to negative, but with a special emphasis on the concept "importance". Furthermore, the extent of importance refers to attaining a specific objective.

We shall adopt here a formal definition of "value" which takes into account the above considerations, and which was first presented by us in 1976 in the monograph: "Values and Attitudes of High School Youth in Israel" (see also Guttman 1982). The approach in this definition--which is repeated below, as is the approach in Guttman's definition of the concept "attitude" (Guttman 1982; Levy 1985)--places the emphasis on a universe of observations of the concept, and mainly on the universe of items:

> An item belongs to the universe of value items if and only if its domain asks for a (cognitive) assessment of the
>
> | | A | | B | |
> |---|---|---|---|---|
> | importance of a | (situational)
(behavioral) | goal in a | (cognitive)
(affective)
(instrumental) | modality |
>
> | | C | |
> |---|---|---|
> | in life area (y) for | (itself as a)
(a more primary) | purpose in life area (z), |
>
> and the range is ordered from (very important that it should) (to) (very important that it should not)
>
> exist for that purpose.

In accordance with this definition, "value" is a special case of "attitude", defined as follows (Guttman 1982):

> An item belongs to the universe of attitude items if and only if its
>
> domain asks about (cognitive) (affective) (instrumental) behavior toward an object, and
>
> the range is ordered from (very positive) (to) (very negative) toward the object.

Value items fulfill the condition of having a range ordered from positive to negative toward the object, and therefore such items automatically belong to the universe of attitude items.

The expression "extent of importance" may be regarded as cognitive assessment. Thus, from the three possible modalities of attitude--cognitive, affective, instrumental--values are limited only to the cognitive modality of assessment. However, the situation or the behavior whose importance is being assessed can be of any type of modality.

In accordance with the definition presented above, the domain of values include three content facets. Assessment of the importance is of a situational or behavioral goal (facet A). For example, we can assess the importance of a situation like "equality" or "happiness", or the importance of a behavior like "helping others". This distinction, to a great extent accords with Rokeach's classification, and with his distinction between "terminal" and "instrumental" values. In terms of the facets in the above definition of values, it appears that for him, a "terminal" value is a situational goal (a situational end-in-itself). Similarly, an "instrumental" value for Rokeach appears to be a behavioral norm, which may be either an end-in-itself or a means to an end.

Our definition distinguishes clearly between types of values whose classification is not so clear by Rokeach's concepts, it being easier to make distinctions among items by the detailed facets. To anticipate, analysis of the data will also reveal a correspondence between the empirical structure of the intercorrelations among values and their content classification by the facets.

Behavior can be of an affective nature (e.g. "to love"), of a cognitive nature (e.g. "to learn"), or of an instrumental nature (e.g. "to make money"). The same is true with regard to a situation, which can be of an affective nature (e.g. "happiness"), cognitive (e.g. "equality"), or instrumental (e.g. "wealth"). This distinction is made in Facet B.

It is possible to assess the extent of importance of a situation or behavior as ends in themselves, or as means to a more primary purpose (facet C). For example, it is possible to assess the extent of importance of "learning achievements" as an end in itself, or as a means for obtaining a good job. Therefore, the meaning of the assessment depends on the goal: "important for what". The assessment of the same behavior (or situation) can change in accordance with the goal.

2. THE DEFINITIONAL FRAMEWORK

Having defined the overall concept of "value", we shall now go on to construct a classification scheme for the particular varieties of value items considered here. Empirical observations are made by mapping the population into the categories of the items. Hence, design of observations implies design of the mapping. A useful technique for expressing this design is that of the mapping sentence. This incorporates both the universe of items--such as defined above for "values"--and the population studied. A mapping sentence serves also as a basis for constructing empirical hypotheses. In our case, the hypotheses will be on the empirical structure of interrelations among values as guiding principles, namely as ends in themselves. The proposed mapping sentence on values as guiding principles is exhibited below. Basically it is very similar to that given above for the general definition for "value" items, but it is more detailed in facets and elements.

The Mapping Sentence for Observations on Values as Guiding Principles

The assessment by respondent (x) of the extent of importance for self (a_1)

B
(1. situational)
(2. behavioral)

of a (1. situational / 2. behavioral) social precept which should be supported by most people

D	E
(1. internal)	(1. cognitive)
(2. external)	(2. affective)
	(3. instrumental)

(c_1) through an (1. internal / 2. external) behavior of a (1. cognitive / 2. affective / 3. instrumental) modality

F
(1. personal)
(2. interpersonal)
(3. impersonal)

toward a (1. personal / 2. interpersonal / 3. impersonal) object, for the purpose of supporting that

H
(1. specific)
(2. general)

precept as an end-in-itself (g_1) regarding a (1. specific / 2. general) aspect of life

J
(1. social acceptability)
(2. religion)
(3. family)
(4. society (social activity))
(interpersonal)
(public order)
(5. government and politics)
(6. leisure)
(7. work)
(8. economics (money))
(9. in general (unspecified))

area (J) ⟶ (positive to negative) assessment of social precepts.

The mapping sentence has nine content facets, four of which were included in the general definition for the universe of value items, namely: social precept (goal) (facet B), modality (facet E), purpose (facet G - "in itself") and life areas (facet J). It should be noted that the type of assessment "extent of importance" in the universe of values can be regarded as one element of Facet A (therefore denoted here as a_1), which may also include "performance" and "attainment" As already mentioned, this paper is devoted only to cognitive assessment of importance. The remaining facets extend and refine the general definition of values and help in subclassifications.

Apart from the content of the observations, the mapping sentence includes the population facet (x), and the range facet which appears after the arrow.

Each question is defined by a structuple composed of one element from each of the nine content facets (a facet element is called a "struct" of each structuple in which it appears). For example, the question "To what extent is it important to you that 'to be rich' be a guiding principle in the life of man?" is defined by the structuple: Importance for himself (a_1) of situational (b_1) social precept which should be supported by most people (c_1) by external (d_2) behavior of the instrumental (e_3) modality, toward a personal (f_1) object in order to support the social precept itself (g_1), from the specific (h_1) aspect of life area economics (j_8). All other questions can be classified similarly.

3. THE POPULATION FRAME

The data presented here are part of a comprehensive research on values conducted by the author in Israel in the fall of 1983. The research population is the Jewish adult (20+) population residing in all types of settlements in Israel (excluding kibbutzim). The sample comprised 1162 respondents selected to ensure proper representation of this population.

The fieldwork was done during October 1983. Interviewing was conducted in the home, using a questionnaire in closed form designed in accordance with the above mapping sentence.

4. THE STRUCTURE OF INTERRELATIONSHIPS AMONG VALUES AS GUIDING PRINCIPLES

The respondents were presented with a list of twenty-eight social values and were requested to indicate the extent of importance for themselves that each of these values be a guiding principle in the life of man.

In order to study the structure of interrelationships among the various values, monotonicity coefficients were calculated among the twenty-eight variables (Table 1).

It should be noted that although all these values share the common concept of "guiding principle", "the extent of importance" does not refer to that general concept, but rather to the value itself as a guiding principle. There may be contradictions between various values as guiding principles, especially if they are not recognized as such in the society. Thus, one cannot assume that all correlations among the values will be positive or zero as would be expected by the First Law of Attitude ("value", it will be recalled, being a special case of "attitude"). There may also be negative coefficients.

And indeed, Table 1 shows that although the majority of the coefficients are positive, there are negative coefficients as well. However, while the positive coefficients reach quite high levels (.81), many of the negative ones are close to zero, and never exceed -.17, which is also a fairly low coefficient. Thus, generally speaking, correlational contradictions between values are not frequent, and those that do exist are rather weak.

Table 1

INTERRELATIONSHIPS (MONOTONICITY COEFFICIENTS*) AMONG VALUES AS GUIDING PRINCIPLES

		1	2	3	4	5	6	7	8	9	10	11	12	13	14	15	16	17	18	19	20	21	22	23	24	25	26	27	28
Raise a family	1	--	81	47	09	31	-05	34	30	19	23	35	47	42	46	40	29	37	43	39	17	06	18	32	34	45	21	26	05
Respect parents	2	81	--	65	-03	30	-10	49	45	24	32	50	66	57	51	62	43	60	49	56	27	11	12	60	45	52	41	39	-01
To live a happy life	3	47	65	--	31	42	08	07	48	43	23	47	47	23	03	37	47	60	38	42	31	22	02	45	37	11	24	35	13
To be rich	4	09	-03	31	--	09	36	-03	24	15	-02	-03	24	13	15	-18	-09	-07	32	-13	-13	16	49	-08	04	-04	-04	12	36
Widen horizons	5	31	30	42	09	--	40	44	42	62	17	47	21	05	-01	40	32	37	27	43	38	40	12	48	27	13	43	32	36
Travel and tour abroad	6	-05	-10	08	36	40	--	12	27	33	02	13	06	-17	-17	-06	09	10	10	04	07	35	36	04	01	-08	16	13	43
Voluntary-public activities	7	34	49	07	-03	44	12	--	39	35	29	37	24	36	45	55	42	40	26	43	32	25	11	45	20	55	36	28	04
Achievements at work	8	30	45	48	24	42	27	39	--	67	25	59	42	08	05	30	35	42	37	44	25	31	35	39	46	18	41	43	29
Develop abilities	9	19	24	43	15	62	33	35	67	--	38	57	18	-01	-15	32	40	42	31	43	39	52	17	47	16	06	43	40	34
Accounting of deeds	10	23	32	23	-02	17	02	29	25	38	--	55	26	28	23	37	28	30	25	41	41	23	16	39	31	30	29	26	20
Behave responsibly	11	35	50	47	-03	47	13	37	59	57	55	--	49	15	02	49	49	59	32	66	58	34	06	65	62	26	50	40	13
Respected by acquaintances	12	47	66	47	24	21	06	24	42	18	26	49	--	49	35	46	36	54	56	26	13	21	38	39	29	39	24	29	20
Believe in God	13	42	57	23	13	05	-17	36	08	-01	28	15	49	--	93	46	21	29	50	21	-02	-04	26	22	12	73	12	05	-05
Be religious	14	46	51	03	15	-01	-17	45	05	-15	23	02	35	93	--	42	20	16	44	14	-03	-14	26	12	08	72	-00	-06	-12
Help others	15	40	62	37	-18	40	-06	55	30	32	37	49	46	46	42	--	73	73	41	62	49	31	01	67	49	60	51	36	05
Give love to another	16	29	43	47	-09	32	09	42	35	40	28	49	36	21	20	73	--	83	25	50	53	35	02	60	43	44	47	31	18
Be a faithful friend	17	37	60	60	-07	37	10	40	42	42	30	59	54	29	16	73	83	--	44	58	49	38	06	69	56	41	54	35	19
Live in good neighborhood	18	43	49	38	32	27	10	26	37	31	25	32	56	50	44	41	25	44	--	45	11	22	42	40	31	48	38	18	22
Protect public property	19	39	56	42	-13	43	04	43	44	43	41	66	26	21	14	62	50	58	45	--	71	33	05	70	68	39	64	45	12
Tolerate others' opinions	20	17	27	31	-13	38	07	32	25	39	41	58	13	-02	-03	49	53	49	11	71	--	43	03	68	52	23	48	38	17
Engage in hobbies	21	06	11	22	16	40	35	25	31	52	23	34	21	-04	-14	31	35	38	22	33	43	--	33	45	16	13	57	25	47
Dress fashionably	22	18	12	02	49	12	36	11	35	17	16	06	38	26	26	01	02	06	42	05	03	33	--	15	09	29	11	16	50
Behave courteously	23	32	60	45	-08	48	04	45	39	47	39	65	39	22	12	67	60	69	40	70	68	45	15	--	70	50	65	41	25
Observe the laws	24	34	45	37	04	27	01	20	46	16	31	62	29	12	08	49	43	56	31	68	52	16	09	70	--	33	51	46	10
Contribute to charity	25	45	52	11	-04	13	-08	55	18	06	30	26	39	73	72	60	44	41	48	39	23	13	29	50	33	--	43	15	-06
Protect fauna and flora	26	21	41	24	-04	43	16	36	41	43	29	50	24	12	-00	51	47	54	38	64	48	57	11	65	51	43	--	39	29
Follow national affairs	27	26	39	35	12	32	13	28	43	40	26	40	29	05	-06	36	31	35	18	45	38	25	16	41	46	15	39	--	26
Have leisure time	28	05	-01	13	36	36	43	04	29	34	20	13	20	-05	-12	05	18	19	22	12	17	47	50	25	10	-06	29	26	--

*Decimal point omitted

Moreover, the existing contradictions are not scattered throughout the Table, but are limited mainly to three values: the two religiosity values ("believe in God", and "to be religious"), and "to be rich".

The religiosity values--especially "to be religious"--are negatively correlated with the variables relating to leisure, both 'external' (e.g. "travel and tour the world" and "devote time for recreation"), and 'internal' (e.g. "develop talents" and "widen horizons"). In other words, the life areas "religion" and "leisure" are at polar ends. This might be expected, since leisure may be regarded as idleness, or neglecting the study of the Torah. Thus, these two life areas express different orientations: order and discipline (religion) versus permissiveness and freedom (leisure). Polarity is not between the life areas per se, but in the population's perception of the variables examined for these life areas. Support of this can be found in the contrasting trend between religiosity and "tolerance of others' opinions". But the coefficient here is close to zero: though the contrast is not strong, these two variables are not compatible. This is the only negative trend that was found between religiosity and the social variables.

Unlike religiosity, "to be rich" was found to be negatively correlated with all the variables relating to the area "social life", be it social activity ("voluntary work", "contributing to charity"), human relations ("to be a good friend", "to love another person", "to be courteous toward others") or public order. With all the other variables the coefficients of "to be rich" are positive, though generally rather weak.

The above finding accords with the interpretation of "to be rich" as being basically of an egotistical-personal nature, and of a "taking" orientation. Accordingly, it is remote from the majority of the other values, and is a polar opposite to social values that imply "giving" of any type, be it interpersonal ("to respect parents" in the family sphere), communal, and even public impersonal (such as "protect public property", and "protect fauna and flora"). Economic egotism is apposite to social altruism. Here, too, the polarity does not stem from the life areas themselves, but from the orientations expressed in these life areas.

We find, then, that two pairs of life areas are of polar opposites, where the polarity stems directly from the orientations expressed in the subsets of variables that were examined: religion versus leisure (order versus permissiveness), and economics versus social (egotism versus altruism). This phenomenon is fundamental to the understanding of the structure of the values sets in general. It is worth reiterating that many of the negative coefficients are close to zero: the polarization is not great.

5. SIMILARITY STRUCTURE ANALYSIS (SSA)

To comprehend the overall structure of correlations, we shall make use of the geometric method of Similarity Structure Analysis (SSA; formerly called Smallest Space Analysis) (Guttman, 1968; Lingoes, 1968, 1973). In SSA, each question is represented by a point in a space. The greater the distance between two points, the lower the correlation between the variables represented; and the smaller the distance between points, the higher the correlation between the variables. This is true for each possible pair of variables.

The SSA-I revealed that it is possible to present the matrix of interrelationships among the values in a three-dimensional cylindrical space, but four dimensions were required in order to obtain good fit for observing the correspondence between the regions of this space and elements of the facets in the mapping sentence. (The cylinder itself occupies three out of the four dimensions; surrounding it is "noise", or lack of correspondence.) Each value is represented by a point inside the cylinder. The cylinder's vertical axis corresponds to the facet of situational versus behavioral type of guiding principle (facet B). The circular order corresponds to the values in the life areas of the polarizing facet J, and to the behavioral mode and modality of the values (facets D and E) that modulate distance from the origin.

This cylindrical structure is shown schematically in Figure 1.

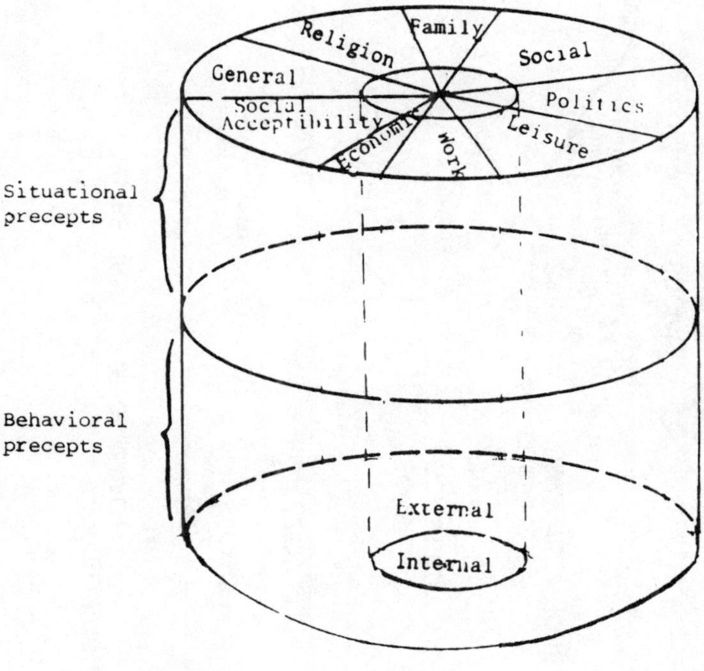

FIGURE 1. THE SCHEMATIC CYLINDER FOR GUIDING PRINCIPLES

Let us now examine in detail the correspondence between the cylindrical structure and the content facets of the mapping sentence. Figures 2a and 2b present the four dimensions of the space of smallest dimensionality and the cylindrical structure of the values.

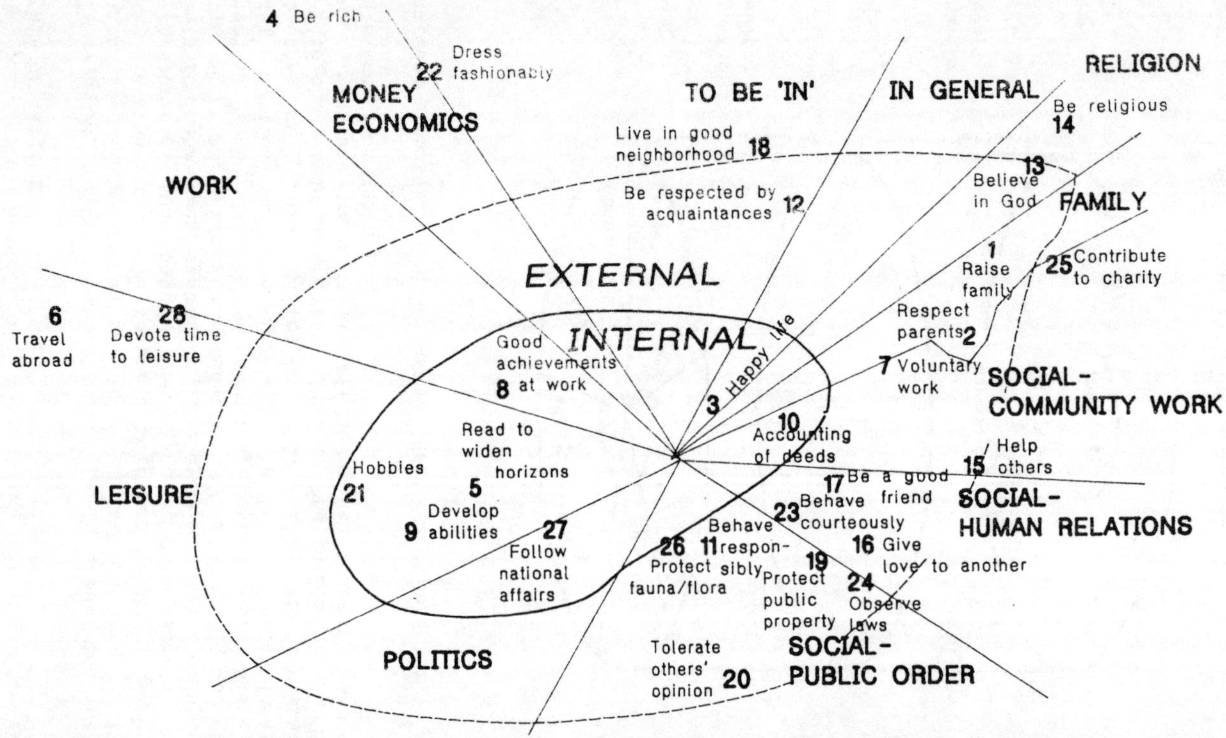

Fig. 2a. Base of SSA cylinder of guiding principles: life area and mode.

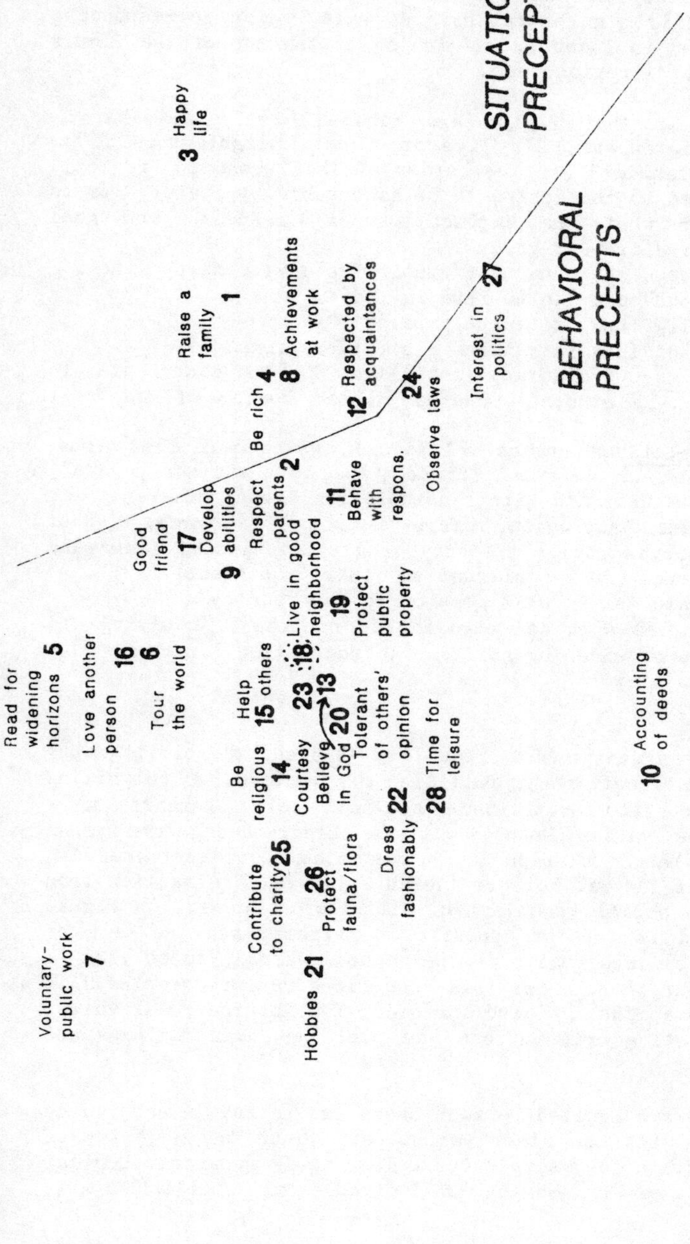

Fig. 2b. Axis of SSA cylinder of guiding principles: situational vs. behavioral.

The Circular Base of the Values

In Figure 2a is presented a projection on two dimensions out of the four, revealing the circular order of the values. The space is divided into eleven regions emanating from a central origin, each region corresponding to one life area as listed in Facet J. Beginning at the top of the Figure and moving clockwise, the 11 regions are:

Social acceptability - in this region are located the values "to be respected by acquaintances", "to live in a good neighborhood", "to dress according to fashion" (on the border of the 'economic' region). All these are related to the desire to be acceptable by society--or to be "in"--no matter what the implication of "respect" or "good neighborhood" is for different groups.
In general - here is located the general variable "to live a happy life".
Religion - "to be religious" and "to believe in God".
Family - "to raise a family" and "to respect parents".
Society - this region is divided into three clear subregions:
1) Social activities: "voluntary activities", "to contribute to charity", and "to help others"--located on the border of the next social subregion.
2) Interpersonal relations (human relations), which includes values such as "to be a good and faithful friend", "to love another person", and "to behave courteously and with consideration toward others".
3) Public order: This subregion refers to both the formal aspect (law-abiding, protecting public property, and protection of fauna and flora) and the informal (to be tolerant of others' opinions).
Politics - "to take an interest in what goes on in the country"
Leisure - includes variables such as "engaging in hobbies", "studying and reading for the sake of widening horizons", "recreation", etc.
Work - "Good achievements at work"
Economics (money) - "To be rich"

Thus, in this study, as in many others (see Levy 1985 and the bibliography therein), the life area facet again fulfills the role of a polarizing facet. Furthermore, the life area items are not only elements of a polarizing facet in the values space, but the order among the areas actually stems from the basic polarization between the above-mentioned two pairs of life areas: religion vs. leisure (Torah study vs. distraction from study) and economics vs. social (egotism vs. altruism). Indeed, in Figure 2a, the area of religion is a polar opposite to leisure, and the area of society (three subregions) is opposite to the economic area ("to be rich"). We have, then, a partial rationale for this specific circular order of life areas: contrasting orientations. [A circular order for interpersonal values which stems from contrasting orientations can also be found in Lorr and McNair (1963).]

The remaining life areas are located between these two pairs, in accordance with their correlations with the other variables. Since the majority of the other life areas contain only single variables, their geometric regions degenerate into a single point, making it difficult to establish stable boundaries for them.

Another aspect of the circular order is the modulation of distance from the origin. The modulation is portrayed by the circles in the space. As already stated, this modulating partitioning corresponds to the type of behavior and modality of the values (facets D and E). Values of the internal-personal behavior type (d_1) are located in the inner circle (marked by a full line) closest to the origin. They include the following values: "to make an account of one's deeds"; "to live a happy life"; "to develop one's talents"; "to read and study for the sake of widening horizons"; "to engage in hobbies", etc. Values outside this circle express external behavior. In the outer circle, the values closest to the periphery are of the "instrumental" modality (e_3). This partition is marked by the broken line. All the values outside the broken-line circle are instrumental: "to be rich"; "to dress according to fashion"; "to live in a good neighborhood"; "to be religious" (which, unlike "to believe in God" is basically instrumental and implies fulfilling the religious obligations); "to contribute to charity"; "to travel abroad", etc. The cognitive values (and the few affective) are all located inside the broken-line circle. Hence, we have here a double modulation from the origin.

It should be noted that the economic values, being of the instrumental modality, tend to be towards the periphery. Accordingly they are less correlated with the value of happiness than are familial and other interpersonal social values.

The Cylinder Axis: Situational Versus Behavioral Social Precept

The direction of the axis--or the length--of the cylinder corresponds to the type of purpose of the value: situational or behavioral. In Figure 2b is presented the projection on the two remaining dimensions out of the four, one direction in this two-space corresponding to the axis of the cylinder, and the other departures from this representing 'noise'. Actually, three dimensions were sufficient for observing the cylinder, but not as clearly as with a four-dimensional space which allows for noise. It should be noted that only a minority of the values refer to situational objectives such as "to live a happy life", "to be rich", "to be respected", etc. However, as may be seen in Figure 2b, there is a clear distinction between these values and the behavioral ones. All the values on the right of the full line refer to situational values, while those on the left refer to behavioral values (with but one exception, namely, "to live in a good neighborhood"). In other words, the cylinder's axis partitions the values space into two levels, in accordance with the type of value (situational or behavioral).

6. THE POSSIBILITY OF FURTHER LAWFULNESS

In sum, the location of the values in the SSA space corresponds to the similarity or difference between values, in accordance with their content as expressed in the mapping sentence. Thus, in predicting the proximity or distance among the various values, at least four facets from the mapping sentence should be considered simultaneously. The remaining facets did not lead to distinct lawfulness even in a higher dimensionality. This is largely due to their technical confounding with other facets that did produce lawfulness. For example, Facet H--"specific" versus "general"--is to a great extent congruent with Facet D--"internal" versus "external" type of behavior--as well as to a certain extent with modality Facet E, the instrumental values being mostly "specific". A more complete selection of variables possible for the facet design would remove this confounding, and possibly reveal further lawfulness in a higher dimensional space.

REFERENCES

Albert, Ethel, M. 1968. Value systems. In the International Encyclopedia of the Social Sciences. Macmillan & Co., The Free Press, Vol. 16, pp.287-291.

Guttman, L. 1968. A general nonmetric technique for finding the smallest coordinate space for a configuration of points. Psychometrika, 33:469-506.

Guttman, L. 1982. What is not what in theory construction. In R.M. Hauser, D. Mechanic and A. Haller (editors) Social Structure and Behavior. Academic Press, New York; pp. 331-348. Also in I. Borg (ed.) Multidimensional Data Representations: When and Why. Ann Arbor, Mathesis Press, 1981; pp.47-64.

Kluckhohn, C. 1951. Values and value orientations in the theory of action: An exploration in definition and classification. In T. Parsons and E.A. Shils (eds.) Toward a General Theory of Action. Cambridge, Mass.: Harvard University Press, pp.388-433.

Levy, S. 1985. Lawful roles of facets in social theories. In D. Canter (ed.) Facet Theory: Approaches to Social Research. Springer-Verlag, New York; pp.59-96.

Levy, S. and L. Guttman, 1976. Values and Attitudes of Israeli High School Youth. Second Research Project. The Israel Institute of Applied Social Research, Jerusalem. (Hebrew, with summary in English)

Lingoes, J.C. 1968. The multivariate analysis of qualitative data. Multivariate Behavioral Research, 3:61-94. Also in Lingoes, J.C., Roskam, E.E., and Borg, I. (editors) Geometric Representations of Relational Data. Mathesis Press, Ann Arbor; pp.575-608.

Lingoes, J.C. 1973. The Guttman-Lingoes Nonmetric Program Series. Ann Arbor, Michigan; Mathesis Press.

Lorr, M. and McNair, D.M. 1963. An interpersonal behavior circle. Journal of Abnormal and Social Psychology, 67:68-75.

Parsons, Talcott 1954. Essays in Sociological Theory. Rev. Ed., Glencoe, Ill.: Free Press.

Parsons, Talcott, 1964. Social Structure and Personality. New York: Free Press.

Rokeach, Milton, 1976. Beliefs, Attitudes and Values. Jossey-Bass, San Francisco.

Scott, William, A. and R. Scott, 1965. Values and Organizations. Chicago: Rand McNally and Company.

Williams, Robin, M. Jr. 1968. The concept of values. In The International Encyclopedia of the Social Sciences. Macmillan Co. & Free Press, Vol. 16; pp.283-287.

Postmaterialist Values and Socialisation

Joachim Scholz

Paper presented at the 11th IAREP Annual Colloquium

9-11 July, 1986

Haifa, Israel

Postmaterialist values and socialization

Why do certain individuals hold postmaterialist values, while others prefer materialist goals provided by the economic system? This paper intends to contribute to a better understanding of the determinants of postmaterialism. The analysis goes beyond socio-demographic variables, looking at socialization experiences.

Notwithstanding massive criticisms (BÖLTKEN + JAGODZINSKI 1985) on INGLEHART's work about the "Silent Revolution", the existence of "new values" along the materialism-postmaterialism dimension is broadly accepted in the social and political sciences. An extensive research effort has been undertaken in order to demonstrate that INGLEHART's political/public postmaterialism is correlated with personal life goals and individual characteristics (SCHNEIDER 1981, LAFFERTY and KNUDSEN 1985, MOHR 1984). BARNES and KAASE (1979) have shown that the postmaterialism/ materialism dimension can explain more variance in protest potential than the conventional left-right continuum. A number of mainly socio-demographic variables are offered to explain individual propensities towards postmaterialism. INGLEHART (1977) argues that individuals who have been socialized during their formative years under prosperous economic conditions, will express higher (in the Maslowian sense) immaterial needs and political preferences. Higher levels of education seem to favor postmaterialism. Other authors see employees in the service sector (BRAND 1982), who do not work under the restrictive conditions of private profit aims, prone to postmaterialism.

COTGROVE and DUFF (1981) in their comparative study of industrialists and environmentalists have shown that socio-demographic factors cannot explain the divergent values of the members of the two groups compared (1). They assume that postmaterialists have been socialized in families with parents working in the human service sector, transmitting their basic values to the children. The research on the socialization background of student activists in the late sixties in the United States points in the same direction, and KENISTON (1968) argues that activists' fathers are professionals rather than businessmen. The parents may have held liberal political orientations, albeit less radical ones than those of the student protesters. Student protesters are often seen as the predecessors of today's postmaterialists. They both feel as protagonists of social changes. Besides "manifest" expressions of political socialization the so-called "latent" political socialization seems to exert an important influence on value orientations.

The impact of child-rearing practices

Three child-rearing practices are commonly distinguished (CAESAR 1972): power-assertive, love-withdrawal and inductive child-oriented.

Power assertive discipline techniques impede an equilibrated personal development of the child. The child becomes anxious and aggressive, being strongly dependent of authorities. The individual is incapable of developing

---

1) The multivariate LISREL-analysis of new German representative data has shown that socio-demographic variables account for less than one fifth of the variances in political-economic values. Relatively important are education (pro PM) and the occupational status 'self-employed' (+ Mat).

political/ social attitudes which do not only reflect personal and egocentric advantages. As KOHLBERG (1969) has shown, power assertive child-rearing practices produce low, preconventional moral standards. Only when sanctions are imposed, the individual accepts societal norms. HAAN et.al (1969) have demonstrated that these individuals hold extremely conservative views combined with strong resentments against social or ethnical minorities. The extremely low level of empathy corresponds with the refusal of prosocial behavior.

Love-withdrawal discipline techniques favor the development of a strong super-ego and a weak, but existent ego. The child internalizes parental norms in order not to be sanctioned with love withdrawal. Later, as an adult, he will in the same way internalize social norms without personal reflections. These individuals are called "rigid conventionalists". They are less aggressive and hostile (OESTERREICH 1974) towards minorities but still incapable to develop orientations which are in contrast to prevailing conventional norms. They are resisting to social change. According to KOHLBERG these individuals show conventional, rigid moral standards. Law and order are seen as unchangeable "eternal" norms which have to be strictly observed. Conventionalists are moderately conservative.

Inductive discipline techniques favor an integrative personal development. The child learns to structure his environment according to his needs. Inductive discipline techniques are not equal to anti-authoritarian child rearing practices. The behavioral options of the child are restricted, but not arbitrarily. Prohibitions will be explained to the child. This discipline technique favors postconventional moral standards and liberal political attitudes. The individual according to high ethic norms (protection of human life, mankind) and is highly emphatic. These individuals are found to be the protagonists of unconventional social change.

Empirical results

The following results are based on the analysis of 50 qualitative interviews with German male employees within the age range from 25 to 45 years. Most individuals holding strong materialist views reported being socialized through power assertive discipline techniques. Many respondents even say that their childhood and youth was characterized by the absence of well-defined child-rearing practices and principles. The parent-child relationship was cold and distant.

The materialist orientations encompass a strong preference for economic growth, for a higher standard of living, for further technological progress and in some cases for less aid to the so called "third world". A change in consumption styles - at the societal and individual level - is not perceived as necessary and desirable. The preconventional moral standard is expressed by the basic, purely materialistic orientation: All I can get, I will take. Conservative ideologies are accepted because they represent the views of the most powerful of the society. Like the parents, all strong authorities are seen as objects of anxiety and submission. The caused aggressiveness is turned to those who are apparently weak within a society, such as unemployed and the foreign workers. The strong striving for individual advantages - due to a fairly low level of internal control and personal autonomy - leaves no room for empathy and solidarity.

The group socialized by love withdrawal discipline techniques holds "balancing-inconsistent" economical-political beliefs. 'Green', postmaterialist sentiments are combined with materialist, technocratic arguments (v.KLIPSTEIN, STRÜMPEL 1985). The early internalized social norms transmitted through the parents and other agents have produced a strong developed "super-ego" and a relatively low level of personality development. Although the "balancing-inconsistents" feel uncomfortable on the affective level with the purely industrialist and materialist goals of the society and economy, they are, because of their psychological dispositions, incapable to develop orientations on the cognitive level which are deviant from the social norm. To reduce this cognitive dissonance they speak out for nuclear power plants, although they favor fewer plants and higher standards of security. They realize that economic growth is bad for the physical environment. But according to their view, we still need economic growth in order to create new jobs and to be successful competitors on international markets.

For a very small group of our respondents, postmaterialist values are a product of liberal-inductive child-rearing-practices. Virtually all postmaterialists had been socialized by love withdrawal discipline techniques. But their later socialization experiences differ significantly from those of the "balancing-inconsistent". In the very important period for the definitive formation of adult personality and of political and economical values they all experienced a characteristic biographic event, discontinuity, or turning point with lasting consequences for their belief systems. The "conversion" occurred mainly when the respondents left their homes and began their academic studies. Postadolescence, especially for university students, is seen as favoring the embracement of new values. Young people can experiment with adult roles without having to care for an own family or being tied to a full-time job. As DÖBERT and NUNNER-WINKLER (1976) point out, a biographical crisis can compensate for deficiencies in socialization caused by child-rearing practices based on love-withdrawal. These biographical changes are due to different "catalysts": The student movement, the women's emancipation movement, the anti-nuclear movement etc.

Our respondents showed - retrospectively measured - a relatively stable value pattern after their 'conversions'. Postmaterialists express preferences for less competition and a greater sense of community in social life. They give priority to ecological aims and perceive high external and social costs in case of a further increase in industrial production. On the individual level postmaterialists strive for a new balance between work and the private sphere. Some of them show a strong preference for less working time, a small group has already shifted to part-time jobs. After their individual conversion they want the whole society to convert to a more natural and human way of life. Postmaterialists manifest relatively high levels of empathy.

But not all individuals who had been exposed to discontinuities, express postmaterialist values.

The high level of material well-being and security, the increased intergenerational mobility and higher levels of education, have increased individual opportunities to choose among a set of differing values and life styles. For this reason, values and life styles cannot be predicted by socio-demographic factors only. Even socialization experiences and child-rearing practices cannot be seen as core determinants for the variance in value orientation. But child rearing practices provide the basis for later psychological dispositions. Thus, child-rearing practices will not tell us directly which economic values the individual holds. However, some value configurations will help the individual to overcome - at least in his belief system - the limits of prevalent social norms and economic goals. In addition to economic resources, there has to be a psychological basis for the recognition that there is a real choice of values and life styles available. There is no economic or socialization determinism of values, but child rearing practices and biographical crises can enable an individual to choose among different values and life styles. How this choice is made can hardly be predicted. Those who give high priority to their new unconventional values seem to be able to organize their lives according to their value orientations.

For example, individuals incisively socialized by the events of the late sixties avoided careers in private business (FENDRICH 1974, PARKIN 1968, SIEBENSCHÖN 1986). Those who had changed only superficially their attitudes might have returned to their old materialist values in favor of career opportunities.

REFERENCES

BARNES, S.H.; KAASE,M. et.al.(1979): Political Action. Beverly Hills.

BÖLTKEN,F.; JAGODZINSKI,W.(1985). In an Environment of Insecurity: Postmaterilsm in the European Community, 1970 to 1980. In: Comparative Political Studies, Vol. 17, No. 4, January, pp. 453-484

BRAND,K.-W.(1982): Neue soziale Bewegungen. Entstehung, Funktion und Perspektive neuer Protestpotentiale. Opladen

CAESAR,B.(1972): Autorität in der Familie. Reinbek

COTGROVE,St.; DUFF,A.(1981): Environmentalism, Values, and Social Change. In: British Journal of Sociology, Vol. 32, No. 1, pp. 92-110

DÖBERT,R.; NUNNER-WINKLER,G.(1976): Adoleszenzkrise und Identitätsbildung. Frankfurt

FENDRICH,J.M.(1974): Activists Ten Years Later: A Test of Generational Unit Continuity. In: Journal of Social Issues, Vol. 30, No. 3, pp. 94-118

HAAN,N. et al.(1968): Moral Reasoning of Young Adults: Political-Social Behavior, Family Background, and Personality Correlates. In: Journal of Personality and Social Psychology. Vol. 10, No. 3, pp. 183-201

INGLEHART,R.(1977): The Silent Revolution. Princeton

KENISTON,K.(1968): Young Radicals, New York

KLIPSTEIN,M.v.; STRÜMPEL,B. (Eds.) 1985: Gewandelte Werte - Erstarrte Strukturen. Bonn

KOHLBERG,L.(1969): Moral Development

LAFFERTY, KNUDSEN (1985): Postmaterialism in a Social Democratic State. In: Comparative Political Studies, Vol. 17, No. 4, January, pp. 411-430

MOHR, H.-M.(1984): Postmaterialismus in der Bundesrepublik? Arbeitspapier Nr. 141, Sonderforschungsbereich 3, Mikroanalytische Grundlagen der Gesellschaftspolitik. J.W.Goethe-Universität Frankfurt und Universität Mannheim

OESTERREICH,D.(1974): Autoritarismus und Autonomie. Stuttgart

PARKIN,F.(1968): Middle Class Radicalism, Manchester University Press.

SCHNEIDER,M.(1981): Postmaterialistische Wertorientierung und Persönlichkeit. In: Politische Vierteljahresschrift, Vol. 22, Sonderband 12, pp. 153-167

SIEBENSCHÖN,L.(1986): Wenn du die Freiheit hast... Die antiautoritäre Generation wird erwachsen. Köln

RATIONALIZATION OF ACTION THROUGH VALUE DEVELOPMENT

Guje Sevón

Swedish School of Economics and Business Administration

Helsinki, Finland

> "The idea that one´s welfare depends crucially upon conditions beyond one´s control - upon luck or the caprice of a saint - and that one can at best only improve upon good fortune, not create it - this idea must certainly be checked on initiative. Its influence on economic life is obvious: one who lives in so capricious a world is not likely to save and invest in the expectation of ultimate gain. In politics, too, it must have an effect. Where everything depends upon luck or Divine intervention, there is no point in community action. The community, like the individual, may hope and pray, but it is not likely to take its destiny into its own hands."
> (Comments by Banfield /1/ concerning the culture of the village Montegrano)

Understanding behavior is crucial to people of all kinds. It is believed that if people understand the reasons behind behavior, they can control both their own behavior and the behavior of others, or more exactly, they can control the achievement of desired goals which are the consequences of behavior.

The belief in comprehensible goal-directed behavior is essential not only in everyday life. The very same belief has laid claim on a theoretical status within social science.

A model of goal-directed behavior is built on certain assumptions. One of them relates to goal-values: it concerns the judgments of the desirability of the goals. The model presupposes that a certain behavior is chosen in accordance with the values of possible goals to attain, and, in addition, that these values are known, stable and exogenous, i.e. not affected by the choices they control (see for example March /2/, for an extensive discussion of this assumption).

Behavior as a <u>prerequisite</u> to change in the value-belief system has not attracted much attention among students of decision making, but there are some exceptions. It was shown already twenty-five years ago in a group of consistent studies that attitude change occurs in a situation in which the individual has been induced to engage in behavior discrepant with some attitude (Cohen /3/; McGuire /4/). However, this change in attitude proved to be short-lived, which, in turn, has lead scientists to infer that the results of the studies were of no greater interest. This unwillingness to interpret information about unstable beliefs as main features of decision makers is discussed by March /5/ and by Fischhoff, Slovic and Lichtenstein /6/. They stress that unstable values should be taken seriously as expressions of the lability of values, but also as context-dependent values.

The aim of this article is to discuss an alternative to assuming values as stable, known and prior to goal-directed behavior. I will refer to now classical research in order to demonstrate that earlier discussions of the state of values should be re-evaluated. I will argue that both behavior theory and value theory could benefit from a conception that values are functionally learnt.

One hypothetical mechanism for value development will be focussed on. Reasons will be put forth for the belief that subjective values of goals of action are developed in a situation in which there is a demand for understanding action in retrospect and a need for justification of actions in accordance with the prevailing cultural context.

THE OLD STORY OF VALUES

The awareness of values is old. We find a story about values in the Holy Bible, in the First Book of Moses, when Adam and Eve had eaten of the tree of knowledge:

> "And the Lord said, Behold, the man is become as one of us, to know good and evil..."

Since then, values are taken for given. Lay people as well as researchers treat values as independent rather than dependent variables in their causal behavior models. As a consequence, there are on one hand lack of research on the development of values and on the other a large amount of research which is assuming that certain values inevitably result in a certain behavior.

Why is the belief that values are stable and known so prevalent in today´s professional and everyday life? Reasons for that may be found in a need of a goal-directed behavior model for planning activities in society, but there are other reasons as well. The circularity of the value-behavior model itself and the intuitive character of people´s values also support the survival of the belief.

The Circular Value-Behavior Model.

The value concept is often used in circular models; it is then used both to explain and to predict behavior. It appears in a reasoning which allows both that peoples´ values are inferred from their action ("They take care of their old parents. Consequently, they must be altruistic") and allow that their actions are predicted from the same, derivated values ("They are altruistic. Of course they will take care of their old folks"). Circular reasoning makes a perfectly untestable model, as it cannot be falsified.

There is a strong belief that values control behavior. That shows when researchers assume that peoples´ values precede their actions even though an experimental setting in a study would provide that the causal relations were interpreted as opposite in direction. For example, when Rokeach /7/ suggests that the value of honesty is a predictor of honest and dishonest behavior, he is referring to an empirical study of prison inmates compared to a national sample, in which the criminal or average American behavior is preceding in time the ranking of honesty as a value in life.

Intuitiveness of Values and Retrospective Attention to Them

People are seldom aware of whether their actions are controlled by an evaluated goal, or not. Presumably, decision makers will think that there is such a reason behind their choices, even when they cannot state the goal-value explicitly at the time of the choice. When it is important that the reason is found, the decision-maker may even engage friends, or a therapist to find it. The belief that behavior is systematically based on values is thus often effective after a decision is made, as it provides an understanding of the behavior in retrospect.

RATIONALIZATION OF BEHAVIOR THROUGH VALUE ASSESSMENT

Several researchers, among them Bandura and Rokeach, assume that the system of values precedes and causes behavior. Bandura /8/ views self-efficacy as one of the important mechanisms underlying behavior. (Self-efficacy is a belief that behavior can be successfully executed to produce desired outcome.) Bandura states that perceived negative discrepancy between performance and standards creates dissatisfaction that motivates corrective change in behavior (and not in value, which theoretically also is possible). Rokeach /9/ states that a value should undergo change if maintenance or enhancement of self-conception is at stake, and its having undergone change should lead to systematic changes in other related cognitions within the belief system and should then culminate in behavior change.

People believe that there is a consistency between values and action, but they cannot rely on there always being circumstances in which the value-consistent choice to be made is available, or that a certain choice will result in the expected goal-attainment. We can imagine the effects of the conventional goal-directed model in a society in which not all actions lead to desired goals. The model would generate unhappy people, as their values do not change in accordance with feed-back information about failure.

In real life, there is a restriced number of possible action alternatives to choose between, but the possibility to reflect, and thereby to develop the values is less restricted. Therefore it is meaningful to view labile (and/or unknown) values as functionally pertinent solutions to the individual adaption in a society with restrictions on what actions can be taken and a society with conditions in which desired consequences do not follow unproblematically from choice.

March /10/ assumes that we often rationalize action by managing posterior constructions of preferences. That has a similarity to the process of legitimation, which is an objectivation of meaning (see Berger & Luckmann /11/).

The view of value assessment as a means for matching justifying reasons to previous behavior partly resembles Bem´s /12/ model of attitude change, in which attitude change occurs as a result of one´s own counterattitudinal behavior when such behavior is perceived as important, and when one feels personally responsible for the outcome. The basis for Bem´s radical behavioristic view is a single empirical generalization that beliefs and attitudes are inferred from public behavior and accompanying stimulus cues upon which the socializing community has relied in training the individual to make such self-descriptive statements in the first place. In this respect, Bem´s view is applicable to the concept of legitimation of behavior.

SELF-EFFICACY, LOCUS OF CONTROL, AND VALUE DEVELOPMENT

A process of retrospective selection of purpose of action is guided by some rationales. One is the following:

It is obvious that people in the Western societies, generally speaking, want to do important things, and to a certain degree also believe they are doing that. Consequently, people attach important purposes to their action, when the actions are described and explained. One basis for this observation is the attribution studies carried out in Western cultures, especially in the U.S.A. The research differentiates between stated reasons that are internal and external to a person. Whether an internal or an external reason is stated for an action may depend on which of them gives the most positive or negative image of the person. The research has shown that when the reason is inferred from own behavior, there is a clear dominance of reasons which give a positive image: internal reasons for successful actions, and external ones for unsuccessful actions. The inferences are reverse when the explanations concern other persons´ behavior. (see Attribution theory, e.g. Jones et al /13/).

When explaining actions in retrospect, people may either choose an important goal among a set of possible goals of different importance, or they may attach a high value to a given goal. Both ways action is justified, following this principle:

> "Conditions over which I have control tend to be more important than those over which I have no control"

By that justification people stay happy in a society in which one is supposed to do important things. People prefer the consequences of their actions, and dislike the goals they cannot achieve.

The principle of doing important things is considerd to be a main feature of the Western industrialized culture. Other cultures may have other principles. In Eastern cultures there is a more fatalistic view, according to which a desired behavior is in agreement with a predictable cycle of events and contrary to a belief that one should influence events to one´s own advantage (Phillips & Wright /14/). A somewhat similar view of external control, a melancholy fatalism is, however, recorded also from the Western hemisphere, from the village Montegrano in Southern Italy (Banfield /15/):

> "In the Montegrano view, action is the result more of forces playing upon the individual than of motivations arising within him. The individual is indeed naturally impulsive; his impulses incline him toward bodily pleasures and in general toward self-indulgence. Unless checked by other forces, they lead him - from heedlessness rather than malice - to do wrong. Usually, however, impulses are checked and action is redirected by external forces."

However, in most parts of the Western culture, in which people are supposed to do important things, if values are labile or unknown, people may assess important values in relation to their <u>self-efficacy</u>. Consequently, importance assessments should be related to beliefs about action-outcome contingencies, namely the <u>locus of control</u>.

The validity of this assumption was established in a yet unpublished Finnish study carried out by Sevón /16/. In the study the degree to which people could influence certain economic and social events varied between decision situations and between individuals. In other words, the external and the internal locus of control varied. It was found that more controllable situations are seen as more important than less controllable ones are, and that people who think that they have a great control over the occurrence of events tend to ascribe higher importance-values to these events compared to other people.

The present study supports the argument that values are important for understanding actions in retrospect. Simultaneously it argues against the view that values precede and control behavior. Consequently, behavior in situations which are based on the assumption that values control behavior, as investment models in economics and election models in political science, should be reinterpreted in accordance with the notion that values are adaptable to what is considered to be possible to achieve through action. For those types of situations, the reinterpretation is most urgent, considering that they often concern peoples´ peripheral values which are more labile than central values are (Rokeach /17/).

REFERENCES

/1/ Banfield, E.C., The Moral Basis of a Backward Society. New York: Free Press, 1967, p. 109.

/2/ March, J.G., Bounded Rationality, Ambiguity, and the Engineering of Choice. Bell Journal of Economics, 1978, 9, 587-608.

/3/ Cohen, A.R., Attitudinal Consequences of Induced Discrepancies between Cognition and Behavior. Public Opinion Quarterly, 1960, 24, 297-318.

/4/ McGuire, W.J., The Nature of Attitudes and Attitude Change. In: Lindzey, G. and Aronson, E. (eds.), The Handbook of Social Psychology (Vol. 3). Reading, Mass.: Addison-Wesley, 1969.

/5/ March, J.G., Bounded Rationality, Ambiguity, and the Engineering of Choice. Bell Journal of Economics, 1978, 9, 587-608.

/6/ Fischhoff, B., Slovic, P. and Lichtenstein, S., Knowing What You Want: Measuring Labile Values. In: Wallsten, T. (ed.), Cognitive Processes of Choice and Decision Behavior. Hillsdale , N.J.: Erlbaum, 1980.

/7/ Rokeach, M., The Nature of Human Values. New York: Free Press, 1973, 134 ff.

/8/ Bandura, A., Self-efficacy: Toward a Unifying Theory of Behavioral Change. Psychological review, 1977, 84, 191-215.

/9/ Rokeach, M., The Nature of Human Values. New York: Free Press, 1973.

/10/ March, J.G., Bounded Rationality, Ambiguity, and the Engineering of Choice. Bell Journal of Economics, 1978, 9, 587-608.

/11/ Berger, P. L. & Luckmann, T., The Social Construction of Reality. London: A Lane, 1966.

/12/ Bem, D.J., Self-Perception. An Alternative Interpretation of Cognitive Dissonance Phenomena. Psychological Review, 1967, 74, 183-200.

/13/ Jones, E.E. et al (eds.), Attribution: Perceiving the Causes of Behavior. Morristown, N.J.: General Learning Press, 1972.

/14/ Phillips, L.D. and Wright, C.N., Cultural Differences in Viewing Uncertainty and Assessing Probabilities. In: Jungermann, H. and de Zeeuw, G. (eds.) Decision Making and Change in Human Affairs. Dordrecht: Reidel, 1977.

/15/ Banfield, E.C., The Moral Basis of a Backward Society. New York: Free Press, 1967, p. 131.

/16/ Sevón, G., Value Development as Related to Rationalization of Action. Unpublished manuscript.

/17/ Rokeach, M., Beliefs, Attitudes and Values. San Fransisco: Jossey-Bass, 1968.

LIFE VALUES: THEIR STRUCTURE AND RELATION TO LIFE SITUATION

Henry Montgomery and Ulla-Stina Johansson

Department of Psychology, University of Göteborg, Box 14158
S-40020, Göteborg, Sweden

1. INTRODUCTION

It is commonly assumed among behavioral scientists that people adhere to a number of basic values such as security, freedom, and personal development. As pointed out by Rescher [1] values are manifested in two ways, viz. (a) on the side of talk or (thought) to justify one's own or other people's actions and (b) on the side of overt action inasmuch as we expect a certain consistency between people's values and actions. This Janus headed function of the value concept distinguishes "values" from the related concepts "needs" and "motives" which primarily are used in line with sense (b), i. e., to explain human action.

Values are expected to characterize a person's vision of "the good life" or at least his or her vision of how life ought to be lived [1]. Needs and motives, on the other hand, are not necessarily seen as good and hence are not so closely related to "the good life" as is the case for values. This implies that people's experiencies of the quality of their lives should be particularly closely related to values. Obviously, the more a person experiences that he or she attains values that are important to him or her the greater is his or her experienced quality of life.

A large number of questionnaires have been developed to assess the experienced quality of life or the subjective well-being (for a review, see [2]). However, to our knowledge none of these questionnaire are explicitly based on values in general. Instead they are based on more restricted aspects of life such as feelings of well-being (e. g., [3]) or satisfaction with different life areas (e. g., [4]).

In the present paper we report on our work to develop a questionnaire on how people view their life situation in terms of a number of values. More precisely, we ask people to rate their *attainment* of different values and how *important* they think each value is. The response pattern within and across these two types of tasks may give information of how people experience the quality of their life but also, obviously, of the structure of their value system. In fact, in the present paper the focus will be on structural aspects. Our aim is to develop and test a conceptual framework which may shed light on similarities and differences between particular values. However, in order to test the validity of our framework in its present shape we will report some preliminary tests of whether the framework may be used for giving a meaningful description of the quality of life of people in different life situations.

Our research is restricted to such values that may be used for distinguishing the life situations of individual people in a given society. We call these values life values. Hence societal values such as peace or equality are not included in our investigation. In the following section we discuss briefly how life values may be characterized and classified. This discussion summarizes and develops ideas that were put forward in a previous paper [5], in which possible ways of classifying life values were highlighted.

1.1. Possible principles for classifying life values

A fundamental assumption in the following discussion is that life values more or less directly reflect different types of relations which a person experiences in relation to some object or objects. We will denote such relations as personal relations. More specifically, we will assume that there are three principles for classifying values involving personal relations, viz (a) whether the stress is on the personal relation as such or on states within the person him/herself or on objects in the environment, (b) the type of object that is involved in the personal relation, and (c) the contents of the personal relation to a given object.

As for our first classification principle it may be noted that many life values seem to focus on the personal relation as such. To exemplify, we will consider the psychologist Rokeach's [6] well-known list of 18 "terminal" values (desirable end-states of existence) and 18 "instrumental" values (desirable modes of conduct). The values are given in Table 1. A total of 33 of the 36 values in the list may be considered as life values (i. e. personal rather than societal values) the exceptions being "a world at peace", "equality", and "national security". Moreover, with exceptions for "happiness" and "inner harmony", all these life values primarily denote relations between a person and an object rather than desirable mental states or environmental objects. For example, true friendship obviously corresponds to a certain type of relation between a person and other people, freedom implies that the environment allows a person to do various things and so on. We have already given examples of values which primarily seem to be desirable mental states (happiness and inner harmony). Values which focus on the object in a personal relation correspond to external resources of different types such as having a good private economy, having a good (physical) health, having good housing etc. It is interesting to note that Rokeach did not include any value of that type in his list.

It should be noted that the border-lines between the three types of values mentioned above are fuzzy. In particular, external resources as well as desirable mental states may give associations to particular personal relations. For example, to have good friends, which obviously is a resource, is also closely related to experiencing friendship, which is a personal relation. Happiness, which is a mental state, may also express a certain attitude towards the environment, e. g., that one is satisfied with life.

To exemplify our second classification principle - the type of object involved in the personal relation that may be associated with a value - we will again consider Rokeach's list of values. Consider first the values "self-respect" and "self-controlled". Here the object obviously is the person him/herself or the person's picture of him/herself. That is, the person respects him/herself or he or she controls him/herself. Consider now the values "helpful" and "polite". In this case the object is some other person or persons. Consider, finally, the values "a sense of accomplishment" and "responsible". Here the object is not necessarily another person but unspecified with respect to whether it is a living person or not. One could say that the object is "ahuman".

The examples now given imply that different life values involve at least three types of objects, viz. (a) the person him/herself, (b) other persons and (c) "ahuman" objects which primarily are not living individuals. The latter type of environmental objects could correspond to various physical objects, to cultural objects like a musical piece or a drama, to the nature, to the society or to parts of the society, or to objects which simply are unspecified, like in the expressions "to accomplish something" and "to create something". An important object for many persons is God. Whether God primarily is seen as a person or as something more abstract and "ahuman" may vary across individuals.

TABLE 1

Rokeach's [6] list of 18 instrumental and 18 terminal values

Instrumental values	Terminal values
Ambitious	A comfortable life
Broadminded	An exciting life
Capable	A sense of accomplishment
Cheerful	A world at peace
Clean	A world of beauty
Courageous	Equality
Forgiving	Family security
Helpful	Freedom
Honest	Happiness
Imaginative	Inner harmony
Independent	Mature love
Intellectual	National security
Logical	Pleasure
Loving	Salvation
Obedient	Self-respect
Polite	Social recognition
Responsible	True friendship
Self-controlled	Wisdom

The contents of the personal relation to a given object - our third classification principle - was discussed in some detail in our previous paper [5]. By inspecting values from previous research we found 12 different types of contents in personal relations. These were no control (e. g., tolerance), control (e. g, influence over others), transaction (e. g., to help), rule following (e. g., honesty), positive feeling (e. g., love), positive evaluation (e. g., social status), knowledge, trust, participation (e. g., task involvement), harmony, stimulation, and development (e. g., personal development). Moreover, we found that for a given content there may be different types of "orientations" of the personal relation. That is, the relation is oriented from someone or something to someone or something. If we also take the type of object involved into account we obtain seven different value orientations. That is, the relation could be oriented from the person to the person (e. g., self-controlled), from the person to others (e. g., helpful), from the person to the environment in general or to more specific "ahuman" objects (e. g., broadminded, caring for nature), from others to the person (e. g., social recognition), mutual relation between the person and others (e. g., true friendship), from the environment in general or from more specific "ahuman" objects to the person (e. g., an exciting life, access to nature), and mutual relation between the environment in general or more specific "ahuman" objects and the person (we have no example of such a value).

It may be hypothesized that different contents and orientations of personal relations could be reduced to combinations of values on a few basic dimensions. For example, to help others could be seen as a reflecting some degree of control and some degree of positive evaluation of others. To find such basic dimensions one may draw from the research on the structure of social behavior. Benjamin and her associates [7, 8, 9] developed a model which summarizes and extends a number of theories in this area. In Benjamin's model social behavior includes behavior directed towards the person him/herself and behavior directed towards other people. That is, in this model social behavior covers two of the three types of categories that are included into our second classification principle (type of object). In her model Benjamin distinguishes between three basic dimensions or aspects in social behavior, viz. (a) focus, (b) interdependence, and (c) affiliation. The focus in social behavior could be on another person (e. g., to help someone), on the self in a relation to another person (e. g., to trust someone) and, finally, it could correspond to an intrapsychic relation, i. e., how the person views him/herself (e. g., to accept oneself). Benjamin [7] asserts that focus on the self in the relation to another person corresponds to passive childlike behaviors whereas focus on the other corresponds to active, parentlike behaviors. In this way focus is related to the passive-active dimension emphasized by several social psychologists (e. g., [10, 11, 12]). The affiliation dimension ranges from hate to love and is expressed in different ways depending on the type of focus involved. For example, when the focus is on the other love will be manifested as nurturing behaviors whereas when the focus in on the self love will be manifested as seeking contact with and enjoying another person. Interdependence ranges from independence to dependence and concerns the independence/dependence of the focused object. For example, when the focus is on the other independence implies that the other's independence is accepted or encouraged whereas when the focus is on the self independence denotes one's own independence.

There are a number of differences between Benjamin's and our approach: First, Benjamin is not explicitly concerned with values and as a consequence she includes neutral or negatively loaded behaviors into her model. Second, there is no correspondence to the distinction between attainment and importance in Benjamin's model. Benjamin is concerned with actual behavior or people's experiences of actual behavior. This implies that her model may be more relevant for how people experience their attainment of values than how they experience importance of values. Third, Benjamin's model is restricted to relations to (single) human objects and hence does not include "ahuman" objects. Still, the overlap between our life value concept and Benjamin's view of social behavior is large enough to warrant the hypothesis that the three basic dimensions suggested by Benjamin, i. e. focus (or passive-active), affiliation, and interdependence, may lie under attainment ratings of values.

2. METHOD

2.1. Collection of life values

The values used in our empirical study were selected with the ambition to cover as many life values as was practically possible. In future research, we plan to use the present data to find a limited number of items which mirror the basic structure of life values. To ensure a good coverage of all possible life values in the present study we used three different sources to create a list of life values.

First, in telephone interviews 75 residents in different areas of Göteborg, Sweden, were asked a number of questions about their life values [13]. (Göteborg is Sweden's second largest city with a population around half a million persons). The questions were grouped according to four domains of life, viz life in general, work, family, and leisure. For each domain, four questions were asked, viz. (1) "What do you want to attain in your life / in your family life / in your work / in your leisure?" (2) "What is required by you to attain what you want in your life / in your family life etc.? (3) "What else is required to attain what you want in your life / in your family life etc.?" (4) "How do you feel when you think life is good / your family life is good etc.?" The subjects were also asked what they believed that other people in Sweden wanted to attain in their lives and, finally, the subjects were asked to tell what they meant by happiness. Subjects' answers were coded into 103 categories. Not all of these categories could be regarded as values, however.

Second, values were collected by going through previous research on values and on related phenomena like needs, drives, and motives [14]. We simply searched for authors who had compiled lists of values etc. We mainly searched for psychological literature, but also for literature in sociology, philosophy, and theology. The search in the psychological literature was partly done in DIALOG - a computerized search system. The outcome of these endeavors was a total of 55 value lists comprising a total of 1053 values, which were grouped into 127 value categories. Most of these value categories clearly corresponded to life values.

Third, values were generated from theoretical considerations related to the ideas presented above. A matrix focusing on values bearing on personal relations was created. The matrix was arrived at by combining the 12 different types of contents described above with the 6 "orientations" that we found in our collection of values (from the person to the person, from the person to others, from the person to the environment in general or to more specific "ahuman" objects, from others to the person, mutual relation with others, and from the environment in general or more specific "ahuman" objects to the person). When possible, each of the 72 entries of the matrix was filled in with values collected from the sources described above. For the remaining entries attempts were made to construct values in line with the definition of the entry. In this way, all entries except four were filled in with values.

The final list of values based on the three above sources comprised a total of 159 items.

2.2. The life value questionnaire

Using the list of life 159 values a questionnaire was constructed on how people experience their life situation. The questionnaire was partitioned into the following four sections.

(1) Questions about background variables (e. g., age, sex, education, profession, working hours per week, marital status, number of children, income, housing, access to car).

(2) Questions about attainment of life values. The subject was presented with 159 statements on his or her attainment of each of the life values selected (e. g. "I have knowledge." "Others respect me". "I have a good family life."). The subject was asked to rate the extent to which each statement gave a valid description of his or her life situation. (The term "life value" was not mentioned in the instructions). The ratings were

to be made on a 7-point scale with extremes defined as "To a very small extent" (1) and "To a very large extent" (7). Two intermediate scale values were defined as "To a rather small extent "2 (3) and "To a rather large extent" (5).

(3) Questions about importance of life values. The subject was presented with statements on exactly the same life values as in the preceding section. However, this time each statement was phrased as a clause starting with "that" (e. g., "that I have knowledge." "that others respect me." "that I have a good family life.") The subject was asked to rate how important the circumstances referred to in each statement was for attaining what he or she wanted in life. (Again the term "life value" was not mentioned.) The ratings were to be made on a 7-point scale with extremes defined as "Totally unimportant important" (1) and "Extremely important" (7). Two intermediate scale values were defined as "Rather unimportant" (3) and "Rather important" (5).

(4) Evaluation of the questionnaire. The subject was asked to give his or her opinion of the questionnaire.

The order between the items in each section was randomized. There were five versions of the questionnaire with different order between the items in each version.

2.3. Subjects and procedure

The selection of subjects followed exactly the same principles as in the preceding telephone interview study [13]. A total of 150 persons between 16 and 75 years of age were sampled from five areas in the city of Göteborg. Thirty persons were sampled randomly in each area from official registers of all persons living in the pertinent area. The five areas were selected to represent different types of housing (single-family houses, terraced houses, privately owned houses, and rented apartments in two areas).

The questionnaire and a letter giving information about the investigation was mailed to each of the 150 persons. It was pointed out that the investigation was a pilot study conducted in order to construct a questionnaire on how people experience their life situation. Full anonymity was guaranteed to those who participated in the investigation. Each person was informed that he or she would be paid by Sw Cr 75 (approximately $ 10) for filling out the questionnaire. An envelope with free postage was enclosed for mailing back the questionnaire.

Those who did not respond were contacted by mail and/or by telephone and were encouraged to participate in the investigation. A total of 82 persons finally filled out the questionnaire.

3. RESULTS

3.1. Computation of value variables

Due to the large number of items in the questionnaire the attainment and importance ratings were first reduced to a more manageable number of value variables that were used in ensuing data analyses. The aim of this data reduction was to create a set of homogeneous and comparable value variables for attainment and importance ratings, respectively. The computations were conducted in the following four steps. 1. The items were partitioned into eight classes, viz. external resources, the six value orientations mentioned above, and mental states. 2. For each class of items the attainment and importance ratings, respectively, were factor analyzed with varimax rotation for factors having eigenvalues of 1.00 or higher. If a factor was not interpretable the factor analysis was repeated with a reduced number of rotated factors. This procedure was repeated until all rotated factors could be interpreted. 3. Using the factor solutions resulting from step 2 groups of items were selected from each value class that would yield homogeneous value variables for both attainment ratings and importance ratings. The homogeneity of the attainment or importance ratings of a selected group of items was tested by factor analyzing the ratings of the selected items. If all items had loadings of 0.50 or higher in the first unrotated factor then the group of items were assumed to form a homogeneous value variable. This procedure was repeated with new selections of items and, in a few case, with changes of the set of the items in the relevant class of values until each item could be referred to a group of items yielding a homogeneous value variable for both attainment ratings and importance ratings. 4. Value variables were created by computing means of the attainment and importance ratings, respectively, of the items in each of the groups identified in step 3.

The factor analyses (step 2 above) resulted in factor solutions that were moderately similar across attainment and importance ratings. The factor solutions for the importance ratings tended to comprise fewer factors than was the case for the importance ratings. In particular, this was true for social values (i. e., value orientations involving relations to other persons). The number of interpretable factors for the three classes of social values (from the person to others, from others to the person, mutual relation with others) were 6, 4, and, 3. The corresponding number of factors for the importance ratings were 2, 1, and, 2. The selection of items for homogeneous value variables (step 3 above) largely could be performed by using a "split and conquer" strategy. That is, the factor solution with the greater number of factors (usually the solution for the attainment ratings) could be used for selecting items yielding homogeneous value variables for both attainment and importance ratings.

Table 2 shows the set of value variables that was identified as a result of the procedure described above. As can be seen, a total of 43 value variables were identified from the original set of 159 value items. The variables are ordered in relation to our grouping of the values into eight classes. It can be noted that the great majority of value items and values variables were classified into one of the six value orientations. Only a few values were primarily seen as mental states. As for the external resources it can be seen that most variables consisted of only one item. Hence, in most cases it was not possible to construct homogeneous value variables comprising more than one item. This reflects the fact that the external resources exhibited more covariation both within and across attainment and importance ratings than was the true for the other values. Another interesting observation is that most items in the class "Mutual relations between person and others" form one homogeneous value variable whereas for the other two social orientations the items are rather evenly spread into four or five different classes. Finally, it can be noted that moral values emerge as a separate class in at least three of the six value orientations (cf value variables 20 (Honest to o), 22 (Responsible), and 34 (Mutual morals). In the value orientation "From others the person" the variable denoted as O honest (No. 32) also contain some values that are not clearly moral.

TABLE 2

Value variables and items for each variable. The variables are grouped into eight different classes (1-11: external resources, 12-16: intrapersonal relations, 17-21: from person to others, 22-28: from person to environment, 29-32: from others to person, 33-35: mutual relation between person and others, 36-41: from environment to person, 42-43: mental states)

Variable	Items
1. Material standard	I have a high material standard. I have much money
2. Enough money	I have enough money
3. Satisfying job	I have a job which I am happy with
4. Having time	I have time to do what I want
5. Housing	I have a nice home. I have access to nature
6. Education	I am educated
7. Family life	I lead a good family life
8. Well-being nearest	Those nearest to me lead a good life
9. Friends	I have friends
10. Health	I am healthy
11. Good-looking	I am good-looking
12. Personal development	I realize myself. I develop myself
13. Caring for oneself	I take care of myself. I look after my health. I am purposeful. I am clean
14. Personal identity	I have a personal identity. I follow my conscience. I have fantasy. I have self-knowledge. I am consistent. I am myself. I have a sense of humor
15. Self appreciation	I like myself. I have self-confidence. I have self-respect
16. Self control	I have self-discipline. I am patient
17. Accepting o	I forgive o. I am tolerant to o. I am considerate to o. I accept o
18. Caring for o	I take care of o. O are important to me I give love to o. I help o
19. Trusting o	I trust o. There is a positive development of my relations to o. I have harmonious relations to o
20. Honest to o	I am honest to o. I am loyal to o
21. Liking o	I appreciate o. I am nice to o. I am polite to o. I respect o. I understand o.
22. Responsible	I am responsible. I am dutiful
23. Motivation	I have faith. I am adaptable. I am interested in what I am doing. I am optimistic. I am involved in something. I have a positive attitude. I am open for new impressions.
24. Capacity	I am wise. I have knowledge. I am intelligent. I am rational. I am efficient
25. Carefulness	I am careful with things. I am orderly. I keep things clean and tidy. I am ambitious
26. Achievement	I accomplish something with permanent

	value. I influence society. I create new and interesting things. I achieve something in society. I am active. I take initiatives. I influence o. I influence my work. I am doing things which produce results
27. Career	I make a career
28. Caring for nature	I care for nature. I appreciate nature
29. O accept	O have harmonious relations to me. O are polite to me. O accept me. O forgive me. O are tolerant to me. O understand me. I receive love from o
30. O help	O help me. There is a positive development of o relations to me. O are loyal to me
31. O pos influence	I know nice people. O influence me positively. O demand something from me
32. O honest	O trust me. O respect me. O are honest to me. I am important to o. O appreciate me. O are considerate to me
33. Good mutual relations	There is a mutual respect between me and o. There is a mutual consideration between me and o etc (in all 15 items)
34. Mutual morals	There is a mutual politeness between me and o. There is a mutual honesty between me and o. There is a mutual loyalty between me and o
35. Love / sex	There is a mutual love between me and another person. I am in love I have a good sex life
36. Freedom / independence	I have opportunities of being alone. I have freedom. I am self-governed independent. I am independent of o. I have courage
37. Security	I live in a place where I feel at home. I lead a harmonious life. I lead a secure life. I feel that I have roots back in time. I am lucky. I feel affinity with my relatives
38. Stimulation	I experience beauty. I lead a varied life. I have access to culture and amusement. There is a positive development of my external life conditions
39. External demands for achievement	I have demanding tasks. I am needed in society. I have a position in society
40. Support from society	I get support from society
41. God	I believe in God. God helps me, God loves me. I am important to God. God cares for me. God has hope for me. God understands me
42. Happiness / inner harmony	I am happy. I have inner harmony. I lead a meaningful life
43. Enjoyment	I enjoy life. I am cheerful. I am full of life. I am satisfied. I have fun. I relax

Note. o = others.

3.2. Basic structure of attainment and importance of values

In order to find out whether the 43 value variables could be described in terms of a limited number of dimensions or components multidimensional scaling of the correlation matrices for attainment and importance, respectively, was performed. Hence, the correlations were seen as corresponding to distances in a multidimensional space where each variable is represented by a point. That is, the lower the correlation is between two variables the greater is the distance between the variables in the space. This implies that closely related variables were assumed to form clusters in the space. Multidimensional scaling is typically used within the so called facet approach to social and behavioral research and has been shown to be a powerful method for analyzing the structure of complex action (cf. the volume edited by Canter, [15]). We also used factor analysis to analyze the two correlation matrices. However, in comparison with factor analysis multidimensional scaling resulted in solutions that appeared to give a better overview of the basic structure underlying the data.

The multidimensional scaling was performed using Guttman's method [16] in the SYSTAT statistical package. In line with the results of the factor analysis performed to construct the value variables it was found that the importance ratings could be accounted for in fewer dimensions than was the case for the attainment ratings. For the importance ratings the stress values of two-dimensional and three-dimensional solutions, respectively, were 0.23 and 0.16. The corresponding stress values for the attainment ratings were 0.28 and 0.19.

Figure 1 shows the two-dimensional solution of the importance ratings. The space in Figure 1 may be partitioned into regions in line with principles which have been found to be applicable in facet theoretical research (cf. [15]). For example, a polar partitioning implies that the space is divided into wedgelike regions emanating from a central origin. In Figure 1 there are six regions which obviously are of that type. Each of them corresponds to a certain life area or type of objects to which values may be oriented. Going clockwise from the upper left corner of Figure 1 these regions are: External self (i. e. how the person appears seen from an outside perspective) , Life in general: responsibility, Other people, Internal self (i. e. how the person appears from an inside perspective), Work and achievement, and Life in general: possibilities. In addition to these regions there are two regions which only comprise one variable each, viz. God and Supporting society. It can be noted that regions located opposite to each other correspond to polarized pairs. Three such pairs may be identified, viz. External self - Internal self, Responsibility - Achievement, and Other people - Life in general. It is also possible to contrast the two Life in general regions, i. e., responsibility and (access to) possibilities. Finally, External self could also be seen as located opposite to Work and achievement. This polarization may be interpreted as reflecting an egoistic versus an altruistic, external world oriented attitude.

Figure 1 also shows two wedgelike regions which overlap with the regions discussed above. One of these regions concerns morals in life in general, in society and with respect to other people. The other region concerns intimacy and corresponds to warm or close relationships to other people or to a positive view of the internal self.

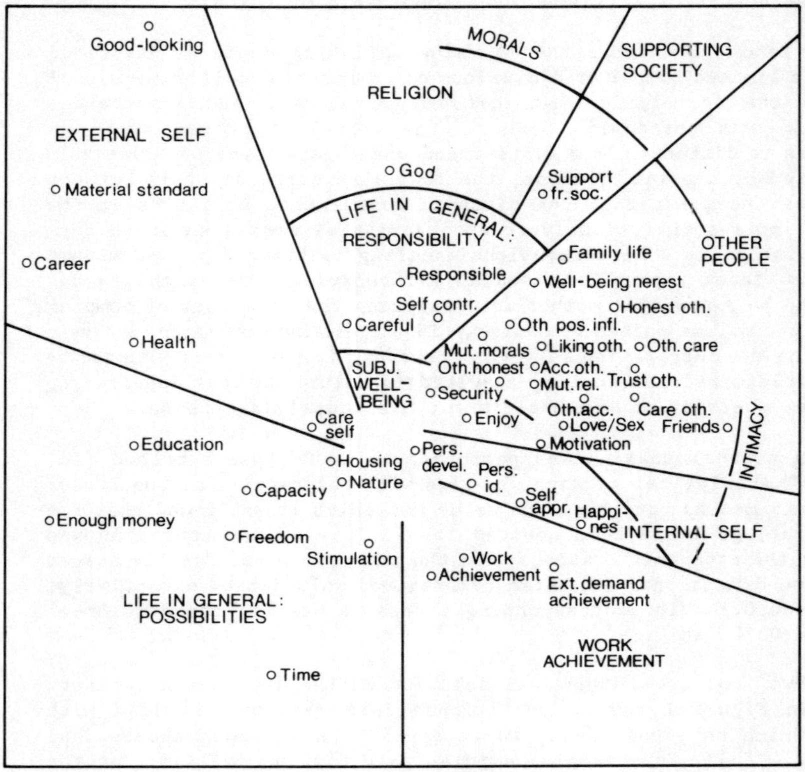

FIGURE 1

Multidimensional scaling in two dimensions of rated importance of life values.

The space depicted in Figure 1 may also be partitioned according to a modular principle, i. e., by means of more or less circular bands around the center of the space. Three modular regions may be distinguished in the data shown in Figure 1 although the borders between these regions are somewhat fuzzy.

The most central region concerns the person's well-being and includes the value variables enjoyment, personal development, and personal identity, and self appreciation. The value variables in this region tend to correspond to mental states or intrapersonal relations. In an intermediate region surrounding the center there are values corresponding to different relations between the person and his or her environment. In the most peripheral region there are various external resources. However, two external resources - housing and nature - are located in the center of the space. On the other hand, happiness which undoubtedly is related to subjective well-being is located rather far out into the periphery. This finding may be irreliable since in another study [17], in which subjects judged the importance of 28 social values, "a happy life" was located almost perfectly in the middle of a two-dimensional projection.

The three-dimensional solution yielded two dimensions which were very close to the ones emerging in the two-dimensional solution. The third dimension tended to distinguish the external resources from the other value variables. This implies that the importance ratings of external resources may have more in common than is shown in the two-dimensional solution depicted in Figure 1.

To summarize, the importance ratings largely seem to be structured in terms of different types of objects to which the values are related and in terms of whether the person, the relation to the object, or the object itself is focused. We will now examine the structure behind the attainment ratings. Figure 2 shows the three-dimensional solution resulting from the multidimensional scaling of the attainment data. It appears that the basic structure of the attainment ratings is fundamentally different from the structure found for the importance ratings. The values now appear to be structured in terms of the type of relation that holds between the person and the object. Figure 2 shows that the type of relation varies along three bipolar dimensions denoted as Active-Passive, Dependent-Independent, and Privacy/Intimacy-Generally positive. In contrast to the polarized pairs of regions found in the importance data the present bipolar dimensions are mutually orthogonal to each other. Rephrased in facet theoretical language the three bipolar dimensions correspond to facets that play an axial role (rather than a polar or a modular role, cf.[18]). The axial organization of the data implies that the three-dimensional space may be partitioned into eight cubes corresponding to the eight possible ways of combining values oriented to either pole on each of the three dimensions. In Figure 2 each of these cubes is shown in a two-dimensional projection (i. e., as a quadrant) for the Generally positive and Privacy/Intimacy halves of the space, respectively.

We will now briefly comment on the nature of each of the three bipolar dimensions shown in Figure 2. Active-Passive denotes activity or passivity, in general, and hence not necessarily whether the person is active or not. For example, stimulation is an active value although that value does not characterize the person. By contrast, Dependent-Independent refers to how the person relates to his or her environment, that is, whether the person is dependent or not on his or her environment. It can be noted that all social values not involving morals have been interpreted as being dependent values. It seems hard to imagine how good social relationship could exist without the person being dependent on the other persons involved. The moral values, on the other hand, correspond to independence when the person's own morals is concerned (Honest to others, Responsible) but to dependence when the morals of others is concerned (Others honest). However, mutual morals which concerns both the person's and others' morals corresponds to independence in Figure 2. It is interesting to note that in Figure 2 work is a dependent (and passive) value located close to various social values whereas achievement is an independent (and active) value located far away from the social values. Thus, the two values are very far from each other in the space. By contrast, these values are closely related to each other with respect to their importance (see Figure 1). These results seem to imply that what people actually get from having a good job (i. e., social relations) differs from why they think a good job is important (i. e., possibility to achievement). The third dimension Generally positive - Privacy/ Intimacy concerns at least two somewhat overlapping distinctions. One of these distinctions is the one between people or objects in general vs specific people (e. g., one's marital partner) or specific objects (e. g., nature). Another distinction related to the third dimension is the one between an altruistic vs. egocentric attitude. Hence, Privacy/Intimacy values tend to be more advantageous to the person him/herself than the case is for Generally positive values. In this way some of the Privacy/Intimacy values are focused on a specific person, viz., the person him/herself.

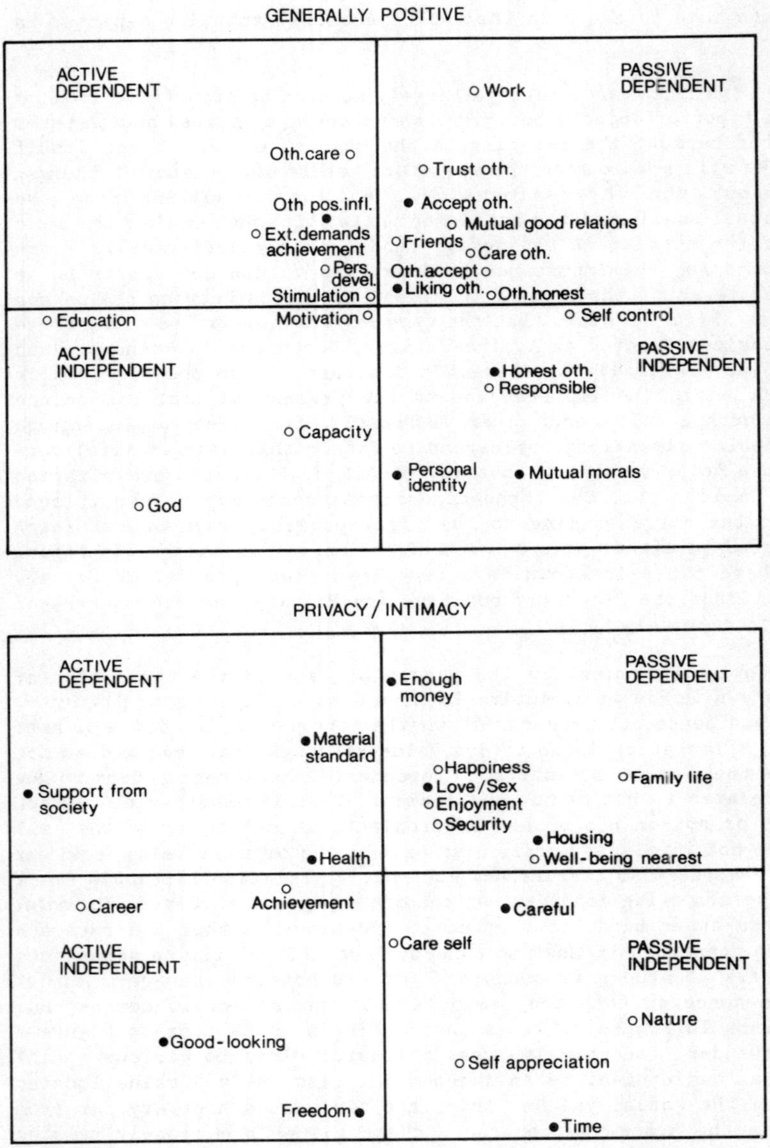

FIGURE 2

Multidimensional scaling in three dimensions of rated attainment of life values. (Filled circles = extreme levels of the dimension Generally positive-Privacy/Intimacy.)

Table 3 gives an overview of how different levels of the three dimensions in the attainment space relate to various regions in the two-dimensional importance space. In some cases the different types of attainment variables are spread out quite evenly in a given importance region. This is true for Internal self, Work and achievement, Life in general: Possibilities, Subjective well-being, and perhaps for Intimacy and External resources. By contrast, External self values are always private/intimate and usually passive. Relations to other people (i. e., social values) are located towards the passive, dependent, and generally positive poles of the three dimensions. Morals (including Life in general: responsibility) are always passive values and tend to correspond to independent and generally positive values. Finally, relations to environment tend to correspond to generally positive values. It can be concluded that there are some clear relationships between different categories of importance and attainment but in many cases there are no obvious correspondences across the two types of ratings.

TABLE 3

Cross-tabulation of importance and attainnment categories of life values (see Figures 1 and 2)

	Attainment					
Importance	Act	Pass	Ind	Dep	Gen P	Priv
External self	4	1	3	2	0	5
Religion	1	0	1	0	1	0
Life in general: Resp.	0	3	3	0	2	1
Supporting society	1	0	0	1	0	1
Other people	2	13	2	13	12	3
Morals	0	7	5	2	5	2
Internal self	1	3	2	2	2	2
Intimacy	2	6	3	5	3	5
Work/Achievement	2	1	1	2	2	1
Life in general: Poss.	4	4	5	3	3	5
Subj. well-being	2	5	3	4	3	4
Relations to environment	11	14	11	14	17	8
External recourses	4	7	3	8	3	8

3.3. Life values and life situation

Table 4 shows how attainment and importance of different life values relate to subjects' life situation in terms of three demographic background variables, viz. sex, age, and marital status. The data given in Table 3 are significant product moment correlations ($p<.05$) between life values and background variables. First, it can be noted that importance is more often significantly correlated with background variables than is true for attainment although this tendency is restricted to correlations involving and age. In general, women and young persons tended to give higher attainment and importance ratings than was the case for males and old persons. Married persons made relatively high attainment ratings on a number of variables (in particular with respect to love/sex) although they rated their attainment of self control and freedom as relatively low. Hence it seems that those having the most positive view of their life situation among our subjects were young married females. It is interesting to note that attainment of happiness was not significantly related to any of the three

TABLE 4

Means and significant correlations ($p<.05$) with sex, age and marital status for value variables based on attainment and importance ratings respectively, and correlations between attainment and importance ratings ($r_{A,I}$)

Value variable	Attainment ratings				Importance ratings				
	Mean	Sex[a]	Age	Mar.[b]	Mean	Sex	Age	Mar.	$r_{A,I}$
Material standard	4.2			24	4.3				27
Enough maoney	4.6			30	5.7				08
Satisfying job	4.9				6.0	36	-32		29
Having time	4.7		25		5.9	37	-40		19
Housing	5.7				5.9	31			33
Education	4.5		-37		5.3				12
Family life	5.4			42	6.3			23	52
Well-being nearest	5.5				6.3				46
Friends	5.2	27			6.0	26	-27		57
Health	5.3				6.1	21			22
Good-looking	4.3		-27		4.3				46
Personal development	5.1	26	-23		5.5	33		-32	35
Caring for oneself	5.3		-25		5.7	30			47
Personal identity	5.3		-29		5.7	31	-39		44
Self appreciation	5.0				5.6	31	-37		34
Self control	5.1			-25	5.6			-24	36
Accepting o.	5.3				5.6	26			56
Caring for o.	5.4	28	24		5.7	29			65
Trusting o.	4.8			23	5.6	41	-23		58
Honest to o.	5.6				5.8	28			32
Liking o.	5.1	31			5.3	25			61
Responsible	5.9	23			5.7				51
Motivation	5.3	22	-30		5.7	34	-32		59
Capacity	4.9				5.3		-28		58
Carefulness	5.3				5.4				46
Achievement	4.4		-42		5.0	22	-46	-26	67
Career	3.1		-32		3.9				29
Caring for nature	6.1				5.9				43
O. accept	5.0	24		39	5.4	39	-31		56
O. care	4.6	31	-30		5.3	28	-27		52
O. pos. influence	5.0	23	-26		5.2	26			56
O. honest	5.1				5.7	38	-32		55
Good mut. relations	5.0	27			5.6	37	-33		58
Mutual morals	5.2				5.6	30			38
Love/sex	5.0			45	5.6	26	-36		29
Freedom/independ.	4.9			-24	5.3	28			32
Security	4.9			25	5.4	30			44
Stimulance	5.0		-27		5.4	33	-30	-31	40
Ext. demands for achievment	4.3		-46		4.4		-33	-24	69
Support from society	2.8				4.3				37
God	2.8				3.0				87
Happiness	4.9				5.6	40	-43		14
Enjoyment	4.9	22			5.7	36	-23		53
Mean all items		28				41	-26		

[a] Male=0, female=1 [b] Single=0, Married or co-habiting=1

background variables. Thus a global well-being measure such as happiness may fail to mirror variations in specific aspects of the experienced quality of life.

The patterns of significant correlations for attainment and importance, respectively, coincide to some extent. However, this does not imply that the attainment and important ratings generally are strongly correlated with each other. The rightmost column of Table 4 shows that there is a considerable variation in the size of the correlations between the two types of ratings for specific life value variables. The correlations are rather high for the social values (with an exception for honest to others), but they are low for many of the non-social resources. It may be concluded, that attainment and importance ratings may tap different types of information of how people experience their life situation.

Table 4 also presents arithmetic means across all subjects of each value variable for attainment and importance ratings, respectively. The means of particular value variables are not of primary interest in the present study although they may say something about the values of ordinary people in today's Sweden. However, with regard to the over all pattern of the data it may be noted that high/low attainment ratings tend to go together with high/low importance ratings. For example, housing, family life, morals, and caring for nature are highly rated with respect to both attainment and importance whereas material standard, good-looking, career, and God are rated low in both respects. This covariation may reflect that people to some extent are able to attain those values that are important to them but it may also mean that people bolster or de-emphasize the importance of values which they attain or do not attain, respectively. It is also possible that both attainment and importance are affected by social desirability. That is, if it is socially desirable to regard a value as important (which may be the case for, say, honesty) then it may also be socially desirable to say that one behaves in line with that value and vice versa for socially undesirable values. However, whatever the reasons are for the covariation between attainment and importance *across values* it should be remembered that variations in attainment and importance *across individuals* seem to be follow different principles as is illustrated in Figures 1 and 2.

4. DISCUSSION

To a large extent, the present data support our conceptual framework for classifying life values. When values are seen in terms of importance then our first and second classification principles seem to be relevant. Hence, there is support for the tripartite distinction mental states (or subjective well-being) - relational values - external resources as well as for the idea that values may be characterized in terms of types of objects to which values may be associated. As hypothesized, it seems relevant to distinguish between the person him/herself, other people, and "ahuman" objects. Moreover, the present data suggest further distinctions between objects such as the one between the external self and internal self.

Our third classification principle - the contents of a personal relation that may be associated with value - is reflected in the structure underlying the attainment ratings. It is interesting that although our items largely differed from Benjamin's [7] items in her studies of interpersonal relations we found approximately the same three basic dimensions in the present data as Benjamin found in her data. It appears that also for values which do not seem to focus on personal relations (i. e., external resource values and desirable mental states) people still think in relational terms when they regard such values from the point of view of attainment. Also, it may be noted that the same three dimensions seem to suffice for describing value relations to "ahuman" objects as well as to human objects. (Benjamin only studied relations to human objects.)

It may be concluded that the present results imply that a step has been taken towards the formulation of an empirically based classification system for life values. However, we think that more data are needed in order to establish the details of such a classification system. In any case, it seems safe to conclude from the present data that life values are structured differently when they are seen in terms of importance and attainment, respectively. Why is it so? We can only speculate. When importance is stressed the focus is on the fact that values offer guiding principles for behavior. Obviously, the more important a person judges a value to be the more he or she commits him/herself to act in line with that value. Perhaps, it is more natural to be guided by the importance of concrete objects or of particular life domains (at least on a conscious level) than by the rather abstract dimensions found in the attainment data. The dimensions underlying attainment may reflect basic aspects in people's experiences of what they get and what they do not get in their lives. However, the fact that people's experiences vary in line with these aspects does not necessarily imply that they also regard these aspects as guiding principles. Still it seems reasonable that each of the poles of the three dimensions reflect fundamental aspects in the quality of life. It may be speculated that the good life should exhibit some balance between activity and passivity, between independence and dependence, and between intimacy/privacy and a more general positive attitude. People may be more or less successful in finding such a balance dependent on which objects or life domains toward which they orient their behavior. It is quite clear from our data that there indeed is a relation between orientation towards particular objects or life domains and particular patterns of attainment across the three dimensions. When the appropriate balance is not attained people may restructure their evaluations of particular objects or life domains in order to find new means to obtain such a balance. Hence the three dimensions underlying the attainment ratings may function as higher order guiding principles that to some extent determine which objects or life domains toward which people orient their behavior.

Finally, we will briefly comment on the relation between value variables and objective life conditions. Our data suggest that by considering the rated attainment and importance of a number of specific life values one may get a rather diversified picture of how people experience the quality of their life. We experience our findings on the relations between value variables and life conditions as promising with respect to the possibilities of constructing a useful quality of life questionnaire in line with the ideas discussed in the present paper.

ACKNOWLEDGEMENTS

This research was supported by a grant from The Swedish Council for Research in the Humanities and Social Sciences. We wish to thank Dr Louis Guttman for his constructive criticism of a previous version of the paper.

REFERENCES

[1] Rescher, N., Introduction to Value Theory (The Free Press, New York, 1969)

[2] Diener, E., Psychological Bulletin (1984, Vol. 95) 542.

[3] Kammann, D.L., & Flett, R. Australian Journal of Psychology (1983, Vol. 35) 257.

[4] Campbell, A., Converse, P.E., & Rogers, W.L. The Quality of American Life (Russel Sage Foundation, 1976)

[5] Montgomery, H., & Johansson, U.S. Göteborg Psychological Reports (1986) No. 7.

[6] Rokeach, M. The Nature of Human Values (The Free Press, New York, 1973)

[7] Benjamin, L.S. Psychological Review (1974, Vol. 81) 392.

[8] Humphrey, L.L., & Benjamin, L.S. American Psychologist (1986, Vol. 41) 979.

[9] McLemore, S., & Benjamin, L.S. American Psychologist (1979, Vol. 34) 17.

[10] Biermann, R. Psychological Bulletin (1979, Vol. 72) 338.

[11] Chance, E. Content Analysis of Verbalizations about Interpersonal Experiences, in: Gottschalk, L. and Auerbach, A. (eds.), Methods of Research in Psychotherapy (Appleton-Century-Crofts, New York, 1966)

[12] Osgood, C.E., Suci, G.J., & Tannenbaum, P.H. The Measurement of Meaning (University of Illinois Press, Urbana, 1957)

[13] Montgomery, H., Drottz, B.M., Gärling, T., Persson, A.L., & Waara, R. Conceptions about Material and Immaterial Values in a Sample of Swedish Subjects, in: Brandstätter, H., and Kirchler, E., (eds.), Economic Psychology: Proceedings of the Tenth IAREP Annual Colloquium, Linz, 1985)

[14] Johansson, U.S. Psykologisk Forskning kring Värden (Psychological Research on Values) (University of Göteborg, 1986)

[15] Canter, D. (ed.), Facet Theory: Approaches to Social Reesearch (Springer, New York, 1985)

[16] Lingoes, J.C., & Roskam, E.E. Psychometrica Monograph Supplement (1973, Vol. 19)

[17] Levy, S. The Structure of Social Values (The Israel Institute of Applied Social Research, Jerusalem, 1986)

[18] Levy, S. Lawful Roles of Facets in Social Theories, in: Canter, D. (ed.), Facet theory: Approaches to Social Research (Springer, New York, 1985)